D0922411

More praise for this book

Wolfram Kistner

"Prof. Duchrow's book conveys a message of hope. The economic and political structures of the prevailing global economic system, however powerful and destructive, are human constructs. They can and must be changed according to principles of justice safe-guarding and promoting the life of all humans and creation. Christians walking in the footsteps of Christ are empowered by this Lord to take up this struggle. They can derive guidelines from the biblical traditions for developing strategies of resistance against the powers of death as well as for finding new models for an economy for life." Dr. Wolfram Kistner, Former Director of 'Justice and Reconciliation'/SACC, South Africa

Jim Wallis

"Economics is too important to be left to the economists alone. It is high time to apply biblical theology to the crisis of our global economy and to search for sustainable alternatives that affirm life, protect the earth, and build human community. Ulrich Duchrow has done that brilliantly and gives us a place to start a new discussion on economics. This is a book whose time has come. Let the conversation and the experiment proceed." Jim Wallis, Editor in Chief, *Sojourners Magazine*, USA

Franz J. Hinkelammert

"Ulrich Duchrow's *Alternatives to Global Capitalism* is certainly the most thorough book on this subject to be published in recent years. Economics has to be 'economics for life' if life on earth is to continue. Life today, for people and for nature, is endangered by an increasingly totalitarian and ferocious capitalism.

Duchrow's highly intelligent analysis of today's world market and its history is complemented by a surprising and new interpretation of biblical texts. As a result, he offers realistic strategies for developing alternatives to the prevailing global economic system.

Duchrow, with his long history of working on many levels within the civil rights and ecumenical movements, is singularly competent to write on both complex economic problems and theological interpretation." Prof.Dr. Franz J. Hinkelammert, Departmento Ecumenico de Investigaciones, Costa Rica

Dedicated to the Sisters of Grandchamp and all base communities and grassroots groups which nourish the hope that solidarity and a life-sustaining economy are possible

Alternatives to Global Capitalism

Drawn from Biblical History
Designed for Political Action

Ulrich Duchrow

International Books
with
Kairos Europa

CIP-GEGEVENS KONINKLIJKE BIBLIOTHEEK, THE HAGUE

Duchrow, Ulrich

Alternatives to global capitalism : drawn from biblical history,
designed for political action / Ulrich Duchrow ; [transl. from the German:
Elaine Griffiths ... et al.]. – Utrecht : International Books. – Ill.
Transl. of: Alternativen zur kapitalistischen Weltwirtschaft : biblische Erinnerung und
politische Ansätze zur Überwindung einer lebensbedrohenden Ökonomie. – Gütersloh :
Kaiser ; Gütersloh : Gütersloher Verl.-Haus, 1994. – Publ. in association with Kairos
Europa.
ISBN 90-6224-976-0
NUGI 635
Key words: capitalism / world economy / religion and politics.

Translated from the German by:
Elizabeth Hicks, Keith Archer, Keith Schorah and Elaine Griffiths

© Ulrich Duchrow, 1995
Reprinted, 1998

International Books
A. Numankade 17, 3572 KP Utrecht, The Netherlands
tel. 31 (0)30-2731840, fax. 31 (0)30-2733614
in association with

Kairos Europa
Hegenichstrasse 22, 69124 Heidelberg, Germany
tel. 49-(0)6221-780718, fax. 49-(0)6221-781183

Contents

Foreword to the English edition   9

Introduction   11

First Part
Background to the present situation:
Pauperisation and the global dominance of finance   19

Chapter I
The birth of the market economy, its structures and development   20
1 First principles   20
2 Principles and consequences of a capitalist market economy
   in which labour, land and money are treated as commodities   29
   2.1 Labour 31
   2.2 Land 34
   2.3 Money 35
3 The political conditions necessary for a capitalist market economy   43
   3.1 Property and contract law 44
   3.2 The money system 48
   3.3 Foreign (trade) policy 49
4 The ideology of market-minded people (homo oeconomicus)   51

Chapter II
The resistance of victims and societies   57
1 Resistance outside Europe   57
2 Resistance within Europe   59
   2.1 The market and regulation 61
   2.2 Socialism, Fascism and Keynesianism 65

Chapter III
The current situation in the neo-liberal capitalist global system   69
1 The transnationalisation of markets and market actors   69
2 Domination of global finance and its effects in the South,
   the East and the West   75
   2.1 In the South: the debt crisis – the tip of the iceberg 77
   2.2 Eastern Europe: the identical debt traps of industrialisation
        and de-industrialisation 82
   2.3 In the North (the West): casino capitalism, growth without
        jobs, the gulf between rich and poor, and the powerlessness
        of the nation-state 83
   2.4 Around the globe: destruction of the basis of life for this and
        future generations by the money-accumulation economy 92
3 The international institutions involved in global domination
   of finance: the Bretton Woods system and its metamorphoses   95
   3.1 The International Monetary Fund (IMF)
        and the World Bank 103
   3.2 The General Agreement on Tariffs and Trade (GATT) 103
   3.3 G7: the seven leading industrialised nations and the
        "World Economic Summit" 105
4 The role of the military in ensuring the global dominance
   of finance   106
5. The media's role in spreading the ideology of the global dominance
   of finance   112

Second Part
Biblical recollection of the future of life
Preliminary considerations   121

Chapter IV
The socio-economic and political-ideological context
of the biblical traditions   127
1 Economy in the ancient Near East   127
2 Politics and ideology   127

Chapter V
Economy for life – biblical approaches   142
1 Israel's emergence as a "contrast society"   143
2 The attempt to "tame" the kingship system by prophecy and
   law   149
3 Alternatives after the collapse of kingship and the transformed
   society in a corner of the Persian Empire   160
4 Resistance to the totalitarian Hellenistic and Roman Empires
   and small-scale alternatives in apocalyptic writings   175
5 The Jesus movement and the early Christian messianic
   communities as the salt, light and leaven of the Kingdom of God
   in Israel and among the peoples   180

Chapter VI
Resistance to the kingdoms of the world and alternatives for life
What does it mean today?   203
1 Five biblical rules for recollecting the past   203
2 False paths: "state theology" and "church theology"   207
3 Three legitimate approaches to being the Church and to taking
   steps towards a life-sustaining economy   208

Third Part
Life-giving economic alternatives – today   211

Chapter VII
From the empires to the global economy   212
1 How can one compare the social configurations of
   ancient empires and the global capitalist system?   213
2 Have the churches the right to speak up at all, in view of their
   2000-year history?   214

Chapter VIII
Rejecting the totalitarian structure of the world economy   230

Chapter IX
Small-scale networked alternatives on the basis of a new vision   240
1 The vision of an economy for life   242
2 An economy for life in community   246

3. Alternative micro-economics   251
    3.1   Alternative companies and company networks   253
    3.2   Alternative technologies   255
    3.3   Alternative land use   256
    3.4   Alternative micro-financial systems   259
    3.5   Alternative trade   267
4   Alternative consumption   268
5   Fairer distribution of income   271
6   The networking of small-scale alternatives   274

Chapter x
Alternative economic policy for life   278
1   Chances for politics under a totalitarian system
   or the relationship between prophetic and apocalyptic writings   278
2   Alternatives to the current world economic and
   financial (dis)order   288
    2.1   The UN and the Bretton Woods institutions
      (IMF, World Bank, GATT)   288
    2.2   Ending modern-day debt slavery   294
    2.3   Combating capital and tax flight and all economic crime   298
    2.4   Riding the tiger, or, can TNCs be tamed?   300
3   Strategies for life at local, national and European levels   302
    3.1   The local level   302
    3.2   The national level   304
    3.3   The European level   307

Conclusion   316

Bibliography   318

Foreword to the English edition

There is no alternative – so it appears following the collapse of socialism in Central and Eastern Europe. The winners in the now global capitalist economy are enjoying the victory. The losers – that is, the poor, not only in the East, but also in the South and the West – feel powerless in the face of world market powers now mightier than ever before. Many feel completely lost. Only a few still dare to be critical and ask what the reasons are for the present threat to the lives of human beings and to nature, and whether there are any alternatives. This was the reason for writing this book.

The year 1994 was marked by the fiftieth anniversary of the Bretton Woods conference, which created the institutional framework for the US-dominated phase of global capitalist economics in 1944. Many non-governmental organisations (NGOs) in all parts of the world have used this occasion to raise critical questions about the present global disorder and also to work out alternatives. In Europe the grass-roots movement Kairos Europa has started a campaign for continuous action, awareness-raising and lobbying from local to international levels. My book is intended to provide orientation in this context, and stimulate further discussion.

My thanks are due to many people for various kinds of support during preparation of the book. Firstly, I would like to thank my wife, Ulrike, and the many participants in discussion groups and various seminars. Amongst my colleagues in theology, I would like especially to thank Israel Batista, Jürgen Kegler, Wolfram Kistner, Theo Kneifel, Philip Potter, Luise Schottroff and Ton Veerkamp. In the field of economics Martin Gück provided welcome corrections and stimulating comments, as did Anselm Duchrow concerning agriculture. For the creative translation of the three parts I thank Elizabeth Hicks, Keith Archer and Keith Schorah. Elaine Griffiths displayed not only professional expertise but also personal friendship in integrating the whole of the English text. I am grateful to Elisabeth Witte for her competent and meticulous care in the production of the final form of the text.

Amongst the many religious and grass-roots communities to whom this book is dedicated, I wish to make special mention of the Grandchamp Com-

munity in Switzerland, not only because they bear living testimony to the existence of alternatives, but also because they have over the last ten years supported both church-related and social movements with their spirituality of resistance and prayers, lending hope to those concerned.
Ulrich Duchrow, October, 1994

Foreword to the second edition
Three years after the publication of this book the profile of the problems described here has even sharpened. Those neoliberal flagships, the South East Asian „tigers", have collapsed and they are grappling with serious financial, economic and social problems. The capitalist shock therapy administered to central and eastern European countries has split societies into impoverished majorities and super-rich minorities, in Russia even leading to the proliferation of mafia-type practices. The debt burden weighing on most southern countries has been compounded by the IMF's imposition of structural adjustment programmes (SAPs). In a similar development, most western European governments have been implementing austerity policies in an effort to fulfil the convergence criteria for the single currency. They would do better to try to hinder the flight of capital and large-scale tax evasion which is contributing to growing budget deficits. Faced with mass unemployment, some governments praise flexible labour policies which in fact often lead to wage-levels too low to feed a family. The lobby of transnational capital tried via the OECD to reach a Multilateral Agreement on Investments (MAI) by which governments would lose their last instruments for the social regulation of capital investment. Fortunately the NGO community raised a worldwide protest with the result that MAI has been postponed - but not dropped.

In the light of the double strategy promoted in this book, the good news since 1995 has been the increasing mobilisation of civil society. Local alternatives have gained ground (see Douthwaite and Korten), as has networking for political intervention. Starting in France organisations of the unemployed launched Euromarches against unemployment, job insecurity and exclusion, climaxing at the EU summit of Amsterdam in June 1997. Kairos Europa has issued a European Kairos document to strengthen the process of alliance-building and has called on leftwing governments to regain control of transnational capital. Otherwise the European Union and other power-centres will not have the strength to create sustainable employment and a coherent social policy. The consequence could be an even greater disaster than the breakdown of the classical liberal system at the beginning of this century. For those seeking social, ecological and participatory alternatives the time to act is still now.

Introduction

The present western economic order, which was born in 1944 at the conference of world powers at Bretton Woods, USA, is half a century old. We have known for a long time that under this system "the poor become poorer and the rich richer," but up until now this problem has normally been associated with the dichotomy between the poorer countries of Africa, Asia and Latin America, and the industrial societies of the rich North. It has also been seen as a matter merely for idealists concerned to help the "Third World." But now more and more people in the East and even in the rich West are sinking into poverty. In the European Union the figure has reached 50 million.[1] A person is defined as poor if he or she receives less than 50 per cent of the average income. Income, however, is only *one* aspect of poverty, even if it is the deciding factor. Alongside income (as we learn from poverty research), one has to take into account a number of other factors.[2] These include work, education, housing, health and social relations, and also personal considerations such as emotional satisfaction, or loneliness, depression, and anxiety. At issue is the uncertainty of being able to meet one's basic human needs. Worldwide this first means food and clothing, although the poor in Western Europe are generally provided for, at least with the bare necessities.

Many people in Western Europe believe that we have a social market economy, and therefore these problems affect us only minimally, if at all. Perhaps we are aware of the pauperisation in the United States under Reagan and Bush and in Thatchers Britain – but could it happen in *Germany*? Of course the transient problems of reunification and the economic recession must be overcome, but the German system is basically a good one and can be usefully applied to other countries – this at least was the sentiment of a report from the German Protestant Church on the subject of the economy. In fact, since the eighties, pauperisation in Germany has been increasing at a great rate – espe-

---

1 See the report of the German National Conference on Poverty (Nationale Armutskonferenz) in the Frankfurter Rundschau, 20.1.1993.
2 See the methodical approach in reporting on poverty in D. Döring et al., 1990, pp.18ff.

cially since the Conservative-Liberal coalition came to power in 1983. Since then average wages in real terms of those who remained in work have just been maintained and only recently declined below zero growth, while there has been a sharp increase in the number of those out of work and rapid deterioration in their living standards.[3] The number of unemployed in western Germany now stands at 3 million – not to mention the situation in former East Germany, where real unemployment is running upwards of 50 per cent. Housing is in increasingly short supply and homelessness a growing problem. Health care is being reduced. Poor families are getting deeper into debt, as are local authorities and other public bodies. These are just some examples of what is happening – the trend is obvious.

At the same time, the large-scale pauperisation of *the "other two thirds" of the world* has reached a point of terrible misery. More and more people find they have not got enough to eat. For us the starving millions of children and adults have become a mere statistic. In Latin America people talk about the decomposition of societies, meaning their fragmentation into ungovernable, warring factions. These are sometimes called "postcatastrophic societies."[4] The West's interest in Africa seems to be limited to using it as a rubbish dump and/or a training ground for neo-imperialist military exercises. In Asia the situation is more complex, as we will see later. Overall we have seen the opposite of "development" – a word that is still invoked in pious speeches to try to give us a clear conscience.

And now there's the *East* as well to consider, as it follows the South in the pauperisation of the masses. Socialism as practised in the eastern bloc attempted to bring about a fairer distribution of resources than existed under western capitalism, and in this had a degree of success. Now it has collapsed, partly because the people rightly wanted not only social justice but also political power, and partly because state-run capitalism does not work in economic terms. Now these countries have the opposite problem. In most cases their governments are pinning their hopes on market forces before the necessary political, legal and cultural structures are in place, not to mention the as yet unknown effects of the world market on western politics. The result is "Manchester capitalism" and mafia-style white-collar crime. The social consequences are there for all to see and are worsening daily, exacerbated wherever

---

3 See ibid. and R. Hickel et al., 1993, and E.-U. Huster in the Frankfurter Rundschau, 19.1.1993.
4 R. Kurz, 1991.

there is war. In China, too, the direction that transition to a market ecomony is taking – although different from the developments in the former Soviet Union – is unclear.[5] The upshot of all this is that the western system has now spread all over the world, albeit with marked regional variations. A recurring feature of its development since the eighties has been increased pauperisation (to varying degrees), accelerated by the collapse of socialism in the eastern bloc. Hand in hand with this goes increased destruction of the environment.

The increase in pauperisation and destruction of the natural environment has been accompanied by a horrific rise in the concentration of wealth. In Germany the disposable income of the self-employed not working in agriculture (5.9 per cent of all households) rose by 47 per cent between 1979 and 1989.[6] Income from business rose by 65.9 per cent gross, i.e. by 75 per cent net. Increased income from financial investments is of particular importance, which we will come back to later. The present German government is promoting this trend with tax concessions for the rich and tax burdens for the poor. As I write, it has just approved cuts to the tune of 20 billion deutschmarks, most of which is to come from reducing unemployment benefit and social security payments. It also announced cuts in top taxation rates.

> "This means that the social distribution in Germany is more unequal than ever. With 57 per cent of the total national household income, the richest third of private households has more than the other two thirds, together only accounting for 43 per cent. Then there is also a great difference between these two lower groups. The poorest third of all households receives 16 per cent of the total household income, i.e. only half of the fair share. But the middle third, at 27 per cent, also remains below the 33 per cent it would receive if income were evenly distributed."[7]

If we look at the global relationship between the South and the North, or at the unequal distribution within the majority of countries in the southern hemisphere, the dichotomy appears even more severe. Since 1990 the UN has been developing a tool to clarify this issue: the annual Human Development Report.[8] The 1992 report (p.48) states that the creditor banks and countries

---

5   See I. Kollin-Hüssen, in: M. Massarrat et al. (eds.), 1993, pp.103ff.
6   E.-U. Huster, op. cit.
7   Ibid.
8   UNDP (United Nations Development Programme), 1990-1994.

extract from the indebted countries an annual US$ 50 billion in debt servicing alone. Yet, through the present rules governing world markets the poor countries lose *at least* US$ 500 billion to the rich countries *annually* – ten times as much as they receive in aid. And that is not even considering the load this places on the economies of these dependent countries.

> What this means in practical terms for the average German has been the subject of a study by Heinz-Werner Hetmeier of the Federal Office of Statistics in Wiesbaden.[9] Since 1980 the worsening trading conditions for countries producing raw materials have brought Germany a trade surplus of at least 30.9 bn deutschmarks.

Reliable statistics for eastern European countries are hard to come by, but the trend is the same as that in the South.

In *global* terms at any rate, this "development" has led to the skew distribution of income shown in the following figure from the front page of the 1992 Human Development Report (see diagram 1).

This means that in global terms we have a situation of apartheid, in which the proportions of the haves to the have-nots is roughly 1 to 4. Add to this global energy consumption, CO_2 emissions, the amount of waste produced, pollution and other environmental factors, and it becomes obvious that this same 20 per cent of the global population is also responsible for 80 per cent of the destruction of our planet. There are a number of reasons for making a careful initial examination of the present state of the world.

1. Most people experience and understand small parts of the whole, the things that occur in their locality. For example, they are put out of work, or take a drop in their social security benefits or wages in real terms; they cannot find anywhere to live or they get into debt; they migrate to escape poverty in our relatively rich society and in doing so come up against racial prejudice; they hear about wars and conflicts somewhere in the world and are told that troops must be sent in; they hear about famines and are asked to donate money for relief work, etc. Does anybody grasp the connections between these events? Economists do not publicise the links. Most politicians either do not know about or do not care to mention them. The media gloss over the issue – with few exceptions. In fact the victims are played off against one another. Hardly anyone tells them that they are *victims of a whole intercon-*

---

9   See Frankfurter Rundschau, 28.6.93 (summarised by R. Bunzenthal).

World population arranged by income

Distribution of income

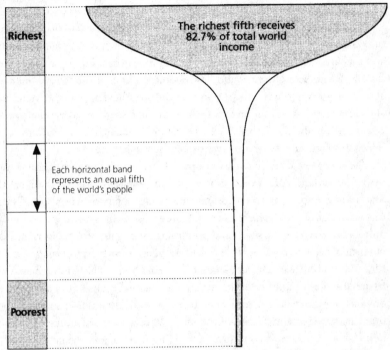

Richest

The richest fifth receives 82.7% of total world income

Each horizontal band represents an equal fifth of the world's people

Poorest

The poorest fifth receives 1.4% of total world income

The design shows the global distribution of income. The richest 20% of the world population receives 82.7% of the world income, while the poorest 20% receives only 1.4%. Global economic growth rarely filters down. The global income distribution by quintile is as follows:

World population		World income
Richest	20%	82.7%
Second	20%	11.7%
Third	20%	2.3%
Fourth	20%	1.9%
Poorest	20%	1.4%

Diagram 1: The global distrubution of income

Source: UNDP, 1992

nected system extending all over the globe and varying only in degree. They might join forces!

2. Not only the obvious victims could join forces. The *future victims*, or the present unwitting victims, could wake up to the situation. Up until now the "Third World question" has seemed not to have much to do with us. If it were to become clear that the very global mechanisms which cause pauperisation and human devastation in Africa, Asia and Latin America are also responsible for cuts in our social services and destruction of our environment, solidarity could also grow in the North. Support for the obvious victims could increase, and victims and those in solidarity with them could work together on *alternatives* to bring about a political change of direction, before the catastrophe which humankind is working towards looms even larger.

3. The *churches* are particularly important here. The cultures responsible for the above situation are rooted in western Christianity (basically the United States and Europe, with an exception being made for Japan on this point). For this reason the churches have a particular responsibility to face the facts – not only external economic, social and political facts, but also what all this means in terms of their own ideological, political and economic responsibility. Until now most mainstream churches have refused to do this. The reason given was frequently the complexity of the situation. Today, the connections are more obvious than ever before, and must be publicised. In addition, biblical approaches have remained largely untapped. When taking a critical look at the political importance of economics we will find them of great value.

4. Finally, it is impossible to work on *alternatives* without understanding which part of the whole one is tackling, what possibilities are open, and how one should relate to those involved in tackling other parts. To put it in concrete terms, if I want to work on alternatives, I have to understand the strategies and mechanisms of the present economic system and its actors in order to know what forces I am up against. I must know what my political options are at the local, national, European and global levels, to avoid disillusion and disappointment.

Naturally one book by a single author – even an interdisciplinary work based on close contact with victims from many parts of the world – cannot claim to give a complete picture of the present economic system, explain biblical, theological and ethical critiques, and then come up with practical proposals for a life-enhancing economy. However, what it can do is to provide a framework and some useful ideas for groups, communities, churches and social movements to continue working on economic alternatives, both locally and in conjunction with other groups.

The reason for writing this book is that *the year 1994* offered a unique opportunity to deepen not only our understanding of the links between global, national and local events, but also to exert political influence. As I mentioned above, 1994 saw the fiftieth anniversary of the present world economic order. In July 1944 the world powers, dominated by the USA (which had emerged victorious from World War II), determined the new world economic order at a conference in Bretton Woods. They decided to set up the International Monetary Fund (IMF) and the World Bank (WB) to regulate the international system of finance, and some time later the General Agreement on Tariffs and Trade (GATT) to regulate world trade. The national economies and the rules governing their function are often regarded as natural or even God-given. It could therefore be useful to take a careful look at the historical developments leading to this world economic order, what its consequences were and what viable alternatives there might be.

Secondly, 1994 was – at least in Germany and in Western Europe – a marathon election year in which local, national and European elections were held. The air was thick with election propaganda persuading people to vote against their own interests. The Right was able to make political mileage out of this, attempting to win over the victims and those fearful of decline. This does not only require explanation and information, but also the organisation of those affected from the grass-roots upwards, to influence the political parties and to win allies if possible. So 1994 – marking 50 years of global economy as "western-style economy", and an election year in Western Europe – was an opportunity to strengthen small-scale coalitions working against economic, social and ecological destruction and for economic alternatives, at all levels. Many people in many places are already active, including "Kairos Europa – Towards a Europe for Justice," a network of independent organisations of victims, solidarity groups, churches and church organisations. In addition, the European churches are planning a second Ecumenical Assembly for justice, peace and the integrity of creation for 1997, following the one held in Basel in 1989. This book aims to make a contribution to these and other efforts – for the sake of our endangered life.

FIRST PART

Background to the present situation: Pauperisation and the global dominance of finance

"Labor and land are no other than the human beings themselves of which every society consists and the natural surroundings in which it exists. To include them in the market mechanism means to subordinate the substance of society itself to the laws of the market."

Karl Polanyi[1]

Our point of departure and reference is human beings, most of whom nowadays are living in increasing misery, and nature, the basis of all life on our planet and now in danger. We could describe the suffering in detail and list the facts. But these "wild facts"[2] are known to all who wish to know. They also operate deep down on the minds of those who are not yet aware of them, or do not wish to be. The fact is that more and more people are now saying, "We have the feeling that something is very wrong." More than anyone, children worry greatly about the future.

This does not quite fit in with the victorious cry, "The market economy has come out on top!" or "There is no alternative to the market economy." However, both of these statements contain a grain of truth: following the collapse of bureaucratic socialism as an alternative project, the now global capitalist market economy has to take responsibility for structural developments worldwide (a fact which was already obvious to those who cared to look). Therefore it is imperative to understand what the dominant form of market economy is, how it operates, and what it has to do with pauperisation, decline in social services and destruction of the environment, if we are to develop life-giving economic alternatives.

---

1   K. Polanyi, (1944) 1957, p.71.
2   See Daly and Cobb, 1989.

Chapter 1

The birth of the market economy, its structures and development

1 First principles

One important cause of people's feeling of powerlessness in the face of things that bring suffering and destruction today, is the widespread belief that the economy runs according to certain natural "laws." Everyone is taught that the complex situation has its own "logic." Only experts can possibly know what it is all about and how things might develop in the future. One can only discuss matters "objectively", they say, and not "emotionally", i.e. from the standpoint of those affected. Anyone wishing to be taken seriously must keep to purely economic arguments. Ethical, theological or other "external" viewpoints are branded as "moralizing" and are therefore not to be taken seriously; they may even be ridiculed.

Here it is useful to look back through history and see that the economy prevalent today is by no means the only form of market developed and practised by human beings. Basic information on this subject can be found in the work of *Karl Polanyi*. In his book *The Great Transformation*[1] he shows that the transition to the modern capitalist market economy arose out of quite specific historical conditions, which in turn have their own history. The differences between the pre-capitalist markets and the present capitalist market are most easily seen by reference to the brilliant and prophetic insights of the Greek philosopher Aristotle.[2]

Aristotle analysed the *difference between the need-oriented household economy and the money-accumulation economy*.[3] The basic point is that Aristotle

---

1   K. Polanyi, (1944) 1957.
2   Aristotle, Politics, Book 1, Chapters 8-13; on this see K. Polanyi, op. cit., p.53ff.; Altvater, 1992[2], p.74; H.Chr. Binswanger, 1991, pp.113-117, 125-135 and elsewhere; Daly and Cobb, op. cit., pp.138f. and pp.191ff.
3   Polanyi, op. cit., pp.53f., calls this distinction arguably the most prophetic statement ever made within the social sciences: "...it is certainly still the best analysis of the subject we possess."

regarded the "oikonomia", the household economy, as being designed to supply the basic needs of the members of the household and of the community as a whole (*koinonia, polis*). This means that the prime goal of a natural economy is to meet basic human needs. In other words, property and goods can be regarded in a strict sense as means of sustaining life, i.e. intended for practical use.

Another important distinction is that between two types of earning and the two corresponding ways of using money. On the one hand, in the natural type of acquisition (*ktetiké kata physin*) naturally occurring substances and goods made out of them can be gathered, processed and exchanged for use elsewhere (and for long-distance trade money can be used as a medium of exchange). Aristotle called this early barter trading by households *metabletiké*. On the other hand, the barter system can be used to amass as much wealth as possible in the form of money for its own sake (*chrematistiké*). Aristotle called this type of acquisition money-accumulation trade (*kapeliké* from *kapelos*, meaning trader or merchant). It developed imperceptibly out of the barter system the moment money was introduced as a practical medium of exchange. In human beings money encounters greed for endless accumulation. They want to live for ever in comfort, and believe that money will make it possible to have an infinite supply of sustenance. Aristotle recognised two forms of this money-accumulation economy: trade for the sake of profit (as opposed to bartering, which can also occur using money, but is not directed at making a profit, but at supplying basic needs); and business to earn interest, by which Aristotle meant money that generates more money (the Greek word *tokos* means both "interest" and "the new-born"). The goal of the first is the creation of monopolies and price speculation, and that of the second is usury. Aristotle regarded both as unnatural and extremely dangerous to households and the community at large. The reason was that under the money-accumulation economy some deprive others of their share of profits from trading (p.1258b). This leads to the destruction of society (of people living within certain limits). People who wish to live for ever, with ever-increasing wealth in the form of money, have not understood what a "good life" is, i.e. a life in community (*koinonia*), and in the end destroy themselves. Here Aristotle points to King Midas, who wished that everything he touched would turn to gold. This was his downfall, since even his food turned to gold and so he starved to death.

How is this relevant to our understanding of different forms of market? Polanyi writes:

"Aristotle insists on production for use as against production for gain as the essence of householding proper; yet accessory production for the market need not, he argues, destroy the self-sufficiency of the household as long as the cash crop would otherwise be raised on the farm for sustenance, as cattle or grain; the sale of the surpluses need not destroy the basis of householding. Only a genius of common sense could have maintained, as he did, that gain was a motive peculiar to production for the market, and that the money factor introduced a new element into the situation, yet nevertheless, as long as markets and money remained mere accessories to an otherwise self-sufficient household, the principle of production for use could operate." (p.54)

This market form can easily be imagined as a *local market* in a "subsistence economy". Household communities engaged in farming and crafts produce goods to meet their own needs, and exchange part of their produce for other goods or for money as a medium of circulation, to improve and extend their supply of goods for their own use. Aristotle also viewed town markets as being there to serve the wider community (*polis*). Such markets existed not only in so-called "primitive" societies, but also well into 18th century European society, by then highly developed. They can be termed neighbourhood markets. Polanyi gives a clear description of how these markets were embedded within societies.[4] They were protected from abuse, and regulated by rites, ceremonies and laws.

The type of market which Aristotle warns against is initially associated with *long-distance trade and the business of loans*. Originally, foreign trade relations certainly did not take the form of a market, but rather that of conquest and piracy.[5] Markets for long-distance trade arose "naturally out of it where the carriers had to halt as at fords, seaports, riverheads, or where the routes of two land expeditions met".[6] This foreign trade supplied specific communities with externally produced goods. It was first and foremost directed towards providing luxuries and prestige items and the necessary equipment for cities or states to wage war. Until well into the Middle Ages local markets were kept strictly separate from the long-distance trade markets.

Naturally, Aristotle was able to recognise the problems, because at that time the Greek economy was already dependent to a certain extent on large-scale trade and credit capital. "In denouncing the principle of production for gain 'as not

---

4 Ibid., pp.61ff.
5 Ibid., pp.58f.
6 Ibid., p.60.

natural to man', as boundless and limitless, Aristotle was, in effect, aiming at the crucial point, namely the divorcedness of a separate economic motive from the social relations in which these limitations inhered."[7]

Polanyi points out that, apart from self-sufficiency-oriented household economies, the attendant secondary local bartering markets and long-distance markets, other economic forms have also existed without any market elements.[8] Here, the economy was embedded in the social behaviour of *reciprocity*. In this case people do not barter – they provided for one another in various ways. The extended family in tribal societies is the best example of an economy embedded in symmetrical social behaviour. Another model, one which is not based on a market, is that of *redistribution*. In this model a large part of the harvest is kept in store by the chief until some large festival, when it is distributed as gifts. The exchange that occurs there is not part of a market but reflects a quite different set of the social relationships and experience.

Summing up, we can say that running an economy in market form is not as old as humankind. Many early societies managed without a market at all. Where a local market arose it was assigned to household economics, and embedded in social relations. Where a market-place for long-distance trade arose it was not essential for supplying the population's basic needs, but concentrated on luxury goods and the necessities for waging war. Such a market was located outside of normal social relations. Until the Middle Ages (and later), local economies were expressly shielded from foreign trade.[9]

How, then, did the capitalist market economy arise and develop?
The most sophisticated theory I know of has been elaborated by *Giovanni Arrighi* in his recent book *The Long Twentieth Century: Money, Power, and the Origins of Our Times* (1994). He makes a distinction between governments as power-oriented and business enterprises as profit-oriented (p.85). Understanding the relation between both is crucial for the understanding of capital-

---

7   Ibid., p.54.
8   Ibid., pp.47ff.
9   The fact that even in Greek and Roman times the foreign trade market created a degree of dependence associated with the disparity between cities and countries led Aristotle to issue his warnings, and will concern us when we come to consider biblical history.

ist history. There is always a "space-of-places" that defines the process of territorial state formation (or formation of inter-state systems) and there is a "space-of-flows of capital" that defines the process of capital accumulation (p.84).

This is the reason why capitalist history can be written as a succession of world hegemonies: the Genoese-Spanish, the Dutch, the British, and the us. Or it can be written as a succession of systemic cycles of accumulation. Both seen together form the "long centuries". Arrighi's book shows not only the interaction between money and power and the sequence of the cycles. He also analyses the inner dynamics and the sub-phases of the long cycles which explain the transformation from the one into the other. These sub-phases also explain the starting point of capitalism as a historical social system.

This "point zero" happened at the end of a tremendous accumulation of capital in the hands of the merchant elites of the northern Italian city-states. Led by Venice, they gained control over the eastern trade route to India in the 12th and 13th centuries, in the context of the Crusades. But in a system of division of labour, Florence, Milan and Genoa each occupied their particular market niche. Around the beginning of the 14th century accumulation through trade stagnated. This created "cut-throat competition" between the city-states in Renaissance Italy, a "war of all against all" (pp.90ff.). This is what Marx called the "over-accumulation crisis". Instead of investing in production and trade, which would not give the expected return in that particular development model, capital was first invested in war-making. The second feature in this situation is that the moneyed interests took over the city-states. Three consequences could already be seen at this early stage: public debt, job losses and wage cuts. Surplus capital was not being reinvested in production and trade but in financial speculation and lending, to make a bigger profit.

Some of the moneyed elites of the city-states developed for the first time a Europe-wide network of banking and diplomacy beyond their own territory, later called "high finance". This was originally a Florentine invention under the Medicis. But as they had put all their eggs into one basket, to assist England in fighting France in the Hundred Years War, and England could not repay the loan, they failed. Not so the Genoese high finance, which invested in Spain's state-making, war-making and the conquista of South America. In doing so they could control the first "long century", the first accumulation cycle from the middle of the 15th to the middle of the 17th century.

This cycle – for the first time showing this structure of capitalist accumulation – had three distinct sub-phases: from the middle of the 14th to the middle of the 15th century the financial expansion, from the middle of the 15th to the middle of the 16th century a new period of material expansion (through production and trade, then under Spanish hegemony) followed again by financial expansion in a time of competition and wars in which the next hegemonic power, the Dutch United Provinces, emerged.

Their "long century" was rooted in the crisis of the previous hegemonic system of capital accumulation (p.127ff.). The bankers all over Europe had organised into "nations" and earned a lot of money through exchange between the many currencies. The Genoese in addition had financed the Spanish war against the Dutch rebels. When Spain lost out the financial centre moved form Antwerp and Seville to Amsterdam. The Dutch built their wealth and power on the "control over supplies of grain and naval stores from the Baltic" (p.132).

The key feature of their regime was to combine money and power in the form which is known as mercantilism, combining the strategies of Genoa and Venice. This combination had three characteristics: "transforming Amsterdam into the central entrepôt of European and world commerce" (p.137) and "the central money and capital market of the European world-economy" (p.138) as well as "launching large-scale joint-stock companies chartered by the Dutch government to exercise exclusive trading rights over huge overseas commercial areas. These companies were business enterprises which were supposed to yield profits and dividends but also to carry out war-making and state-making activities on behalf of the Dutch government" (p.139).

When other nations imitated the successful model of the Dutch, creating a self-sufficient national economy with overseas companies, competition started and the Dutch withdrew into financial expansion. But siding with France in the British-French wars they lost out. The world financial centre moved from Amsterdam to London.

So the third, the British, cycle of capital accumulation started again during the final stage of financial expansion of the previous hegemonic power (p.159ff.). British capital grew through the debt incurred by the British government when waging war against France. This capital, together with the profits from slave trade, was invested in the iron industry (railways and ships) as well as in the mechanisation of the textile industry. At the same time money linked up with the British Empire in the form of free-trade imperialism. The financial houses, especially the Rothschilds, became the "governors of the imperial engine".

When again this model of capital accumulation through material expansion began to stagnate and competition started to grow (this time with Germany), finance withdrew again into speculation and credit. The Great Depression from 1873 to 1896 signalled this financial expansion – the time when the USA started to emerge as the hegemonic power of the next cycle of capital accumulation. But we will leave this period leading to the present day to a later stage in our analysis.

This model of interpreting capitalist history, brilliantly unfolded in detail by Arrighi, deals with the highest layer of capitalist dynamics: the interaction between money and power, high finance and political institutions – invisible to the eyes of most people. Looking at the four long cycles of capital accumulation Arrighi distinguishes two forms of this interaction: state (monopoly) capitalism and cosmopolitan (finance) capitalism. Capital uses political institutions either directly or indirectly for the purpose of accumulation. This already shows that Adam Smith's idea of the "invisible hand" governing the market is really a mystification of the visible hands turning the wheel towards profit-making. Profit-making for capital accumulation is the one logic driving the owners of capital into either material or financial expansion.

However, Arrighi affirms that this sphere of finance capital and political power is not the only level of the capitalist economy. The market and material life are two layers below this key sphere which will deserve careful consideration as we seek strategies for our present situation. So let us turn back to the question of the market and its components.

After the Middle Ages, nascent capitalism by no means led straight away to an all-encompassing market, even though that was what the capitalist merchants wanted.[10] In fact it was direct state intervention that led to the setting up of *domestic markets* covering state territory, alongside the local markets and municipal centres of foreign trade (particularly in the emerging nation-states). This *mercantilism* "destroyed the outworn particularism of local and intermunicipal trading by breaking down the barriers separating these two types of noncompetitive commerce and thus clearing the way for a national market which increasingly ignored the distinction between town and countryside as well as that between the various towns and provinces."[11] These

---

10 On this matter as a whole see Polanyi, ibid., pp.62ff.

measures enabled states to gain control of all resources to increase their power abroad. At home, feudal and civic independence had to be overcome. The tool for achieving this was capital, accumulated private wealth, that was now to be invested in developing trade.

A clear, theoretical mercantilistic model was first put forward by *Thomas Hobbes* (1588-1679). It was he who said that man treats man like a wolf. In saying so, he was merely projecting onto human nature something that historically only emerged when the norms of society were based on private owners striving to increase their power over other owners. This led to a general insecurity requiring the hand of a strong state. "The possessive market model requires a compulsive framework of law. At the very least, life and property must be secured, contracts must be defined and enforced."[12] The state thus takes on absolutist characteristics. Hobbes calls this type of state Leviathan, the beast of the Apocalypse, its lifeblood being money.

John Locke continues the reflexion on this period in his second Treatise of Government (1690). We will come back to his basic arguments when considering property, money and the role of political institutions. Here it is important to remember (with Polanyi) that even in his day, the economic system of the domestic market remained embedded in the overall framework of social relations. The state even controlled foreign trade, through protected trading companies. The best known of these are the Dutch East India Company and the English East India Company. Their triangular trade in finished products from Europe, slaves from Africa and raw materials from Latin America and the Caribbean will concern us later.

How did the idea of an all-encompassing and self-regulating market arise, and how did it take effect? And how did it come about that the market was no longer an appendage of society, but that society was an appendage of a market designed for profit and the accumulation of money?

Enough has been written about this to fill whole libraries. Of course such revolutionary changes are not brought about by just one factor, but by a combination of factors. But still some of them are more important than others. Polyani describes the central point in the following terms:

"We submit that all these [market expansion, coal, iron, cotton, persons dispossessed by enclosures, machines, etc., U.D.] were merely incidental to one basic

---

11 Ibid., p.65.
12 C.B. Macpherson, 1962, p.57 (9ff.).

change, the establishment of market economy, and that the nature of this institution cannot be fully grasped unless the impact of the machine on a commercial society is realized. We do not intend to assert that the machine caused that which happened, but we insist that once elaborate machines and plant were used for production in a commercial society, the idea of a self-regulating market was bound to take shape."[13]

The connection between complex machinery and the factory, on the one hand, and commercial society, on the other, is just another way of defining industrial capitalism as a market society. Let us just remind ourselves what "commercial society" means in this context. A merchant who trades to make a profit (initially in foreign trade, then on rural and urban markets), buys a finished product and sells it again at a profit. This is captured in Marx's formula:

M – C – M' (money – commodities – (more) money)

But if in addition there is production using complex, expensive machinery, then all factors must be available to be bought and sold, otherwise losses cannot be avoided and profits cannot be calculated. What does this mean in practical terms? The merchant turned entrepreneur has to buy the production factors, first and foremost labour and raw materials. Using machinery, energy (together making up machine force, as opposed to labour force)[14] and his product concept (either his own or bought), he goes ahead and manufactures the product. The time that elapses between investment and production is calculated as the cost of the money (interest). This alters the formula for calculating profit from trade:

money – buyable production factors (labour, raw materials, loan capital) –
production with machine force – commodities – (more) money.

However, the effects of this change are not confined to one part of society, namely production. In fact a society in which markets used to play a minor role becomes a society defined by a system of interlocking markets, in other words, a market society.[15] It is not only production that is determined by the prices set by the law of supply and demand. These prices also determine the incomes which in turn form the basis for distribution and consumption. The *interest* is the cost of the money and constitutes income for those who provide

---

13 Polanyi, op. cit., p.40; on the following, pp.41ff.
14 See Binswanger, 1982, p.34.
15 See Polanyi, op. cit., pp.68f.

the money; the *ground-rent* is the price of use of the land (including raw materials found there) and makes up the income for the landowners; the *wage* is the price of the labour and forms the income for the workers; the price of the goods produced minus the cost of production constitutes the *profit* for the entrepreneurs running the business.

This model of interlocking, self-regulating markets presupposes several different expectations and pre-conditions:

- human beings behave so as to achieve maximum profit (rationality);
- as suppliers of one (or more) production factors human beings should be regarded principally as property owners;
- if all human beings were to behave in this economically rational way, it would be to the greatest possible welfare of all – as if controlled by an "invisible hand" (Adam Smith);
- therefore the state, as the organisation of human beings in society, has only to ensure the self-regulation of the markets.

This can be summarised as follows: Aristotle warned against substituting an economy of money accumulation for a household economy and subsistence-related (local) bartering markets. Capitalism reversed this approach with drastic social consequences in its industrial and liberal form – building on the previous cycles of Genoese – Spanish empire-building and Dutch-type mercantilism. The economic motive of subsistence was replaced by the profit motive. All transactions were expressed in monetary terms through prices. Labour and raw materials, i.e. human beings and nature, became commodities (as did money).

2 Principles and consequences of a capitalist market economy in which labour, land and money are treated as commodities

The alternative is not "to have a market or not," or, in conventional terms, to choose between a free market economy or a planned economy. Starting from first principles, or taking a historical perspective, it is possible to envisage markets in which goods of practical utility are exchanged in the interests of the whole community. Also, prices of goods (and services) can function as indicators of demand and of what should therefore be produced and offered for sale. This is called the allocation function of the market, i.e. tailoring the use of resources to the needs that have to be met. The economies of bureaucratic socialism, planned right down to the last detail, have demonstrated the nonsensical consequences of disregarding the problems of allocation.[16] The problem has much more to do with the total market, one whose success is measured by the accumulation of money, as in the classical and neo-classical liberal models. What does this actually mean?

A market of goods and services tends to destroy its own foundations if left to operate according to the principle of maximising money accumulation. It operates according to the theory of competition. According to Adam Smith, the founder of liberalism, this type of market functions because the various driving forces keep one another in check. That, however, assumes that the competing market partners are equally powerful. This power can be expressed in different ways, e.g. control over resources and information. The necessary consequence of competition is, though, that some lose while others win. This initial imbalance leads inexorably to an accumulation of the effects: the strong become stronger and the weak become weaker. Aristotle recognised this phenomenon and described it as "monopoly."[17] Until the advent of mercantilism, this problem received a lot of attention, as I indicated earlier. Neglecting it is the first great weakness of liberal theory. It postulates something which is not borne out by reality.

The decisive factor in the transition to the market economy was, as we have seen, that not only goods, but also labour, land and money were organised to suit the market, i.e. they became trading commodities.[18] But this is either a monstrous abstraction[19] or a monstrous fiction.[20] Obviously labour, land and money are not physical commodities produced to be bought and sold.

> "Labor is only another name for a human activity which goes with life itself, which in its turn is not produced for sale but for entirely different reasons, nor can that activity be detached from the rest of life, be stored or mobilized; land is only another name for nature, which is not produced by man; actual money, finally, is merely a token of purchasing power which, as a rule, is not produced at

---

16 R. Kurz, 1991, provides a detailed and convincing analysis of this weakness of the fully planned economy.

17 See the recent work of Daly and Cobb, op. cit., pp.49f.

18 In addition to Polanyi, op. cit., see also E. Altvater, 1992^2, pp.70ff.

19 See Daly and Cobb, op. cit., pp.25-117, on the analysis of "misplaced concreteness" in the economy.

20 Polanyi, op. cit., pp.72ff.

all, but comes into being through the mechanism of banking or state finance. None of them is produced for sale. The commodity description of labor, land, and money is entirely fictitious. Nevertherless, it is with the help of this fiction that the actual markets for labor, land, and money are organized."[21]

This points to the fundamental problem of the capitalist market economy: it is highly abstract, not based on real life, but forcing real life into the iron mould of the money-accumulation mechanism.

2.1 Labour

The historical effects of this fiction on labour are well known and have been the subject of many studies. After the organisation of land and capital along market lines, the introduction of the labour market was delayed because of the experience of the brutal mechanisms of impoverishment which accompanied industrial waged labour.

An attempt to rectify these effects was made in England in 1795, with the introduction of the Speenhamland System, designed to ensure the poor a minimum income, the "right to live." However, it had the opposite effect, causing widespread pauperisation and demoralisation, and it indirectly favoured the employers, who exploited this state-guaranteed minimum wage as a way of reducing wages. For this reason the "right to a living" was replaced by the Poor Law Amendment Act in 1834. The Poor Laws saw the introduction of the free labour market. "Never perhaps in all modern history has a more ruthless act of social reform been perpetrated; it crushed multitudes of lives..."[22]

These processes are known to Germans as Manchesterism. The problem of the free labour market was not a purely economic one. Part of the working population were financially better off. The decisive factors were social destruction, vulnerability and exclusion.

Applied to the working population, the fiction of the market brought about the destruction of people's social environment. Was this due to a lack of

---

21 Ibid., p.72.
22 Ibid., p.82.

historical awareness, accident or design? Let us turn to *Adam Smith* himself, as
an impartial witness, to answer this question. In his famous work *Inquiry into
the Nature and Causes of the Wealth of Nations*, he starts by investigating the
composition of the price of a product.[23] Here he notes that although the work
put into it is the only real reason for a product's surplus value, i.e. net profit,
three groups share this value added or profit: the workers receive a *wage*, the
owners of capital receive *capital gain* and the landowners receive their income
through *rent*. In this regard Smith concedes that the workers are in the weakest position in the struggle for their share. (I.viii):

> The law allowed only combinations of masters, not combinations of workmen;
> the owners of land and stock can hold out much longer in disputes; the masters
> make secret agreements amongst themselves which even have the support of the
> government; combinations of workmen are always abundantly heard of; they are
> loud but end in nothing, and laws are passed to have them punished.

Despite the greater power of the employers, Smith seems to think that the
wages of workers and their families cannot be kept below the poverty line for
a prolonged period (in which calculation he includes a child mortality rate of
50 per cent !). Only in exceptionally favourable circumstances does he expect
wages to be "above this rate; evidently the lowest which is consistent with
common humanity" (for which read subsistence level) (I.viii). These favourable economic conditions lead to population growth amongst the working
classes. If a downturn in the economy follows, then the demand for labour
falls and workers try to undercut one another by offering their services more
cheaply. This in turn leads to overwork and deterioration of their health, and
finally to high child mortality. In times of stagnation the minimum wage is
the most an employer will pay. When a country's economy is shrinking, the
lowest strata of society will be plagued by hunger and death until the demand
for labour recovers. "It is in this manner that the demand for men, like that *for
any other commodity*, necessarily regulates the production of men" ! (I.viii, my
emphasis). Smith does not investigate whether the life expectancy of land and
capital owners is also reduced in times of scarce employment.

He then turns his attention to the advantages these owners enjoy, and closes
by stating that the interests of capital owners are fundamentally opposed to
the interests of the community at large, because their whole activity is geared

---

23 A. Smith, 1776, Chap. 1.

towards generating profit, i.e. towards expanding the market and reducing competition. Therefore no government should trust the owners of capital, when passing legislation, because employers try to deceive and oppress the public (I.xi).

This means that even for Adam Smith, economic growth does not automatically lead to the steadily increasing welfare of all – not to mention the life-threatening conditions during stagnation and recession. In fact the owners of capital and land have the most power and can extract profit (through the labour of others) from the distribution of the value added, and – in principle – leave the workers only just as much as is necessary from them to reproduce themselves, i.e. to maintain the existence of the labour force. Anything over and above that is due to rare favourable circumstances. The workers and their families are a commodity whose existence depends on the supply and demand of the labour market.

In her book *The Influence of Adam Smith on Marx's Theory of Alienation* Margaret Alice Fay shows that Marx used Smith's work as the basis for his first fundamental dialectic criticism of capitalist political economy.[24] He brings conflicts between the three participants in trade who "share" the net profit (value added) into sharper focus. This mechanism, previously put forward by Smith, leads, according to Marx, to alienation of the workforce and their labour, because the owners of capital and land are also the owners of the production factors (Smith had already mentioned this, although he did not reflect upon it). Not only are those who do find work forced to accept the lowest possible wages, but the consequences for those out of work are misery, hunger and death. That is the systematic effect of the capitalist market economy, not pure chance, nor the moral depravity of one particular employer. So there is not only social inequality between workers and capitalists when it comes to exchange and the distribution of the products or their trading value. In the production process itself, there is greater inequality between those who own the means of production and those employed, which we will come back to later.

---

24 M.A. Fay, 1980.

2.2 Land

To call the soil, the land and all its life-supporting resources, commodities to be used for wealth accumulation, is an abstraction, a fiction, whose grave consequences we are only beginning to comprehend today.[25] The origins of this fiction date back to *Descartes* (1596-1650) and his dualism of the human mind (subject) and mechanical matter (object), which has determined "modern" thought right up to the present day. Land is matter and the animals on it are small machines. All thought based on mathematical abstraction aims at physical domination of matter.

John Locke continues this approach in his second Treatise of Government (1690), ascribing value to land in that it is worked by human beings. He realises that only the introduction of money allows one person to acquire more land than he can work. Indeed, Locke understood this accumulation as part of the commandment contained in the book of Genesis (1:28): "...be fruitful and multiply, and replenish the earth and subdue it..." Here, too, the notion of property plays a central role. It is worth mentioning that in the 17th century, *Sir William Petty* (1623-1687) stated that strongly male viewpoints were behind this interpretation. He termed labour the active principle of wealth and land the passive principle.

Liberal theorists since *Adam Smith* have directed their main interest very much away from the land (even as a production factor, a view which is itself an abstraction), to the question of ground rent. For them, money is the common denominator of labour and land, and the accumulation of money is the goal of economic activity through market mechanisms.

It is remarkable that *Karl Marx* also clearly understood the consequences of subordinating land to the fiction of being a commodity in industrial capitalism:[26]

> "In modern agriculture, as in the urban industries, the increased productiveness and quantity of the labour set in motion are bought at the cost of laying waste and consuming by disease labour-power itself. Moreover, all progress in capitalistic agriculture is a progress in the art, not only of robbing the labourer, but of robbing the soil; all progress in increasing the fertility of the soil for a given time, is a progress towards ruining the lasting sources of that fertility. The more a

---

25 See Daly and Cobb, 1989, pp.97ff.; E. Altvater, 1987, 1992 and 1992[2]; H.Chr. Binswanger,1991; L. Mayer, 1992.

26 K. Marx, MEGA Vol. II/9, pp.442f.; see also E. Altvater, 1992[2], p.268.

country starts its development on the foundation of modern industry, like the United States, for example, the more rapid is this process of destruction. Capitalist production, therefore, develops technology, and the combining together of various processes into a social whole, only by sapping the original sources of all wealth – the soil and the labourer."

The result is that the ground, the natural resources and the environment are only of interest to the capitalist market economy in terms of their monetary value – or to be more accurate, in their potential for accumulating money. This is precisely what leads to their destruction.

So what does it mean to say that money, this "common denominator" of labour and land, is also subordinated to the abstract fiction of being a commodity?

2.3 *Money*

There is considerable debate about the origins of money. In the second part of this book we will be investigating the early importance of money for the levying of tributes and for the temple economy in connection with biblical tradition. At this point we are interested in the relationships between commodities and money. Here again it was Aristotle who put his finger on the problem.[27] As shown earlier, he distinguished between two types of economy: the economy that existed to supply the basic needs of households and the community at large (*oikonomikè*), and the economy that served to increase wealth in the form of amassing money for its own sake (*kapelikè*, buying and selling as part of the artificial art of acquisition, *chrematistikè*). The latter arises from the former inasmuch as money is used as the medium of exchange of essential goods, initially in the form of precious metals such as silver and gold, and later in coin form. For this was the moment at which a human desire (*epithymia*) arose to surmount the limitations of life and its essential needs, by infinitely amassing money to achieve infinite supplies of the necessities of life and excessive pleasure. "...for all getters of wealth increase their hoard of coin without limit." (1257b)

---

27 See above pp.10f.

With this analysis Aristotle also determines two functions of money:

1 Money as a medium of exchange and circulation;
2 Money as the medium of wealth accumulation through making profits.

Later European tradition built on this distinction. Until well into the time of the Reformation, the people continued to follow Aristotle in condemning the money-accumulation economy, fighting it and preventing its spread with both moral and legislative means. Such measures included banning the payment of interest, demanding fair prices that were not manipulated by a monopoly, and limiting the right to property.

The great change occurred with the advent of mercantilism in the 17th century. Here again, *John Locke* provided the basic philosophy of the emerging bourgeois society. He turned Aristotles' values on their head.[28] His aim was precisely to justify and extend the individual right to property for the purposes of accumulating wealth through capitalisation. In his second Treatise of Government (1690) he says, in a nutshell, that God not only gave men the earth, but commanded them to rule it, i.e. to take possession of the earth and to utilise it (according to Genesis 1:28-29). This should be achieved via hard work and consumption. Initially, supplies exceeded what could be processed and consumed. Accordingly, what individual people could process and consume was their private property. All agreed that introducing money would be of general benefit. Certain individuals could acquire more land using non-perishable money, on condition that they did not allow any portion of what was raised to perish, but instead passed it on to others by trading. This could only lead to increasing the yield for everyone.

"And thus *came in the use of Money*, some lasting thing that Men might keep without spoiling, and that by mutual consent Men would take in exchange for the truly useful, but perishable Supports of Life." (Book II, Chapter 5, § 47)

Binswanger aptly summarises Locke's theses:

"The money we are speaking of here is obviously not the same money as is used merely for the mutual exchange of surpluses (in the sense of *oikonomikè*), but is the money with which one can purchase land and other production factors (in the sense of *kapelikè*), thus transforming land and the other production factors into a money value (capital) which can be used to generate a sum of money

---

28 See Binswanger's seminal work (1982).

(profit). This money value (of land and other production factors) is then the capitalised money yield. The ascension of the economy based on money leads to a re-evaluation of property, by its being transformed into capital. This in turn leads to a change in the laws governing the value of things, which in the last analysis are based on the regulation of property. The consequence of this is a concentration of ownership of *non*-multipliable resources such as land. However, if one correctly projects *Locke's* views onto the economic development of the industrial revolution, this also leads to the increasing appropriation of raw materials and energy, whose consumption can be increased annually, as long as supplies exist. So in addition to the *concentration* of property, there is a general *increase in the amount* of property. This means that money influences both the distribution and the growth of the national product. Here the decisive factor is that this tendency toward concentration and increase of property can continue indefinitely."[29]

Locke explains interest in terms of the unequal distribution of money:
"Locke wrote that money is able to bring the borrower of credit, if he invests it appropriately, more than six times its original value, in the same way that land, along with the labour of the tenant, can produce a harvest greater in value than the dividend paid to the landlord."[30]
Binswanger summarises: "It becomes clear that interest is therefore nothing other than the dealer's or tenant's share of the profit. However, this profit is explained ... in terms of the basic characteristics of an economy aiming at acquisition, on which *Locke* bases his considerations. This means that interest is, in the same way as profit, a *monetary factor*. It presupposes the capitalisation of goods in trade and of agricultural land, i.e. storehouses, like land itself, appear primarily in terms of their money or capital value and only secondarily in terms of their usefulness or natural productive potential."[31]

Binswanger shows how *John Law* developed Locke's theory in two ways in his major work *Money and Trade* (1705), namely "with reference to the economic reasoning behind the productive power of money, or credit."[32] The basic idea was this: the introduction of paper money (and later of the account system, i.e. demand deposits at banks) makes it possible to increase the money supply

---

29 Ibid., p.100(tr.).
30 Quoted from Binswanger, op. cit., p.11.
31 Ibid.(tr.).
32 Ibid., p.116(tr.).

over and above the value of the gold and silver reserves. The bank thus becomes an issuing bank (i.e. it can issue more credit than it holds in deposits.) Under Law's system banknotes are covered by the national debt and the profits of trading monopolies. If a larger amount of money is now invested productively in trade, a mechanism of extending production and trade is set in motion, which stimulates economic growth through credit.

Law aimed this mechanism at opening up new trading routes, the colonisation of the New World and tapping new sources of raw materials. He compares money with blood (as Hobbes did before him). For Law, the relevance of this image is that the circulation of money throughout the state is vital to the economy. "However, the issuing bank is, in economic terms, the heart of the state. Law used this image to introduce the concept of circulation into the national economy."[33]

Although the system set up in France in 1717 failed due to the mounting speculation fever, the Bank of England adopted a similar approach and as English hegemony increased, it developed into a type of world bank, a banks' bank, providing the basis for the later development of today's system of central and commercial banks and for the international currency institutions.

To summarise, mercantilism entailed not only a revision of values in view of the positive attitude to the accumulation of money for its own sake, but also far-reaching changes in the monetary system. This system was now able to boost economic growth for the purpose of accumulating wealth.

This revolution in attitudes to, and the form of, the money-accumulation economy under mercantilism between the 16th and 18th centuries, as expressed in the writings of John Locke and John Law, is the fertile ground which fed the capitalist market economy burgeoning at the moment of industrialisation. Polanyi speaks of the "commercial society," from which the market economy arose the moment the complex machine began to make its presence felt, in that in addition to land and money – as under mercantilism – labour was also fully transformed into a commodity on the "free market".

Only *Karl Marx* develops Aristotle's critical line. He unveils the mechanism of money accumulation, the "secret of making a plus," as he calls it, in economic development up until the advent of industrial capitalism through

---

33 Ibid., p.123(tr.).

recognition of three fundamental aspects. Firstly, he explains the distortion of reality due to the abstractness of the money accumulation mechanism by analysing the fetishisms of commodities and capital. All rules and institutions of this system that remain invisible but which have the power of life and death over human beings and the earth, ultimately serve the accumulation of capital and are therefore regarded as sacrosanct (taboo). Secondly, at the same time, he refines the Aristotelian distinction between money as money (exchanged for useful goods needed to meet human needs, i.e. to be consumed), and money as capital (in the sense of unlimited and excessive accumulation of money for its own sake). Thirdly, he also comes up with a basic analysis for something realised earlier by Luther, that accumulating money as trading capital or as industrial or interest-bearing capital, i.e. surplus value, is achieved by the exploitation of labour. (Today one would have to add the exploitation of the environment, which Marx also hinted at). He, like Adam Smith, saw that only as much of the profits reached the labour force as was necessary to maintain it at a minimum level. Neither the earth, nor human beings, and their needs which extend beyond reproducing the labour force, are of any interest to self-expanding capital. This is the root of human misery and the destruction of the environment.

A detailed account of Marx's *fetishism analysis* in *Capital* is beyond the scope of this book. The reader is referred to *Franz Hinkelammert's* excellent "The ideological weapons of death: a theological critique of capitalism"[34] which develops the issue from today's perspective. What does Marx analyse in his fetishism theory? He analyses the rules, institutions and power relationships governing the division of labour and the distribution of goods within society. In particular, these rules are kept secret in capitalist society, because they are hidden in the terms applied to commodities.

> The more pressure society puts on the workforce, the more the value of an item is seen in terms of its money value rather than its usefulness in satisfying human needs. (Aristotle expressed this in the distortion of the natural economy of acquisition, *ktetiké*, into the money-accumulation economy, *chrematistiké*; tellingly, the Greek *chrema* means both "thing" and "money.") So this fetishism has developed in various periods in history.[35]

34 F.J. Hinkelammert, 1986, pp.5-61.
35 Ibid., p.16.

There is nothing mysterious about the usefulness of an object. Wheat is there to be eaten, clothes are made to be worn. However, under a system of labour division based on private property, wheat becomes a means of exchange for obtaining shoes, and vice versa. (Incidentally, Hinkelammert also shows that under bureaucratic socialism relationships were still expressed through commodities, a point which must be left out at this stage).[36] However, through the system of exchange the goods themselves begin to develop a network of relationships of their own reflecting the social relationships.

This process is exacerbated if the commodity money becomes a common denominator for the exchange value of all other goods. Money is then the *commodity,* with a value of its own. Symbolised by silver and gold, money is the depository of value. Laying up treasure corresponds to this stage of the fetish. It was this that Aristotle described as greed for unlimited accumulation of money.

Under capitalism the fetishism reaches its pinnacle of development and acquires its all-inclusive character. For under capitalism *everything becomes a commodity to be used for money accumulation.* Of course this means money itself, but also includes land (and increasingly the means of industrial production) and, most importantly, labour in the form of waged labour.[37] In other words, everything is transformed into capital. So what is capital?

Marx contrasts two formulas to explain what capital is. Under a barter system money facilitates the exchange of two commodities required by human beings to satisfy their basic needs. The first formula reads: Commodity 1 – Money – Commodity 2 (c-m-c'). Money becomes capital if it becomes the starting point and goal of the economic process, while the commodity is reduced to a means of increasing the amount of money. This gives the formula Money – Commodity – (more) Money (m-c-m'). As shown above, one or more identical cycles of this type are hidden in the production process of the commodity.

> "Buying in order to sell, or more accurately, buying in order to sell dearer, m-c-m', appears certainly to be a form peculiar to one kind of capital alone, namely, merchants' capital. But industrial capital too is money, that is changed into commodities, and by the sale of these commodities, is re-converted into more money.

---

36 See the recent work of R. Kurz, 1991.
37 Cf. Hinkelammert, op. cit., pp.27f. with reference to K. Marx, and Polanyi, op. cit.

The events that take place outside the sphere of circulation, in the interval between the buying and selling, do not affect the form of this movement. Lastly, in
the case of interest-bearing capital, the circulation M-C-M' appears abridged. We
have its result without the intermediate stage, in the form M-M', "en style lapi-
daire" so to say, money that is worth more money, value that is greater than itself. M-C-M' is therefore in reality the general formula of capital..."[38]

Marx uses this statement to point out that in the modern bourgeois money-
accumulation economy the value added in the transaction from money via
commodities to more money is exploited labour. The waged worker can no
longer take his labour to market in the form of a concrete product he has
made, but must sell his labour, i.e. himself. The owner of capital has control
of the production factors, the machinery etc. But he is also the owner of the
products, that is, the means of survival for all non-capital-owners, i.e. and
therefore also for the farmers who do not own land, the unemployed and
other marginalised groups.

"The consumption of labour-power is at one and the same time the production
of commodities and of surplus value."[39]

However, capital – by its very nature money-accumulation for its own sake –
"ensures the livelihoods only of those workers necessary for its (capital's) survival."[40] The misery of unemployment, for example, has no place in the calculations of capital – just like child labour at one time – as long as the opposing
forces are not strong enough. This is how capital seems to a non-capital-
owner. Capital itself gives the impression of being the source of everything
productive. Its destructive mechanism of self-generation is presented as the
source of life.

"The relations of capital assume their most externalised and most fetish-like
form in interest-bearing capital... Capital appears as a mysterious and self-crea-
ting source of interest – the source of its own increase. The thing (money, commodity, value) is now capital even as a mere thing, and capital appears as a mere
thing. The result of the process of reproduction appears as a property inherent in

---

38 K. Marx, MEGA, Vol. II/9, p.135.
39 K. Marx, MEGA, Vol. II/9, p.152; see also Hinkelammert, op. cit., pp.28f.
40 Hinkelammert, loc. cit., p.30.

the thing itself. It depends on the owner of the money, i.e. of the commodity in its continually exchangeable form, whether he wants to spend it as money or loan it out as capital. In interest-bearing capital, therefore, this automatic fetish, self-expanding value, money generating money, are brought out in their pure state and in this form it no longer bears the birth-marks of its origin... This too becomes distored. While interest is only a portion of the profit, i.e., of the surplus value, which the functioning capitalist squeezes out of the labourer, it appears now, on the contrary, as though interest were the typical product of capital, the primary matter, and profit, in the shape of profit of enterprise, were a mere accessory and by-product of the process of reproduction. Thus we get the fetish form of capital and the conception of fetish capital."[41]

The two formulae used by Marx, M-C-M' and M-M', are the theoretical expressions of what Arrighi has described as capital accumulation through material expansion and through financial expansion. The latter hits workers even harder than the former. Mobile capital can just go to where it gets the highest returns. If production and trade do not make enough profit they move into speculation and loans until a new, profitable mode of production and trade has been found.

It was none other than Goethe who really developed the subject of the exploitation of the natural environment by the money mechanism, only hinted at by Marx. In his book *Money and Magic*, Binswanger has shown that *Faust*, Part II deals with precisely this topic.[42] He states that paper money has the same function as alchemy: to turn dross into valuable material. This means that it is only covered if "earth" is transformed for this purpose. This is the aging Faust's great project with the aid of technology. Concentration on money accumulation causes the destruction of all other economies and the people living in them, such as Philemon and Baucis with their subsistence economy. Faust also destroys himself. He goes blind. The digging, which he thinks is part of the great project, is the digging of his grave.

---

41 K. Marx, 1974, Vol. III, pp.391f. See also Hinkelammert, op. cit., p.32.
42 H.Chr. Binswanger, 1994. See also 1990 and his extensive work on today's ecological problems, 1991. The connection between the dynamics of the capitalist system of money and environmental problems is emphasised by the school of Silvio Gesell and has been taken up in detail, most recently by H. Creutz, 1993, pp.295ff.

The result of this is that under mercantilism, important elements for the revolution of industrial capitalism were put into position. Locke provided the theological and philosophical legitimation for the accumulation of wealth and property, while Law invented a new system of paper money, thus providing the economic basis for extending the monetary economy. The transformation of working people, the land and money, as a means of exchange, into the fiction of being commodities left society at the mercy of the capitalist market, dividing it, destroying nature and allowing money to become a fetish, as Karl Marx showed.

The introduction of paper money demonstrates again that the state also has functions to perform in a capital-accumulation economy. Initially it has to guarantee the quality of the coins and later cover its banknotes. We will now turn our attention to these functions.

3   The political conditions necessary for a capitalist market economy

According to the pure form of liberal theory, all social matters are best regulated by the markets themselves. The state then only has to ensure that the markets really do regulate themselves without any external interference. This approach assumes strict duality, even separation, between bourgeois society and the sphere of politics. It corresponds to the distinction between the citizen as a member of society (*bourgeois*) and the citizen as a political force (*citoyen*). Here again, the traditional positions, as described by Aristotle, are completely reversed: according to him, those performing economic functions in the community (*koinonia*) or the household (*oikos*), and politicians responsible for society *(politikos)*, are supposed to prevent the development of the money-accumulation economy and its destructive effects on households and the fabric of society.

So how does the state assist the smooth functioning of the capitalist market economy, which aims at the accumulation of money? The main factors here are property, contract law, the organisation of money and foreign (trade) policy.

3.1 *Property and contract law*

The turning point is again marked by *John Locke*. In his second Treatise of Government, this pioneering philosopher of the bourgeois society defines a human being as a natural property owner.[43] His definition of property includes:
– one's own life, one's person, most importantly one's work potential
– goods (first and foremost land and money)
– certain liberties.[44]
Under Locke's system, therefore, slaves did not have to be regarded as human beings with the rights of citizens, but as legitimate prey – captured in a just war and subject to the whims of their masters.

> "*Slaves*, who being Captives taken in a just War, are by the Right of Nature subjected to the Absolute Dominion and Arbitrary Power of their Masters. These men having, as I say, forfeited their Lives, and with it their Liberties, and lost their Estates; and being in the *State of Slavery*, not capable of any Property, cannot in that state be considered as any part of *Civil Society*; the chief end whereof is the preservation of Property."[45]

So Aristotle's philosophy did find some favour with Locke! His justification of slavery is largely taken from the same volume of *Politics* that has a later chapter containing the prophetic warnings about the wealth-accumulation economy, which Locke, as I have mentioned, turns upside down. It may be useful here to take a look at some passages verbatim from Aristotle, since they clarify the continuity between the imperialist, patriarchal, xenophobic and environmentally damaging culture of the ancient empires and of the European Modern Age, which we will have to turn our attention to later. This is what Aristotle has to say:

> "...we may firstly observe in living creatures both a despotical and a constitutional rule; for the soul rules the body with a despotical rule, whereas the intellect rules the appetites with a constitutional and royal rule. And it is clear that the rule of the soul over the body, and of the mind and the rational element over the passionate, is natural and expedient; whereas the equality of the two or the rule of

---

43 J. Locke, (1690) 1988, Book II, Chap. 5.
44 E.g. ibid., Book I, Chap. 9.
45 Book II, Chap. 7, § 85.

the inferior is always hurtful. The same holds good of animals in relation to men; for tame animals have a better nature than wild and all tame animals are better off when they are ruled by man; for then they are preserved. Again, the male is by nature superior, and the female inferior; and the one rules, and the other is ruled; this principle, of necessity, extends to all mankind. Where then there is such a difference as that between soul and body, or between men and animals (as in the case of those whose business is to use their body, and who can do nothing better), the lower sort are by nature slaves, and it is better for them as for all inferiors that they should be under the rule of a master. ... Nature would like to distinguish between the bodies of freemen and slaves, making the one strong for servile labour, the other upright, and although useless for such services, useful for political life in the arts both of war and peace." (1254b)

"And so, from one point of view, the art of war is a natural art of acquisition, for the art of acquisition includes hunting, an art which we ought to practise against wild beasts, and against men who, though intended by nature to be governed, will not submit; for war of such a kind is naturally just." (1256b)

The analogy between the emotions, tame animals and women, on the one hand, and the body, wild animals and human beings destined by their very nature to become slaves, on the other, along with the predestination of both these groups to be ruled, belongs to the most persistent legacies of the Ancient Greeks and Romans that have found their way into European tradition. Indeed, in a way, the horrific consequences of this idea have become even worse since the beginning of the modern era, i.e. the 16th century – everything that Aristotle defined as requiring to be ruled is now subordinated to the merciless rationality of the money-accumulation mechanism, which Aristotle in fact condemned.

This is expressed in the notion of property, which Locke and Aristotle define differently. The latter also defines slaves as possessions (*ktesis*), but ascribes this property to the *oikonomia*, the household economy. All household property is characterised by the fact that it is limited, and that its only function is to meet human needs. Locke, on the other hand, is concerned with actually justifying unrestricted accumulation, amassing possessions via the unrestricted money-accumulation mechanism. This is exactly what Aristotle rejected as unnatural and destructive.

Behind Locke's concept of property lies the Roman legal idea of "dominium." This is equated with absolute power and gives the owner the right to do as he pleases with his property: "Ownership is the right to use and consume property, as long as this is within the law."[46] However, this reference to legal compatibility is not to be understood as social acceptability, but rather as compliance with contract law. In bourgeois society, the chief purpose of the state is, as stated in the quote on slavery above, the protection of private property, and thus its unlimited accumulation, both at home and abroad:

> "...thus the Commonwealth comes by a power to set down, what punishment shall belong to the several transgressions which they think worthy of it, committed amongst the Members of that Society, (which is the power of making Laws) as well as it has the power to punish any Injury done unto any of its Members, by any one that is not of it, (which is the power of War and Peace;) and all this for the preservation of property of all the Members of that Society..."[47]

In justifying property, its unlimited increase through the mechanism of money, and the definition of the law and of the state as the protectors of property, Locke is primarily concerned with land and money, although labour potential as property is expressly mentioned as one of three types of property. But here we are dealing with an unparalleled cover-up, whose consequences only come to light when waged labour under industrial capitalism becomes the principal form of work as dictated by market laws. Equating labour potential, land, money and goods (as production factors and as commodities), not to mention liberties, with forms of property, the liberal economic theory of Locke and his successors suggests that all people are thereby equal in respect to property. Robert Heilbronner, in his book *Behind the Veil of Economics*, gives a precise analysis of this impression. He refers the reader to the differing values attached to various forms of property:

> "...is an unequal construal of the meaning of 'property' when it refers to the means of production (land or capital) and when it refers to labor power – the ownership by the individual of his or her laboring capacity, including the precious right to withhold that capacity if desired [in a strike, U.D.]. Although these property claims appear to be identical, they are not. For the right to claim the product of the means of production conjoined with labor power is entirely vested in the first owner, not in the second. The capitalist farmer owns the crop raised on his land and the capitalist manufacturer the output produced in his factory. In exchange for a wage payment, the worker surrenders all claim to this out-

---

46 "Dominium est ius utendi et abutendi re sua quaterus iuris ratio patitur." See Locke, loc. cit., Book II, Chap. 5, and Binswanger, 1982a, p.33.
47 Locke, op. cit, Book II, chap. 7, § 88.

put, even though it would appear – and many conventional economists claim – that labour and capital as 'factors of production' exist on an entirely equal conceptual footing, one with the other. Thus the uncontested ownership by capital of all value added is evidence that the market system incorporates a system of asymmetrical disposition of its product – a disposition that reflects the presence of social domination, however unrecognised, within its operations."[48]

That has far-reaching consequences for the role of the law and the state in a bourgeois market society. A legal system and a state that restrict themselves to setting up the basic conditions for the protection of property and self-regulation of the market, must necessarily protect inequality, despite the formal equality of all before the law. The owners of land and capital as means of production own more powerful property than those who can only take their own (potential) labour to market, not to mention the case of slaves under mercantilism, who have no rights at all. And this is not a random side-effect of the bourgeois market society, but is consciously intended, as the writings of Locke show. He gives a theoretical rationale for the actual effects of the market economy, i.e. the accumulation of land and capital in the hands of a restricted number of people who own these production factors. Indeed, Locke justifies this theologically as being a rational and industrious response to the divine command to subdue the earth.

And this perception of reality is not merely a thing of the past. The constitution of the United States from 1776 and bourgeois constitutions from the French Revolution, right up to the West German post-war constitution in 1949, are all based on John Locke's fundamental ideas.[49] The fact that Napoleon incorporated property law as expounded by Locke into his legislation had particularly far-flung effects, as this legislation was then used as the basis of all subsequent civil codes. Binswanger has this to say on the subject:

"In the *Code Napoleon*, the civil code Napoleon created, article 544 reads: 'Ownership is the right to enjoy and use things in the most absolute manner' (La propriété est le droit de jouir et de disposer des choses de la manière la plus absolue), the only proviso being that the owner may not use his property in a way

---

48 R. Heilbronner, 1988, p.30.
49 See C.B. Macpherson, 1962, pp.194ff.; M. Beaud, 1981, pp.33ff. For an assessment of the importance of this tradition for the German constitution see A. Krölls, 1988. A critical history and an ethical judgment of property law from Aristotle to present-day social teachings of the Catholic church is given in G. Lantz, 1977.

that contravenes the rest of the civil and criminal law. The *Code Napoleon* was to become the model for civil codes the world over. This new property law – the *dominium* of Roman law – differs fundamentally from the original conceptions of property, all of which are based in some way in the idea of *patrimonium*: the duty to tend nature."[50]

At this point we are not concerned with the hard-won social corrections to the western constitutions, but with the original approaches in the definition of the role of law and the state in the emerging bourgeois market society. As in the case of defining land, money and labour as commodities, the concepts of property and of liberty to enter into contracts as one wishes, and their protection, are also abstractions which do not take account of the real power relations and the attendant inequalities and restrictions on freedom in the real world.

3.2   The money system

Binswanger points out that in *Faust* Goethe presents the introduction of paper money as a suggestion made by Faust and Mephistopheles to "the Emperor."[51] The emperor is to be freed from his financial worries by issuing these notes, which are both covered by the gold deposits in the ground and endorsed with the emperor's signature. This means that the emperor is at the same time sanctioning the paper money as a blank check. Faust is then supposed to mine the gold deposits in a great project. The complete process is presented as alchemy, as something of lower value is transformed into a something of higher value. Here Goethe is making an allusion to the Duke of Orleans, who engaged John Law, the inventor of paper money, and then dismissed his court alchemists, saying that he had now found a better way of acquiring money.[52] Goethe put an emperor in his play instead of a duke because he had Napoleon in mind.

This also has a deep symbolic meaning, which we will discuss in more detail in the second part of this book, i.e. how the European Modern Age followed on from the empires of antiquity.[53] Even Emperor Charles v had

50 Binswanger, 1994, p.32.
51 Ibid., pp.10ff.
52 Ibid., p.31.

tried to unite Europe in a single empire. He rose to power using the trading and financial capital of the Fuggers and the Genoese merchants, and sought to finance the creation of his empire with gold and silver plundered from South America. After the failure of this attempt, the mercantile territorial states were formed. They practised accumulation of capital with the aid of their own trading companies (exchanging finished products from Europe, slaves and raw materials in triangular fashion). In the classically liberal phase of the 19th century private finance capital took over the leading role. In other words, the empire had shifted completely from the realm of politics to the anonymous power of capital, and Goethe could treat the creation of paper money as the actual founding of an empire. Binswanger summarises as follows:

> "As the nineteenth century advanced, the creation of paper money and bank
> money combined with the spread of the new property law to provide the support
> for the industrial revolution and the growth in trade that developed out of it.
> Faust's enterprise has become the global plan of the economy. It is *the* modern
> economy."[54]

3.3   Foreign (trade) policy

The origins of European trading policy go back to the Crusades. Normally we associate the Crusades with the alliance of the Cross with the sword, forgetting the role that money also played. The banks and trading institutions of northern Italy had an ulterior motive. They – in particular Venice – became rich, not only through the enormous sums of money collected by the Pope and their high-interest loans to help fund the Crusades, and by supplying equipment for the Crusaders. More importantly, with the military expansion towards Palestine, they gained control of the trading routes to the East, principally to India, the most important goal of foreign trade.

The "*conquista*," the Genoese-Spanish conquest of America, was based on this *reconquista*, the reclaiming of the Holy Land (and of the whole of Spain). (It is ironic that Columbus came upon America whilst looking for a second trading route to India – with the intention of finding as much as gold as possible, to finance another Crusade.)[55] The foreign relations of the European

---

53 See U. Duchrow, 1992, Part I.

54 Binswanger, 1994, p.33.

55 See U. Duchrow, 1992, with suggestions for further reading. See also Le Goff, 1988,

city states and then of the kingdoms of Spain and Portugal, and of the Habsburg Empire until well into the 16th century, consisted initially of plundering expeditions with disastrous effects on the countries and peoples on the receiving end. During the first 70 years of Spanish rule, approximately 70 million native inhabitants met their deaths, i.e. ninety per cent of the indigenous population. This led to the early development of the equally murderous slave trade, importing slaves from Africa to South America and the Caribbean, to replace the dwindling numbers of workers in the mines and on the plantations. The mercantilist states of the 17th and 18th centuries based the triangular trade on precisely this combination of factors – first under Dutch leadership, then English (in competition with France) – trade which provided the most important source of capital accumulation in Europe. (Incidentally, John Locke also earned his money from the slave trade.) During this phase the state trading monopolies were the main actors in economic foreign relations between states, supported by their armed forces and the colonial administrations.

Whilst this early phase is associated with the use of military force, during the liberal era of the 19th century capital indirectly dominated the globe. If one particular country did not want to participate in the free world market, (English) capital financed proxy wars. To take an example, London financed the war by Argentina, Brazil and Uruguay against Paraguay, to put a stop to that country's self-sufficiency. The side-effect of this was debts on their part, i.e. subsequent dependence of the warring countries on English capital.[56]

Once one has an overview of the transformations (a) of societies with markets to market societies, (b) of land, capital and labour into commodities, and (c) of legal and political institutions serving the market of owners, the fundamental question emerges, what happened to the people during this historic metamorphosis?

---

according to whom the doctrine of Purgatory and the purchase of indulgences was developed to allow bankers, who had broken the ban on charging interest by capitalising on the Crusades, to enter Heaven, simultaneously diverting a proportion of the interest earned into church coffers.

56 See ibid., p.26 and Galeano, 1985, p.221.

4 The ideology of market-minded people (homo oeconomicus)[57]

Macpherson characterises the view of human beings (anthropology) in the emerging market society as "possessive individualism."[58] To be more precise one would have to say "property-accumulating individualism," or to be even more exact, "money-accumulating individualism."

Let us turn our minds back once again to Aristotle. He, too, assumes that humankind needs possessions (*ktesis*) in order to live. But this property is associated with the household (*oikos*), community (*koinonia*) and the surrounding political community (*polis*). For this reason he defines people as political beings (*zoon politikon*). They can only live, survive, and meet their essential needs if they accept that the community is finite. Anyone wishing to amass individually the means of everlasting life by accumulating money, will destroy not only the community, but also him/herself. That is the moral of the tale of King Midas, who starved amid mountains of gold. That is why Aristotle repeatedly calls the greed for wealth accumulation (*epithymia*) and its mechanism an "illusion", as opposed to truth, i.e. that which lasts to the end. When he contrasts the blind, destructive striving towards endless life achieved through the unlimited accumulation of wealth with "good life," this is not a moral category in the sense of modern abstract "ethics", but an ontological, political category. Life can only be lived and maintained within the limitations of a concrete human community.

This piece of wisdom has been preserved in the non-western remnants of African, Asian and Indian cultures. In western Europe it crumbled away in the *mid-14th century*, at a time that we now celebrate as the beginning of the Renaissance. There are many theories about reasons for this *break*. The learned poet *Francesco Petrarca* is celebrated as the "first modern man". Following on from Augustine, who has incidentally been wrongly accused of reducing theology to "God and the soul," and from Cicero, he describes in hymns the new individual relationship with nature and history. However, when referring to the continuation of theological and philosophical traditions, one must explain why this "discovery" of the individual occurred at this precise time.

---

57 See also Daly and Cobb, op. cit., pp.85ff.
58 C.B. Macpherson, 1962.

K.G. Zinn points to two factors in economic history in particular: the *plague* and the invention of *firearms*.[59] Both make people keep their distance from others. The Great Plague of 1348-1352 wiped out half the population of Europe. The plague made people keep away from others through fear of infection, through the scapegoat syndrome[60] and a growing "save yourself" or "every man for himself" mentality. The invention of firearms, apart from reducing the immediacy of killing, also had an extraordinary economic effect. It reinforced the turn away from a very productive period of farming that also benefited the general standard of living, to the ascendancy of towns and cities, whose development was powered by the arms industry.

Such a dramatic change is caused by the interplay of a myriad of factors. So it cannot be any surprise that the drastic change started principally in those cities which had already grown rich by financing the Crusades, i.e. the northern Italian city states, including Venice, Florence, Milan and Genoa. Witnessing the cut-throat competition between them, Machiavelli was the first to declare that power, and striving for power, were the root of all politics.[61]

However, *Thomas Hobbes* and *John Locke* are the founding fathers of the economic theory that human beings are property- and wealth-accumulating beings in competition with one another.[62] We should be clear on how Hobbes arrives at his statement that man is "by nature" a mechanical system striving for power over others, and therefore a violent struggle must ensue if a strong government does not intervene. This argument, that human beings are simply made that way, has been used by ideologists of the capitalist market economy right up to the present day. It justifies the view that the market economy is natural. Anyone claiming the opposite must be an ideologist, at best an idealist not to be taken seriously. However, Macpherson has shown persuasively the manner of Hobbes' argument.[63] He takes the condition of the emerging market society, determined by competition, and projects it backwards onto a supposedly natural state, re-applying it to society and then drawing political conclusions.

---

59 K.G. Zinn, 1989.

60 This was the time of the first systematic pogroms against the Jewish minority, justified by the claim that the Jews had poisoned the wells.

61 See E. Barincou's readable illustrated biography, *Niccolò Machiavelli*, (1958), 1988, pub. by rororo.

62 See Macpherson's extensive treatment of this, op. cit.

63 Ibid., pp.17ff.

What is his artificial model of the human condition like? From the abstraction of bourgeois society he gleans the three important, supposedly natural causes of conflict for people striving for a good and comfortable life. These are competition, distrust and the desire for glory. So, to protect themselves from others, people need the state and its laws.

> "The Passions that encline men to Peace are the Feare of Death; Desire of such things as are necessary to commodious living; and a Hope by their Industry to obtain them."[64]

> In the initial chapters of *Leviathan* Hobbes justifies this construct both physiologically and psychologically. A human being is very similar to an automatic machine, an *automaton* intent on continuing its movement. Movement "towards" is greed, while movement "away from" is disinclination. '...because Life it selfe is but Motion, and can never be without Desire, nor without Feare, no more than without Sense', each man must seek continual success in obtaining those things which he from time to time desires and will desire."[65] So he reaches the definition of power and the postulate that all human beings strive for ever-new power over others: "The Power of a Man ... is his present means, to obtain some future apparent Good." "So that in the first place, I put for a generall inclination of all mankind, a perpetuall and restlesse desire of Power after power, that ceaseth onely in Death."[66] As an example of power he mentions the characteristics of the market: wealth, large undertakings, important goods and offices. "Every man is in the market for power."[67]

> "The possessive market society, then, does meet Hobbes's requirements. It is a society in which men who want more may, and do, continually seek to transfer to themselves some of the powers of others, in such a way as to compel everyone to compete for more power, and all this by peaceable and legal methods which do not destroy the society by open force." [68]

This is really still only the mercantilist model of the market society, in which the state has the important function of regulation. *Locke* also develops his

---

64 Hobbes, *Leviathan*, chap. 13; see also Macpherson, loc. cit., p.29: "Natural man is civilized man only with the restraint of law removed."

65 Ibid., p.33 on *Leviathan*, Chap. 6.

66 Chapters 10-11 and also Macpherson, op. cit., pp.35ff.

67 Ibid., pp.38f.

68 Ibid., p.59.

similar theory against this background. He perceives the state, however, not as being imposed by a single ruler, but instead based on the agreement, or contract, of the community. In addition, he adds to Hobbes' basic viewpoint the importance of money for continual increase in property. First and foremost, though, he uses the divine command to homo sapiens to subdue the earth as a legitimation for the wealth-accumulation mechanism. So reason is interpreted in the sense of rational accumulation of money.

That refers us back to two other philosophers who played a decisive role in the birth of the Modern Age in Europe: *Francis Bacon* and *René Descartes*.[69] In his *New Organon of the Sciences* (1620), Bacon describes three stages of human striving for power. The first stage is, "to claim one's own power in one's own country," the second is, "to increase the respect and power of one's own country," while the third is concerned with "the power and dominion of the human race over the whole of nature." This seizure of power is made possible through science and technology (Novum Organum 1, paragraph 129).[70] The apparently harmless proverb "Knowledge itself is power" comes from Bacon, and in this case "power" can be interpreted as power which can be used against members of the same society, against other races – *primitive* races, as the native inhabitants of America and Africa are called – and against nature itself. So it was no accident that as Lord Chancellor Bacon was responsible for the trials of so-called "witches." When he says that Nature must be tortured in order to extract her secrets, it is all too apparent that this language springs from violence against women.

Descartes should also be mentioned here once more. It is well known that he defined mankind as "master and possessor of nature" (maître et possesseur de la nature). The thinking of human beings transforms their own corporeality, and the whole world, so that they become mechanically viewed objects of violent scientific method and technical manipulation. For us here it is especially important to note that this pure knowledge is of a mathematical nature. The whole world was regarded in the abstract terms of mathematics. Revealingly, Descartes developed probability theory in association with the calculation of interest. The economic future of the human race was subordinated to the mathematics of money accumulation.

---

69 See also U. Duchrow and G. Liedke, (1986) 1989, pp.69ff.
70 In this connection it is interesting to remember that one of Aristotle's ways of distinguishing between the wealth accumulation economy and the household economy was the former's use of artificial methods.

From this point there is a direct link to *Adam Smith*, the founder of modern national economics. He regarded himself as the Newton of economics. This simply means that the theory of economics and human economic activity is represented in a similar way to classical physics. Like Hobbes before him, Smith regarded human beings as automatons striving to make a profit. The difference here is, however, that the state is no longer required to regulate the market; under the liberal conception of industrial capitalism, the market regulates itself. To be fair one should add that Smith genuinely regarded himself as a moral philosopher and as such introduced two conditions for his calculations, which are generally ignored by proponents of neo-liberalism. Firstly, in much the same way as Descartes started from a vision of God as the wise watch-maker who made the earth and set it running, Smith uses the concept of the "invisible hand," keeping the market working harmoniously, to the greatest common good. Secondly, he assumes that people, being blessed with reason, are also blessed with solidarity towards their fellows which keeps the whole system in check. Whenever this natural solidarity breaks down, as in the paragraph on selfish employers quoted above, Smith does in fact see a need for the state to take action.

However, Smith's philosophy and the mechanistic traditions on which it was based sowed the seed of the view that the economy has autonomous laws, and therefore also of the assumption that scientific economics and its techniques are essential in recognising and controlling economic processes and interpreting human behaviour within the economy ("Only the experts...").

Let us summarise the unparalleled abstractions and re-evaluations associated with the economic view of human beings as market-minded people, i.e. money-accumulators and consumers:

— Market-minded persons do not strive to satisfy their limited needs for survival, but, for fear of death, seek to fulfill their unlimited, artificial desires, and to acquire more and more money and goods; they are unlimited consumers and capital accumulators.
— Market-minded people are, naturally, power-minded. They strive egoistically to increase their property at the expense of others, since this allegedly guarantees the wealth accumulation of the whole national economy.
— Market-minded people possess their own labour, which is of value in that they sell it on the market for money.
— Being business people, the market-minded calculate rationally and imaginatively, aiming for maximum profit.

— Being thinkers, the market-minded are mathematicians in that they perceive certain patterns in (natural and human) reality, which they learn to manipulate by means of technology.
— The market-minded are individuals striving to escape the restriction of time, space and community with the aid of artificial technologies. The fact that they are destroying themselves and the world is kept quiet.

In the light of the above, it should be obvious that economics and anthropology of this type are highly ideological, if they do not reflect on their own assumptions and limitations. Firstly, they are based upon the abstraction of economic and human processes.[71] In connection with this we will turn our attention in the Third Part to the unexamined criteria for measuring economic success. The way human beings are regarded is also an abstraction. It completely removes them from their natural and social relations and limitations. Evidence provided by another discipline, depth psychology, is enough to counter the view that human beings are just greedy for increased possessions and personal power. This is untenable, because human nature also has a complementary positive side which is at least as strong: from early childhood positive emotions govern relations and cooperative behaviour.[72] The most important point missed by mercantilist and classical economists and their theory of human nature is that their suppositions, which they draw from the emerging market society and then declare to be universal, are strongly laced with sympathy for the massive power interests of the winning social classes. And as economics presents this combination of partial recognition of the true state of affairs and power interests as a universal scientific truth, it has an interest itself in gaining power over the market and in stabilising existing market relations.

---

71 See Daly and Cobb's fundamental criticism of economics as a science, with regard to the lack of reflection on the methodology and the corresponding catastrophic effects of the abstractions on real life (1989), pp.25ff.
72 See among others B. Heilbronner, 1988, p.20 and elsewhere.

Chapter 11

The resistance of victims and societies

1 Resistance outside Europe

It is an age-old custom that the winners get to write the history books. For example, in the version of history taught in Western Europe, only small minorities know about the periods of suffering and resistance of the victims of the gradual spread of the capitalist global market. Which of us is familiar with the Moslem view of the Crusades?[1] Or the struggle of the American Indians or that of Africans deported to America as slaves?[2]

1992 brought a welcome improvement in this regard.[3] Not only did we witness the European and international campaigns against the 500th anniversary celebrations of Columbus' "discovery" of America, under such catchwords as "500 years of oppression *and resistance*", but, in Latin America and the Caribbean, 1992 also saw self-help groups being set up by the indigenous population, in some cases spanning the whole continent, and also large-scale projects on re-writing history.[4] The award of the Nobel Peace Prize to Rigoberta Menchú has also drawn more people's attention to the struggle of native Americans.

A deeper-running form of this struggle to resist and survive does not even express itself through words, nor does it have a visible organisation. Words are much too dangerous in the situation of total oppression by the Europeans. One form of expression is the liturgy used in church services, whether it be in the form of Afro-Brazilian cults such as Ubanda, or Afro-American spirituals. Another form is wonderful dances like the Capoeira, still practised in Brazil today. They are forms of self-defence. So is the drum language, which enables

---

1 See A. Maalouf, 1983, or K. Armstrong, 1988, and others.
2 For older works of non-fiction see F. Fanon, 1981; E. Galeano, 1976 and 1983-1988; W. Rodney, 1972; T. Todorov, 1985; E. Williams, 1967 and 1971; E. R. Wolf, 1982. For fictional works see R. Schneider, (1952) 1990; A. Seghers, (1976) 1981[4].
3 See U. Duchrow, 1992, with bibliography. Also from the numerous works on this subject: D.N. Hopkins and G. Cummings (eds.), 1991; H. Gründer, 1992.
4 The current CEHILA project to write a comprehensive new history of the church in Latin America must be mentioned here.

people to communicate over great distances. Solidarity within the extended family was another form of resistance against the conquering market culture – in short, manifold cultural forms have allowed the few survivors a survival in resistance.

Let us recall some examples. It was precisely during the above-mentioned first phase of financial expansion, when capital moved out of production and trade in order to finance domestic and foreign debt, that *workers in Florence* became impoverished and subsequently rebelled. The so-called revolt of the Ciompi of 1378 was even successful in seizing state power. However, the employers, like today, hit back by dividing the workforce, locking out the lower-level workers and cooperating with the more qualified ones. They also transferred cash surpluses from the productive to the monetary sphere.

Secondly, *Bartolomé de Las Casas* deserves mention as the prime figure in the resistance to the Spanish and Portuguese imperialism in the 16th century, which was characterised by plundering and murder. Admittedly he was only one of a sizeable minority of members of holy orders who joined the native population in their struggle. But his strategy of resistance is important, because it includes aspects which can give clues for action that can be taken today, as we will see in the Third Part.[5] For example, he condemned the systematic crime of the war against the Indian population and of the capitalist slavery of the "encomiendas"[6] in mines and plantations.

For the period of transition from mercantilism to liberalism at the time of the French Revolution, particular mention should be made of *Toussaint Louverture* in French Saint Domingo (today Haiti), who is the only (known) case of liberation of slaves by their own efforts.[7]

Toussaint Louverture was a slave who lived in the area where Columbus founded his first settlement and also where Las Casas developed his settlements with the native Indians. He was allowed to use the library of his priest, where he read not only about the the Good News of liberation and the tradition of Las Casas, but also about military strategy, as chronicled by Julius Caesar. When news of the French Revolution and its new principles of "liberty, equality and fraternity"

---

5   See also U. Duchrow, 1992, pp.10f. and esp. Mires, 1989, and Gutierrez, 1990.
6   "Commenda" from the Latin "commendo," *to entrust*. The king "entrusted" the conquering settlers with native Indians to be looked after and converted to Christianity. The conquerors exploited this arrangement, forcing the natives to work as slaves.
7   U. Duchrow, 1992, p.19 and bibliography.

reached the receptive ears of the slaves, they started using guerilla tactics and under Toussaint's leadership defeated the attacking English and French.[8] Although Napoleon captured Toussaint by trickery and let him die miserably, the armies of slaves beat Napoleon's soldiers, and despite all the Europeans' countermeasures were able to preserve their independence into the 20th century, when the United States occupied the island and then installed the Duvalier dictatorship.

Paraguay, too, managed to maintain its independence for quite some time before it was forced into the "free market economy".

In summary, there were three phases of European global conquest until the First World War: (1) plundering, murderous imperialism of the 16th century, (2) the subtle, mercantilist triangular trade in the 17th and 18th centuries, and (3) the liberal global system under English control until the heyday of colonialism in the 19th century. The result was the underdevelopment and subjugation of those countries that we still sometimes call the Third World. That does not mean to say that the history of resistance was pointless. It is the potential which we have to draw on today (see Third Part). But none of the counter-strategies of the non-European peoples have been able to really resist or tame the deadly power of the European and, later, the North American, capitalist market society – apart from Japan, which copied the West and now operates with identical methods.

In western Europe and the United States itself development took a somewhat different course.

2   Resistance within Europe

Polanyi has pointed out that it is a pure fiction to assume that the self-regulating capitalist market economy is somehow by nature essential, grew out of historical necessity, or even occurred anywhere in pure form.

---

8   Philip Potter is of the opinion that the Europeans have never forgiven the slaves for driving their proud armies out of Haiti – which is why they do not refer to this period of resistance.

> "No society could stand the effects of such a system of crude fictions even for the shortest stretch of time unless its human and natural substance as well as its business organization was protected against the ravages of this satanic mill."[9]

That is to say, although liberalism and neo-liberalism claim that the market regulates itself, it was in fact not only introduced and regulated by a mercantile state, but also always immediately produced protective moves, forcing the market to accept regulatory measures which varied depending on the strength of resistance. The best-known example of this is the birth of the labour movement in the 19th century. After the failure of the Speenhamland System following the introduction of waged labour into industry, and the creation of the free labour market by the abolition of the "right to live" in 1834, "now the labouring poor were being forced into...a class by the pressure of an unfeeling mechanism."[10] At the same time the self-protection of society began with the passing of legislation governing factories and social conditions. Even if the country's ruling classes were not active in passing legislation through the legislative process to further their own ends, they were sufficiently worried about the increasingly radical attitude of the workforce, and later about the victory of socialism, to enter into a compromise. One classic example of this is Bismarck's combination of laws to govern social conditions and to control the socialists.

Of course opinions on these laws and other measures to regulate the market vary to the point of direct opposition. The view of liberal economists is diametrically opposed to that of institutional economists like Polanyi:[11]

> "It is agreed that the liberal movement, intent on the spreading of the market system, was met by a protective countermovement tending towards its restriction; such an assumption, indeed, underlies our own thesis of the double movement. But while we assert that the inherent absurdity of the idea of a self-regulating market system would have eventually destroyed society, the liberal accuses the most various elements of having wrecked a great initiative. Unable to adduce evidence of any such concerted effort to thwart the liberal movement, he falls back on the practically irrefutable hypothesis of covert action. This is the myth of the antiliberal conspiracy..."

---

9   Polanyi, op. cit., p.73.
10 Ibid., p.83.
11 Ibid., pp.144ff.

Admittedly resistance solely in terms of class interest, because society in its entirety suffers and is therefore involved in opposition in various ways, including through cultural expression.[12] However, one cannot deny the fact that the dependence of industrial capitalists on labour gave the opposing force of the labour movement its strength and forced social compromises onto the market system. In addition, Polanyi interprets the failure of the gold standard in international trading in goods and foreign exchange as a failure of the pure market economy.[13] Lastly he interprets the global economic crisis of 1929 and the early 1930s as being the breakdown of the attempt to introduce a pure market economy along the lines of classical liberalism.

This requires us to take another long, hard look at the way the market is "embedded" in society, and the political conditions for this.

2.1 The market and regulation

Since society cannot be seen abstractly as a set of interlocking, self-regulating markets – independent of and quite separate from the realms of politics and culture – we must take a another look at the elements involved, in order to grasp the historical processes and also the possible options for action. Prevailing neo-liberal economic theory does not offer any assistance in understanding the way in which the economy is embedded in the whole of society and nature. Things are different in the case of that branch of economics known as institutional economics (in the broadest sense of the word).[14] Of the authors quoted above, first and foremost economists such as Polanyi, Heilbronner and Daly have been interested in asking these questions. A related branch of economics is regulation theory. Following their tradition, *J. Hirsch* has attempted, in his book *Kapitalismus ohne Alternative?* (No alternatives to capitalism?),[15] to analyse and interpret the meaning of capitalism against the background of all the various forms of societies that have existed. He identifies three basic categories, whose different physical forms determine the prevailing form of capitalism at any particular time in history:

---

12   Ibid., pp.151ff.
13   Ibid., pp.192ff.
14   See U. Duchrow, 1987, pp.151ff.
15   J. Hirsch, 1990.

1   the capitalist production relationship itself,
2   the mode of accumulation,
3   the mode of regulation.

> "The *capitalist production relationship* is a mode of socialisation, largely deter-
> mined by private production of goods (made possible by exchange), by the separ-
> ation of the producers from the means of production, and by waged labour. This
> forms the basis of the capitalist class division and social dynamics dictated by the
> production of value added, profit maximisation and accumulation, all enabled
> by competition. This mode of socialisation is the basis of the 'objective' social
> forms (value, money and capital), which arise behind the individuals' backs
> whilst at the same time determining their actions."(pp.32f., tr.)

This is a short summary of the introduction of the special type of market
economy as linked with industrial capitalism. It again shows that even the area
of production does not exhibit a purely economic structure, but has far-reaching social consequences. It contains a social production *relationship*, i.e. the
separation of the workers from the production factors, buying them off with
wages, and the maximisation of profits for the investors. These conditions
opened up a rift between the different social classes. I would, however, join
Binswanger, Altvater, Daly and Cobb and others in adding that the capitalist
production relationship is determined by the transformation not only of the
waged labour of others, but also of (wherever possible unpaid for) natural
resources into money value. This has a lasting effect on the whole of society
with its natural life-support systems, not only on one particular social class
(the waged workers).

What Hirsch means by the accumulation enabled by competition is ap-
plicable to both areas of society – i.e. the relationship between the capital
owners and the waged workers, and the economic transformation of nature
(land) into money value. This means that when society has in principle accepted the capitalist production relationship, individuals cannot change anything about this basic mechanism by themselves, and the production of value
added, profit maximisation and accumulation all occur "behind their backs."
That has far-reaching consequences for ethics, theology and counter-
strategies, which we will come back to later.

However, as we have seen, this capitalist production relationship has never
existed in pure form. The first important observation which Hirsch makes in
connection with this is that although the capitalist production relationship

has been dominant ever since its emergence, other production relationships have always existed alongside it, e.g. the subsistence economy of farmers, production for local markets and housework. It must be said that these forms are not independent of the dominant capitalist production relationship. The families affected also participate in the exchange of goods, or housework (by women), which is utilised by capitalism as a reproduction factor for waged labour. The question is, though, whether there exist degrees of freedom to take action, and we will return to that later.

The capitalist production relationship expresses itself not only in the concrete historical processes, but also in various *modes of accumulation.*

> "By *accumulation process* we understand the general organisational and technical conditions of social value, its distribution and re-allocation. This includes the method of producing a net profit (organisation of labour, labour qualifications, production technology: the productive forces), the volume of capital invested and its distribution among industries and sectors, the length of utility cycles, the distribution of the social product over the various social classes, individual and collective (class-specific) forms of consumption, and norms of consumption." (p.34, tr.)

Accumulation must occur in the capitalist production and re-production relationships. But just how it occurs is not predetermined. In the case of production, for example, labour-intensive or capital-intensive technologies may be employed, or the relationship between capitalist and non-capitalist production relationships may vary. In the distribution struggle the organisation of the workforce may be good or not so good. Concerning consumption, individuals or populations can follow different cultural traditions or habits. This means that the method, or "regime," of accumulation (as Hirsch terms the method prevailing in a given situation) is not completely determined by the abstract capitalist production relationship and law of values, nor is it totally free, as it has to remain within the structure of this production relationship and is therefore continuously determined by it.

As the capitalist production relationship necessarily contains opposing class interests (and brings about the destruction of nature, on which it itself relies), if it is in equilibrium at all, then this must be a dynamic equilibrium with continual conflicts and crises. This is why it needs to be *regulated* to remain stable, and throughout history this *regulation* has taken various forms.

"In its most general and abstract form, the capitalistic system of regulation is founded on a form of socialisation of the capitalist production relationship: private production, exchange of goods, separation of capital and waged labour. This leads to the emergence of money, civil law, competition between capitalists and waged labourers, to the development of legal subjects as legally free participants on the market and citizens of the state, the social values of subjectivity, liberty, equality and progress. These factors provide the basis for the general form and structure of the regulatory institutions: the *business* as an expression of private ownership of the means of production, the *family* as the social location of the reproduction of the workforce, (which is separated from the capitalist production), the *market* (including the labour market), the *freedom to enter into contracts,* the system of *private* and *public law*, the freedom of association for individuals to protect common interests (societies, employers' organisations and trade unions) and the *state* ...

The physical configuration of the relationship between determinants of institutional and normative regulation is influenced by these general factors, but has historically taken on a variety of different forms: the specific modes of regulation. These are dependent upon the degree of implementation of the capitalist production relationship, but also on national political and cultural traditions, and on the balance of political and social power." (pp.36f., tr.)

Once more this shows that in the different ways of organising the regulatory system, there is room for flexibility – admittedly only within the basic framework of the capitalist production relationship and its compulsive accumulation of money. This theory of regulation renders obsolete the erroneous alternative of either "pure market" or "pure plan," along with the distinction between economics and politics. But it also belies the assumption that the whole social process is the result of conscious, intentional action. The whole process lacks a guiding hand. Within the interplay of production relationship, and methods of accumulation and regulation, however, there are social actors in a highly contradictory developmental process, which is threatened by crises, and the power relations between these actors determine the physical form of the social process at any given point in time. So in principle the process is not guaranteed. "The reproduction of the capitalist society might possibly fail." (p.40, tr.)

2.2 Socialism, Fascism and Keynesianism

Armed with these theoretical tools, it will now be easier to understand how the various opposing movements and attempts to curb the capitalist market economy went about it.

Socialism did not come in the guise envisaged by Karl Marx. However, *socialism* as practised in the eastern bloc was founded on the basic tenet that the production relationship was the decisive underlying structure. Private ownership of the means of production was abolished, so that no class of land and capital owners could have sole power over them, over what was produced, or over the surplus product. And even after the failure of this attempt at socialism it is indisputable that a certain degree of success was achieved. When one considers something like the meeting of basic human needs or the fairness of the distribution of property among a fifth of the world's population in China before and after the revolution, or the difference between China and India, or between Cuba and other Latin American countries, there can be no question about who was the more successful when judged on these criteria.

Quite apart from the conscious strategies of the western capitalist world aimed at preventing the success of this alternative model, it is admittedly clear by now that there were also internal reasons for the downfall of this system. They led, for example, to the emergence of a new class of polit-bureaucrats, who in their turn syphoned off surplus value and engaged in political oppression. But it is also clear that the economic approach itself contained serious flaws. Even before its downfall it had been pointed out that also under eastern-bloc socialism the economy was organised in terms of commodities. In his book *Der Kollaps der Modernisierung – Vom Zusammenbruch des Kasernensozialismus zur Krise der Weltökonomie* (The collapse of modernisation – from the breakdown of barracks-socialism to crisis in the world economy), Robert Kurz has proved that the abstract form of labour and money accumulation remained the decisive factors. The difference was that the market was replaced by a central plan along the lines of the Prussian war-time economy, a strategy condemned to failure in a complex economic situation, for reasons that we cannot go into in detail here. In any case the term "state capitalism" is more fitting than Marxist socialism. With regard to the environmental consequences of eastern-bloc socialism, it should be pointed out that "state ownership" still assumes the concept of ownership in both the Roman and Lockean sense of the word, meaning total power over the object. In addition, the capitalist model of development was adopted in regard to consumer expectations.

Industrialism under state capitalism was even more disastrous for the environment than private capitalism. And when consumer expectations are maintained, with less efficient means of production, it is no wonder that people are drawn to the capitalist centres (while a veil is drawn over the increase in misery on the periphery).

Similarly, the type of protection against the world market practised in *Nazi Germany* was also a type of state capitalism – though admittedly it was even more clearly based on the logic of capital accumulation than the socialist experiment in Eastern Europe.[16] Evidence for this is provided by the unconditional support for Hitler on the part of the German capital-owners, with the Deutsche Bank and I.G. Farben playing a particularly criminal role in the process, as is well known.[17] Still, it is important for our investigation to be aware that Nazism was able to profit from depicting itself as the people's protection against a global market intent on exploitation (under British hegemony). Apart from that, it mobilised non-economic, i.e. social and cultural values suppressed by the liberal market economy. It also exploited victims of the liberal system, in particular the unemployed, for its own ends – a truly cautionary tale in the light of our present situation at the end of a neo-liberal phase.

Fordism and Keynesianism are also relevant here. After the Soviet Union had turned its back on "laissez-faire" in 1917, not only Germany, but also the United States, which for reasons connected with the First and Second World Wars was beginning to take over from Britain as the leading power in the world, used the collapse of the liberal-capitalist world market to do the same. This is first expressed in Roosevelt's *New Deal*. We must take a closer look at the constellation that arose here, which remained characteristic until well into the 1960s. It is also a prime example of the interplay between a simultaneous transformation of the modes of accumulation and modes of regulation within the capitalist production relationship.

The change in the mode of accumulation is associated with the term Fordism. This is the name given to the following accumulation regime.[18] Based on the rationalisation of the production process through the introduction of the production line (Taylorism), relatively high wages were paid to that section

16　See R. Kurz, 1991, pp.63ff.; Polanyi, op. cit., pp.243ff.

17　See R. Gordiano, 1989, and the reports of the OMGUS investigations of the Deutsche Bank and I. G. Farben, 1985 and 1986.

18　See Beaud, 1981, p.156; J. Hirsch and R. Roth, 1986; J. Hirsch, 1990.

of the workforce that was prepared to accept this type of discipline, in the hope that the workforce would then be divided and attention would be diverted from more far-reaching economic and political demands; increased production. The fact that higher wages took the form of increased mass buying power led to greater profit and simultaneously, through mass consumption, transplanted one section of the workforce into the middle class.

The new *methods of state regulation* in the *New Deal* took on corresponding forms, however weak at that time. [19] They included new regulations for banks, trade and industry and strengthening infrastructural measures. First and foremost, though, they included a fresh historical compromise between capital owners and the conformist sections of the workforce. Under this system the state not only intervenes by passing legislation designed to bring protection and security for the workers in the production process, but also – primarily in times of recession – through an employment policy, in order to curb unemployment and support the economy by means of public investment. This includes a policy of low interest rates in the money sector. This method of regulation was first developed in detail by the English economist John Maynard Keynes and still bears his name.[20]

In Germany, this model has been adopted particularly by social democracy. But important elements of it, combined with Eucken's so-called ordoliberalism, have found their way into the concept of the "*social market economy.*" Alfred Müller-Armack is the classic proponent of this position.[21] He summarises it like this: "The point of the social market economy is to combine the principle of market freedom with that of social equalisation". Here the starting point is the insight "that as a means of organising large societies, the principle of competition is only viable if a clear set of conditions is present to ensure competition" (ibid.).

Müller-Armack lists four factors which in his opinion grant "a varied and complete [sic!] system of social protection" in the "social market economy." Firstly, "consumers can ... control the economy according to their needs" through the system of pricing (ibid.); secondly, "a necessary increase in productivity ensured by the system of competition effects an improvement in social conditions." (Here growth is again identified with an improvement in welfare, or at least parallel with it, as in Adam Smith's writings.) Thirdly, an

---

19 See J. Hippler, 1985; W. Greider, 1987, pp.304ff.; G. Arrighi, 1994, pp.274-280, 319ff.
20 J.M. Keynes, 1936.
21 A. Müller-Armack, 1956 (p.390,tr.).

"institutional guarantee of competition" is implemented to tackle "monopolies, oligopolies and cartels"; and lastly, "the income process under a market economy offers social policy a viable basis for a state incomes policy, which in the form of social services, pensions and allowances, construction grants, subsidies, etc., correct the distribution of incomes" (p.391, tr.). It is important to be aware of the assumption underlying these social measures: "Competition must be understood primarily as a form which should realise, preferably with the least possible hindrance, technological and economic progress. Its justification is therefore the continual increase in production. A policy of having a social market economy demands a deliberate policy of economic growth" (ibid.). This means that in this concept of growth the environmental consequences of running an economy are forgotten as are the global economic preconditions of increasing production (e.g. cheap raw materials and labour in two thirds of the world).

Summing up, we see that after the Soviet Union broke out of the liberal global market under English hegemony in 1917, the other world powers also tried, following the collapse of the global market in 1929, to develop a (nationally) regulated form of capitalism. Germany, and other countries, opted for the fascist form, the western industrial nations for the Keynesian form. The latter – alongside "ordo-liberal" elements – also determined the introduction of the "social market economy" in West Germany after the Second World War.

Many people today, at least many of those living in Germany, assume that the concept of the social market economy describes reality and policy in Germany and western Europe just as it has done in the past – indeed, one only has to apply this successful model to the rest of the world, and all our current problems will be solved. Does this view match the real situation?

Chapter III

The current situation in the neo-liberal capitalist global system

1 The transnationalisation of markets and market actors

The collapse of the liberal international economic and finance system in 1929 had led the nation-states to expand their control functions. This was open to misuse by national imperialism as occurred in Nazi Germany. Yet it had a positive effect on the mechanisms of social protection and redistribution – due to the growing labour movements and also to pressure from the competing system of communism.

This was also the background for the first phase of the recovery of a capitalist global economy after the Second World War. National and international regulatory mechanisms were, amongst other things, intended to combine the accumulation interest of capital with social interests, in a combination of Fordist and Keynesian methods (without giving much thought to ecological questions at this stage). The idea was to create the political conditions necessary for the economy, albeit with severe restrictions imposed by the capitalist production relationship. In a way this also applied to the African, Asian and Latin American countries that became independent after the War.

At this point let us take up again Giovanni Arrighi's *The Long Twentieth Century*, because we are dealing with the central stage of the US dominated fourth systemic cycle of capital accumulation in the history of capitalism. As mentioned in the first chapter, the Great Depression from 1873 to 1896, linked with financial expansion and the increasing competition among the old capitalist powers, marked the take-off point for the rise of US economic and financial power (pp.269ff.). The two world wars gave the USA the chance to boost its industry to provide England with the equipment necessary for war-making. In addition it lent money to the British government, which gradually led to a shift of financial power from London to New York.

However, just as after the first Genoese-Spanish cycle of cosmopolitan finance capitalism the Dutch switched to state (monopoly) capitalism, the pendulum also swung back after the free trade-imperialism of the British cycle of accumulation. Roosevelt's New Dealism was trying to regulate more in favour of state control and social redistribution. In the Glass-Steagall Act of 1933 he even separated commercial and investment banking – a "fatal blow to the House of Morgan's domination of US financial markets" (p.279). Bankers and financiers were also absent at Bretton Woods in 1944. And the Federal Reserve Bank was not in New York, near Wall Street, but in Washington, next to the government.

The key feature of the US accumulation model was the giant corporations. The secret of their strength was the vertical integration of all elements of production, trade and financing. The opening up of the world market after the Second World War gave them the unique opportunity to expand on a global scale by penetrating the other national economies through private foreign investment ("internalisation of the world market"). This led to twenty years of material expansion in the 1950s and 1960s. But their inter-nationalisation (still at least partly regulated by national and international political institutions) led to transnationalisation. This in turn gave high finance the chance for a comeback, which has resulted in a new period of financial expansion – at the same time signalling the decline of the US cycle of accumulation. This is what we have to understand in more detail.

During the late 1960s and 1970s the relationship between economic and political power was turned right round. This swing was continued in the eighties and now determines the situation of humankind and the environment all over the globe: the economy dictates government policy. "Market deregulation" has become the great motto. How did this come about? What mechanisms are at work? What became of the political institutions? What are the consequences and how are they connected?

It is obvious that such a momentous and global process is determined by a myriad of individual factors, which are often confusing. As it concerns questions of life and death of the majority of people alive today, and of succeeding generations, it is vital to understand the essence of this development. And it can be demonstrated that the same mechanisms are causing the pauperisation of the majority of human beings and the destruction of the environment, and at the same time bringing increased wealth to a minority. It is not greedy individuals causing the change, but a new mode of capital accumulation and de-regulation.

The essence of the change is that productive, trading and monetary capital can be trans-nationalised (globalised), while the political instruments of regulation remain either national or inter-national.

The choice of this term is intended to illustrate that the world capital market was able to establish itself *beyond* national regulation, i.e. *trans*-nationally. Even when national governments get together and set up international institutions *between* nations, these cannot intervene in the trans-national markets, as long as they are not associated with any country's territory – which is explained below.

In addition, finance capital assumed the leadership. The result is that the accumulation of money assets is now the absolute, immutable yardstick for all economic, social, ecological and political decisions. It is no longer just an aim, but a concrete mechanism. With the transnational finance markets as the agents of the owners of money assets, the capitalist market economy has made significant progress towards its goal of running world society as an appendage to self-regulating markets. Anyone looking for life-enhancing alternatives must first grasp this reality. Perpetuating illusion and ignorance only hinders counter-strategies.

The main actors on the transnational markets are the *transnational companies* and the *commercial banks*. Businesses, as we have seen, are part of the system of regulation of the market economy, and as such, an expression of private ownership of production factors. They process the practical aspect of increasing the money value. The banks are actors on the monetary side of wealth accumulation, money being understood both as a means of payment for the flow of goods and as interest-bearing credit. The first phase after the Second World War was still determined by large national companies following the model of the U.S., which replaced Britain as the leading power.

In his book *The Work of Nations*, *Robert B. Reich*, the influential economic advisor to Bill Clinton and his present Labor Secretary, has described the situation at that time very clearly, to distinguish it from the present situation.[1] Approximately 500 major companies were responsible for half the industrial production in the United States. The largest of these, General Motors, made up 3 per cent of the United States' gross national product in 1955. Because of their importance, these companies were *the* "national champions." After the war their importance increased sharply, in line with North American expansion. European recovery and the development aid propagated by president Truman show that business and national interests went hand in hand (pp.63ff.).

1　R.B. Reich, 1991, pp.46ff.

In the most up-to-date publication on this question, *Multis, Markt & Krise*, (Multinationals, market and crisis), *M. Gück, K. Heidel and U. Kleinert* have described the various phases of internationalisation.[2] They see the first phase – still in the so-called "old international division of labour"[3] – typified by intensified foreign trade, with the express purpose of safeguarding markets and raw materials (pp.244ff.). This means that in this phase there is an international economic structure in which national economies relate to the international system through foreign trade. The first phase of GATT (the General Agreement on Tariffs and Trade) provided the political framework, which will be discussed in greater detail later. Although the trading conditions it contained were certainly to the disadvantage of the so-called developing countries, they enabled the industrialised countries to deregulate and expand trade to their mutual benefit.

This also applies to the money side during this phase. The currency of the United States, the strongest economic power, became the "global currency" – the dollar, linked to gold (the gold-dollar standard). But the individual countries have their own, controlled, currencies, linked to the dollar by fixed rates of exchange. Similarly, they can use Keynesian methods to adapt their monetary policy to the requirements of their national economies to a certain extent, not only by controlling the money supply, but also interest rates. This means, for example, cutting interest rates to stimulate the economy and create jobs. In its early life the International Monetary Fund (IMF) provided for short-term balance of payments.[4] In the late 1960s and 1970s there was a significant change from the internationalisation to the trans-nationalisation of the world market. As far as production and trade were concerned, something emerged which Fröbel, Heinrichs and Kreye have termed the "new international division of labour".[5] The background to this new wave of globalisation was a series of changes in certain elements of the global economic structure:

–   Firstly, the dominance of the United States in trade and direct investment was weakened around the globe by the increasing strength of Japan and western European countries, as well as a few "newly industrialised countries" (NICs) (with their largely labour-intensive production using stand-

2   Werkstatt Ökonomie, 1992; see also R. Barnet and J. Cavanagh, 1994.
3   See also E. Altvater, 1992, pp.144ff.
4   For more detail on the first phase of the Bretton Woods system see [pp.95ff.] below.
5   Fröbel, Heinrichs and Kreye, 1977 and 1986; see also the critical work of Werkstatt Ökonomie, 1992, pp.245ff.

ardised techonology). This meant an increase in competition, but also in monopolisation.

- Secondly, the boom that followed the Second World War ended, growth rates slumped, and overcapacity rose. Then in the early 1970s the oil crisis also pushed up the price of energy.
- Thirdly, disadvantaged industries and regions in the industrialised countries were threatened by the liberalisation of the world market, and called for new protectionist measures.

Corporations were no longer able to apply the old strategies. It was not enough just to increase production and turnover. The question was not now, "How can we meet the demand through increased buying power?" but "How can we reduce costs?" The answer was by transnationalising production. Whole ranges of products were physically removed to areas of cheap labour and raw materials, and low taxation (horizontal specialisation), or individual stages of production were moved to developing countries (vertical integration). The watchword of the emerging transnational corporations (TNCs) is *global sourcing*, meaning scouring the globe for the most cost-effective location of production factors.

This is the phase that Rudolf Strahm publicised in his widely circulated diagrams in various editions of his book *Warum sie so arm sind* (Why they are so poor).[6] Here are a few examples: developing countries as the location of production using cheap labour (p.144); domination of the market by foreign corporations (p.150); cartel agreements amongst the corporations (p.152);[7] the North profiting from the TNCs (p.158); transfer-price manipulation (1975, p.103). But apart from profiting from transfer-price manipulation, in which the corporations fix an arbitrary price in order to disguise their profits and reap tax advantages, they also profit from the creation of so-called free trade zones. Using these methods prices can be re-adjusted, via spurious companies, without the goods ever having been in that place. In other areas the large corporations control trade by calculating higher freight costs for the raw materials from the developing countries than for finished products from the industrialised countries.[8]

---

6   R. Strahm, (1975, originally under the title "Überentwicklung-Unterentwicklung") 1985. For the whole complex see also R.J. Barnet and E. Müller, 1975.
7   This diagram is based on the information on the exposed Lausanne cartel bureau, evaluated in R. Mirow's book *Die Diktatur der Kartelle*, 1978.
8   See Strahm's diagram "Sechs Handelsgiganten beherrschen den Getreidemarkt"

In principle more serious and with more far-reaching consequences, indeed revolutionary for the methods of accumulation and regulation in the capitalist market economy, was the *transnationalisation of the financial markets* during this period. Basic reading to gain an understanding of this process is Alexander Schubert's book *Die internationale Verschuldung* ("The international debt").[9] The process of transnationalisation of production and trade led to an increase in the money requirement for international payments and interest-earning loans. The procedure that was actually planned for this dealing in money was that the commercial banks of the different countries would handle international transfers under the surveillance, guidance and control of their national banks, using US dollars as a common currency, i.e. via the US money market. As early as 1957, when the British government introduced foreign currency restrictions, some British banks began to trade in dollars themselves, i.e. to make loans in dollars without converting to pounds at all. This has led to the creation of so-called "free-banking zones," also called "off-shore," "Euro" or "xeno" banking. This should not be misunderstood as meaning a particular geographical location. In practical terms it means that a bank, say, in London or Frankfurt, will divide its book-keeping into two sections, to reflect the division of the global money market. One section concerns transactions subject to national control, while the other deals with trans-national transactions that are not subject to controls. Of course banks then set up subsidiaries in so-called tax havens such as Luxembourg or the Bahamas, so as to avoid incurring national taxes on the deposits they hold on account.

With regard to the transnational granting of dollar loans, the free bank markets give banks and owners of financial assets the following advantages:
– the banks enjoy tax concessions;
– for these (transnational) loans the banks are not required to deposit a certain minimum reserve with their central bank, with the effect that they gain more interest;
– the equity requirement is lower, leading to a relative increase in turnover;
– the banks can specialise in large-scale business.

The consequence of the expansion of the "free" banking markets was a rapid increase in the volume of money on the now trans-national financial markets – money not subject to political control and generally not taxed, which

---

("Six trading giants control the cereal market"), 1985, p.62.
9   A. Schubert, 1985; see also Arrighi, 1994, pp.299ff.

sought only one thing: a way of earning the greatest return on investment in the shortest possible time. This trend was reinforced, but not actually caused by the glut of petrodollars from the rise in oil prices in 1973.

This had two immediate results:

– The transnational flood of dollars reinforced the inflationary development of the dollar brought about by the US government's financing of the Vietnam War. It was therefore forced to abandon gold coverage (abandoned provisionally in 1971, and finally in 1973). This simultaneously put an end to the fixed exchange rates between the dollar and other currencies. The so-called flotation of the dollar, that is, the deregulation of the currency markets, led to more transnational money being used for currency speculation.

– In addition to this, the banks were trying, with advantageous interest rates, to persuade as many countries as possible to borrow for industrialisation, as a channel for the flow of money. In contrast to early industrialisation, these countries now channelled only part of these investments into so-called import substitution, i.e. the production of industrial goods for their domestic markets with the aim of independence from expensive foreign imports. Instead, the money was used principally for prestige projects such as building dams, atomic plants, etc., or else to produce goods for export, which were seldom competitive on the world market. Many southern and eastern European countries (e.g. Poland) fell into the debt trap. But most importantly, something happened in 1979 that caused the outbreak of the debt crisis, that made it impossible to solve within the system as it stood, and that determines the global situation economically, socially and politically, to this day: the introduction of monetarism.

2 Domination of global finance and its effects in the South, the East and the West

If the transnationalisation of the financial markets in the early 1970s had influenced the deregulation of the currency markets, in 1979 it also contributed to the changes in United States' policy on the money supply and interest rates. In his New York Times best seller *Secrets of the Temple. How the Federal Reserve Runs the Country*, whose 800 pages are as exciting as any detective story, *William Greider* describes how President Carter was forced to allow sweeping changes to US monetary policy. He appointed Paul Volcker as direc-

tor of the Federal Reserve Bank, a man who could be relied upon to implement a monetarist economic policy. In this case, this means that the Federal
Reserve Bank only guaranteed a stable (i.e. restricted) money supply, but no
longer controlled interest rates. In fact the bank made a conscious decision to
leave interest rates to the mercy of the free market, which – given the restrictions on the money supply – caused them to soar. (So there is always a political
element present in the neo-liberalism of the "free-market economy" which is
generally played down.) The financial markets were now in a position to push
interest rates to historic heights, as much as 20 per cent or more. The policy of
high interest rates was again reinforced by the greatest stock-piling of armaments ever seen in peace time. The Reagan adminstration financed its armaments programme on borrowed money and was therefore forced to attract
international capital into the United States by raising interest rates as much as
possible.

So behind this development there lay a variety of interests:

– the interests of the owners of financial assets, who regarded the low interest
  rates of the early 1970s as not sufficiently attractive and saw a chance of
  earning a better profit with higher interest rates;
– the interests of the banks, who could exploit this opportunity of using their
  power over the market to increase the difference in borrowing and lending
  rates;
– the political interests in the form of those forces that led to the Reagan
  administration;
– in addition, the switch to the doctrine of monetarism was gathering
  momentum, set in motion by the inflationary development existing since
  the Vietnam War.

By this time the political climate was so influenced by monetarism, that Congress itself, dominated by the traditionally Keynesian Democrats, simultaneously repealed the laws brought in to prevent usury.[10] So the way was clear
for the "triumph of money," as Greider calls his last chapter.

What does the rule of money involve? This has to be examined. In simple
terms, the rule of money means that maintaining the stability of wealth accumulation has top priority in all economic decisions. In other words, the financial markets have a decisive influence over the non-variable factor, i.e. interest
rates, the "price of money," to which all economic, social, and environmental

---

10 See Greider, 1987, pp.170f. and 251ff.

decisions, as variables, have to adapt. But as all decisions are made with interest rates restricted by the financial markets, it depends on the relative strength or weakness of those affected, how much room for manoeuvre they can gain for negotiations. The central banks have adopted a position that is somewhat ambivalent, about which more later. With respect to social class, the rule of money means that the owners of financial assets have priority over the workers; internationally it means countries with hard currencies have priority over those whose currencies are "soft".

Let us now take a look at the consequences of the move to monetarism or neo-liberalism:

2.1 In the South: the debt crisis – the tip of the iceberg[11]

The first victims were naturally the weakest links in the chain: the countries in debt, which in any case had been exploited and disadvantaged for 500 years, and their corrupt elites, installed and/or supported by the West, who had made deals with the banks and corporations. These countries' debts rocketed due to the increased interest rates. They had signed credit agreements, so-called "roll-over contracts", in which changes in interest rates could in some cases be back-dated. In 1982 Mexiko became the first of these countries to reach the threshold of bankruptcy. A lot has been written about the debt crisis.[12] Here we are only concerned with the development of the underlying mechanism.[13]

The debt crisis is not a conventional debt cycle (credit – investment in production – creation of added value – payment of interest and repayment of debt). It is the crisis of the Fordist development model and its methods of regulation, on a global scale. The following figures demonstrate that the debts are not paid off in the normal way, but continue to increase:

"The patient is not cured – on the contrary, the patient's condition deteriorates. The extent of this is made obvious in that in the period from the outbreak of the

---

11 An inclusive overview has been attempted in "Die Dritte Welt und wir," edited by M. Massarrat et al., 1993.

12 In addition to Schubert and Greider, see primarily G.A. Potter, 1988; Susan George, 1988 and 1992; E. Altvater et al., 1987; in M. Massarrat et al. (eds.), 1993, pp.10ff.; W. Bello, 1994.

13 On the following see primarily Altvater 1992[2], pp.219ff., and 1992, pp.168ff.

debt crisis in 1982 to the end of 1989, the poor countries of the Third World had paid the rich countries of the 'First World' US$ 236.2 bn net (World Debt Tables 1989/1990, p.9), development aid in reverse. The figures for the countries that are heavily in debt are even more dramatic. From 1982 to 1989 they had to transfer a net US$ 124.79 bn to the creditor countries, and yet their debt increased from US$ 433.519 bn in 1982 to US$ 624.984 bn (World Debt Tables 1989/90, Vol. 1, p.122 ff.)."[14] Today the debtor countries of the poorest two thirds of the world owe approx. US$ 1,500 bn. According to 1992 statistics they are transferring US$ 50 bn net capital to the creditor banks and nations annually.[15]

What structural changes have taken place here? The owners of financial assets and their agencies, the banks, could not find sufficiently profitable opportunities for investment in the industrialised countries. So a portion of these assets sought suitable opportunities on the transnational financial markets. For one section (another section will concern us with reference to speculation in finance) the banks found ruling classes in the developing countries, who took out loans with the aim not only of "modernising" their countries (i.e. Fordist industrialisation), but also so that they themselves could enjoy the benefits of mass-produced consumer goods, including arms. The interest to be paid to the owners of financial assets is an unassailable fact fixed by the global credit market. *The interest payments to the global money market force all the different nations of the world to adapt to one and the same system.*

> "The various economic levels throughout the world, the diversity of production methods and life-styles in different regions of the world, and the manifold attitudes to time in various types of societies are all being subjected to the one and the same restriction: the 'tough' monetary budget restriction, which requires and enforces a specific monetary and concrete economic efficiency (which is simply the profitability of the capital investment), along with 'systematisation' by the creation – corresponding to the tough budget restriction – of social institutions."[16]

What does that mean in practical terms? The countries affected have no time to develop globally competitive industries, banking systems, state taxation

---

14 Ibid., p.219(tr.).
15 See UNDP, Human Development Report, 1992, p.89; see also ibid., pp.48ff. and Altvater, 1992, p.168.
16 Altvater, 1992, p.170(tr.).

schemes, labour qualifications, etc. Instead, they are forced to come up with hard currency to service their debts within the stated period – which is, of course, impossible. This applies just as much to the countries of the South as to the central and eastern European countries, which are now suffering the shock of being left to the mercy of the mechanisms and the tough profitability criteria (on the measure of the industrialised countries) of the productive and monetary world market. The results are devastating. Because the hard currency needed to "service" the debts *cannot* be generated, the ruling elites squeeze the money out of the nations that are all the while becoming poorer, axe public and social services, and in turn take their financial assets back to the transnational markets, thus draining capital from the debtor countries. The economic effects of attempted modernisation then go into reverse. Countries such as Chile, Argentina and Brazil revert to the status of suppliers of raw materials, or else they make sure that even at Christmas, consumers in the big cities can have asparagus and other fresh vegetables on the dinner table, next to fresh cut flowers. Unemployment rises to as much as 80 per cent. More and more people are forced out of the official economy into the hidden economy, where mafia-style methods prevail. For the traditional subsistence economies and social networks were destroyed by modernisation. The slide into chaos set in motion by the global money market is completed by increasing violence and crime. As mentioned above, the Latin Americans speak of "decomposition," i.e. the destruction of societies right down to their smallest components.[17]

> "The 'logic' of Fordism is unrelenting, when it employs monetary relationships as a 'vehicle' ... Societies (in the same way as individual companies) unable to raise the money to pay the interest are failures, since this is the only valid yardstick. Before the norms of a regime can have any effect, the monetary budget restriction must be taken into account."[18]
>
> "The development of productive power is being sacrificed on the altar of 'dollarisation' of national currency systems, along with the future of a whole generation of Africans, Asians and Latin Americans, for the purpose of maintaining a hypertrophic international loan system. The rationality of the *formal* market destroys the living conditions of the populations of whole continents..."[19]

---

17 Paulo R. Schilling offers an excellent and comprehensive account of the history and present situation of the economic development of Latin America in his critique of the neo-liberal domestic market, *Mercosur*, 1993.

18 Altvater, 1992, p.173(tr.).

This merciless logic of the transnational financial market reaches a pinnacle of perversity when one reads the UN figures and discovers that in the 1980s, "the effective interest rates averaged 17 per cent in the developing countries and 4 per cent in the industrialised countries". [20] This relationship has not only to do with the higher interest rates for loans involving greater risk, but also with the falling prices of products from developing countries on the world market, as opposed to rising prices of products from the industrialised countries. Falling income from Third World products manufactured on credit causes the effective interest rate to rise. While, say, a German firm can increase the prices of industrial products manufactured with borrowed money, the price of coffee from a plantation established in the same way falls. Monetary and productive market processes interlock through these unjust terms of trade, which we must therefore follow up here.

"From 1975 onwards (with a short interruption in 1979), the prices of raw materials fell by 40 per cent in relation to the prices of industrial goods – a tendency which can be expected to last until the end of the century."[21] One obvious reason for the increasing severity of the problem of unfair terms of trade is, cynically enough, the form in which the developing countries are required to pay off their debts: tailoring their national economies to export to earn the hard currency needed for interest payments. The more coffee, soya and raw materials find their way onto the market, the greater the decrease in prices, according to the law of supply and demand. This means that while the northern industrial corporations come closer to being monopolies, and continually push prices up, countries exporting raw materials are driven into a state of competition that continually forces prices downwards. This mechanism is reinforced by another tactic of the owners and accumulators of financial capital: speculation in raw materials (which are bought up at low prices and sold again when the prices are higher, e.g. following harvest cycles).[22]

The roots of this mechanism date back to the distribution of power between the conquering nations of the West and the conquered nations of the South from

---

19 Altvater, 1992², p.221(tr.). The term "sacrifice" will concern us in its theological sense later.
20 UNDP, Human Develpment Report 1992, p.48; for commentary see Altvater, 1992, p.174.
21 Ibid., p.175(tr.); see also Strahm's diagrams, in particular 1st ed. 1975, p.46.
22 See also Strahm's diagrams, 1985, pp.116ff.

the time of the murderous Hispanic exploitation and the mercantilistic triangular trade. With this foundation, the industrial nations succeeded in using various mechanisms to turn their dependence on raw materials into the dependence of countries exporting raw materials on them. These countries had to transform themselves into "extraction economies," whose products of practical use are undervalued in trade controlled by capital.[23]

Another major reason for the ever-widening gulf between the industrialised and the so-called developing countries caused by the drop in the price of goods, is the conditions of international trade. The industrialised countries preach free trade when it comes to breaking into the economies of the weaker countries. But they also indulge in the opposite practice of *protectionism*, either in the open or in secret. For example, non-processed goods incur lower customs tariffs than semi-finished products; the transfer of technology is either hindered, restricted or else made so expensive as to be out of reach of the developing countries; in the case of textiles and farming the domestic market is completely isolated from outside influence, etc. But restrictions are also imposed on the free labour market and on immigration from the developing countries.

The UN calculated in 1992 that, all in all, the developing countries were *losing* US$ 500 bn annually by having to service their debts and through market restrictions and manipulation.[24] When one realises that only a few factors have been included in this calculation, and that an institution such as the UN has to use the lowest possible figures, to avoid being shown to be wrong, debt payments of US$ 17,000 to 53,000 bn by the South to the countries of the North in the period 1956 – 1990 are nothing like as unrealistic as it might seem at first – and that is not even taking account of the 500 years of exploitation.[25] This shows who is in debt to whom.

---

23 For details see Altvater, 1992, pp.178ff.
24 UNDP, 1992, pp.48ff.
25 H. Sabet, 1991, esp. pp.81ff.

2.2   *Eastern Europe: the identical debt traps of industrialisation and de-industrialisation*

As early as 1988, Ton Veerkamp drew attention to the fact that "the debts are devouring socialism."[26] Altvater gives figures for the net increase in the debts of eastern Europe and the USSR of US$ 68.8 bn in 1983 and US$ 99.2 bn in 1989. These figures include US$ 35.2 bn for Poland alone and US$ 11 bn for the former German Democratic Republic.[27] However, as he rightly points out, it would be an over-simplification to say that the collapse of eastern-bloc socialism was solely due to the burden of foreign debts. In fact the problem was that the socialist economies were drawn into the world market with its level of productivity and competition, which they simply could not cope with. And in addition, the western economic powers could of course use their market muscle to manipulate the world market, as the following example demonstrates.

> At that time a Heidelberg wholesaler could, for DM 16.24, acquire a pair of jeans
> manufactured in North Korea using metal parts such as buttons and zips from
> (former) East Germany. The wholesaler sold the labelled and repacked jeans for
> DM 60 to a retailer, who then sold them in the High Street for DM 120.

R. Kurz[28] takes this analysis even further, by drawing attention to the fact that eastern-bloc socialism – in contrast to Marx's fundamental criticism of production for the purpose of wealth accumulation (as opposed to practical value) – was organised in the strict sense of state capitalism, following the same basic principles as private capitalism (the only difference being the ineffectual central planning), and could not therefore succeed on the world market. The attempt to revitalise these economies through the western economy is doomed to failure.[29] According to Kurz the western system, now spanning the globe, resembles a pyramid, with only two victorious economies at the top – Germany and Japan. The others are falling behind, although the United States is also managing to maintain a position at the top.[30] The "post-catastro-

---

26 T. Veerkamp, 1989.

27 Altvater, 1992², pp.48f.

28 R. Kurz, 1991.

29 See T. Veerkamp, 1989.

30 Against Kurz, it should be borne in mind that the United States is certain to remain one of the countries at the top. It is less dependent on exports, for example. And

phic societies" of the "Third World" and the eastern bloc, which has joined this group, simply lack the structures necessary to attain the level of production of the world market. Only the production units which succeed in doing this with the required concentration of capital can still produce a genuine profit, while all other production units are being destroyed. They can sometimes be kept afloat artificially by loans, but once the exponential interest payments have sapped them, disaster is imminent. There are less and less resources for capital to exploit, which wipes out non-competitive production, and the buying power dependent on it, along with the markets for domestically produced goods in more and more parts of the world.

Owing to this inability to be competitive at the level of productivity required on the world market, the de-industrialisation of eastern Europe is already apparent. The West encourages this trend, principally by concentrating its financial transfers on the acquisition of raw materials. In this case investments are made with the obvious motive of simultaneously gaining transnational control over industrial exploitation. Here the most coveted prizes are the oil and natural gas to be found in the Commonwealth of Independent States.

If there is less and less to be "devoured" in the South and East, where does capital then turn in its quest for self-accumulation?

2.3 In the North (the West): casino capitalism, growth without jobs, the gulf between rich and poor, and the powerlessness of the nation-state

At the present time there are two ways of analysing the repercussions of the western-dominated world market on the industrialised western countries themselves. In the first place, the question is, "What are the repercussions of the destruction taking place in the South and East on the big cities?" The second question is, "What are the effects of the transnational world market, i.e. monetarist Fordism, on the societies in the North?" Both of these approaches are important, especially as together they can provide us with important impulses for raising awareness.

Susan George follows the first approach in her book *The Debt Boomerang: How Third World Debt Harms Us All*,[31] which has been the basis of a campaign

---

Germany now has severe problems with its national debt, similar to the United States since the Reagan presidency.

31 S. George, 1992; see also L. Mayer's book title *Ein System siegt sich zu Tode. Der*

of the same name to cancel these debts by the Transnational Insitute (TNI) in Amsterdam. She describes the repercussions of the South's debt crisis on the centres of capitalism with respect to the environment, drugs, taxation, unemployment, migration and instability:

– The *environmental* effects of the debt crisis include increasing the destruction of the rain forests, with disastrous consequences not only for the earth's atmosphere, but also for the extinction of species essential for our future food and medical supplies.

– The destruction of human life and the fabric of society through *drugs* will continue to increase, as long as the South is prevented from producing alternative goods at fair prices and its societies are forced into poverty by western creditors' extraction of interest payments.

– Western *taxpayers* pay enormous sums to the commercial banks, who adjust the value of their debts via tax write-offs and thus attract indirect public subsidies, while in some cases the money diverted out of the country avoids tax because it belongs to foreign citizens. Taken together, all these items generate at least US\$ 26-30 bn annually.

– *Jobs* are lost in western industries and agriculture, because the countries in debt can no longer buy products from the North, instead they have to use their money for interest payments to the banks (loss of buying power and of markets).

– The destruction of the economies with debts deprives the local populations of their basic resources, with the result that many make their way into the few remaining centres of prosperity as refugees or itinerant workers. *Migration* caused by the present global economic and financial system will remain one of the burning topics of the immediate future. This "boomerang" is fuelling right-wing extremism in the West, especially when irresponsible political parties divert the attentions of those caught in the poverty trap away from its basic causes and direct their aggression onto immigrants.

– Social and political *instability* is another consequence of the debts and leads to growing numbers of military conflicts with increasing repercussions for us.

These separate effects of the boomerang from the debt-ridden countries pale into insignifance, however, when viewed against neo-liberal, monetaristic, transnational Fordism's direct effects on the populations of the industrialised

---

Kapitalismus frißt seine Kinder (A system achieves its own death. Capitalism devours its children).

countries and their socio-economic and political institutions. This is the aim of the second mode of analysis.

The *dissociation of the financial markets*, that is, the monetary aspect, from the concrete economic aspect, has probably had the most far-reaching consequences of any change since the 1980s. The financial markets have not only contributed to the development of the debt crisis, but are having tremendous *effects* both globally and on individual regions:

– As *investment* in the deregulated transnational financial markets brings the owner of financial assets more profit through interest payments and speculation than investment in a manufacturing company, investments are *shifting from the productive area to that of pure money*. In 1981 – the monetarist policy of the United States Federal Reserve Bank under Paul Volcker – raised average interest payments to 14.2 per cent on short-term borrowing and 13.2 per cent on long-term borrowing, paid to the industrialised countries. For the period 1980-1987 the average interest rate stood at roughly double the rate of growth of the GNP.

Today, of the US\$1,000-2,000 bn passing through the transnational currency markets daily, only 5 per cent are associated with genuine production of goods! The rest goes into speculation. To add to this there are the so-called "financial innovations" such as futures, options and swaps, i.e. "derivatives" for risk protection and for speculative profit-taking, which now even worry the national central banks, because they are causing more and more instability on the financial markets, to the point of threatened collapse.[32] Financial speculation primarily draws the money available away from productive projects producing an income for many, to the casino of the wealth-accumulating owners of financial assets – hence the name "casino capitalism."[33]

– This situation, however, exerts a direct influence on the *behaviour of companies*. Between 1980 and 1987 interest payments exceeded profit margins. Today companies give more than half their profits back to the banks in interest payments. So the companies themselves are starting to *channel their money*

---

32 A good summary of the intensive discussion existing since the crisis of the European Monetary System (EMS), which was accompanied by speculation, and the attendant speculation is to be found in an article by Wilhelm Nölling, formerly director of Hamburg Central Bank: "Die Finanzwelt vor sich selbst schützen" ("Protecting the world of finance from itself") (in Die Zeit, 5.11.93, p.35).

33 See A.G. Frank, 1988; F.F. Clairemonte, 1989; Altvater, 1992[2], pp.157ff.; Le Monde diplomatique, May 1995.

into the financial markets instead of investing it in concrete projects.[34] In addition, they are no longer interested in long-term investment but in deals that bring the fastest financial profit. This development climaxed in the fashion in the United States of using dubious financial practices to buy up large firms, extract everything possible out of them and then sell them off at a profit – the so-called "leveraged buy-out" with junk bonds, i.e. destructive take-overs on speculative borrowing. Interest restrictions are also instrumental in causing companies to cut costs by rationalising wherever possible. The result is lean production and lean management.[35] These cost-cutting strategies do not only have detrimental effects on the suppliers, but also on the workers. First and foremost they squeeze wages and create unemployment.

– *Unemployment* is not simply the necessary consequence of rationalisation, as is often claimed. Full employment is one parameter within the so-called magic square or magic triangle of economic policy, the others being stability, equilibrium in the balance of payments and "appropriate growth." A Keynesian approach gave priority to full unemployment and maintaining a balance of payments equilibrium, in order to achieve the demand for the "appropriately" growing mass production and a balanced global economy. However, this presupposes that in an emergency economic policy decisions can keep interest rates down anticyclically. In contrast, in the neo-liberal monetarist approach top priority is awarded to the stability of monetary value. The central banks keep a tight hold on the money supply, and the deregulated transnational markets can push interest rates up as a first move. This relegates full employment and equilibrium of the trade balance to secondary importance. The owners of financial assets and the countries with strong currencies profit, and the workers and the countries with weak currencies lose out, because individual states are powerless against the monetary restrictions imposed by the world market.[36] Here the American and West German model is gaining prevalence, whereby the central banks practically amount to a second non-elected government regarding economic, social and employment policy.

– The employers, too, use the external pressure (and the income via the money markets) to *increase their profits* and *keep real wages down*. This fact would set off a storm of social protest, if the general public were to see through

---

34 Altvater, ibid. The profits of the Siemens company are now only 30 per cent derived from production, 70 per cent from operations in finance.

35 Described and analysed in detail by Werkstatt Ökonomie, 1992, pp.79ff.

36 See Altvater, 1993, pp.38ff. and 52f.

it politically. Since the 1980s there has been a gigantic process of redistribution away from the dependent workers to the owners of financial assets under the pressure from the deregulated transnational financial markets. Altvater summarises this as follows:

"The effects of this lack of regulation are there for all to see: in all industrialised countries, monetary income (profit through interest) is of increasing importance in comparison to the 'real' incomes from waged labour and productive capital. In the decade 1980-1990 the average annual rise in the gross income of the employed in West Germany was 4.7 per cent, and the gross income of manufacturing companies rose by 6.3 per cent ..., the average return on fixed-interest government bonds still to run for at least three years (index for long-term interest rates) over the same period was 7.65 per cent ... [this] means an interest rate above all other growth rates, [and] that interest cannot entirely be covered by growth in incomes but only by incomes being redistributed in favour of the owners of financial assets."[37]

– The *main losers* in this process are *those in debt* – not only in the South and East, but also in the North. In the United States consumer debts amounted to US$ 756 bn at the end of 1987, i.e. 24 per cent of disposable personal income, with mortgages at 60 per cent of this. The total debts of United States households amounted to 97 per cent of income.[38] H. Creutz has presented the debt development in Germany in a series of clear diagrams and explanations.[39] Though in contrast with the United States, personal consumer debt was for a long time frowned upon in Germany, it has shown a rapid increase – it is now 300 times what it was in 1950. It now constitutes 6 per cent of all debts within Germany, with 46 per cent from production, 23 per cent from housing, and 24 per cent from the public sector. But the greatest burden is borne by the weakest members of society.[40] In 60 per cent of cases where excessive debt led to termination of the loan, unemployment was the cause. Many households have too little or too variable an income to cope with unforeseen circumstances. The principle causes of getting into excessive debt are advertising and new electronic payment systems.

---

37 Altvater, 1993, p.64.
38 Altvater, 1992[2], pp.157f.
39 H. Creutz, 1993, pp.167ff.
40 On the following material see U. Groth's (1991[8]) excellent presentation, esp. pp.16ff.

– The *increasing public debts* of the rich countries since the Reagan administration, now developing dramatically in Germany, has been taking on socially destructive forms. Nowadays, 15 per cent of taxes paid by Germans goes to owners of financial capital as interest payments. A few figures will give a clearer idea of what this means. In 1992 the working population paid an average of DM 3,500 per head to the owners of financial assets via the state – a figure that might equal what an employee earns per month. To put it another way, the state pays DM 317 million in interest every day of the year. With this amount of money it could, for example, build 1000 family houses or 1,500 flats.

– Instead, the ruling Conservative-Free Democrat coalition in Germany is following Reagan and Thatcher with its policy of *social cuts* under pressure from the government debt (the level of which is also indirectly influenced by the mechanisms of transnational financial markets). U. Schneider is therefore justified in calling his new book on the subject *Solidarpakt gegen die Schwachen – der Rückzug des Staates aus der Sozialpolitik* (Solidarity pact against the weak – the state's withdrawal from social policy).[41]

– This process is even more irresponsible in that the financial asset-holders not only enjoy tax cuts, but can simultaneously legally *avoid tax* by transferring money out of the country, a practice tolerated by the state. Anybody in Germany can at any time invest their money, through a bank, in the transnational financial markets, e.g. in Luxembourg, so that it does not count towards the allowance of DM 6,000 tax-free income from interest. The government rejects the Social Democrats' demand for spot checks, which are normal practice in virtually all industrialised countries, on grounds of bank secrecy.[42] The few checks on companies that were in fact carried out by the German tax authorities resulted in supplementary tax demands and thus extra income for the state exceeding DM 115 bn.[43] But as our banks remain uncontrolled, and in any case profits from speculation on the transnational markets cannot be assessed, the state loses a vast amount of tax revenue from financial asset-holders, while the dependent workers have their taxes automatically deducted from their wages. To get an idea of the dimensions involved, since under German law exact figures cannot be calculated, Huster makes the following comparison:[44]

---

41 U. Schneider, 1993.
42 See Frankfurter Rundschau, 3.6.1992.
43 See D. Eissel, in: E.-U. Huster, 1993, p.91(tr.).
44 E.-U. Huster, 1993, p.27.

In 1986 the Deutsches Institut für Wirtschaftsforschung (German Institute for Economic Research) recorded financial assets of DM 22,336 bn gross and DM 2,113 bn net. However only DM 375 bn of this was taxed. Assuming interest at 6 per cent and a 30 per cent tax rate (that is, without taking account of higher interest rates in 1986), that means a minimum of DM 31.6 bn in lost tax revenue. These financial assets have by now more or less doubled (to approx. DM 4,000 bn), giving a corresponding tax gift of at least DM 60 bn (in addition to all the other tax benefits). The vastness of this sum can be visualised when one sees in the taxation distribution table that in 1990 only DM 6.3 bn from financial assets was paid to the state in taxes on profits, i.e. 1.1 per cent of all revenue from taxation, in contrast to the dependent employees, who paid DM 177.6 bn, i.e. 35.1 per cent of income from taxation. This is quite apart from what they then had to pay on top of that in taxes as consumers, not to mention the whole battery of dubious practices and tax dodges which the self-employed and the owners of financial assets use and which are sanctioned by the state through legislation protecting "bank secrecy" and the lack of resources for tax investigation.[45]

– This is also the reason for the progressive disappearance of the dividing line between the legal and the illegal in such as competitive system as the neo-liberal monetarist system of the 1980s and 1990s. The best known example of white-collar crime in economics is the laundering of money from drugs or tax evasion.[46] Hans See calls this area "capital crime" in the title of his book *Kapital-Verbrechen. Die Verwirtschaftung der Moral* (Capital crime: Marketing morals).[47]

One of the most impressive examples of this and of the cooperation between capital, the judicial system, the state and even the EU itself is that of Stanley Adams, who reported the company he was working for, Hoffmann-La Roche, to the then EEC for illegal transfer-price manipulation – as this contravened the official free trade agreement between Switzerland and the EEC (the corporation had, amongst other things, reported a profit of 6 per cent instead of 79 per cent earned from selling its product Librium to the Bolivian government). Instead of

---

45 On the whole complex see D. Eissel, in: Huster, op. cit., pp.94ff.(tr.).
46 See J. Ziegler, 1992 (TB), with the wonderful title "Die Schweiz wäscht weißer – Die Finanzdrehscheibe des internationalen Verbrechens". The personal consequences he suffered in the wake of his publications are described in his autobiography (1993).
47 H. See, 1992, and Couvrat and Pless, 1993.

taking proceedings against the company, the Swiss authorities arrested Adams and he was sentenced to 12 months imprisonment, suspended for three years, for "industrial espionage." In addition, he was expelled from the country for five years, had to pay his own legal costs and lost his bail. He was blacklisted by Big Business throughout Europe, with the result that his career was in shreds. The EEC also let him down, even though the European Court did in fact fine Hoffmann-La Roche £ 150,000 for breaking the law – a sum that the company could pay out of its petty cash.[48]

This aspect of criminality, even when sanctioned to an extent by the state and the courts, as this example shows, is by no means a secondary problem. Instead, because there is no real distinction between what is legal and what is illegal, it is the expression of a system whose top priority is wealth accumulation.

– The *net result*, summarising the factors mentioned above, along with others, is that in the last decade *the gulf between the owners of financial assets and those dependent on a wage* (and even more so the unemployed and those excessively in debt) *has widened greatly.* Creutz's diagram gives a good overview, showing clearly that in contrast to the nominal gross national product, which by 1990 had increased to 3.6 times its 1970 level, net wages only increased by a factor of 2.9, and per capita income by a factor of 2.6, while interest earnings rose by a factor of 6.8 (see next page).[49]

It should be noted here that nearly 50 per cent of the total assets included in the calculations are owned by the richest 10 per cent of households (and hardly any information on foreign assets held by German nationals is included here), whereas the poorest 50 per cent of households own barely 2.5 per cent.[50] Women are under-represented among the wealthy.[51] The same distribution has spread, following German reunification, from eastern to western Germany,[52] due to the national policies of the ruling conservative-liberal coalition (see diagram 2).

---

48 H. See, op. cit., pp.110ff.
49 Creutz, 1993, p.226.
50 Huster, 1993, pp.14 and 21.
51 See A. Weinert in the Frankfurter Rundschau, 26.8.1993.
52 See Hickel, Huster and Kohl, 1993; see also E.-U. Huster's short summary of the distribution mechanisms from the bottom upwards and from East to West, in the Frankfurter Rundschau, 19.1.1993.

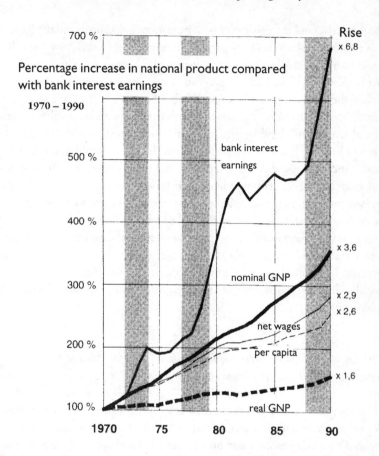

Diagram 2: Percentage increase in national product compared with bank interst earnings
                                                    Source: Creutz, H., 1993

– The final question is that of the role and *opportunities* for the nation-state and democracy in the current money-dominated global capitalistic system.[53] Is it a pure coincidence that the Keynesian welfare state has been progressively dismantled since the mid-1970s? One could be forgiven for thinking that it was a purely political shift of power that caused these processes of redistribution from South to North, from bottom to top and from East to West. However, the global nature of this development casts doubt on this theory. Indeed,

---

53 See R.B. Reich, 1992.

the debt crisis and the collapse of both bureaucratic socialism and the Keynesian model have been running parallel. In other words, even if we and other societies had elected a more socially oriented government, which would in fact be desirable, these national governments would not be able to resist completely the forces imposed from outside by the transnational financial markets. Were they to tackle the situation with legislation and control measures, capital would withdraw via the transnational financial markets (if it really were to lose the battle in the public arena, despite controlling most of the media and propaganda). The Keynesian national welfare state and the so-called social market economy have been brought down principally by the transnationalisation of the capital markets, as has the concept of development in the South (and in the East, which will become more and more obvious as time goes by). "Keynesian intervention presupposes the nation-state; the concept and scope of 'coherence' clearly refer to, and are confined to, a national territory."[54] So it only remains for the question of a new democratic international order to be posed – not merely for social reasons, but also primarily for ecological ones.

2.4 Around the globe: destruction of the basis of life for this and future generations by the money-accumulation economy

With regard to money and the natural environment there exists an amazing degree of agreement in a number of excellent recent publications on this topic. There is agreement not only about the basic approach, but also on many details of analysis and interpretation. The much more difficult question of how the recognition of the obvious danger to life from the present capitalist market economy can generate alternative strategies, will concern us in the Third Part of this book.

The authors of the books mentioned above are Altvater, with three large studies, Daly and Cobb, Binswanger, Lothar Mayer and Creutz.[55] They all regard running an economy for the purposes of wealth accumulation as the root of modern destruction of the environment. Interestingly, they nearly all follow on from Aristotle's distinction between the household economy cover-

---

54 Altvater, 1993, p.45.
55 Altvater, 1987, 1992² and 1992; Daly and Cobb, 1989; Binswanger, 1991; L. Mayer, 1992; H. Creutz, 1993.

ing basic human needs and the chrematistic trade-based economy for the purposes of infinite wealth accumulation. Most of them likewise share Karl Marx's similar criticism of the transformation under industrial capitalism of labour and land (raw materials) into commodities and money. (In contrast, Creutz starts from Silvio Gesell's criticism of interest earnings.) There is also a newcomer on the scene, a scientific consideration that should make debate absolutely essential for those who, for whatever reasons of prejudice, consider Aristotle and Marx to be obsolete – the principle of *entropy*, from the second law of thermodynamics.[56]

> In this case entropy is "the amount of energy unfit or unavailable to do work in an enclosed system" (Mayer, p.18, tr.). In this sense the capitalist economy exhibits a continual increase in entropy. "The increase in entropy is greatly accelerated by the economic process; social progress consists of producing more and more machines for turning raw materials into waste and energy into waste heat. In terms of thermodynamics economic growth is simply a race for the remains of low entropy [which Altvater calls syntropy, U.D.], so that they can be transformed into entropy, i.e. into waste, as quickly as possible." (Mayer, p.19)

Binswanger summarises the strain on the environment from the economy as follows:[57]

"*1* Thanks to the opportunities offered by the economy, the human race is multiplying out of all proportion to other creatures ... thus reducing the habitat of other creatures;

2 Economic capital is replacing ecological capital;

3 The waste is leading to deterioration and disruption of the environment;

4 Natural resources are continually being removed from ecological cycles and ecological capital." This process, which takes the form of an exponential curve due to the dynamics of money, *must* collide with the ecological curve at some point in time (t), as the latter has stabilised in the form of steady curve following the development of the ecological web (through a type of ecological equilibrium). The result is a pre-programmed collision (see diagram 3):[58]

---

56 This approach goes back to N. Georgescu-Roegen, 1971.
57 Binswanger, 1991, p.62(tr.).
58 Ibid., p.63(tr.).

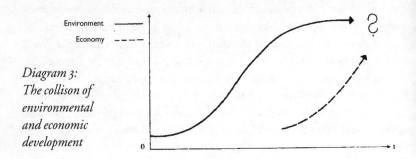

Diagram 3:
The collison of environmental and economic development

Altvater recognises five areas of incompatibility of economy with ecology:[59]

1 the incompatibility of quantity and quality, driven by the money-accumulating capitalist economy;

2 the incompatibility of time and space with the timeless, non-spatial abstract rationality of the capitalist economy;

3 the incompatibility of reversibility with irreversibility: capital always reappears having increased in quantity, to enter a new cycle of self-proliferation, whilst natural processes are irreversible (as in the case of non-renewable raw materials such as fossil fuels);

4 the aims of making profit and earning interest in the money-accumulation economy render zero capital growth impossible, while at the same time the accumulation of capital with high throughput of materials and energy is bound to increase entropy;

5 the incompatibility of rationality and irrationality: the logic of capital demands growth of profit through the (greatest possible) transformation of natural resources into marketable commodities, which is highly irrational with regard to the environment, while on the other hand a non-profit-making economy, serving basic needs and placing fewer demands on the environment, is therefore ecologically rational, but is regarded as irrational by western utilitarian reason."

Altvater concludes that "[it] is therefore complacent and naive ... to expect the solutions to the ecological problems from capitalistic methods of production" (tr.). He goes a step further than the other authors (who agree with this conclusion) in that he does not start from the money-accumulation economy, but also includes the implications of the most recent neo-liberal developments of the capitalist market economy in his analysis. In the light of what has been said above, it comes as no surprise to learn that the transnationalisation of capital markets increases both the scope and the speed of damage to the environment. This process is simply the successful attempt of capital to free itself from every type of control, precisely for the purpose of stimulating wealth accumulation. Maintaining high interest rates not only sets off mechanisms of increasing debt, unemployment and reductions in social services, thus promoting an increase in financial assets world-wide, but also facilitates the destruction of as much of the natural world as possible, with resources being syphoned off for money accumulation which would otherwise be used for environmental purposes.

So not only is ecological criticism of the capitalist market economy urgent in a logical sense, but nature itself demonstrates the cost of the deadly effects of this type of economy almost daily. Those who cannot or will not hear the cries of the starving and dying will witness the death of natural life-support systems, either in person or through their children. Here, too, the powerlessness of individual states to take control of the money mechanism and its global ecological consequences comes to light, perhaps even more so than in the case of social matters. We are again faced with the pressing question: are there any international or global institutions to protect the human race and the environment from the money-accumulation mechanism?

3   The international institutions involved in global domination of finance: the Bretton Woods system and its metamorphoses

3.1   *The International Monetary Fund (IMF) and the World Bank*

In 1944, a conference took place at Bretton Woods in the United States that was to have more and greater effects on the second half of the 20th century even than Yalta. The East-West division resulting from the Yalta conference has proved itself to be relatively short-lived in comparison to the global economic order which had its origins in Bretton Woods.[60] The conference was intended to discuss a comprehensive set of new international regulations designed to prevent a repetition of the mistakes that led to the collapse of the liberal international system in 1929. A *plan* to this effect was submitted by *J.M. Keynes*, the leader of the British delegation. His proposals were aimed at setting up an International Clearing Union with its own currency, along with facilities for correcting member countries' deficits and surpluses in their balance of payments and for supporting weaker countries. The aim was to achieve, as far as possible, balanced global development. (This was to occur within the Fordist model of mass production, mass buying power and mass consumption accompanying full employment.)

> "J.M. Keynes' original proposals to the conference included an International Clearing Union as a reserve bank and an overdraft facility for the national banks. Reserves were to be held and clearing conducted in an international, 'stateless' currency created by the Union, bancor, the predecessor of today's special drawing rights (SDRs). Keynes also put forward an original system for balancing international payments: not only countries with debts (overdrawn accounts), but also those with surpluses would be penalised with progressive rates of interest. This was intended to apply pressure, not only on countries running a deficit, but also on those running a surplus, to balance their books and thus avoid driving their partners on the world market into the red. From the start a policy of growth led by exports along the lines of Germany and Japan was to be avoided. The result would have been even more expansion of the global economy, and decreasing reserves of bancor would have been needed to balance payments ... To make the system acceptable to the structurally weaker developing countries (a term Keynes introduced into the discussion), Keynes also proposed setting up an International Bank for Reconstruction and Development funded by subscriptions from the richer countries."[61]

Under pressure from the United States, not only was this plan watered down but important aspects of it were altered. The United States pushed its White Plan through. Britain, now weakened by the Second World War, and the other participants in general, were hardly in a position to prevail against the capital

---

60 On the following see the concise, but outstanding, description by G. Granados and E. Gurgsdies, 1985, sections 23.1ff. and 24.1ff.
61 W. Hankel, 1992, pp.22f.(tr.).

interests of the United States, itself now in a position of strength (following the war). After all, it now controlled 80 per cent of the world's gold reserves.

The central aspect in the mechanism for achieving equilibrium of national trade balances was dropped completely. The core of the Keynes Plan was that it aimed to further not only the short-term interests of creditors, but also the long-term economic balance by achieving a balance between debtors and creditors. The key to this, however, was balancing trade deficits against trade surpluses. To this end, the Plan recommended that money gained by one country via a trade surplus should be either spent on the purchase of foreign goods or services within a certain time limit, or else cancelled.[62] This would have put a lasting shackle on the development of the notorious gulf between the strong and weak countries and currencies, and could possibly have prevented it altogether. Instead, the White Plan merely included adjustments for debtor countries.

Nonetheless, under the hegemony of the United States the Bretton Woods Agreement still contained some central controlling elements during the initial phase up until 1971-73. The aim was to build up international trade again in the most smoothly-running form possible. The devices for achieving this were to be (a) short-term borrowing facilities for countries with a temporary balance of payments deficit, and (b) a system of fixed exchange rates. But bancor was dropped as an international unit of account and its role taken over by the US dollar, which in turn was linked to the gold standard (at US $ 35 per ounce). This was to allow expansion of the money market via the dollar, whilst simultaneously providing security through gold. The other member countries linked their currencies to the dollar in a system of fixed exchange rates, with fluctuations confined to 1 per cent of their par values. If this could not be maintained then the central banks of the member countries would have to resort to buying up that currency to support it – a principle also adopted later by the European Monetary System in Western Europe, prior to being severely jolted recently by speculation on the financial markets and the monetarist economic policy of the German Bundesbank.

These functions were not to be carried out by an international central bank, but instead by the newly created International Monetary Fund (IMF).

---

62 This idea is reminiscent of the propositions of the Gesell school of thought, which calls for a monetary system governed by taxation rather than rewarded with interest, to prevent stock-piling and to establish money purely as a means of circulation. See H. Creutz's new and comprehensive work, 1993.

Its funds for granting loans were supplied by quotas, or subscriptions, from the member countries. Here lies the second fundamental flaw in the system, which, similarly to the lack of a Keynesian mechanism of maintaining equilibrium, has had catastrophic effects ever since: the undemocratic structure of the IMF.

> Voting rights within this institution of decisive importance for the economic lives of nations are not equal for all members, as in the UN, but are determined by the subscription quotas. Countries that make larger contributions have more votes. I call this plutocracy, rule by the rich (from the Greek *plutos*, rich, and *krateia*, rule). The United States keeps almost 20 per cent of the quotas for itself. This means that in the system where an 85 per cent majority is required for important decisions, the United States has a de facto veto right. The "Group of Ten," i.e. the ten richest industrialised countries, commands 54 per cent of the quotas, so that all IMF decisions can be taken by this group alone (which now includes the USA, Germany and Japan as the most powerful three, followed by Britain, France, Italy, Canada, the Netherlands, Belgium and Sweden). And not even all the agreed control bodies have been set up.[63]

In addition to all this, it was not a structural fund that was set up, but the International Bank for Reconstruction and Development (IBRD), normally called the *World Bank*. Its chief function was to be to make funds available for economic recovery in Europe. The former European colonies were conveniently forgotten at this point. Or rather, their interests, along with global equilibrium, were forgotten. In the new world view under the emerging hegemony of the United States, they were subsumed under the term "underdeveloped" and requiring development according to the US model, as testified for the first time comprehensively in President Truman's declaration on 20th January 1946.[64]

It is undeniable that compared to the more recent developments of rich countries' global (market) policy, the initial phase of the Bretton Woods system was able to claim a degree of success. International trade reached unprecedented proportions, bringing with it the well-known prosperity to the metropolises – and also to the bulk of the population in rich countries. But as

---

63 See D. Budhoo, 1991.
64 See W. Sachs, 1992, pp.887f.; concerning the World Bank, cf. S. George, 1994.

there was no built-in system for maintaining equilibrium or hindering concentration of wealth and power by the strong members, the system was gradually eroded from the inside. The real turning point came, as it did in the other global economic developments described here, at the beginning of the 1970s.[65] Here is W. Hankel's summary of the collapse of the Bretton Woods system:

> "The collapse of the Bretton Woods system (which was definite by the spring of 1973) was ostensibly caused by two contraventions of the rules, these being the United States' inflationary policy of running a deficit, and the counter-productive policy of high interest rates followed by the German Bundesbank and other EEC countries. In the last analysis both of these 'fouls' were the result of currency competition that had become a free-for-all. The United States misused its privilege as the country of the reserve currency and financed its continuous deficit by accepting foreign debts against the dollar, which could be conveniently devalued later. Under the monetary leadership of Germany, the EEC bloc compounded the United States' problem and deficit through premiums earned from high interest on funds diverted out of dollar holdings into other currencies. Coupled with periodic gains from revaluation of their currencies, this ensured the 'blow-up' of the global currency system."[66]

The free-for-all competition between currencies had in fact a lot to do with the free-for-all on the transnational financial markets, as indicated above. The dollar was left floating while the Europeans fixed their exchange rates within the European currency snake (later replaced by the European Monetary System), so that they were able to present a united front against the dollar.

From this point on the "developing countries" were left in the position of increasingly helpless victims, though to different degrees, according to the market law that the weakest suffer the most. Indeed, some (of the stronger "developing" countries) have managed the transition to "newly industrialised countries." This is often cited as disproving the dependence theory, which held that those peripheral countries that have become dependent on the centres since colonial times have no chance of developing.[67] This argument overlooks the fact that some of these countries, in particular the so-called

---

65 See F.E. Aschinger, 1978; W. Hankel, 1992.

66 Hankel, ibid., p.10(tr.).

67 For example see U. Menzel and D. Senghaas, 1986. For damning criticism of this position see Altvater, 1992, p.143 and elsewhere. See also G. Arrighi, 1994, pp.333ff.

Asian "tigers", (South Korea, Taiwan, Hong Kong and Singapore) all had special conditions. In particular, all were anti-communist front-line states and were therefore granted special terms by the West for geo-political reasons. The extremely high social and political costs of this development model were kept quiet. For example, under the neo-liberal aegis of Pinochet and Milton Friedmann Chile has increased the proportion of its population living below the absolute poverty line from 20 per cent in 1973 to 40 per cent in 1992, so that an ever-shrinking elite can enjoy the blessings of Fordist prosperity.

In any case, the debt-ridden countries of the South were on a continuous downward slide instead of developing. In the face of this situation, the IMF and the World Bank radically revised their original functions. They changed their task to keeping the countries heavily in debt within the mechanisms of the capitalist world market, in the interests of the creditor nations and banks. The developing countries would have to gear their entire economy and society to servicing their debts, so as to avoid the collapse of international and transnational credit systems. Altvater has written a good summary of this situation:

> "Now, however, it is less important to regulate the buyer-seller relationships to countries becoming fixed in the role of either creditor or debtor than it is to bring the long-term debtors into the sphere of regulation by the institutions of the industrialised world. The motive is obvious: to prevent the debt crisis from turning into a credit crisis, and to save the lending banks from being encumbered with debts which are non-serviceable and must therefore be written off. After all, an international loan crisis could spread to the existing Fordist system if financial assets were not increased through interest but instead decreased through bankruptcies of debtors."[68]

In other words, the IMF has become a financial policeman working for the owners of financial capital. It squeezes as much money as possible out of the poor debtors and only grants or authorises further loans when their exports have been increased to the maximum and their social services have fallen to the minimum – and this then merely earns interest for the creditors. The result is the above-mentioned net capital transfer of US$ 50 bn from the debtor countries to their creditors every year. The aim of the IMF is now the reverse of Keynes' original concept. The poor are financing the rich.

---

68 Altvater, 1992, p.172(tr.).

This is achieved via "adjustment measures," which under the White Plan only the debtors, and not the creditors, were required to implement. One of R. Strahm's diagrams, "the IMF's programme of recuperation affects the poorest countries," gives a good overview (see diagram 4).[69]

What is not obvious from the diagram, and what will concern us later in more detail, is the fact that those becoming poorer are driven to action that has disastrous effects on the environment, to make money at any cost, but also purely and simply to survive (deforestation and fire-wood). Additionally, the "development projects" supported by the World Bank in these countries are aimed principally at earning hard currency, and, in flagrant contradiction of all rhetoric to the contrary, neglect creation (e.g. by building large dams!). But first and foremost they are only granted to those countries accepting the structural changes imposed by the IMF.

Another perfidious device used by the political and economic coalition of creditors (the financial asset owners and their agents) is debt-for-equity swaps.[70] Under such swaps, the countries in debt have to relinquish the most profitable parts of their national economies to the transnational corporations in exchange for the cancellation of part of their debts (which, of course, at the same time are still rising under the effect of compound interest).

"Privatisation" is hailed as a cure-all for reforming the economies of the countries in debt – at a time when the UN is aleady warning of the "seven sins of privatisation."[71] But with their help it is no longer necessary to possess countries as the old empires did in order to exploit them – this is easily done via computer from the comfort of an executive office in a far-off country.

The catastrophic failure of this neo-liberal monetarist approach, which ensures wealth accumulation by the owners of financial assets at the cost of the majority of human lives, is now even recognised by the European Parliament and the relevant UN body, the United Nations Development Programme (UNDP).[72] The UNDP has stated plainly that neither the IMF, nor the World

---

69 R. Strahm, 1985, p.108.

70 See Altvater, 1992, p.175.

71 UNDP, 1993, pp.5of.

72 See the declaration of the European Parliament, "New World Partnership", (No. PE 201.304, May 1992). It is however very interesting to compare this with the Progress Report of the European Commission to the Council of Ministers, "On the EEC Participation in the process of structural adjustment programmes in the ACP states", i.e. within the framework of Lomé IV. Here, in one seat of real power in the EU (unlike the European Parliament), the ideology of structural adjustment can work unhindered

wage freezes
buying power is reduced

social spending cuts
hospitals, schools and social services are
affected

removing subsidies on foods
the price of staple foods increases

currency devaluation
prices of exports fall – prices of imports rise
exportation instead of consumption

profits are diverted elsewhere
corporations benefit

Diagram 4: Conditions set by the IMF for debtor countries in
Structural Adjustment Programmes (SAP's)

Source: IMF

Bank, nor their divisions responsible for interest-free or low-interest loans to
the poorest countries, the members of the International Development Association (IDA), are fulfilling their original mandates. Kunibert Raffer pointed
out (orally) that if these institutions serving the rich nations were to be judged
according to their own economic criteria and made financially responsible for
their policies, they would have ceased to exist long ago. In a attack on the
World Bank and the IMF, which he left for reasons of conscience after many
years as an executive, Davidson Budhoo has publicised how the the IMF's
highly-paid technocrats, who stick to the book to gain power over the econ-

(EEC Document SEC (91) 2320 final, 8.1.1992). – In contrast, the UNDP Human
Development Report 1992 expresses its criticism in no uncertain terms (pp.74f.).

omic and social policies of the debtor countries, do not merely fiddle the figures in order to subordinate these countries to imf regulations – they are also personally involved in corruption within this system of the arrogance of power.[73]

3.2 The General Agreement on Tariffs and Trade (GATT) and the World Trade Organisation (WTO)

The Bretton Woods conference was also supposed to launch the planning of a set of regulations governing international trade. Subsequently a Havana Charter was drafted, including the proposal for an International Trade Organisation (ITO). In 1947, as a provisional measure, the part of the charter benefiting the industrialised countries was implemented by the setting up of the General Agreement on Tariffs and Trade (GATT) to reduce barriers to international trade. However, no more action was taken because the United States and some other countries failed to ratify the Charter.[74]

GATT was founded on three basic principles: the avoidance of preferential trade agreements (the "most-favoured nation principle"), a ban on trade quotas and the abolition of import tariffs – in theory at least. In reality, the practice of making exceptions ensures that the stronger trading nations can, and do, further their own interests, while the weaker are forced to abide by the rules.

> "The *most-favoured nation principle* ... states that any import or export concessions awarded to one country must also be awarded them to all other member countries. However, this principle does not apply ... to the creation of free trade zones and economic blocs such as the EU. Its practical effects are therefore severely limited.
> The *imposition of quotas* is ... prohibited on principle. Nevertheless, exceptions can be made to this principle at any time to protect the national trade balance and domestic producers. In practice this means that virtually any infringement of this rule can be justified."[75]
> The third element, the *rounds of negotiations aimed at reducing tariffs*, have led world-wide to reductions – as far as these are advantageous to the rich, strong,

---

73 D. Budhoo, 1991. For the critique of the ideological and even religious character of this system see below, Chap. III.5.

74 See Hardes, Rahmeyer and Schmid, 1985, pp.49f.

75 Ibid.

industrial nations. The Uruguay Round of negotiations resulted in a worsening of conditions for the increasingly ravaged poor countries, despite the fact that some concessions were made in the World Trade Organisation (WTO) replacing GATT.[76]

In a nutshell, free trade under GATT/WTO means freedom for the strong to make inroads into the national economies of the weak – protectionism by the strong against competitive products of the weak (the best-known example being the EU's Common Agricultural Policy).

Another feature of the transformation of the international political institutions into the neo-liberal, deregulated market system (with state intervention in the interests of the strong) is the progressive stripping of power from the UN, that is (in principle) all-embracing and democratically organised. The relevant UN agency for such matters, the United Nations Conference on Trade and Development (UNCTAD), has been gradually sidelined by the institutions of the rich, i.e. the IMF, the World Bank and GATT. Their latest masterstroke has been to incorporate the UN Centre on Transnational Corporations into UNCTAD, so that the TNC-friendly "World Investment Report 1993. Transnational Corporations and Integrated International Production" was published under UNCTAD's name. In the 1970s it was still possible for developing countries to build coalitions within UNCTAD calling for the creation of a New International Economic Order (NIEO). Since the assumption of absolute power by the world market and its crisis managers, the governments of the rich industrialised nations, this voice has fallen silent.

---

76 See M. Windfuhr, in: Werkstatt Ökonomie, 1992, who shows how the transnational corporations have influenced the Uruguay Round. The most misguided GATT decisions include the rules for patenting knowledge and intellectual property for the monetarisation of science and technology (to deny the developing countries easy access to such knowledge) and for the monopolisation of certain types of genetically engineered seed; the liberalisation of agriculture, which leaves the North's political instruments for guaranteeing its farmers' incomes intact whilst undermining those of the South for tackling hunger and famine; the introduction of the World Trade Organisation (WTO) to police the neo-liberal regulations in such a way that countries infringing GATT rules in one area can be penalised in another, particularly vulnerable, area – a rule naturally targeted only at the weaker members. See ICDA, 1995, summarising the NGO-critique of the WTO.

3.3 *G7: the seven leading industrialised nations and the "World Economic Summit"*

The crisis managers call themselves the Group of Seven (G7), the group of the seven richest industrialised countries. Its members are the United States, Germany, Japan, France, Britain, Italy and Canada. Since 1975 their heads of government and ministers of finance have held an annual economic summit, to turn the never-ending crisis in a world economy which can no longer be controlled by the existing institutions to their own benefit. They have not been elected to do this. They represent 12 per cent of the world's population, and act as if they were at the helm of the global economy. Quite apart from the fact that they themselves are largely subject to the dictates of the transnational capital markets, the "summit" is the ultimate in arrogance of wealth and power, a pinnacle of plutocracy. Arrighi aptly calls it "a committee for managing the common affairs of the world bourgeoisie".[77]

Regarding political regulation of the market in the neo-liberal monetarist phase of the Fordist accumulation model, it can be concluded that Keynesian regulation of the market was only partially successful in the context of nationally regulated economies and under the pressure of a labour movement embodying real power in the accumulation process. Through the transnationalisation of the markets, primarily the financial markets, interest rates (and other factors) were subject to decisive external influence, and tax flight and price manipulation were favoured. Since the 1970s, financial expansion has become the key feature of capital accumulation. The automation of production has undermined workers' leverage. The combination of transnationalisation and automation results in domestic economies, national legislation and trades unions being relegated to secondary importance, with conditions imposed on them by the deregulated world market. The capitalist market economy has become a truly global market economy. Keynesianism has – so far – failed as an international regulatory model, not to mention that it was based on maximum economic growth and limited to

---

77 See Arrighi, 1994, p.331. See also the criticism of the lack of balanced representation of the Group of Seven in UNDP, 1992, pp.74f. G. Mapp encapsulated the situation wonderfully in the Braunschweiger Zeitung (27.1.1993): "Die Marktwirtschaft ist die Planwirtschaft der Reichen" (The market economy is the planned economy of the rich). The New Economics Foundation in London and other NGOs try to build up a counter-publicity to the annual "summits" by "The Other Economic Summits" (TOES).

the workforces in industrialised centres. Keynes' vision after the Second World War – of a international economic order aspiring to equalisation – has become a disorder destructive to the majority of the world's population both socially and ecologically,[78] supported by the political institutions of the wealthy. What remains of the order is now having to be protected with the increasing use of force by the handful of winner nations.[79]

4 The role of the military in ensuring the global dominance of finance

The use of force to protect economic interests is nothing new. It occurs at the beginning of the history of the empires, which we will examine more closely in the Second Part of this book. 500 years of western European history have certainly brought new developments in the form of weapons of mass destruction. But apart from weapons technology, which in this century has progressed to the stage where we can cause permanent damage to the planet, security and defence systems have changed in parallel with the capitalist modes of accumulation and regulation. Let us consider history since the Second World War.

The initial post-war phase, up until the 1970s, followed the patterns of classical hegemony quite closely. Apparently legitimised by the "threat presented by communism to the free world," the United States (at times accompanied by the other ex-colonial powers such as Britain and France) sent troops into areas it considered politically important because of their location or because of raw materials found there without, a flicker of embarrassment. Vietnam is the best-known example. The United States simultaneously installed governments, principally military governments (with special help from the CIA), e.g. in Persia, Brazil, and especially around the beginning of the

---

78 The potential importance of UNCED for global control of the environment is investigated in the third part.

79 The whole of Altvater's book *Der Preis des Wohlstands* (The price of prosperity), 1992, is dedicated to clarifying this dialectic. The negative side to the prosperity and the relative order enjoyed by an (albeit dwindling) majority in the rich western countries is that in the monetarist system they generate chaos. His summary of the failure to internationalise Keynesianism was published in 1993; Altvater and Mahnkopf *Gewerkschaften vor der europäischen Herausforderung* (Trade unions facing the European challenge), pp.46ff.

1970s, in other Latin American countries. Noam Chomsky and Edward S. Herman have documented this period in detail in their classic work *The Washington Connection and Third World Fascism – The Political Economy of Human Rights*.[80] That was all more or less out in the open. People knew what they were dealing with. Those in positions of power in the United States were aware from the very beginning that the only way to protect their wealth was with tough power politics. The State Department Policy Planning Study of 24th February 1948 (as recorded by George Kennan) contains the following passage:

"... we have about 50 per cent of the world's wealth, but only 6.3 per cent of its population ... In this situation, we cannot fail to be the object of envy and resentment. Our real task in the coming period is to devise a pattern of relationships which will permit us to maintain this position of disparity without detriment to our national security. To do this, we will have to dispense with all sentimentality and day-dreaming; and our attention will have to be concentrated everywhere on our immediate national objectives. We need not deceive ourselves that we can afford today the luxury of altruism and world-benefaction ... We should cease to talk about vague and – for the Far East – unreal objectives such as human rights, the raising of living standards, and the democratization. The day is not far off when we are going to have to deal in straight power concepts. The less we are then hampered by idealistic slogans, the better."[81]

Parallel to the swing to deregulation of the financial markets and to neo-liberal monetarism, another, more subtle, security strategy also developed. Not only the disaster of the Vietnam War caused US strategists to look for indirect methods of securing the dominance of the United States. They found them in *low intensity conflict strategy* (LIC) and, more recently, in *mid intensity conflict strategy* (MIC). G. Eisenbürger, J. Hippler and I have published the confidential strategy documents of the North and Latin American military commanders with a commentary under the title *Total War Against the Poor*.[82] What follows are the main points.

Right from the start these secret documents make it clear that even though the Soviet Union under Gorbachev could no longer be billed as the Enemy

---

80 Chomsky and Herman, Vols. I and II, 1979; see also K. Nair and M. Opperskalski, 1988.
81 Quoted from N. Chomsky, 1985, p.48.
82 U. Duchrow, G. Eisenbürger and J. Hippler, 1990.

and the economic, political and military superiority of the West was plain, the real fundamental conflict across the globe remained, namely the struggle for *"domination and distribution of natural resources and strategic raw materials"* (p.55). This bears a startling similarity to the modern western view of the human race, as expressed in the words of Descartes, that mankind is the "master and possessor of nature". Equally startling is the continuity of interests with the State Department in 1948. The addition of the words "strategic raw materials," the foundation on which Fordism is based, i.e. energy from (non-renewable) fossil fuels.[83] Fordist industrial capitalism can only increase production and thus generate profit and prosperity (for some) by using energy to turn the greatest amount of resources into goods. The fact that at present this energy comes from fossil fuels, mainly oil, means that political and military relations to oil production are of fundamental importance. The secret documents accordingly demand that in the battle for control of resources the forces trying to alter the status quo be resisted "at all levels (of power)," i.e. militarily, politically, economically and socio-psychologically.

> The interesting thing is, though, that in 1987, the secret services and military commanders of the North American and Latin American armed forces attending the conference where the documents were presented appeared to be relatively certain of their position, as far as the military, political and economic aspects were concerned. Their main interest was directed at what they termed the "socio-psychological" or cultural level (of power), that is, people's "hearts and minds." In practical terms this meant that the main battle against the "international communist movement" would now have to be fought in churches, schools, universities, and, more than anywhere else, in the media. Their main opponents would accordingly be the local churches, liberation theology, human rights groups, international solidarity organisations such as Amnesty International, the World Council of Churches, the International Fellowship of Reconciliation, Bread for the World (in Germany) and others, which work with the poor. The head of the Philippine security forces once described his archetypal enemy in a single sentence to the liberation theologist Edicio de la Torre during an interrogation (using torture): "We are suspicious of anyone who does good and does not get rich." The social movements are subject to defamatory campaigns of misinformation, their activists obstructed, or murdered by death squads, e.g. the fate of

---

83 See Altvater, 1992, pp.81ff.

the Jesuits in El Salvador or the fiercest low intensity conflict in South Africa be-fore change.[84] This strategy naturally includes the conventional tactics of sup-plying weapons and training soldiers and death squads acting on behalf of the United States, as well as destabilisation programmes. Nicaragua, El Salvador, Haiti and other central American and Caribbean countries are the best-known recent examples.

In connection with this it is important to note the metamorphosis of both the concept and practice of *democracy*. In 1948 the view of the State Department was still that the power struggle might sometimes require democracy to be publicly abandoned, but now democracy itself has been transformed into an tool serving the power struggle.[85] Essential to the understanding of this pro-cess is the Sant Fé II document of the Inter-American Security Council, a policy paper for President Bush in January 1989. The document defines "free enterprise and free national capital markets allowing independent societies" as "democratic capitalism." With regard to politics, the document states that we have concentrated too much on the question of elected governments, as they are in any case only "temporary governments." The main institutions of this "democratic regime", which according to the document must be streng-thened, are the agencies of "permanent government," i.e. the military, the police, the judiciary and administration. And the document recommends that this concept be channelled into the hearts and minds of the population through the churches, schools, universities and the mass media – which the authors term the cultural "war."

With regard to the real situation in the islands of prosperity within the capitalist market economy, the importance of these statements cannot be over-estimated. This is because the specific methods mentioned above support the system by preventing people from seeing clearly just what is happening – and that totally legally. They do not realise how they are being manipulated and often do not even see a heightened awareness as being in their own interests.

We will shortly consider the ideological and cultural dimension of the capitalist market economy in greater detail, but first we must return to mid-intensity conflict. Since the Gulf War it has been revealed that the concept of low intensity conflict has been extended[86] with the aim of preventing the ad-

---

84 See Minnaar, A., et al. (eds.), 1994.
85 See Duchrow, Eisenbürger and Hippler, op. cit., pp.33ff. and pp.189ff. ; and the recent study on this subject, ed. 7. Hippler, 1995.

vancement of those "Third World" countries rich in resources which, with western technology, especially armaments, could attain sufficient leverage to threaten the industrialised countries' monopoly of the world market – such as Iraq with regard to the price of oil. That has been peddled as the "new world order." There are some excellent analyses of the subject.[87] Altvater perceives many direct links with the unipolar neo-liberal type of Fordism following the collapse of the Soviet threat. The states with high-tech weapons, which are to be forcibly disarmed through wars in the interests of western hegemony, obtain their weapons from precisely those centres of capitalism which, in the face of over-production of goods and the eradication of the buying power of the impoverished societies, compensate through selling arms, in their inexorable drive to accumulate. Altvater puts this succinctly:

> "The deregulation of the market over the last twenty years is not the only reason why the export of arms has been subject to less and less political control, and has been left more and more to the 'free market forces,' thus making a profit for the arms producers." (p.213)

These producers of arms make a double profit, through alternate stock-piling and enforced disarmament. The Federal Republic of Germany has now become the second-largest exporter of arms on the world market (after the United States).[88] And now, just like the USA, it is setting up an imperial intervention force to take action anywhere on the globe to preserve its economic interests, as is openly admitted in the defence ministry's strategy documents. The intention is camouflaged by "humanitarian aid" all over the world. "The states of the 'orderly' hemisphere are creating the conditions for the growing chaos of the other hemisphere."[89]

Of course this disruption is not only caused by the arms trade, but also by the destruction of the economic and social fabric of the poor countries as described above. But the way these countries are perceived in the West is also changing, as pointed out by W. Sachs.[90] The developing regions are turning into areas of risk. The "Third World" is no longer regarded in terms of development, but in terms of security. The notion of development in the context

---

86 See T.M. Klare, 1991.
87 See J. Hippler, 1994; J. Nelson-Pallmeyer, 1992; Altvater, 1992, pp.206ff.
88 See Frankfurter Rundschau, 25.10.1993.
89 Altvater, 1992, p.214(tr.).
90 W. Sachs, 1992.

of the neo-liberal world market has become pure ideology, totally removed from reality. We should be speaking not of developing countries but of decomposing countries. The West has shifted from "hegemony of progress to hegemony for stability." Correspondingly, it is trying to make itself indispensable as a humanitarian policeman.

> "The scenario is obvious: the military world order provokes the creation of a 'caring imperialism', while at the same this very role of 'guardian' of vast areas demands a permanent military presence. The result of such a new world disorder at once militaristic and humanitarian, would be anything but a form of civilised capitalism, even if (or because) military intervention is backed by the democratic parliaments of the rich countries ... That would be a new era of war, in which the dominant countries would maintain simultaneous order and chaos confined to different parts of the world by the use of military force and humanitarian aid. The Cold War would be followed by a period of 'Warm War', with continual interventions without them ever encroaching onto the territory of the rich countries and escalating to a state of 'Hot War'. Wars would be phases of a cycle of arming and forcibly disarming the armed military states when, with their military power, they posed a threat to the 'new world order'. They would also be the tried and tested means of periodically limiting the 'disorder' within the order, at the same time providing the necessary conditions for maintaining the division of the world, which is itself an essential precondition (and also a side-effect of) global Fordist systematisation."[91]

As many of these armed states are dependent on oil from the Middle East (e.g. Iraq and Iran), the image of the "Enemy Islam"[92] held by the West since the time of the Crusades can be revived, and comes as a welcome substitute for the lost communist enemy stereotype. So we have come full circle, back to the origins of global domination by Europe and capitalism, to find that domination and power always contain an element of ideology.

---

91 Altvater, 1992, pp.215f.(tr.).
92 See Hippler and Lueg, 1995.

5   The ideology of the global dominance of finance and the media's role

Every form of rule must have some basic legitimation, and legitimation is achieved through ideology. We will return to this point in more detail in the second part of this book, concerning theology, starting with the empires of the ancient Near East. The ideology of the present system is what Franz Hinkelammert calls the "metaphysics of capitalism."[93] We touched upon this previously, when examining the emergence of the capitalist market economy and came upon the "fetishism" regarding money and commodities, the automatic mechanism of money accumulation through production, circulation and consumption of commodities in a self-regulating market. We are not concerned to analyse this fundamentally here, but rather to locate these problems as they occur in our present-day society and also in the institutional media that construct and disseminate ideologies.

The goal of global capitalism is the accumulation of money via (supposedly) self-regulating markets. This is why money is at the centre of the ideology. It is shrouded in secrecy and treated as the Holy of Holies. People accept more than just "bank secrecy." Paul Frank, a former official in the German Foreign Ministry, draws attention to bank architecture such as that in Chicago, where a bank was recently built in the style of a romanesque cathedral:

> "Customers ... will probably find that this cult-like form of self-presentation is in keeping with the fact that the ethics of late capitalist society ascribe the utmost importance to the unlimited acquisition and possession of money. Money has top priority. So it is only logical that this society accepts its own demise in the interests of making a profit. This is the 'mechanism' inherent in capitalism which causes its destruction. The quantitative growth rates make the reduction in quality appear to be an improvement."[94]

When the German Bundesbank appears on television it comes across as a temple to the deutschmark. Many central banks are built in a similar style. This is why Greider entitled his book on the proceedings within the United States' Federal Reserve Bank surrounding the 1979 changeover to the monetarist policy of high interest rates *The Secrets of the Temple*. Evidently the

---

93 F.J. Hinkelammert, 1986.
94 P. Frank, 1991, p.351(tr.).

public has no difficulty in accepting that the powerful board of a central bank does not have to be elected, although it determines the conditions within which the democratically elected government has to operate its economic and social policies. There is also evidence that those at the very core of the system cannot be called to account by those affected by it. They are answerable only to the owners of capital assets, i.e. to their interest in accumulating money.

This is the form in which real democracy, even today, is confined to the owners of assets. Locke made it clear that from the beginning this was the intention of the bourgeois state. Bourgeois rights are based on property. Slaves, as non-owners, were naturally excluded. Those who owned only their labour potential, and none of the means of production, initially had correspondingly fewer rights, even down to not having the right to vote. Nowadays the dependent waged workers do have the right to participate in electing a "temporary government," but – if they are not owners of financial assets – they have no influence over the power of money, which sets the harsh background for any formal social, economic or ecological policy decisions.

That leads us back to the concept of democracy, as expounded in the Santa Fé II document drafted for President Bush. However, in the word *freedom* it contains another indication of an ideological connection. Freedom is defined here as freedom for private enterprise and the capital market. Apparently this is regarded as the foundation of all social freedom, whereas in fact, under the liberal and neo-liberal conceptions, freedom means market freedom.

> Market freedom in the sense of freedom for the accumulation of property and money – which Locke not only honestly propounded, but also required men of reason to practise, in fulfilment of the commandment to subdue the earth – contains inherent inequality. Market freedom can only lead to the strong becoming stronger and the weak becoming weaker. That is why Keynesian Fordism consciously demanded that the social state work against this trend. But now, under neo-liberalism, the markets are deliberately being deregulated and social services systematically run down. This reduces the market chance of all those who do not own financial assets. Indeed, the more they are sidelined, the more they are excluded from the formal market (which has now happened to the majority of the world population).

This shows that "freedom" under market liberalism and neo-liberalism is an ideological illusion. Market freedom for the strong does not only destroy the political freedom of being able to reach common decisions about fundamental social issues such as justice and preservation of the environment for future generations, but also destroys itself, i.e. the freedom of the weaker market participants. All those who do not conform to this ideology of freedom for money accumulation, and instead demand economic democracy as the basis for political democracy, are branded as socially undesirable radicals incapable of participating in the consensus – which is the simplest form of ideological warfare. When society itself becomes active and these "radicals" gain too much power, low intensity conflict is made to escalate, even going as far as murder.

If the bankers are the high priests of that Holy of Holies, the money accumulation system, then the academic economists (who try to be "objective") are the teachers and elders. It is no accident that Germans have their "council of the Wise Men" who give the periodic analyses of the economy. It is their business to explore and teach the laws of the self-regulating market within the liberal and neo-liberal concept. Not for nothing did Adam Smith regard himself as the Newton of national economics. The new notion of mechanistic, mathematical laws governing science and technology that typified the Age of Enlightenment is an abstraction which is forced onto the whole of human, social and natural life.[95] And the most fundamental law is the rationality of capital accumulation.

Correspondingly, the norm of commodity and income growth, abstractly expressed as the monetary value of the gross national product, has now become the yardstick for measuring economic performance and success, without anyone asking whether this type of achievement is genuinely useful to life. It is well known that road accidents and river pollution, for example, both increase the GNP. We shall return to this question when we come to consider the alternatives.

Susan George and Fabrizio Sabelli have written a book with the telling title *Faith and Credit: The World Bank's Secular Empire*. It shows how in various ways the Bretton Woods institutions are "the visible hand of the programme of unrestrained, free market capitalism" as a belief system (p.248) administered by church-like hierarchical organisations. The programme of "structural adjustment" have proven wrong and detrimental to all countries involved as debtors (not to the creditors, to be sure). All predictions of improvement through these lines of development have proven wrong. A science would have

---

95 See the outstanding and ideologically critical analysis of economics and other disciplines by Daly and Cobb, pp.25ff., and F. Hinkelammert, 1986. R. Cockett (1994) has aptly described the rise of the neo-liberal *Economic Counter-Revolution*.

to correct its assumptions and theories after they had been disproved. Not so the faith system of the neo-liberal ideology of the Bank and the IMF since the 1980s. On the contrary, it is pressed through with the iron fist of an organisation resembling a one party system or a religious sect.

> There are "striking similarities between the development vision of the Bank and the neo-conservative, right-wing fundamentalist religious agenda on the rise in many northern countries in the 1980s...the missionary is replaced by the neo-classical economist...helping the underdeveloped to tread the long road to salvation...Debt payments are one offering, a kind of tribute; the structural adjustment measures which ensure that these debts can and will be paid, act as a kind of ritual cleansing through sacrifice...only one interpretation of the Word is allowed. Proposals of alternatives to adjustments are dismissed by its proponents as dangerous, unrealistic, or irrelevant. If the invisible hand of the market, like the divinity, is beyond the control of mere mortals, if the road to redemption requires sacrifice and penance, then no human agency, much less any individual, can be considered responsible for the consequences of the markets operations." (pp.96f.)

Here the point is to show that a supposedly objective, neo-liberal science of economics is itself intrinsically ideological, if it claims responsibility for all economic life. This is not a theoretical question, but one of gargantuan relevance in practice. On the one hand, it is connected with ordinary people's belief in experts, which hinders them from perceiving and deciding on issues that have a fundamental effect on their lives. On the other, the ideology of there being natural laws governing economic processes leads to the notion that "sacrifices have to be made" for the sake of future growth, as if to some idol, without anyone asking what is supposed to grow and for whose benefit. This ideology induces the social victims to believe that they are victims not of social and political decisions but of natural disasters which just happen. The Latin American liberation theologians have discussed intensively the way in which the neo-liberal concept of the total market claims its victims.[96]

As well as mentioning schools and universities, the secret service documents speak of the *media* as the cultural battleground for "domination and distribution of natural resources and of strategic raw materials." This has both

---

96 See H. Assmann and F.J. Hinkelammert's summary, 1989.

an obvious and a more hidden motive. The obvious one is the power of advertising. Advertising is a direct expression of the market, market forces and market ideology. In our analysis, it calls on the desire for unlimited accumulation of money and of (real or imagined) means of life-support, i.e. consumption. This monstrous mechanism drives not only those with great purchasing power, but also those who desire it. For example, under socialism in Eastern Europe, people were driven by the desire for deutschmarks and consumer goods – without looking at the negative effects of these tempting goodies. Apart from areas such as East Germany, where financial benefits have been made available to alleviate the social situation for political reasons, people living in the "economies in transition" are suffering a particularly rude awakening.

Indeed not only actual advertising, but also the very structure of the mass media benefits the market. With few exceptions, information is divided up into and disseminated as minute portions, so that background, links between issues and alternatives remain hidden. In addition, the news agencies utilised here are all in western hands. The Third World agency IPS is deliberately – and scandalously – under-used.

This did not come about by accident. The media market is dominated by a shrinking number of large companies.[97] The most dangerous thing about them is the destruction they inflict on individual independent cultures through the world culture they market, whose only aim is to produce profits and which weakens people' capacity for social resistance.[98] Added to which, the banks have developed their own information network, which is faster even than that of the governments.[99] E.S. Herman and N. Chomsky have summarised the situation of the "political economy of the mass media" in their book *Manufacturing Consent*.[100] Their thesis is that the media in the present-day neo-liberal market society serve only to mobilise support for dominant interests in the economy and the state. This is the explanation for what the media do not report and where they distort or hide the truth, especially where they manipulate the recipients at a subconscious level. This analysis was written within a US context, but in Europe public broadcasting is also adapting rapidly to the style of the private media.

---

97 See J. Tunstall and M. Palmer, 1991.
98 See H.I. Schiller, 1989.
99 See C. Hamelink, 1983.
100 Chomsky and Herman, 1988.

Last but not least, the secret strategy documents on low intensity conflict mention churches and theology as an important area in the battle for power over people's hearts and minds. For this reason, at least, even those who do not find the church or theology very important should not neglect the Second Part of this book.

6 Summary

The power system

Transnational		Global Finance Market:	**Transnational**
(under little or no political control)	exploiting, blackmailing	– currency and interest speculation – tax and capital flight – capital drain from the real economy, large profits	
		World Market of Productive Industry	**Transnational**
		– global sourcing: production using the cheapest labour and raw materials by playing them off against one another and – developing technology for maximum profit	
			Transnational
		– global supermarket: most lucrative sales and – rubbish disposal (of toxic waste) in the South and East	

International		
a. economic	dictating / manipulating / waging war	→ "Plutocratic" **Bretton Woods institutions + G7** (the "Group of Seven", the seven richest industrialised countries)
b. political		→ **UN-System:** – weakening of UNCTAD, UNDP, UNESCO – manipulation of the UN Security Council
c. military		MIC arms exports LIC
d. ideological		Advertising, media, science, "capital theology"

Regional	**THE WEST**
	USA + Canada — competition — EU + Western Europe — competition — Japan
	"Fortress Europe"

National	**Governments**
	– cooperate on capital-promoting economic order – control mobile capital only to a limited extent – lose large sums in taxation - national debts – have only limited influence on the central banks – suffer under currency speculation – convert financial pressures into decline in social services – support capital-promoting governments in the South and East

Societies		
	– Are divided into:	fewer and fewer winners: – owners of financial assets – those employed in the world market sector — ca. 1/3
		unstable group benefitting a little: 1/3
		growing number of losers and excluded (unemployed, homeless, people in debt, pensioners, etc.): 1/3
	– Rising crime	

Environment	– Destruction: – is only slightly reduced and repaired – the West produces 80% of the waste – the West consumes 80% of the resources and energy

Future Generations	– lose their means of life-support

Result	**A DEATH-BRINGING ECONOMY**

of the global neo-liberal capitalist economy

Finance	**Aim:**
(Actors: commercial banks, insurance companies etc.)	unlimited wealth accumulation for – owners of financial assets – owners of means of production
Production	**Means:**
(actors: transnational coporation/TNCs	– private ownership of means of production – competition amongst the weak – monopolies amongst the strong – compound interest mechanism – unlimited growth – loss of political control
Trade	
(actors: transnational corporations/TNCs	

▼ ▼ ▼

IMF (International Monetary Fund) – World Bank
+ GATT (General Agreement on Tariffs and Trade)
now: WTO (World Trade Organisation)

financial police force | (structural adjustment = social decline) | free trade for the strong | protectionism against the weak

~US$ 50 bn
    net capital transfer to the West
~US$ 450 bn
loss to the West through market disadvantages

THE SOUTH		THE EAST	
Newly industrialised countries	analo-	Newly industrialised countries	
	decomposed countries	gous to	decomposed countries

——— **Boomerang effects**: environment, drugs, taxation, unemployment, migration, instability

Governments

– have little influence on the international economic order
– have little or no control over mobile capital
– suffer under (and sometimes indulge in) even more tax and capital flight ———→ debts
– suffer enormous pressure from hard currencies
– suffer under currency speculation
– convert financial pressures into decline in social services
– receive political support from the West

– **Are divided into**
    ┌→ tiny minority of winners – owners of financial assets   ca.
    │   – those employed in the   5%
    │   world market sector
    ├→ small group that benefits   15%
    └─ large number of losers and excluded (unemployed,
            homeless, people in debt, starving, etc.):   80%

– **Become ungovernable and extremely violent**

– **unbridled destruction** (e.g. the rain forests)
– **is the West's rubbish dump**

– **lose their means of life-support**

if no resistance or U-turn occurs

SECOND PART

Biblical recollection of the future of life

> *"This 'God' is a distant rumour, a rumour about that liberty which exists in autonomy and equality."*
>
> Ton Veerkamp[1]
>
> *"The epidemic in our neighbourhood is forgetfulness."*
>
> Nagib Machfus[2]

Preliminary considerations

In the face of the life-endangering structures of the existing world system and the apparent lack of any way out, hopelessness is widespread. All the varied victims struggle with despair. Those who have fought or are fighting for change are less and less clear about what paths to take. Many of those even who have long believed that the key to the problem is the social taming of the market economy are wondering why things are actually going downhill in every area of society and why in spite of our greater awareness ecological degradation continues apace.

Here *ethics* offers its help. "Economic ethics" is booming, professional chairs are being established, books are being written,[3] big companies even are employing theologians and philosophers and organising seminars on the theme. Ethics is about people's behaviour, be it the behaviour of individuals in personal issues (when we speak of Individual Ethics) or the behaviour of individuals and groups in social and political contexts and structures (when we speak of Social Ethics). Elmar Altvater even avers that of necessity, as "positional goods" can no longer be distributed by the allocation mechanisms of the market economy, a "'re-moralising' of reality, the application of ethical principles to the allocation and distribution of resources, (is) unavoidable".[4]

---

1 T. Veerkamp, 1993, p.369(tr.).
2 N. Machfus, 1990, p.213(tr.).
3 Cf. the research report by U. Duchrow, 1993.
4 Altvater, 1992(2), p.346 (tr.).

This approach is confronted by a fundamental problem, formulated by, of all people, an advocate of liberal capitalism, Max Weber. He writes:

"In virtue of its 'impersonal' character, the capitalist economic system cannot be regulated by ethics, unlike all other forms of government. Even externally it mostly appears in so 'indirect' a form that it is impossible to tell who the 'ruler' really is or to confront him with ethical demands. In the relationship of house-holder and servant, teacher and pupil, landowner and staff, master and slave, pa-triarchal prince and subjects, it is possible to present ethical postulates and to in-sist on adherence to concrete norms, since these are personal relationships and the services to be performed are a product and integral part of the relationship... *The factors determining conduct at the decisive points* (within the capitalist system) are the 'competitive capacity', the market (labour market, money market, pro-duction market), i.e. 'objective' considerations, factors which *are neither ethical nor unethical but simply an-ethical, ethically neutral, at a level where ethics are irrele-vant* (my *emphasis* U.D.), where impersonal authorities come between the human beings engaged. This 'slavery without slaveowners' into which capitalism en-snares workers or borrowers *can be discussed in ethical terms only as an institution* (my *emphasis*, U.D.) but this is certainly not – in principle – the personal beha-viour of an individual – either among rulers or ruled – behaviour which has been prescribed for him in all essentials on pain of punishment by objective situations and (this is the decisive point) having the character of 'service' in respect of an im-personal *material goal* (M.W.'s *emphasis*)."[5]

"Just as rational economic and political action obeys its own inherent laws, so too every other form of rational action within the world remains inescapably tied to the conditions of the world which are inimical to fraternity but which must necessarily be its means or ends, and thus finds itself in a relationship of tension with the ethics of fraternity."[6]

After the historical and analytical results reached in the First Part, there can be no doubt that Max Weber is right when he states that a pure market system leaves no room for ethics. It is about "service" to an impersonal, objective goal: that of making money. "Debt servicing", the necessary payment of inter-est and principal, is an example of this. Debtors either pay or they go bank-rupt, they become un-creditworthy, their property and goods are seized – or

---

5   M. Weber, 1972(2), pp.708f.(tr. David Lewis).
6   M. Weber, 1963, p.552 (tr. David Lewis).

in ancient times they and their family had to go into slavery. In the case of an indebted state, there are no insolvency regulations to guarantee its people a minimum standard of living like the provisions that exist today for private bankrupts. It has to squeeze the last drop out of its citizens, even if the price is starvation and chaos – unless a solution is found other than at the economic level of the market. In the market economy ethics is excluded – at the price of economic downfall, as Max Weber says.

Only as a total institution is the liberal (i.e. supposedly self-regulating) capitalist market economy "worthy of ethical discussion", according to Weber. That simply means that one may accept it ethically or not. Weber himself had no experience of attempts to intervene in the market by political regulation, which would make for a different, ethical kind of debate. However, what applies to his classical liberalism applies equally today to the transnational financial markets, which have freed themselves from political regulation – as is only right, according to neo-liberal and monetarist ideology.

In view of this (which, unfortunately, few people today admit as honestly as Max Weber did), an ethical approach to the "real-capitalist" market economy is in principle too superficial to assess its problems and set alternatives against those of its structures and effects which endanger life.

This throws light on a more fundamental problem, which we have often run into. A good number of our modern problems have come about because the whole of life is not held in view; instead, it is carved up into components, each of which can then be held in the manipulative grip of expertise and technology, posing as tools of common sense. When considering life on this planet as a whole we must not lose sight of the whole complex of relationships in society. And at the very least that includes its economic, political-military, cultural and ideological aspects. Now it is again too superficial to calculate their sum by simply adding these aspects together. It is much more a matter of their interconnection and interplay. What in any specific situation in society is the nodal point about which the whole is organised? Weber, interestingly, calls it "service" of a purpose. The Greek language knows two words for what we describe by the single word "service": *latreia* and *diakonia*. *Latreia* concerns the "service of God" in the sense of the "worship of God". That means: what is the ultimate concern of a society and the individuals who comprise it, to what authority do they feel ultimately bound, what do they follow, to what do they owe obedience? *Diakonia* concerns the relationships people have with one another. Clearly, the two are related in a way that needs explanation.

It means no more and no less than that the question of God is ultimately about a society's constitution. So when, according to Weber, the capitalist market economy defines as its nodal point "service" of an impersonal, objective purpose, it makes in its own context a statement about what in pre-modern cultures was called "God". Thus it does not matter whether in modern economic, political or cultural-ideological texts the word "God" appears or not – Adam Smith still discerns an "invisible hand" at work in the market. But even economists who in modern, scientific style do without the "working hypothesis of God" are thereby saying something about their theo-logy, their talk about what does and does not concern them ultimately. Something is also revealed of their conceptions of human (and environmental) relationships; Weber excludes "brotherliness", for example, when a society operating as a capitalist market economy ultimately "serves" an impersonal, objective purpose.

Now this same Max Weber, as everyone knows, claimed that capitalism grew essentially upon the ground of Christianity, particularly that of Calvinism. In his famous work *Protestant Asceticism and the Spirit of Capitalism*[7] he looks into the contributions Protestantism has made to the development of the rational culture of the West in terms of capitalist economy, science, technology and politics. We shall not examine this thesis in detail here.[8] Historically Weber's derivations cannot be maintained, as the elements of early capitalism were all there before the Reformation. But it is indisputable that the capitalist form of economy and society came from Europe and that the capitalist world market is to this day dominated by the West – along with westernised Japan. It is incidental to this, but not unimportant, that in step with the change to neo-liberalism an explicit re-theologising of the ideological discourse has taken place. The secret service papers mentioned above and the two Santa Fe documents for Reagan and Bush witness to this,[9] as well as many more recent publications on the theme of "theology and economics". These observations and considerations alone serve to show that when dealing with the question of where an economy is going it is essential to work seriously on the Christian traditions.

On the other hand, it is a fact that the victims of Western capitalism in the "Third World" have for years been researching the biblical and theological traditions intensively. They have come to the conclusion that the victims can

---

7   In: W.G. Runciman (ed.), 1978, pp.138ff.
8   Cf. for a critical view on it H. Lüthi, 1967.
9   Cf. Chap. III, 4 and 5, above; also U. Duchrow, 1993.

draw from these traditions clarity, certainty and strength in their struggle against the capitalist style of economy, society and life. They have rejected as an abuse and slander of God all attempts to legitimise this system with the help of the Bible or theology, or even to suggest it should be tolerated. Now that is not a minor or academic question, if only because the contrary is clear from the fact that the USA in secret, and many Latin American governments in public, oppose liberation theologians and even have them killed. An example of this is the Jesuits in El Salvador, whose head and leader, Ellacuria, was mentioned explicitly in the American secret service papers before his assassination.[10] Also not to be overlooked is the role in this life-and-death struggle of the Vatican and certain protestant sects that come mostly from the USA: to which we shall return later.

So we have the situation that in the capitalist system both the dominators and the dominated appeal to the Bible and theology, the one for legitimation of the status quo, the other for the sake of protest and resistance to it. Clearly this situation needs clarification, which raises the extraordinarily difficult question of how to proceed methodologically. How can we explain and assess biblical traditions and relate the results we obtain to the apparently wholly incomparable modern situation? This is the concern of hermeneutics, the problem of translating for our time texts and utterances about life from the past.

Here we are fortunate in that *Ton Veerkamp* has solved the problem admirably, at least for the biblical traditions after the collapse of kingship from the sixth century BC onwards. We will draw on his insights, first examining his approach as developed in his book *Autonomie und Egalität*[11] (Autonomy and equality).

He starts from the premise that, when we compare *texts* from different epochs and societies, what we compare is not only forms of expression of the life of people in society but *societies* themselves (p.21). Proceeding like this is not at all the normal practice, though it obviously should be. Many theological disciplines claim to work in a "historical-critical" way, but what that means is often just philological-critical, i.e. they operate above all at the level of concepts. Dogmatics and ethics do so even more. The essential role of "context", i.e. social reality, in our understanding of the Bible, the history of

---

10 Cf. Duchrow, Eisenbürger and Hippler, 1990, p.133.
11 T. Veerkamp, 1993.

theology and the theological enterprise today is an insight and practice we have rediscovered only by doing theology with the West's victims, with the liberation theologies of Latin America, Asia and Africa. It is true that in European and North American biblical criticism "sociological" exegesis is gaining more and more ground; but there are important distinctions to be made here, to which we must return. At all events, if we wish to improve our judgement and orientation on economic issues by reference to older traditions, it is clear that we cannot understand ancient witnesses simply at an abstract level. It can only be within a nexus of social realities.

Chapter IV

The socio-economic and political-ideological context of the biblical traditions

1 Economy in the ancient Near East

The difficult question here is whether it is possible to compare societies at all. Does not the modern age take pride in having progressed to the point of being completely different from older societies? Helpfully, Ton Veerkamp starts from a very simple fact. There is an indisputable continuum in the history of all societies in that people have to find a means to sustain their lives. And that is precisely what this book is about. "A life-giving economy" – in the plainest sense of the term – is, whatever else may be said about human life, an absolute necessity as the basis for all other things. So our theme is the basic continuum of all human history and also a reference point for all eras of this history.[1] The fundamental question is: What are we to eat, what are we to drink, how are we to be clothed? Whether this question is also significant for the biblical writings will have to be demonstrated by interpreting the texts. What are the elements of economic activity common to the economies of all eras? Veerkamp enumerates five:

1 the satisfaction of basic needs;

2 the emergence of new needs;

3 the continuation of life through procreation;

4 cooperation in the production and reproduction of human life with the help of productive labour, hence the relationships of production as social relationships;

5 the need for those who work productively to achieve a surplus, as for reasons that will be explained later there are always various groups of people who do not work productively and must therefore be provided for communally.

A formula may help us understand the relationships of production and society:

Veerkamp cites in this context Karl Marx, MEW 3, p.28.

P (total production) = R (reproduction) + S (surplus) (p.22).

There were three different groups for which the surplus achieved by the producing families ("houses", home economies) could be put to use. One was that group of people who for some reason or other could not/could no longer provide for their own livelihood, e.g. widows and orphans. Here we would speak of social welfare. In addition, social structures arose in the ancient Near East whereby groups within society established themselves as ruling cliques and by various kinds of coercion were able to take away from the producing families the surplus value they had created. This happened above all as centres were formed in the shape of *city-states and empires.*[2]

Internally they developed a *class society.* H.G. Kippenberg has given a classic description of this process in his work *Die Entstehung der antiken Klassengesellschaft* (The emergence of the ancient class society).[3] A military, bureaucratic and state-priest apparatus emerged with a king at the top, who was imagined to be either particularly close to the state god or himself divine. In a significant text Israel's God, through his prophet Samuel, warns the people of what will happen if they, like other peoples, introduce the kingship system. It describes most vividly "the rights of the king":

> "He will take your sons and assign them to his chariotry and cavalry, and they will run in front of his chariot. He will use them as leaders of (sections of) a thousand and leaders of (sections of) fifty; he will make them plough his ploughland and harvest his harvest and make his weapons of war and the gear for his chariots. He will also take your daughters as perfumers, cooks and bakers. He will take the best of your fields, of your vineyards and olive groves and give them to his officials. He will tithe your crops and vineyards to provide for his eunuchs and officials. He will take the best of your manservants and maidservants, of your cattle and your donkeys, and make them work for him. He will tithe your flocks, and you yourselves will become his slaves." (1 Sam 8: 11-17)

Military service, services to the court (including manual jobs), forced labour, slavery, the large-scale accumulation of property for officials, and taxes and duties (tribute) in the form of "tithes" of produce and cattle – that is how the state class raked off the surplus the small farmers had made and lay claim to land and labour, the means of production. Temple and priests are not men-

---

2   Cf. for an overview S. Breuer, 1987, pp.82ff.
3   H.G. Kippenberg, 1977; cf. also 1978; and Breuer, loc. cit.

tioned here, since historically they only entered the debate later (at the time of Solomon). So in economic terms this vivid picture shows three basic characteristics of the kingship system, city-states and empires:

- the accumulation of land as a means of production, and
- the accumulation of (slave) labour as a means of production, and also
- the appropriation of surplus value in the form of duties and tribute for the non-productive state class.

Thus we have two kinds of goal for which the profit created by productive work may be used:

1 Social or community purposes: this includes the social welfare we have already mentioned, but also self-defence which the community has to organise. When in the days before the kings the "tribes" of Israel organised themselves communally for protection against attack, they naturally had also to feed the men involved in this from the surplus they had produced. But it is a different matter to seize it for:

2 the power purposes of local elites. This was done by force, and it was an additional burden on the productive part of the population, particularly small farmers and (rural) craftsmen.

Since in the case of an existing monarchy care of the poor, the social welfare of those who could no longer make their own living, was also the king's responsibility, this function of his was often extravagantly praised in kingship ideology, together with his protection of the poor from the rich.[4]

Externally city-states and empires began to *behave as conquerors*. In economic terms this behaviour was characterised by three main things: direct oppression by the *looting campaigns*; forced labour, or *slavery*; and institutionalised oppression through the imposition of duties, or *tribute*.

- The *looting campaigns* aimed at the extension of territory and thus the accumulation of land as a means of production; the seizure of raw materials (above all gold, metal ores and minerals, either in ready-mined form or in the form of long-term control over areas with raw materials); finally the capture of slaves.[5]

> "The great powers of antiquity based their dominion...on a system of widespread territorial conquest for the extensive, mainly short term, exploitation of agricul-

---

4   Cf. below p.(137f.) on Egypt.
5   Cf. (e.g.) B. Breuer, op. cit., p.90, who in Egypt's case talks of "thoroughgoing police raids on neighbouring countries" (tr.).

tural resources, and mineral wealth. Anyone who opposed this would be threatened militarily."[6]

– *Enslavement* was the exploitation of labour for all aspects of the economy, but particularly for large-scale projects of empires for which the local labour potential was inadequate. Biblically the classic case is the slave-labour done by the Moses group for the building of Egyptian granary-cities and the cultivation of state plantations in the Nile delta. Slaves were always a mixture of (poor) indigenous and foreign workers (press-ganged or "voluntarily" enslaved because of poverty). We shall have to investigate the causes of poverty leading to slavery.

– *Tribute* to a foreign power was doubly destructive for local producers on top of exploitation by their own elites.[7] Local elites did in fact perform some functions useful to the community, and if they abused their power too much they could be subjected to pressure and, ideally, removed. Some of the surplus value they creamed off did flow back into the local economy. Tribute paid to the great power outside was extorted by sheer force, and it was totally withdrawn from local economic circulation. Its effect was like that of channelling financial resources today into the transnational finance markets, which are not rooted in the real, productive economy but work through the interest mechanism purely for their own growth. As with the transnational money mechanism, the amount of tribute was not dependent upon income: it had to be "serviced" no matter how great or small (for instance) the yield from the harvest.

There were two ways in which duties were extracted. The village community as a whole might be liable for them to the ruler; but since Babylonian times the practice had also existed of taking the means of production out of the farmers' hands and having the landowner make decisions about the use of land and the sale of produce. In this way individual families were even more directly sucked into the vicious spiral of poverty, debt and bonded labour.[8]

Tribute of this kind had weighty consequences for subject peoples in two respects. The local elites had to discharge their duty to the great power after they had collected their own taxes and duties from the producers. If the overall burden became too great, the producers could die. Then the local rulers

---

6   J. Kegler, 1986, p.10(tr.).
7   Cf. Veerkamp, 1993, pp.25ff.
8   Cf. Veerkamp, 1977, pp.30ff.

were in a tight spot, because non-payment, whatever the reason, was always seen as rebellion and punished militarily. Secondly, overburdening with tribute had the strongest effect on the weakest producers, so that they had to give up the land and could no longer feed themselves. So tribute resulted in increasing inequality or, as we say today, a widening gap between rich and poor. Veerkamp, therefore, compares tribute to regressive taxation. Instead of increasing the burden on the better-off progressively, as in a proper welfare state, tribute, being unrelated to income, increased the burden on the weak regressively. Thus tribute was "recurrent robbery, 'legitimised' by quasi-treaties."[9]

Let us summarise, along the lines of Veerkamp,[10] the complete production/tax complex in one formula. Production (P) is divided between reproduction (R) and the various objects for which the surplus is used, with shares for community tasks (C), the taxes of local elites (L), and tribute to the great power (T). The result is:

$$P = R + (C + L + T).$$

There is, though, another mechanism, as well as forced tribute, which can burden the producers or in most cases even destroy them: the debt mechanism.[11] It is important here to work out the difference between this and debt mechanisms in the capitalist economic system, as Veerkamp does, in order not to short-circuit the application of the biblical traditions to our situation. Let us imagine that a peasant, who is under the demands of reproduction – subsistence farming, that is – and duties C, L and T, has a bad harvest. It can happen that his family, in order not to starve, has to use the seed corn as food and consume it. He goes to his wealthier neighbour, who has more "padding", and borrows seed corn from him; in effect he takes out a loan. If he has to guarantee to give back after the harvest as much seed corn as he borrowed (repayment), he must do this too out of a surplus that has been thoroughly skimmed off anyway. Nevertheless, he mays perhaps manage it. But if the giver of the loan takes an "increase" (Heb. *tharbith* or *marbith*), what we today call "interest", the ruin of the receiver of the loan is pre-programmed. It is practically impossible to pay out of the surplus not just community duties and the doubled state tribute but also a private tribute in the form of "interest" as

---

9   Ibid., p.261(tr.).
10 Veerkamp does not admit community duties into the formula as such but subsumes them under duties to the local elites.
11 Ibid., pp.28ff.; cf. also Kegler, 1992, in: M. Crüsemann and W. Schottroff, 1992.

well. That is why Lev 25:35ff. calls this "increase" taken on top of the repayment a "bite out" (Heb. *neshek*) – of the living flesh.[12]

> Veerkamp rightly draws attention to the difference from what we call interest in
> capitalist economics. To summarise briefly: here capital and labour (and land)
> are invested in the production of goods; which presupposes, for example, expens-
> ive machines, to obtain which a loan must be secured. Through the sale of the
> goods, a surplus is created that is greater than the sum of wages, rent and the
> share of the profit on which the entrepreneur lives, enabling the payment of in-
> terest. In other words: it is included in the cost calculations right from the start.
> "In this case interest is nothing other than an agreed share of the company's
> profit" (p.29,tr.). This, therefore, involves economic growth, and part of the
> growth element is taken as interest. (We have already seen that under certain cir-
> cumstances the market can extort too much interest, i.e. at a rate above the real
> growth rate. We shall have to return to this in the Third Part.)

Anyway, in the pre-capitalist economy interest demanded a share of the profit
that did not exist since production as a whole remained the same (with the
technology of the time improvements in productivity were conceivable, if at
all, mainly over long spans of time). So interest was, like tribute, "quasi-legal
robbery". Veerkamp labels the complete servicing of debts – repayment and
"interest" - D. The formula for the demand on the surplus product, then, is
this:

$$P = R + (C + L + (T + D)):$$

But this now is no longer an equation, since everything in the brackets can no
longer be "paid" out of the surplus product: i.e.

$$P < R + (C + L + (T + D)).$$

The consequence of this was poverty, step by step. As a rule the creditor made
his loan only against securities, normally in the form of pledges. If the family
concerned was no longer able to turn the means of reproduction into tribute,
as they would then starve, the land fell immediately to the lender, who of
course extended his land holding. All the family were forced into slavery one
by one: daughters, sons, wife, husband. Nehemiah 5:1-5 gives a classic description of this process:[13]

---

12 One is reminded of Shakespeare's *The Merchant of Venice*, where the creditor
demands a pound of flesh from the insolvent debtor's living body.
13 Cf. also Kippenberg, 1977, pp.41f.

"The ordinary people and their wives began complaining against their brother Jews. Some said, 'We are having to barter our sons and daughters to get enough corn to eat and keep us alive.' Others said, 'We are having to mortgage our fields, our vineyards, our houses to get corn during the famine.' Still others said,'We have had to borrow money on our fields and our vineyards to pay the king's tax (i.e. for tribute payments, in this case to the King of the Persians: U.D.); and though we are of the same flesh as our brothers (the creditors: U.D.), and our children are as good as theirs, we are having to sell our sons and daughters into slavery; some of our daughters have even been raped! (Then too women were the first to suffer under unjust economic structures: U.D.) We can do nothing about it, since our fields and our vineyards are now the property of others.'"

The critical point, obviously, is "to keep us alive". If they wanted to counter the tribute system's exploitation mechanisms, which endangered people's livelihoods and divided nations externally into centres and peripheries and internally into the rich and powerful, and the poor and powerless, they needed *autonomy* in external relations and *equality* at home ("brotherliness" between equals as in a family, in the Nehemiah passage). This is precisely what Max Weber regards as incompatible with capitalism. That is why Ton Veerkamp uses these two terms, autonomy and equality, for the title of his book in which he illuminates economics, politics and ideology in the Bible.

But before we can turn to the biblical texts and traditions, we must once more address a central economic element which gained more and more significance in the course of biblical history: *money*.[14] We have already noted that Aristotle was of the opinion that money had been introduced to make exchange easier. The view today is that it originated out of cultic commerce and the tribute system, though indeed with an element of exchange.

– If people could not pay their Temple *dues* in the form of natural produce, they were supposed to "turn them into silver" so that this could be exchanged back into sacrificial animals at the Temple (Deut 14:24f.). Thus there was a manifest connection between money and "sacrifice" to the deity, from which the priesthood, if it wanted, could profit in various ways – as one can see from the gigantic temple treasures that existed, which were naturally attractive to conquerors. This also makes clear the role played by the Temple as a place of commercial exchange. Anyway, either the "sacrifice" meant reducing one's

14 Cf. T. Veerkamp, 1993, pp.32ff., following H.G. Kippenberg, 1978, p.51.

consumption, to the extent that it could be reduced without jeopardising reproduction, or yet another burden on the surplus product besides state and private tributes.

– As for *tribute,* it was the Persian king Darius (Darius 1, 522-486) who changed the basis of payments to money. As well as centralising the imperial civil service and the military he introduced state-guaranteed money in the form of coins as a universally valid means of accounting, as a "world currency". Thus a real empire arose, for the first time covering the whole of the Near East. By this means tribute could be raised in the same way, through all the seasons and in all parts of the realm.

"Cultic commerce and tribute turn general goods into money," says Ton Veerkamp[15] and investigates money's various functions and ways of acting: as a means of exchange, as a means of accumulation, as a means of maintaining worth, as a mobiliser of resources, as a means of exploitation, as God.

> To be able to pay tribute in money, the producers had to produce not for their own basic needs and, by exchanging goods, a bit extra too, but for *money-seeking exchange* on the market. That not just changed the structure of production to money-making products like wine, olive oil, etc. but also made it dependent upon market prices which could not be influenced (just as debtor countries today are forced into an export economy and then punished for it by the – often falling – prices they get.) Along with this the form of business changed to an economy of domains with tenants or day-labourers. And merchants began to extract more and more wealth from the exchange process – something that disturbed Aristotle even when the money economy was just starting, since farming families were becoming poor as a result. Money destroyed not just the economic structure but also the whole traditional social structure.
>
> Money as a *means of accumulation* appears at the moment when those who had become rich on tribute not just increased their consumption (and waged more war) but also bought slaves and land and made more money with these means of production. This change in the way production was organised did not yet lead to a capitalist form of production.[16] But it strengthened the divide between town and country because the money which was made flowed to its owners in the towns. The King of Persia and the Jerusalem Temple illustrate the *value-maintaining*

---

15 Veerkamp, op. cit., p.36(tr.).
16 Cf. ibid., p.39.

function of money. Through tribute and "sacrifices" they heaped up money in the form of treasure and thus withdrew it from the productive economy. Since money, as Aristotle reflected, incites people to make more money, it also stimulates production (of goods) and extends it. In this way it becomes a *mobiliser of resources*. But since money presupposes and causes the universal division of producers from their products, it is also a means of exploitation. "It is the direct expression of the disunity of society, the divide between producers and consumers, between the owners of the means of production and the owners of nothing but their own labour, between the countryside around it and the urban centre."[17]

Finally it has – as again Aristotle saw – the function of a religious, limitless giver of life. Yet he also knew that this function is a sham. This *God* is an illusion, albeit one that destroys life with cruel efficiency.

2 Politics and ideology

As we have already indicated, certain kinds of tribute and work organisation were fixed quasi-legally, mostly to legalise a form of robbery. Political power enforced this law – if necessary by military means, yet the situation of society as a whole was not just legalised, it was also legitimised ideologically, and then internalised.[18]

Ton Veerkamp rightly rejects the popular Marxist and undialectical view that politics and ideology are just superstructure, a reflection of their real base, the economy. This is fundamental for the way we formulate our question. For if everything were determined by the relationships of production, any scope for resistance and shaping something new would be impossible. The traditions of the Bible show that though the political and ideological structures of society are massively determined by economic relationships, resistance and protest against ancient Near Eastern society, and attempts to shape alternatives, are precisely what distinguishes Israel's history from that of other peoples. What characterises the biblical texts is that they portray not only the social process but also the struggle to resist, shape society and create alternatives. Veerkamp calls this the "concordant reading of scripture" (p.49,tr.).

---

17 Ibid., p.42(tr.).
18 Ibid., pp.42ff.

When one uses modern sociological ideas to aid understanding, as we with Veerkamp have done, the resultant readings of scripture must show how far the texts speak of relationships in society and how far they do not.

The same applies to our biblical recollection in terms of modern social processes. Only if we work out where the contexts compare *and* differ can the Bible speak to our situation. That certainly also happens on a direct level when people engage in a concrete struggle in society, as we shall see. Yet in a concrete situation where the Bible speaks to a movement, community or church in struggle, it can be helpful and reassuring to make a clear distinction between context and theology.

So what are the political-ideological contexts in which and against which the biblical traditions speak? Here we are in the fortunate position of being able to consult, as well as Ton Veerkamp's fundamental work on the late period[19] and general historical representations of the empires like that of S. Breuer, some thorough *general studies of Israel in the context of the ancient Near East.* They include the detailed sociological history of the religion of Israel by R. Albertz and concise studies of our problem area like those of N. Lohfink, C.A. Dreher, J. Assmann and W. Dietrich.[20]

Of fundamental importance for understanding the history and texts of Israel is its geo-political position in Palestine. The early city-states, which had imposed tribute on the agricultural areas around them, lay mainly in the valleys of the Euphrates and the Tigris in Mesopotamia and on the Nile in Egypt, though there were some also in Asia Minor and in the coastal plains and valleys of Palestine. Not least because of big irrigation projects, the larger political units formed on the Nile and in Mesopotamia. They were distinguished by high productivity in agriculture but also by a very marked division of labour in society and consequent stratification into hierarchical social classes. Having developed considerable military power upon this basis, both territories – independently of each other at first – expanded into empires.

Between the two imperial regions lay Palestine. Its city-states were marked above all by their key role for trade. The name "Canaanite" originally meant "trader". Since the deserts between Mesopotamia and Egypt were difficult to cross by caravan, the routes had to run through Palestine; and there they met the routes from and to Asia Minor (an important crossroads lay south-west of

---

19 Cf. as well as T. Veerkamp 1993 and 1983, H.G. Kippenberg 1977 and 1978.
20 R. Albertz, 1992; N. Lohfink, 1987, pp.103ff.; C.E. Dreher, 1993; J. Assmann, 1992; W. Dietrich, 1989.

Damascus and south of Tyre, level with Jezreel). With the outbreak of warlike confrontations between the imperial regions – over control of those very trade routes – the Palestinian region took on central strategic significance in military terms. Before Israel stepped into the limelight of history the historical situation in the region may be summarised like this:

> From about 1780 BC the group called by the Egyptians "Hyksos", who had built in Palestine a system of city-states, pushed into Egypt and subjugated parts of it. From 1580 BC onwards the Egyptians began not only to shake off this yoke but actually to press to the North and subjugate the whole region up to Mesopotamia. This is the time of the "New Kingdom". About the middle of the 13th century BC – the time of the Exodus reported in the Bible – the Egyptians were driven back as far as southern Syria by the Hittites from Asia Minor. At the beginning of the 12th century BC came the invasion of Palestine by the "sea people", pirates presumed also to be from Asia Minor – known in the Bible as the Philistines.

At this time, when the Egyptians' influence was restricted, the groups which later belonged to Israel were able to free themselves from Egypt and the Palestinian system of city-states supported by Egypt, and establish themselves in Palestine. They thought of themselves as an alternative to city-states and empires.

From then on *Egypt* was Israel's opposite. It was the power that looted, compelled tribute, enslaved – in the name of the divine Pharaoh. With all this polemic it is most praiseworthy that Jan Assmann has in his *Politische Theologie zwischen Ägypten und Israel* (Political theology between Egypt and Israel) (1992) brought out the ways in which Israel's critique fits the Egyptian system and the ways in which it does not. He opposes the idea, used in older research, of "oriental despotism".

> "The Egyptian state did not understand itself as a non-transcendent, sealed box with Pharaoh as its pyramidal top. Rather Pharaoh, although himself a god, had above him the whole world of the gods with the Highest, the state god, at its peak. He was a symbolic figure, pointing to and representing something higher, just as the top of a pyramid pointed to the sun which set on it." (pp.39f.,tr.).

The unity of the divine and the state-cultic was *Ma'at*, justice, truth, order. In this whole context the Pharaoh was the protector of the poor. Indeed, without state order the strong destroyed the weak. Governance was thus understood

as salvation. That meant that in all stabilising of vertical exploitation structures the political order was also there to guarantee a certain protection and
mediation – within the structure of the state at any rate. Slaves and subjec
peoples are of course excepted. Assmann calls this the principle of "vertica
solidarity"[21] – a concept that must concern us further when we look at Israe
in the time of the kings. However, Assmann also stresses that one of Israel':
criticisms, the impossibility of opposition, is justified:

> "...the unity of governance and salvation, the absence of distance between a relig-
> ious position and power, and the consequent impossibility of distinguishing be-
> tween good and bad rulers (mean that) governance (i.e. politically shaped and in-
> stitutionalised power) is above all criticism". This exceeds even Mesopotamian
> kingship ideology, which did develop criteria for the criticism of rulers
> (pp.40f.,tr.).

Egypt's weakness and the power vacuum between the Great Powers lasted
until well into the 10th century BC, so that in Israel itself a monarchy and a
medium-sized empire developed, with its highpoint under David (1000-961)
and Solomon 961-931. After that this empire split into a northern half (Israel)
and a southern half (Judah) and fell once more between the fronts. First the
Assyrians, then the Babylonians, forced the northern and southern kingdoms
to pay tribute and finally destroyed them.

For the collection of tribute the *Assyrians* introduced a multi-staged vassal
system, which contained clear legal duties and sanctions, as we know from the
reports on Sennacherib's third campaign, 705 (or 704) – 680[22]. The Babylonians took over this system in its essentials:

> The first stage was marked by a treaty for the "protection" of a small state by the
> great king, in exchange for annual gifts.
>
> If a vassal fell away – e.g. through a change of ruler – or was brought down by
> war, governance was transferred to a new family and the old one was taken host-
> age. As well as tribute (natural products, raw materials) they had to pay fines (e.g.
> Hezekiah of Judah had to deliver all kinds of treasure – gold, silver, etc – to Sen-
> nacherib, cf. 2 Kings 18:13ff.) (second stage).

---

21 Cf. also J. Assmann, 1990, pp.200ff. (pp.214f.); N. Lohfink, 1987, pp.122ff., sees it as
a specific feature of the ancient Near East that people and above all the king are expected
to accept the poor and weak *as individual families* – as opposed to Israel, where systems
that make people poor are questioned as such.
22 In: O. Kaiser (ed.), 1982, pp.388ff.

If even more fell away the third stage went into effect: the capital city was destroyed, all those able to bear arms were deported to another part of the empire and, to make conspiratorial activities more difficult, the women were sold as slaves.

It is unnecessary to stress again that this was not a law governing equals – it was rule by diktat and compulsion. The treaties were initiated cultically, statues of gods were exchanged, common rituals of sacrifice were celebrated, symbols of rule were set up. This is the origin of the close involvement of the priesthood with the tributary system of politics and economics. The main theological opponents for Israel and Judah at that time were, after all, not distant Great Powers and their gods, but the Canaanite kingdom with Baal as its legitimating god.

As already indicated, the *Persians* refined the tribute system yet again. Instead of containing half-independent vassal empires or city-kingdoms through treaties, they organised a centralised empire with various provinces and installed governors there. They centralised the military, foreign policy, and above all the currency. Only the cultus remained decentralised. But this too was built into the imperial system in a very subtle way. Ezra 6:8ff. shows that the king took over the cost of rebuilding the Temple and of the sacrifices – for reasons which were obviously not entirely selfless. In v. 10 it says of the Jerusalem priests:

> "...so that they may offer acceptable sacrifices to the God of heaven and pray for the lives of the king and his sons."

Whilst the Assyrians had demanded that treaties be sworn by calling upon their own god but demanded no further cultic obligations, the Persians expected a daily declaration of loyalty.[23] Yet, as we shall see later, the Persians granted the people of Judah a certain amount of freedom, unlike the other Great Powers.

The worst period for Judaea came with the *Hellenistic empires*. The ruler did not just become absolute. Aristotle aptly defined the "one" – not in the Platonic sense of the inexpressible but something very visible – as a principle of rule: "*one* god, *one* ruler, *one* guiding principle in the cosmos, *one* guiding principle in society".[24] The cultus too was centralised. A traumatic period for

---

23 For this point I thank J. Kegler.

the Jews, therefore, was 169-167 BC, when Antiochus IV, the ruler of the Hellenistic-Syrian Seleucids, had a statue of Zeus set up in the Jerusalem Temple – the trigger for a revolution in politics and theology, as we shall see. The *Roman Empire*, heir to all ancient empires, then declared the Emperor himself to be a god. And it was not just the Jews but the Christians as well who resisted emperor-worship as the incarnation of the "aeon of injustice", right up to martyrdom.[25]

Turning to the question of how Israel and the early Christians behaved in the situation we have sketched, we can distinguish *four constellations of relationships in society*, which also involve other forms of conduct, other theological responses and other conflicts. This differentiation will prove very important with regard to possible ways of acting and theological positions in today's situation.

– The first constellation emerged in the period between about 1250 and 1000 BC. This is the time when an autonomous Israel was growing up between the empires and city-kingdoms – as an alternative society.

– The second constellation arose out of the adoption in Israel of the tributary kingship system in competition with the empires and city-kingdoms, between about 1000 and 585 BC, and led up to the destruction of Jerusalem, the deportation to exile in Babylon and the flight to exile in Egypt. This is the period of the (unsuccessful) attempt to tame the kingship system by prophecy and law.

– The third constellation was the partial autonomy of those remaining in the country and those returning from exile between 586 and 333 BC, first under the Babylonians and then above all under the Medes and Persians. In this period an interesting example of social change took place in a corner of the empire.

– The fourth constellation was the Hellenistic-Roman era between 333 BC and 312 AD. This was the period of active rejection of an economically, politically and ideologically totalitarian system and of attempts to create small-scale alternatives.

---

24 Cf. J. Assmann, 1992, p.50(tr.), and T. Veerkamp, 1993, pp.319ff.
25 Cf. in this connection K. Wengst, 1986.

In summary we may say: The history of the faith of Israel unfolded in direct confrontation with the economies, policies and ideologies of the ancient Near Eastern empires and city-kingdoms. They were characterised internally by class structures and externally by a desire for conquest (producing surplus value through slave labour, land accumulation and tribute). Ideologically speaking, the power elite of society was legitimated by gods. From Egypt to the Roman Empire this history may be divided into four political constellations reaching into the early Christian period. They provided the context for Israel, Jesus and the early Christians.

Chapter V

Economy for life – biblical approaches

Sciences develop in jumps. When a whole way of seeing things, a paradigm, has become established, it remains for a long time the framework within which people research and teach. If its inherent difficulties increase to the point where it can no longer explain certain phenomena, the old paradigm is dismantled bit by bit. Then, perhaps, a breakthrough may occur, and a new paradigm slowly build up and establish itself. This is called "paradigm shift".[1] The change from classical, mechanistic physics to modern quantum physics is a popular example of this process.

In biblical exegesis, but even more so in the practice of Bible reading in Latin America, such a paradigm shift has occured. Increasingly, a socio-historical approach is taking the place of a conceptually or theologically abstract form of Bible interpretation or one focussing on individual spirituality. It can build on older research methods such as form criticism. Working sociologically does not mean restricting the meaning of biblical texts to so-called socio-political questions but rather recognising that socio-economic and political structures and ways of acting are, according to the insights of the Bible, to be understood as a decision for or against God. It is the social question that is theologised, and not the God question that is secularised. Socio-historical exegesis thereby follows the revolutionary movement that emergent Israel brought into the world of the peoples of the ancient Near East. On this the Egyptologist Jan Assmann writes:

> "I see the core of this transformation in the shifting of the socio-political spheres of action, law and justice into the theo-political sphere. In this way there emerges the radically new idea of making God himself a legislator. God takes on this function in the place of the ancient Near Eastern kings. ... Israel's all-decisive step was to transpose justice from the social and political sphere into the theological, and to subordinate it to the direct will of God".[2]

---

1   Cf. T.S. Kuhn, 1978(2), and K. Raiser, 1986.
2   J. Assmann, 1992, pp.64f.(tr.), agreeing with H.G. Kippenberg, 1991, pp.157ff.

So socio-historical exegesis does not tackle the biblical text with a method that neglects the theological question. With respect to Israel, this method is truly theological. This will become even more evident as we review the fresh approaches taken by the Israelites in the different socio-political constellations of their history. With regard to what follows, particularly the sources for early Israel, we should state clearly that a historical picture can only be a *reconstruction*, not an "objective" description of the facts. That means the process of reviewing, understanding and acting has to be repeated constantly and is never completed. That is precisely why it is important to pursue the way Israel remembers its history through each new historical constellation. Only in this way can we see whether there is a pattern running through Israel's history and faith. Only in this way, too, can we see whether, with all the individual questions the scholars dispute, we may speak with the Reformers of the "clarity of scripture."[3]

1   Israel's emergence as a "contrast society"[4]

With the disintegration of the Egyptian empire from about 1200 BC the system of Canaanite city-states also disintegrated, as we saw. The fundamental change made possible by the resultant power vacuum is also confirmed by archaeology:

> "Until this time the hills and mountains had hardly been settled. The walled towns on the coasts and in the valleys, which controlled their respective hinterlands, were typical. Most of these Canaanite towns were destroyed around this time and never rebuilt. Or only a village rose over their ruins. In hilly and mountainous areas, on the other hand, village-type settlements covering a large area (and so not protected by a wall) were built. ... If one does not link it in historically, (this finding) can be characterised negatively as decolonisation and de-urbanisation. In positive terms, at least in the hills and mountains, this was the emergence of Israel".[5]

---

3   In addition to the general works cited p.136 n.20 above, cf. F. Crüsemann, 1992.
4   I have adopted this term (German: Kontrastgesellschaft) from N. Lohfink, 1987, p.118, and G. Lohfink, (1988) 1993, pp.55ff., etc.
5   N. Lohfink, op. cit., pp.108f.(tr.).

The groups that settled here were, according to present research, of very varied origins. Many had simply freed themselves from servitude caused by interest payment, forced labour and tribute imposed by the surrounding cities. Others had migrated from the outskirts of the Mesopotamian kingdoms and empires, or from East of the Jordan (as the "stories of the fathers" tell). After their exodus from slavery in Egypt the Moses group had joined them along with impoverished nomads and bands of economic drop-outs scavenging to survive. These marginalised, socially declassified groups were called Hebrews, *apiru*.[6]

Recent ethnological research has drawn a relatively clear picture of these groups. Their societal form is characterised by kinship. Several "father's houses" or families form a grouping of families and these in turn form a tribe. Scholarship speaks of "segmentary lineage systems", segmentary societies. "The lineage system means that the unity of groups is produced not by autonomous political leadership but by their members' orientation towards the genealogical ties of the kinship system".[7] The segments of society were therefore not superior or inferior, but of politically equal rank.

In economic terms this meant family production and self-sufficiency (autarchy).[8] The system was built on rights not of ownership but of collective use. Today we call this kind of thing *subsistence economy*, by which we mean "the production of goods for people's own use and for mutual support".[9] C. Boerma points out that no concept of "poor" is to be found in Genesis; this indicates not great prosperity but the lack of difference between poor and rich.[10]

In political terms we have spoken since Max Weber of *"regulated anarchy"*.[11] The groupings of families were autonomous. That means "that political autonomy is not the incidental effect of the lack of state apparatus found in segmentary societies, but of a conscious wish for self-determination and independence".[12] One should therefore call emergent Israel not "pre-state" but decidedly "anti-state", because that means "anti-ruler".[13]

---

6   Cf. N.K. Gottwald, 1981(2); H. Donner, I, 1984, p.71; Albertz, op. cit., pp.68ff.; recently and extensively R. Neu, 1992, pp.38f. and 97f.

7   R. Neu, op. cit., p.50.

8   Ibid., pp.51ff.

9   Ibid., p.54(tr.) after Elwert and Fett.

10   C. Boerma, 1979, p.10; also Neu, p.56.

11   Neu, pp.60ff.(tr.).

12   Ibid., p.64(tr.).

But the *decisive* thing is that this process of social liberation and new social organisation was identified with the *experience of the god Yahweh*. In the city-kingdoms and empires of the ancient Near East the gods and their cults were the guarantors and props of the system. Yahweh was in radical contrast to this. Yahweh was experienced as the One who frees the oppressed and enslaved. The big group of Moses people, fleeing from Egypt, brought Yahweh with them to Palestine.

> "The emergence of the Yahweh religion is linked inseparably with the process of political liberation of the Exodus group. It is the spark that helps a longlasting, smouldering social conflict burst into flame. The book of Exodus tells in various ways how this conformist, fragmented, politically inept, oppressed group of foreign forced labourers attain through the initiative of the god Yahweh a political leader and a new political hope for the future. These enable them to build solidarity within and loosen themselves from their external social constraints and so make them capable of common action for political liberation."[14]

It appears that Yahweh had been worshipped previously in the wilderness of southern Palestine, by freedom-loving nomads. Yahweh came from outside, was not part of the Egyptian pantheon, and consequently was able to bring various attributes, which people experienced as dynamic (with the attribute of the thunderstorm), into the social conflict. According to Exodus 3, God reveals to Moses the mystery of the name Yahweh: "I shall be with you" – with you, the oppressed. "Not by chance is Yahweh characterised repeatedly in Exodus 1-12 as 'the God of the Hebrews'..., i.e. as a god who in the social conflict that is brewing sides with the social outsiders."[15]

Apart from their liberation from Egypt, the Moses group experienced Yahweh in an appearance on the "mountain of God", as Sinai is traditionally called.[16] This experience established the cult of Israel (first of the Moses group). What is typical here is that in this theophany Yahweh does not tie himself to a place, for example to a city or a temple, but to the group. In Yahweh's utterances, too, the cult is to remain mobile: an "ark" to be carried,

---

13 J. Assmann, 1992, p.72, in agreement with N. Lohfink. Albertz, 1992, pp.46f.(tr.), speaks of "anti-ruler".

14 R. Albertz, 1992, p.76(tr.), on what follows ibid., pp.76ff.

15 Ibid., pp.84f.(tr.).

16 Ibid., pp.85ff.

a "tent". Possibly, even the mobile company of the "Levites", who owned no means of production, date back to this first cultic experience. That could be why, even when Israel got a state temple and a state priesthood, the Levites remained active as a mobile (and often socially oppositional or revolutionary) element.

> The commandments and laws, which are linked in the tradition to this theophany, do not go back in their present form to the early period.[17] The link between God's law and Sinai occurs first only in the prophets' arguments against the sin of kingship at the time of the downfall of the Northern Kingdom (722). They want by relating law-giving to Sinai to establish the Law as being *from outside* the state's sphere of power. Sinai *becomes* by this means *the* basis for the history of Israel's Law, but in these early days of the Moses group it is not that yet. In all probability we may assume for this time simply the old, mutually-supportive laws of clan and custom.

The newly liberated Moses group came across the poor nomads, marginalised groups from the cities, peasants evading the tribute system, and the brigand bands of *hapiru* – all trying to settle in the hill country of Palestine. The solidarity within and between family groups gave rise to the social and legal order of the anarchist *Judges period.* An assembly of the legally free and economically independent family patriarchs became the local political decision-making body. The elders were the representatives and spokesmen in the *"People's Assembly"* of all the tribes. In cases of external threat *charismatic leaders* took over the leadership in common wars of defence and liberation. Yahweh turned out to be a strong ally in times of trouble and was therefore increasingly worshipped as the one God in all the local cults of the god El, who took the form of the different family gods.

> "(The god Yahweh) was, as the southern desert region's only god, not integrated into the polytheistic system. He was, moreover, a god who had proven his divinity in the liberation from state oppression. And finally he was a god who had tied himself exclusively to a group at the bottom of the pile. As such he was positively predestined to become the god of an association of tribes which secured for groups of precisely that kind the freedom they had won from state dependence.

---

17 Cf. ibid., pp.95ff. and in detail Crüsemann, 1992, pp.39-75.

We may therefore suppose that Yahweh was quickly taken on by the rest of the tribes in the association as a welcome strengthening of their world of religious symbols. Yahweh became fused with El, and thus the God of Israel (Judg 5:3-5)."[18]

That means that the protection of the weak and oppressed was from the start not understood as a sociological – or "social ethical" – problem, but as a theological one. Doxology, the act of praising a God who liberates from oppression, is linked inseparably to justice within the liberated and protected community (cf. the Song of Miriam, Ex 15; the Song of Deborah, Judg 5; and Mary's Magnificat, Lk 1:52).

The fact that the structure of socio-political representation in this society is clearly masculine, while the songs of praise for liberation are sung by women, is a warning to us about the question of patriarchy so hotly debated today. There can be no doubt that in the early Israelite period the most important relationship links were through the father, i.e. through men. This pattern is known as "patrilinear". On the other hand Neu, summarising older work, shows that "the religious role of the woman in the acephalous, proto-state societies of the Near East (must be regarded) as extraordinarily multi-layered and meaningful." This may be seen in relation to the woman's leading role in Shamanism. Even though there is no direct trace of that in Israel, women apparently had "much the same access to the area of the sacral...as men".

> "Sociologically, the Old Testament material leads to the conclusion that, even in patriarchal societies, and despite all the later disadvantages, in the early period men and women were more or less equal, and had a differing involvement in religious acts more on the basis of function than of rank."[19]

---

18 R. Albertz, 1995, p.120(tr.). Cf. Neu, 1992, pp.40f.: "At the many Canaanite shrines the god of the fathers took over the traditions of the local deities, which should be regarded as hypostases of El. As in the nomadic period, they are linked with fixed groups of worshippers, composed of the groups of families living in the neighbourhood of a cultic place. At the same time increasing importance is gained by the god Yahweh, who probably comes from the steppes of southern Canaan and is identified with El, which gives him access to the local shrines. Yahweh carries out the function of a god of liberation, who is called upon specially at times of crisis and is worshipped as a giver of charismatic spiritual gifts in wars of defence and liberation. Thus Yahweh rises to become the highest god of the segmentary Israelite society and is - taking over in the process essential traits of El, the gods of the fathers and Baal - worshipped as a divine being."(tr.).

19 Ibid., p.135(tr.).

The works of Yahweh, which women and men glorify in songs of praise, involve the *creation of good, just relationships* at home and abroad. Asymmetrical power relationships, which harm people and make them dependent, are, according to the earliest biblical witness, intolerable to God. God hears crying and sees suffering (Ex 3). This finds expression in some central biblical ideas: justice (*sedaqah*) is understood as "community oriented behaviour"[20], "judge/conciliate" (*safat*) as saving the weaker party in a conflict[21], and "*shalom*" as a condition of health within just relationships[22].

The first form which the people of the liberating god Yahweh take, therefore, is that of a community of nomadic and marginalised groups which are now in solidarity with each other, consisting of (groups of) peasant families, whose security is organised by charismatic leaders ("judges") who Yahweh endows with the Spirit of salvation and conciliation.

> "They no longer needed a state, a bureaucracy, differences between poor and rich: they were able to live in a human way – even if to do so they had, initially at least, to give up some of civilisations's finest products, which originally only a small upper class had owned anyway... The true God became manifest the moment society took on human traits; society changed and became human to the degree that the true God became manifest. There is interplay between the two, and historically at least it will be impossible to say which came first... Economic change was an essential element of the whole process. The rule of the new God was accomplished, not exclusively of course but still in a very decisive way, in a new kind of human economy. The Bible shows us the beginnings of the kingdom of God. As its history continued, Israel fell short again and again of the standards set by this beginning. Again and again it gave in to the temptation to be like other peoples. Again and again God brought it back and led it on along the way towards the definitive revelation of the kingdom of God, above all through the prophets."[23]

---

20 Cf. K. Koch, 1976, pp.507ff.(tr.), and F. Crüsemann, 1987, pp.38ff.
21 Cf. G. Liedke, 1971, pp.62ff.; J. Miranda, 1974, pp.111ff.; F. Crüsemann, 1987, pp.35ff.
22 U. Duchrow and G. Liedke, 1988.
23 N. Lohfink, op. cit., pp.109f.(tr.). Cf. also R. Albertz, op. cit., p.122: "As the god who rules (Israel!), Yahweh is the symbol of anti-rule for early Israelite society. The solidarity-building he creates is non-institutional; it comes from below, on the basis of free will, and is not imposed politically from above."(tr.).

2 The attempt to "tame" the kingship system by prophecy and law

Even the judge/saviour Gideon had turned down the royalty he was offered after a successful defensive battle, with these words:

"It is not I who shall rule over you, nor my son; Yahweh must be your lord" (Judg 8:22f.).[24]

For 200 years Israel kept to this autonomous and egalitarian kind of "contrast society". Only in about 1000 BC did it begin to go hesitantly towards kingship. What were the reasons?[25] Earlier the cause was taken to be growing conflicts with the Philistines, the sea peoples who had penetrated into the coastal region. It has been thought that Israel sought to organise itself more tightly under a king to increase its military strength. More recent investigations, however, have concluded that it was not just this external pressure that played a role, but also internal, socio-economic developments.

The evident economic success of the egalitarian "peasants' republic" led to strong population growth: as much as a fourfold increase, it is estimated, in those 200 years. That led to a westward expansion of the Israelite tribes from the hill country of eastern Palestine to the slopes facing the river valleys and the sea. This made more cooperation necessary to facilitate cultivation (terracing, cisterns, etc.), while regional differences arose (olives and wine in the West, cereals and cattle in the East). Through this opening of the subsistence economy to the market, the society also followed the trend towards social stratification. The emergent better-off groups, profiting from trans-regional trade, were bound to develop an interest in not being destroyed and molested by the Philistines as they expanded. This external factor was thus only the trigger for central political leadership, not its sole cause.

Every step towards political centralisation, and even afterwards, had to reckon with opposition from the free peasants. Two texts reflect this resistance most clearly – Jotham's fable (Judg 9), and the warning about the "rights of the king" (1 Sam 8) which, as we saw, ends with the phrase: "and you will become his slaves". Typically, the criticism of the loss of socio-economic and political

24 Cf. Albertz, op. cit., p.121.
25 On what follows R. Albertz, ibid., pp.159ff., summarising the earlier research, above all F. Crüsemann, 1978, and I. Finkelstein, 1989.

solidarity is identified with the theological criticism: Yahweh is no longer to be king among his people. It is assumed that Yahweh was first given the name "king" in this conflict situation. As the king's party used this name to legitim-ate the king, the opposition party turned this argument around: Yahweh is king, which means criticising the earthly kings for usurping this name.

The first step towards monarchy in Israel was relatively timid. *Saul*, a char-ismatic leader, was first more a "chief" than a king. He probably had no trib-ute at his disposal, just voluntary taxes. The change comes with *David.* At first the tribute he exacted scarcely exceeded what was paid in defence taxes. More-over, the Elders of Judah and Israel had committed themselves to him in a reciprocal agreement that was supposed also to restrict the king's power. But David was building a power base of his own with mercenaries and the con-quest of a city as his own seat, Jerusalem. He entered into wars of expansion and now subjected other peoples to tribute, from which the Israelites them-selves also profited. His son *Solomon* developed from this a sacral kingship on the ancient Near Eastern model. He built up a powerful, modernised army. But since in peace time taxes could not be legitimised by supporting the army alone, this was achieved all the better by building a state temple. This required massive imports of wood (from Tyre) and had the effect, like the foreign trade that was being extended anyway, of making the peasants produce for export. Simultaneously state domains were developed to this end. This, like the emer-gent ownership of land, changed fundamentally the egalitarian structure of the anti-state society.

Society, likewise, became divided *ideologically.* Albertz distinguishes three groups:

- the officials, military people and priests who profit from this development; they represent the official theology of King and Temple;
- a central party, which tries to combine the new with traditional values;
- a party of religious and political opposition with a peasant base, which by going back to the religion of the anti-state period develops a theology of resistance to kingship (a minority position under the monarchy but wide-spread after its collapse, in post-exilic Judaism).

When Solomon's son *Rehoboam* wanted to make forced labour even tougher and the tax burden even higher, the northern tribes broke with the royal house of Judah and in 926 BC formed their own northern kingdom, Israel. Although this too was set up as a monarchy, they at first reduced the burden of taxes. Only after 822 BC, when Omri founded the *Omri Dynasty*, did the tribute system get into full swing here as well.[26] His son *Ahab* married the Phoenician princess *Jezebel* from Tyre, thus creating trade links with the Phoenicians. Ahab in turn married his daughter Athaliah to Joram, heir to the throne of Judah, which opened the trade routes to the South. When the Assyrians pressed southwards for the first time, the normally hostile Syrians were ready to form an alliance so that the eastern trade routes would be kept open again after the Assyrians had been thrown back. Trade, army – "mules and horses" (1 Kgs 18:5) – and court luxury again characterised the situation of the northern kingdom's top people, after they had originally split from the southern kingdom specifically to avoid these problems. The country people, on the other hand, became poor. Famine broke out. To cap it all, the king grabbed the free peasants' family land, which under ancient Israelite law could not be sold – as the story of Naboth's vineyard (1 Kgs 21) shows.

The biblical traditions see this development as coupled with a *falling away from Yahweh*. Omri had already begun to allow different kinds of worship, in order to harmonise the Israelite and Canaanite parts of the population. The internationalising of trade and policy on marriage did their bit to strengthen syncretism. The translation of Baal is "Lord and Master": in social terms Lord or owner of land and therefore Master, most particularly in the sense of being master over women.[27]

This saw the birth of power-critical *prophecy*, which became one of Israel's distinguishing features. There was prophecy before this – as much in Israel's surroundings as in royal Israel, in the shape of court prophets to stabilise the kingdom and cult prophets to stabilise the state temple cult. But now a movement of prophets arose who were obviously recruited very much from the lower classes and relied upon them for support. They supported themselves on their wanderings through miracle healings, exorcism and uttering oracles, and so were independent. Some organised themselves into prophets' cooperatives. Their classic representatives are *Elijah* and *Elisha*. Their criticism is directed at two types of target, socio-economic injustice and political oppression at home, and imperialism abroad; and, secondly, irresoluteness of belief in God. "How long will you sit on the fence?" Elijah asks the people on Mount Carmel when it comes to deciding between Yahweh and Baal[28] – an early form of Jesus' "You cannot serve God and Mammon".

---

26 Cf. the contextual summary in C.A. Dreher, 1993, pp.24ff.
27 On this and what follows cf. the first theo-economic book of Ton Veerkamp, 1983 (on the meaning of Baal see especially pp.323f.); also R. Albertz, pp.23ff.
28 Cf. T. Veerkamp, 1983, pp.40ff.

The prophetic movement of Elijah and his disciple Elisha reacted to what we today would call structural violence from above with counter-violence from below in the name of Yahweh. Not only were the priests of Baal killed at Elijah's own hands (21 Kgs 18); Elisha also allied himself to Jehu, the leader of a military coup, and anointed him the new king (2 Kgs 9). By order of Yahweh Jehu executed the cruel sentence on the house of Omri and the upper class who, with the former king, had seized the land of small, free farmers, and exterminated the rest of the priests of Baal.[29] As much as the redactors of this text praise Jehu's religious and social deeds, they also criticise him for leaving the golden calves of Dan and Bethel untouched. Jeroboam had had them built after the secession from Judah as central shrines for the northern kingdom. As such they were symbols of central power. The fact that they were spared meant, for those who worked on the text, that "Jehu was not careful to follow the law of the Lord the god of Israel with all his heart" (2 Kgs 10:29-31). Later on Hosea further criticises Jehu on grounds other than those of the chroniclers of the books of Kings, for the cruelty of his bloody revenge on the house of Ahab (Hos 1:4).

Without doubt the struggle of the peasants and the prophets against injustice and oppression, against the Baalist kingdom and against the great landowners and officials was of decisive significance for the continuing history of Israel as the people of Yahweh. But the uncertain judgement on Jehu points to the fact that doubt arose early on about whether oppressive power could be overcome only by a violent change of rulers. In fact from 841 Jehu and his successors were forced back into vassal status by Assyria and had to pay tribute.

Only under Jeroboam II (787-746 BC) could Israel again extend its empire and its trade. Again the result was extreme luxury for the court and upper class and poverty for the country population. This is the context in which the prophet *Amos* – again in close cooperation with peasant movements[30] – utters his radical criticism of the injustice and idolatry not just of individual acts by people in power, but of the whole system. The prophet *Hosea* also makes his first appearance now. In graphic terms they roundly denounce the royal system of state and economy with its officials, military leaders, priests and merchants.

---

29 Ibid., pp.242ff.
30 Cf. M. Schwantes, 1991, particularly pp.143ff.

At this same time the *southern kingdom of Judah* was developing along similar lines under the rule of kings Azariah (Uzziah, 767-739 BC), Jotham (739-734) and Ahaz (734-728). These were good days for the upper classes who profited from trade, tribute and Temple revenues, and bad days for country people and the urban poor. A bad situation became worse when in 745 the northern kingdom and in 733 the southern kingdom were forced into tribute to Assyria. Just like Amos (about 760 BC) and Hosea (between 750 and 724) in the North, in the southern kingdom the prophets *Isaiah* (between 739 and 701) and *Micah* (before 701) criticised the structures and processes of society, demanding that people turn away from this deadly system to choose life, which was identical with turning back to the god Yahweh. What specifically were the *objects of the prophetic criticism and message of change?*[31]

– The *socio-economic criticism* was directed at the *increase of large-scale land ownership* (Am 8:4; Is 5:8; Mic 2:9f.). In this connection Micah makes a pointed appeal to ancient Israelite land law: "a man and his house, a man and his inheritance" (Mic 2:2f.). The use by the rich of the *law of credit and pledge* is therefore attacked heavily, since it leads people not just into poverty but also into the loss of their livings and into slavery (e.g. Am 5:11 and 8:6; Is 3:14; Mic 2:2). They convert everything into *money*, even the left-over ears of wheat reserved for the poor:

> "Listen to this, you who trample on the needy and try to suppress the poor
> people of the country, you who say, 'When will the New Moon be over so that
> we can sell our corn, and sabbath, so that we can market our wheat? Then by
> lowering the bushel, raising the shekel, by swindling and tampering with the
> scales, we can buy up the poor for money, and the needy for a pair of sandals,
> and get a price even for the sweepings of the wheat.'" (Am 8:4-6)

The upper class dominated and manipulated the local *jurisdiction* as well and bent the laws governing poor people (Am 5:10,12; Is 5:20ff.). This structural violence gave them the resources for *collecting treasures* in their palaces and their *life of luxury* (cf. Am 3:1 and 6:1ff.).

The criterion for criticism was "law and justice" (*mispat* and *sedaqah*), "the just balance of interests for the good of all; a community founded on solidarity, guaranteeing basic rights for all Israelites" – in other words, the fundamental values of the pre-state/anti-state order.[32] At this point an important

---

31 Cf. Albertz, 1992, pp.255ff.; Dreher, 1993, pp.26ff.; R. Kessler, 1992.

question arises: how do the prophets see the alternative? Should Israel and Judah go back to a kingless, mutually supportive community of equals? Should they transform the whole system into one constituted in a fundamentally different way? Or may kingship be "tamed", may it be reformed in accordance with Yahweh's demands for justice? Isaiah seems to look in the latter direction (cf. Is 1:26).

– The political *system of king and officials* as such came in for criticism from Hosea. Whilst Isaiah had already attacked the king's military alliance policy fiercely as lack of faith in Yahweh[33], Hosea took the scramble for power around the throne as a reason for describing the whole path to kingship since Saul as a blind alley now coming to its end (Hos 9:15;13:10).[34] Whatever their estimation of the reformability of the monarchy, the prophets of the northern kingdom saw the impending doom.

– The *cult* too had a part in the whole social system's corruption. Priests issued their directives and prophets their oracles only for money (Mic 3:1-12). Above all, though, the lavish feasting engaged in by the upper class was a cover for injustice and oppression. In their place Amos demanded law, justice and solidarity (Am 5:24). Amos and Micah announced the fall of the royal shrines of Bethel and Jerusalem (Am 3:14; 9:1-4; Mic 3:12). Under the circumstances it is not surprising that they were rejected by the court priests and prophets and also certain population groups. The priests expressly refused to let Amos speak at Bethel, with these words: "...this is the royal sanctuary, the national temple" (Am 7:13). And Micah interpreted the people's view on what a prophet ought to say like this: "Were there a man of inspiration who would invent this lie, 'I prophesy to you wine and strong drink', he would be the prophet for a people like this" (2:11). One is reminded of the "feel-good" religion of an affluent society.

All this – the economic and social division of society, political oppression, military-imperial posturing, the ideological misuse of religion – has, the prophets say, its basis in the fact that the upper class particularly, but also the people they led astray, have left Yahweh – who chose them specifically so that they should not be like other peoples with their oppressive, state cultic kingship system.

---

32 Albertz, ibid., p.259.
33 Cf. ibid., pp.261ff.
34 Ibid., p.266.

"Listen, sons of Israel, to this oracle Yahweh speaks against you, against the whole family I brought out of the land of Egypt: You alone, of all the families of earth, have I acknowledged, therefore it is for all your sins that I mean to punish you." (Am 3:1f.)

This is why *turning* is the prophets' decisive perspective, turning to justice, law and solidarity, which is identical with turning to Yahweh (cf. Am 4:4ff.; Is 2:27, etc.). "Seek me and you shall live" (Am 5:4) and "Seek good and not evil so that you may live" (5:14) are two sides of the same coin. It is important for our theme that "live" comes up again and again here as the general opposite to the system of kingship, which brings death and destruction.

This *turning* can take *two possible forms*: either changing what exists by way of a *reform* (taming), or its destruction and a *new beginning from a "remnant"*, a "stump", which survives the destruction (cf. e.g. Is 6:13; that would be a fundamental transformation). Both were attempted in Judah.

When in 722 BC the northern kingdom was destroyed by Assur, many Israelites fled southwards to Judah, amongst them Hosea and his followers. There began an intensive discussion about how the southern kingdom could avoid the same fate. A first reaction was the *reform* of King Hezekiah (728-699 BC). It is clear that it included various measures to safeguard the exclusive worship of Yahweh. To what extent it also involved social reforms is a matter for debate.[35]

On the other hand there is a document dating from between 722 and the time of King Josiah (641 BC) which expresses in classic form the unity between exclusive Yahweh worship and social justice: the Ten Commandments, the *Decalogue*.[36] It reminds free landowners of the reason for their freedom: Yahweh, who brought them out of Egypt, the house of slavery. To "preserve this freedom" they may serve no other god (from the enslaving societies about them) and thus make no image of God manipulated by human power. Thus they should keep the Sabbath strictly free of all work, practise care of the

---

35 Cf. Albertz, pp.280ff., who assumes this and therefore regards the Book of the Covenant (Ex 21:1-23:33) as the basis of reform, against Crüsemann, who locates the Book of the Covenant in the same period but argues that there is no evidence of social measures by Hezekiah. I shall not present the Book of the Covenant here even though it contains the earliest Israelite legal statements and represents the basic form of the Torah (cf. in detail Crüsemann, pp.132ff.).

36 Basically Crüsemann, 1983.

elderly as solidarity in the family, and not deprive their free fellow-citizens – by either open or hidden violence – of life, law and livelihood.[37]

But the decisive attempt at reform comes in the time of King *Josiah* (641-609 BC) and the prophet *Jeremiah*.

> To understand these events it is important to remember the special structure of kingship in the southern kingdom. David was a city-king by his conquest of Jerusalem, but at the same time he was king of Judah by legal agreement with the free peasants from the surrounding country under Yahweh. This "covenant" between God, king and people on the one hand can, like the one between king and people on the other, be reactivated at any time. When King Manasseh died in 642/1 his son Amon was killed in a coup soon after taking power[38]. In view of the crumbling power of Assur the free peasants of Judah ('am ha'ares) succeeded in suppressing the coup and installing Amon's eight-year-old son, Josiah, as king. That guaranteed them direct political control at first, supported by loyal officials, prophets and Levitical priests. The members of the upper class and priestly aristocracy who cooperated with Assur for the sake of their own power were shut out of this coalition.

The reform movement is called *Deuteronomic* because the foundation for its policy was formulated in a book of law said to stem from Moses like other law and to have been discovered in the Temple. It appears to contain the essence of the book of Deuteronomy.[39] The book has two great emphases: centralisation of the cult of true Yahweh worship in the Jerusalem Temple, and radical social and political laws. The group behind Deuteronomy is obviously the High Court in Jerusalem, made up of laymen and priests, which is mentioned for the first time here and adopts a position of apparent independence vis-à-vis the king. Deuteronomy fundamentally consists of a constitutional definition of the relative "sovereignty" of free people, which binds the now adult King Josiah (and of course all kings after him) to the people, and all to the

---

37 Crüsemann's sociological exegesis shows how wrong it is to misunderstand the Ten Commandments as the basis of a general ethics. In this way specifically political issues, which are not in the Decalogue because of its consciously clear aims, would be excluded completely. This contextual exegesis, on the other hand, helps relate the Commandments intensively to economic processes.

38 On this and what follows cf. F. Crüsemann, 1992, pp.248ff.

39 Ibid. and Albertz, op. cit., pp.304ff.

liberating and just intentions of God's law. The latter is preserved institutionally by priests and prophets and taught and proclaimed according to the needs
of the hour. Deut 17:14-20 impressively describes the *model of a kingship tamed
and subjected to the common good through law*:

> 1. Yahweh himself must choose the king from among the people; 2. he shall not
> acquire great military power (horses) and so not make Israel like the Pharaonic
> system; 3. he shall not take a large number of wives (and with them the religions
> of the surrounding empires and city-kingdoms); 4. he shall not acquire too much
> gold and silver; 5. he shall let himself be guided by the teaching, preserved and in-
> terpreted by the Levitical priests, of God's commandments (the Torah); 6. he
> shall not raise himself above his fellow-countrymen, that is, he shall listen to the
> voice of the people. 1 Sam 16:13 says: "Samuel...anointed David in the presence of
> his brothers". In contrast it says of Jehu: "...call him aside from his companions"
> (2 Ki 9:2).

(Levitical) priests and prophets oversee the exercise of institutional power
(Deut 18). The prophets face the people and king, like Moses (18:18), so breaking institutionally the absoluteness of ancient Near Eastern monarchy. In
Egypt, as mentioned above in connection with Jan Assmann and N. Lohfink,
this had brought about the principle of "vertical solidarity", from which individual poor families derived a certain protection even within the class society
of the time. But Deuteronomy is about the constitutional taming of kingship
and – to the extent that this is possible in that framework – legally secured
"horizontal solidarity".[40]

Because of the radicalism of its social laws Ton Veerkamp locates Deuteronomy after the collapse of Jewish kingship (587 BC) and understands it as a
draft constitution for the new beginning, though older laws from Josiah's
Deuteronomy have found their way into it.[41] By this understanding the main
group behind it would be "poor country people" (dal ha'am), the lowest
group in rural society ('am ha'ares). Looked at systematically, this socio-historical disagreement over the dating makes no great difference. In both cases
the crucial groups behind Deuteronomy are social movements of rural
people, supported by Levites, prophets, and – in the case of the pre-exilic

---

40 The things the king does for the common good are an expression of knowledge of
God. Jeremiah testifies of Josiah: "'He dispensed justice to the lowly and poor; did not
this show he knew me?' says Yahweh" (22:16).
41 Veerkamp, 1993, pp.55ff.

dating – reform-minded representatives of officialdom. The king – while there is one – is bound by the law to God's will and people. It is impossible to cite all the *individual regulations*. Here are just a few, which are particularly *important examples* in view of the questions before us.[42]

– Crucially the state *tribute*, the tithe, was abolished (Deut 14:22ff.). It had clearly led to poverty, debt and enslavement on the one hand, and large-scale land acquisition and use of slaves on the other. The tithe was now to be spent for two years on an annual pilgrimage and a big feast at the shrine[43], and on feeding the landless Levites living in the various settlements. Every third year it was to be allocated to those with no land of their own to produce with (widows, orphans, foreigners and Levites). This according to Crüsemann is *"the first known social tax"* (p.254,tr.). It is the *"law as laid down by free landowners"* (*ibid*, pp.256ff.,tr.), who do not use what they have saved in taxes for themselves, but contribute to the common good. This also involves:

– a year of remission every seven years for those who, despite the society's supportive structure, have fallen into debt (15:1-11); this also happened as an act of mercy by kings, but here it is taken out of the area of arbitrary decision and turned into a right for debtors[44];

– after six years of work, someone who has become a slave should be released in the seventh year and even receive some start-up capital to help them get on their feet (15:12ff.);

– the poor and weak should also be able to join in the pilgrimage feasts (16:11);

– charging "interest" is forbidden among Hebrews, and also taking pledges from the weak (23:20; 24:17);

– harvest left-overs should remain in the fields for the hungry (24:19).

All these laws are linked with the *reminder about being set free from Egypt,* the house of slavery, by Yahweh, and with the hint that Yahweh will give blessings if they are kept.

---

42 Ibid., and in detail Crüsemann, 1992, pp.251ff., and Albertz, 1992, pp.337ff.

43 This text about the rededication of tribute seems to me to speak clearly for Veerkamp's post-exilic dating. Nothing is said of priests in connection with "the place which he (God) will choose", which suggests that the Temple was already destroyed. But Deuteronomy may well include texts from both pre-exilic and post-exilic times.

44 Cf. ibid., p.340.

This shows up what lies at the heart of Deuteronomy: the uniqueness and *oneness of the god Yahweh*, to whom Israel should bind itself wholeheartedly in the sense of the first Commandment:

"Listen, Israel: Yahweh our God is the one Yahweh. You shall love Yahweh your God with all your heart, with all your soul, with all your strength." (6:4f.)

The people bound themselves to all this in a Covenant (26:16ff.). Thus God stepped formally into the place of the great Assyrian kings, who until this point had dictated treaties of vassalship.[45] Here again the redactors show how the god Yahweh and his people contrast with the tributary kingship systems of the ancient Near East. Keeping the Covenant and its commandments is a matter of life and death for the people (30:15ff.).

In summary we may say that Deuteronomy, with the help of the ancient Israelite traditions about a free(d) people, updated by the prophets, Hosea and Jeremiah in particular, succeeded in reforming the kingship system fundamentally. The monarchy was fully bound into the social system of solidarity and participation and lost its instruments of economic exploitation and political oppression. But it might also have been abolished altogether. Then society would have been transformed – without a state, as it was before 1000 BC. This would have been the New Beginning out of the "remnant" or the "stump", and the prophecies of the prophets, that the southern kingdom would also be destroyed, would have come true.

In fact the collapse of the southern kingdom took place shortly after Josiah's period of reform, after his successors had mostly gone back to the side of the old power elite. The Babylonians, the heirs of Assur, destroyed Jerusalem in 586, and deported the ruling class to Babylon; a group fled to Egypt and took Jeremiah with them. Only the "poor of the land" were left: the "remnant".

---

45 Cf. ibid., p.357.

3 Alternatives after the collapse of kingship and the transformed society in a corner of the Persian Empire

The rural poor who stayed behind in the country were in a better position after the upper class was deported. They all got some land again and were able to organise themselves without a state and temple in an autonomous and egalitarian way, as foreseen by Deuteronomy 14f.[46] They were, however, conscripted to work for the provincial administration (Lam 5:13), so they were only semi-autonomous. Judah was not set up as a province on its own; the Babylonians administered it from distant Samaria, the former capital of the former northern kingdom, which must have reduced the burden significantly. Another problem was that neighbouring peoples were penetrating Israelite territory. Yet this period is an example of the strength of the Yahweh faith and of the fact that under certain conditions an alternative, better way of life, one marked by solidarity, is possible even under imperial rule.

This turning to Yahweh and the transformation of society connected with it was also the big issue for those who had been led off to exile in Babylon and those who had fled to Egypt, known as the Babylonian and Egyptian *gola*. The latter in particular seem to have taken great care of the Deuteronomic traditions.

> We do not know much about the group that fled to Egypt, but we do know that it had supported Gedaliah of the Deuteronomic reform group. The Babylonians had appointed him governor over those who stayed behind in Judah. When he was murdered by the Ammonites, they were afraid that they too would be punished by the Babylonians. They took Jeremiah and Baruch, Jeremiah's scribe, to Egypt with them – although against their will. They had explicitly supported the Deuteronomic reform of Josiah and the groups behind him. We may therefore assume that this tradition lived on among them, although little is known about the Egyptian *gola*.[47] We know that while some of them did military service for Egypt, they also built a temple to Yahweh.

The key presence in theological development along the lines of the prophets and Deuteronomy was the *Deuteronomic Movement*, which actually em-

---

46 Cf. ibid., p.378, and Veerkamp, 1993, pp.55ff.
47 Cf. Albertz, 1992, pp.381f.

braced a number of different groups. The two main ones are the Jeremiah-Deuteronomists (Jer-D) and the compilers of what is known as the Deuteronomic History (D-hist).

The Jeremiah-Deuteronomists (Jer-D) are to be detected in the reworking of the original words of Jeremiah. There were evidently later prophetic movements that studied the words of the prophets after the collapse of the monarchy in order to understand why it went so wrong and gain perspectives for a new beginning. In the case of the Jer-D what we have, probably, is groups which, in the tradition of Jeremiah and the Deuteronomic reform group (of which Gedaliah is the last historical trace), did "missionary work" among those who stayed at home and their descendants – perhaps also among the Egyptian *gola*.[48] Their main object was not just to remind the people who had lived through the downfall of the monarchy that it had been predicted by the prophets. More importantly, they updated the latter's message to cope with a new beginning at home (but also with a new life in diaspora), in the conviction that any syncretism with the gods of tributary kingship systems should be avoided and social justice guaranteed. So the main theme was still turning to Yahweh and to solidarity. They were critical of kingship and the state temple, but did not exclude a reformed monarchy.[49] Seventy years after its downfall they hoped for a turning-point through the forgiveness of Yahweh, expressed in God's putting his law in a new covenant into the Israelites' hearts, so that they may fulfill it from within (Jer 31:31ff.).

The *Deuteronomic history* (D-hist) is the first total presentation of the history of Israel from the taking of the land to the Exile, and thus includes texts that go all the way from Deuteronomy to 2 Kings. Several levels of editing witness to a process of work stretched over a long period of time. From the emphases of this presentation of history we may gather that behind the D-hist there are probably reform groups from the old national-religious leadership: priests and temple prophets (now unemployed), and also elders from among those who stayed at home in Judah.[50] Anyway, the "Levitical" priests, which in the D-hist simply means Jerusalem priests, and the elders play a vital role in this presentation of history, which is critical of kings.

They measure history against the Law of Moses. Yet it must be said that they mainly restrict this to the ban on foreign gods and images, while simply

---

48 Ibid., pp.391ff.
49 Ibid., p.396.
50 Ibid., pp.398ff.

ignoring the social laws.[51] They do indeed report Yahweh's warning about introducing kingship (1 Sam 8), but then they have God accept the wishes of the people. Subsequently they assess the kings less in terms of the fundamental socio-political problem of the monarchy than of their conduct towards foreign gods – quite differently from the critical prophets, such as Jeremiah, who in the D-hist are practically ignored. Instead it shows a strong interest in the Temple. Indeed, the centralising of the state cult in Jerusalem by Josiah is the climax and criterion of all history – thus also for the history of the people after the collapse and for the future of the New Beginning.

> "More important for them was the evidence that only the way indicated by the Deuteronomic reform of the cult, the thoroughgoing centralisation of the Yahweh cult in Jerusalem and the cleansing of Yahweh worship from heathen influence at all levels, offered a chance for the history of Israel to survive the national catastrophe. Thus what the Deuteronomists do in their great historical work is by no means just to work over theologically the state collapse of 587, but also – vitally – to point out to their contemporaries in Judah what they consider to be the only right way out of the crisis – away from the rampant popular syncretism, away from the pre-deuteronomic practices typical of the Samaritans, and towards an exclusive, Jerusalem-centred form of Yahweh worship. In their opinion it was not the comprehensive religious and social renewal of the people for which the Jeremiah-Deuteronomists strove which was the key to a new beginning, but the restoration of the Jerusalem based state cult established so convincingly by Josiah ."[52]

Of course, even after the collapse, there was nothing like a united, general turnabout involving all groups and classes of the people. Beside the identification (Dt 14f.) with the pre-state, ruler-free time of solidarity, and the religious-social Jeremiah-Deuteronomists, there was also the continuation in the D-hist of the (admittedly purified) national-religious tradition. But there were other fresh approaches.

In *Babylonian exile*, after the loss of the foundations for an official state religion, the *family* became an important setting for the worship of Yahweh. As a result of this the pre-state stories of the Fathers acquired new meaning

---

51 Ibid., p.402.
52 Ibid., pp.412f.(tr.).

and were told and retold.[53] In this context circumcision and sabbath observance also acquired special significance, through the efforts made to maintain the identity of the chosen people in diaspora.

In addition in Babylon there was a group of prophets, and their leader, which we know as *Deutero-Isaiah* or Second Isaiah. These prophets sought a new beginning by reinterpreting the prophet Isaiah.[54]

> Their texts are preserved in Chapters 40-55 of the Book of Isaiah. They attempt so to interpret history as to reveal new saving action by Yahweh, and thus hope. Behind this there were obviously temple singers and cult prophets from the destroyed Temple in Jerusalem, as the mixture of hymnic, Psalm-style speech and salvation oracles shows. Originally they must have had a rather nationalist function. But now the prophets of doom were obviously read and interpreted during worship, even though the groups that saw their relevance for their times still encountered sharp resistance, as we can see from the texts.

Central to Deutero-Isaiah is, firstly, a completely new understanding of the relationship between *Yahweh and kingship*. The group asserts that it is Yahweh who has called the Persian king Cyrus to liberate Israel and the other peoples from the yoke of the Babylonian Empire (Is 41:2f.,25; 45:4). Thus God is no longer the national god of Israel but god of all the world. "And he has a tendency to be critical of governance: self-important political power is made impotent and its victims are set free."[55]

Secondly, Yahweh's saving acts no longer affect just Israel but *all peoples*. In this Israel has a mediatory function. But this "no longer comes about through political subjugation as in the old Jerusalem theology (Ps 47:3,9), but by free will and conviction. Yahweh's great invitation goes out to all the nations to turn to him and be saved (45:22)."[56] The so-called "Servant Songs", which are to be interpreted, at least in part, as referring to Israel, show it is precisely Yahweh's saving action towards its deprived population that makes Israel a people able to testify to the uniqueness of its God.

Thirdly, this marks the end of the *"amalgamation of divine and political power"*. The universal *kingly rule of God* becomes a basic belief which "clearly

---

53 Ibid., pp.413ff.
54 On what follows, ibid., pp.431ff.
55 Ibid., p.438(tr.).
56 Ibid., p.441(tr.).

excludes human kingship, i.e. the institutionalised concentration of political power... The old equation of Near Eastern kingship ideology, whereby divine power is reflected in the extent of the state's power, is broken by this".[57] Deutero-Isaiah promises Israel no further restoration of the state. Yahweh himself will be king, he will free the oppressed and strengthen the weak and those who have grown weary (40:29-31; 41:17; 42:22). The departure from Babylon will be a new Exodus (52:12). Power will yield to justice (Is 42:1-4).

> "The mysterious Song of the Suffering Servant Israel (Is 52:13-53:12) goes a step further. Israel has been able to bring salvation for the peoples not in its power, greatness and fame but precisely in the phase of its absolute powerlessness, by bearing their sufferings and sins as a substitute. This is the first attempt to give Israel's loss of political power positive meaning in God's plan for history and is probably the most profound theological interpretation the painful period of exile ever had."[58]

Finally, there was the *reform proposal by a priestly group centred on the priest-prophet Ezekiel* (Ezek 40-48), which came about roughly between 573 and 520.[59] It highlights the holiness of the Jerusalem Temple, in which God will make his dwelling in the midst of his people after the return of the exiles. The most important political conclusion from the heightened concept of holiness is the thoroughgoing "release of the cult from any kind of state guardian-ship."[60] The Temple should not belong to the king again. The priests should be maintained in a new way (with plots of land with which they can look after themselves). There might still be a political leader (*nasi*), but he would be divested of all sacral and priestly office. For his economic base he should be given clearly defined lands (nowhere near the capital city), but he should not lay claim to anything else and not give land to officials' families, so that the fatal concentration of land and impoverishment of the peasants that hap-pened at the time of the kings may not happen again. The land should again be divided equally, as in pre-state times, and now even foreigners should get a share.

---

57 Ibid., p.444(tr.).
58 Ibid., p.446(tr.).
59 On what follows cf. ibid., pp.446ff.
60 Ibid., p.453(tr.).

"All families were supposed to be able to manage on an equal and free basis, un-burdened by state intervention, as they used to before the state existed... In this way the ancient liberating impulse of pre-state Yahweh religion gained ground again under wholly changed conditions."[61]

It is impressive to see the theological strength with which different groups from the destroyed southern kingdom of Judah, whether in Judah itself or in exile in Egypt and Babylon, tried to work through the catastrophe and plan, or implement, a new beginning: Deuteronomists of prophetic and nationalist origin, the prophetic Deutero-Isaiah group and the priestly Ezekiel group. Apart from the nationalist Deuteronomists all of them, for all their differences, agree on one thing: Yahweh proves his uniqueness in that, having broken the political power of the king and the ideological link between cult and king, which had combined to bring about people's economic destruction, political oppression and idolatry, he makes the gift of a *new beginning which involves the hallowing of the cult, and economic equality and political self-determination for the people.* No matter how much of that could or could not be realised in the post-exilic Province of Judaea (now part of the Persian empire) these writings contain a source of faith for the humanising of society that can never be exhausted, and which Deutero-Isaiah thought would attract the peoples in hope to Yahweh, the God of liberation, who strengthens the weak.

What of all this could be put into practice when the *Persians* permitted the exiles in Babylon to return, and (from about 520 BC) to join those who had stayed at home in building a new community in Judah? It is not possible and not necessary here to present in full the very complex picture of all the different competing and cooperating groups and currents. Albertz has done this very plausibly, following Crüsemann.[62] We can restrict ourselves to the essentials and some examples.

The first important fact is that the *pre-exilic theology of king, state and Temple* did not regain currency. There were, to be sure, clear signs that during the Persian period some of the aristocracy and top priestly circles at first opposed social and political reforms where they could. They also did so towards

---

61 Ibid., pp.458f.(tr.).
62 Ibid., pp.463ff.; cf. in particular the detailed diagram on p.467.

the end of this period, and then gained increasing power, above all in the Hellenistic-Roman period that followed.

In the early post-exilic period, however, something came to a head that discredited *radical prophecy* and drove it to the fringe of society, if not underground. At the start the Persians had given the Davidite Zerubbabel the task, as their governor, of organising reconstruction in Judah. But when the salvation prophets *Zechariah* and *Haggai* prophesied the restoration of Davidian kingship along with the building of the Temple, and spread a mood of rebellion among the people, the Persians intervened. All three had to disappear; after this disappointment prophets in general lost their public significance and hived off into little groups, gaining most support probably from those without land, the lowest of the low. Hope for the future became eschatologised: God would intervene radically from outside and end all economic exploitation and misery, and all political oppression (cf. e.g. Trito-Isaiah, Is 55-66).[63] Only in apocalyptic literature did prophecy again play a publicly significant role.

The reshaping of Jewish community life in the Persian period was the work of a coalition of the mass of free peasants (smallholders), and a reform-minded part of the upper class: like Nehemiah and the reform priests from the Ezekiel group. Following the Deuteronomic-Deuteronomist traditions *peasants* and the progressive members of the upper class made up the *Elders' Council,* the leading lay body. It consisted of representatives of the newly formed associations of extended families (clans). The priests were represented in the *College of Priests.* For important decisions the *People's Assembly* was revived. A king was not foreseen, and would not have been allowed by the Persians, who were in charge themselves. The Elders' Council and the People's Assembly clearly followed the models of pre-state times; only the College of Priests was a later invention, now without any link with the power of kings. Thus the *structure of Jewish self-government in the Persian period* was an "attempt at an artificial reconstruction of the social structure of the pre-state period".[64] From the experience of the failure of (the taming of) the kingship system society had been transformed – but *only semi-autonomously,* in a corner of the Persian Empire. This is the first reason why this structuring of socio-economic relationships, rooted in Yahweh, the God of liberation, could not work fully. Tribute had to

---

63 Ibid., pp.479ff.
64 Ibid., p.474(tr.).

be paid to the Persians as it had earlier to the king. The second reason was that some of the *upper class*, who had reached the top during the monarchy, *rejected solidarity*, so that the peasants again had to face worsening degrees of poverty, debt and slavery. For this reason, all the laws and rules of behaviour that developed had less of a constitutive than a corrective character, compared to those in Deuteronomy. Only in this way could the desire for equality and solidarity be expressed at all. Here are *some examples*.

It was not the draft constitution of Ezekiel and his group (Ezek 40-48) that was followed in priestly circles after the return to Judah, but the so-called "priestly document" (P).[65] This probably provided the basis for the priests' position over the re-ordering of relationships in post-exilic Judaea and was part of the context for the emergence of the *Pentateuch* (the Five Books of Moses).

Albertz assumes the following scenario.[66] It has become known that the Persians had the practice of recording the cultic and legal practices of subject peoples in written form. Their object was, on the one hand, to encourage loyalty to the Empire by showing interest in these people's own traditions and, on the other, to be able better to control peoples who were governing themselves according to principles they recognised. The basic documents that resulted then received "imperial authorisation". The two self-government bodies, the Elders' Council composed of "laymen" and the College of Priests, probably commissioned the production of such a basic document. Albertz calls those given this task "theological commissions". Anyway, this is a good explanation of the compromise in the Pentateuch between Deuteronomic-Deuteronomist parties and priestly parties. The two elements together, forming the Pentateuch as Israel's Torah, must have been completed at some time between the end of the Temple rebuilding in 515 BC and Nehemiah's appearance in Judaea in 445 BC. At the time of Ezra's mission in 458 or 398 BC the document was canonised and officially enforced by the Persians. That is why Veerkamp calls this the "Torah republic" model.

Crüsemann sees in the priestly writings of the Torah (P) above all three new accents which, starting from the Creation, make it possible to feel God's

---

65 On this, summarising the earlier research, F. Crüsemann, 1992, pp.323ff.
66 Albertz, op. cit., pp.497ff. in agreement with Blum.

presence and to fashion God's will into law, even in the Diaspora and later in
the semi-autonomy of the Persian Empire:

- "– P loosens the link between God's Law and the Exodus, possession of land,
  and the cult...;
- – P interprets the Exodus in a radically new way (God's presence liberates his
  people for holiness) and thus makes possible the fundamentals of a Law
  which will not be obeyed by free landowners alone;
- – P makes atonement and forgiveness central for the cult and thus integrates
  into the Torah Israel's failure to observe it."[67]

For our questioning about alternative forms of economy, *Leviticus* 25, from
the Holiness Code, is central.[68]

– Lev 25:2-7[69] begins with the rule for the seventh year, here called the *sabbath year*. It should be celebrated, and everyday life should be suspended,
including the normal laws governing the economy – for God, for the land, for
working people, for everyone, including slaves. The reason is that God is the
owner of the land.

– Lev 25:8-31 gives rules on the famous *year of jubilee* (jobel), the seven-times-
seventh year.[70] The "jubilee" is the horn which was blown in public when
specially important events happened, like the advance to Mount Sinai and the
fall of the walls of Jericho (Ex 19:13; Josh 6:3ff.). Veerkamp interprets this
convincingly as an allusion to the gift of the "Magna Carta" of Israel's freedom
on Sinai and as destruction of a city-kingdom, with its division of society into
classes where the wealthy become richer and the poor become poorer. The
crucial event of the year is the return to the original situation of equality.
Everyone goes back to their own land, the basis for the egalitarian freedom of
the families. Those who have accumulated more must give it back. This
should take place on the "Day of Atonement", the "feast of reconciliation",
when the priests "make atonement" for all wrongs by placing the people's sins
upon the scapegoat and driving it out into the wilderness. The emergence of
inequality is obviously interpreted as sin. But people are not abandoned to a
fate of structural economic sins. God has broken down the old structure. This
year is holy because God is holy. Whether this radical restructuring of the

---

67 Crüsemann, op. cit., p.337(tr.).
68 On the texts of the Holiness Code, Lev 17-26, T. Veerkamp, 1993, pp.86ff.
69 Ibid., pp.89ff.
70 Ibid., pp.91ff.; cf. also Lohfink, op. cit., pp.110ff.

system ever fully became reality we do not know. Some think the seven-times-seven number also has something to do with the return from exile after 50 years, with all families receiving the same gift of land to enable them to make a living – as they had under the original egalitarian system before Israel became a state. But the crucial thing, different from all the surrounding cultures, is that it does not concern a one-off act of generosity by the king but a right for every family, granted by God and enshrined in law.

– Verses 14-17 say something about that sacred cow of the market economy, *price*.[71]

"If you buy or sell with your neighbour, let no one wrong his brother" (v. 14). This is about land, the means of production through which families earn a living by farming. The stress is on protecting the seller. In the circumstances of a subsistence economy he normally sells not because he wants to but because he needs to, because of a bad harvest, or high tribute payments or the like. It is in precisely such situations of need that the "supply" to the market is high, so the prices can be squeezed by those in a stronger position. Ezekiel's draft constitution (Ezek 45:8) contains a provision for the most powerful person, the king: "My princes will no longer oppress my people", by extending their lands at the cost of the people (Ezek 46:18). The word *janah*, oppress, means literally "to use violence", the violence of those who are (in market terms) stronger against those who are weaker (cf. Ex 22:10, against foreigners!). The alternative is that the buyer should fix the price not according to the law of the market but according to the land's real value, and that is the sum of the yields of harvests up to the Jubilee year, for the land then returns to the person who sold it (out of need) anyway. Theology still had ideas about the "just price" until the time of the Reformation. Then it capitulated before the market and the Law of the Strong. But:

"You shall fear your God; for I am the lord your God" (v. 17). Veerkamp rightly draws attention to this renewed evidence theology and ethics are not poaching on the preserves of economics. "'God' does not stand on the side of the poor, those who are socially and economically defenceless, as if he could equally have stood on their opponents' side. Rather, the very NAME (U.D.: insert Yahweh, from Ex 3) contains this position. It is the expression of an order in which this exploitation does not and cannot exist... So

---

71 Veerkamp, op. cit., pp.94ff.

theology is nothing but another *language* for expressing the thrust of the chosen economic strategy."[72]

– Verse 23 goes to the theological and eonomic heart of the matter:

"Land must not be sold in perpetuity, for the land belongs to me, and to me you are only strangers and guests."

This sentence is a considerable restriction on the civil law of property. In the ancient Near East, even more in ancient Rome, this was unheard of. Ownership involved a right of disposal, in Rome an absolute right of disposal. The king saw himself as the country's owner. In Israel it is different: people simply have inferior rights when compared to Yahweh. God gives out land for them to use, on lease – not to diminish his creatures, but to protect them against the strong who exploit them. Therefore the question about *who* 'God' is really signifies *what* functions as 'God'[73] – the politically and economically strong, or Yahweh, who frees his people from the house of slavery and protects the weak.

– Verses 24ff. are about the *ge'ulah order*, the possibility of redeeming what has been sold.[74]

"You will allow a right of redemption on all your landed property."

This word is also "redemption" in the Christian tradition, though it has been spiritualised for so long that no-one thinks any more of its socio-economic origins. *Ge'ulah* comes from the root *ga'al*: "to comply with one's family duty with regard to someone". *Go'el* is the "redeemer". In the verses that follow, situations are presented in which a brother is down and out. In these cases *ge'ulah* should come into play: *family solidarity*, which means not just the individual family but the whole of Israel, whose entire social structure is patterned on this. It is that same "ethic of brotherliness" that Max Weber says is impossible in the capitalist market economy.

"Just as the absolute sovereignty of the NAME is the *reason* for equality in Jehudah (Judah) and for Jehudah's autonomy, this structure of relatedness is the *framework* for equality. Jehudah's whole 'civil law' functions only within this *framework* and for this *reason*."[75]

– Verses 25-28 deal with the situation where a brother is down and out and must, *out of need, sell his land.* This emergency mechanism is implicit in the

---

72 Ibid., p.97(tr.).
73 Ibid., p.101(tr.).
74 Ibid., pp.101ff.; cf. R. Kessler in: M. Crüsemann and W.. Schottroff, 1992, pp.40ff.
75 Veerkamp, op. cit., p.101(tr.).

complaint of "the ordinary people and their wives" before Nehemiah. In this case the closest relative should come and, as it were, ransom his brother's property. That these "brothers" can in fact also be women is shown by the Book of Ruth, which tells the classical story of *ge'ulah* order. If no-one in the family redeems the land, the purchaser should buy several successive years' income from the land, but not the land itself. This, if it cannot be bought back before then, reverts to the original family of ownership in the Jubilee year in any case.

– Verses 29-34 concern "*houses*".[76] Houses in towns should have a right of redemption for only one year, houses in villages for ever, and Levites' houses may not be sold at all. Underlying this difference is the fact that in rural areas houses, like land, belong to the means of production. "Again and again the legislator's concern is to guarantee direct producers ownership of their means of production."[77] An exception is made for the town houses of the Levites, since this was their only property.

– Verses 35-38 now deal with the prohibition of "*neshek*", of "taking a bite", of taking more when your brother is in debt to you.[78]

> "When your brother-Israelite is reduced to poverty and cannot support himself
> in the community, you shall assist him as you would an alien or a stranger, and
> he shall live with you. You shall not charge him interest on a loan, either by de-
> ducting it in advance from the capital sum (*neshek*), or by adding it on repay-
> ment. You shall fear your God, and your brother shall live with you; you shall
> not deduct interest when advancing him money or add interest to the payment
> due for food supplied on credit. I am the LORD your god who brought you out of
> Egypt to give you the land of Canaan and to become your God."

We have already pointed out above that *neshek* cannot be identified simply with charging interest in the capitalist economy. The interest is a share of the surplus value that has grown out of completed production – although it is necessary to talk about the size of the share. In the economic system of the ancient Near East, *neshek* bites out of what the person concerned has to live on. Yet according to this text, the criterion in the mind of Yahweh for every economic system is that people should live, not just vegetate; they should be productive and able to provide properly for themselves – even if for a time

---

76 Ibid., pp.104ff.
77 Ibid., p.105(tr.).
78 Ibid., pp.106ff. and J. Kegler, 1992, in: M. Crüsemann and W. Schottroff, 1992, pp.17ff.

(until the Jubilee year) this must happen with the lesser rights of aliens and tenant farmers. Anything else is "Egypt": exploitation, slavery and oppression.

– Verses 39-46: those "reduced to poverty" who *sell themselves*.[79]

"When your brother is reduced to poverty and sells himself to you, you shall not use him to work for you as a slave. His status shall be that of a hired man or a stranger lodging with you; he shall work for you until the year of jubilee. He shall then leave your service, with his children, and go back to his family and to his ancestral property: because they are my slaves who I brought out of Egypt, they shall not be sold as slaves are sold. You shall not drive him with ruthless severity."

This is about the "constant theme of political economy in the ancient world: debt-slavery".[80] It is worth noting here that the priestly document strays from the older laws of Israel at this point. It changes the status of slaves into that of day labourers and tenant farmers, but Veerkamp doubts if that represents a real improvement. Day labourers were the lowest group in society and particularly insecure, whilst slaves were part of the household and could live quite secure lives, in material terms at least. Crüsemann, on the other hand, sees signs of a trend towards the abolition of slavery in general.[81] But both agree that delaying the release of slaves from every seventh year, as in the Book of the Covenant and Deuteronomy (cf. Ex 21 and Deut 15), to the year of Jubilee, the fiftieth year, represents an unequivocal de-radicalising of the laws of Israel and an exacerbation of the position of debt-slaves.[82] There is again an explicit reference to the ground of these laws, Yahweh, who liberated the slaves from Egypt and who himself steps into the place of a king or pharaoh. He does not trample his servants underfoot, however, but protects their lives and their position in society when they are reduced to poverty.

– Verses 47-55 deal with the special case of when Israelites have to sell themselves to foreigners. Then their closest relative should "redeem" them and keep them as day labourers until the year of Jubilee. Here too we find the reminder about the liberation from Egypt.

– The close of the whole thing (26:1f.) is again highly theological.[83]

---

79 Veerkamp, op. cit., pp.108ff.
80 Ibid., p.109(tr.).
81 Crüsemann, 1993, p.353.
82 Cf. ibid., p.332, and Veerkamp, op. cit., p.109.
83 Cf. ibid., pp.113f.

"You shall not make idols for yourselves; you shall not erect a carved image or a sacred pillar; you shall not put a figured stone on your land to prostrate yourselves upon, because I am the LORD your God. You shall keep my sabbaths and revere my sanctuary. I am the Lord."

This economic order is an expression of the first and second commandments. The rejection of other gods is "not an expression of religious intolerance but of the practical *irreconcilability* of conditions in a society that tries to follow the orders of the sabbath and *ge'ulah* in the context of the property accumulation typical of the ancient Near East." Thus says Ton Veerkamp, who continues aptly:

"Anyone who prostrates himself before the gods of the goyim (peoples) accepts the conditions that go with them as god-given." This is not a question of ethics. "Rather, a body of laws that sought to defend the economic interests of a quite specific group of people was tackled. The text has an unequivocal, class-led standpoint; it intervenes in the class struggle in favour of the one whose livelihood and freedom is under threat and against those in whose hands the means of production are beginning to be concentrated. If this is inconsistant in some places, that does not change its unequivocality. When considering theology's part in economics on the strength of this text, we may say that theology does not replace economics but that it makes it *unequivocal*, i.e. theology ensures that economics as economics represents *unequivocally* and therefore also *uncompromisingly* the interests of those who are holy in the eyes of the ONE and ETERNAL God, *the people he led out of the house of slavery*. It is not this text's specific solutions but its absolute clarity that constitutes its appeal for us, even today."[84]

Incidentally, the *Book of Nehemiah* shows that the delay of the release of slaves from the seventh year to the fiftieth year, as proposed in the priestly Holiness Code, was not carried out (cf. Neh 10:32). We shall turn briefly to this book, because it contains a good example of how the laws of Israel, the people of Yahweh the liberator, were followed in practice, even in an environment where the tendency was to divide society into rich and poor. In a classic scene "the ordinary people and their wives"[85] came to *Nehemiah*, the Persians' governor in Judaea (445-425 BC), and complained about the lack of solidarity shown by the upper class, who had got them into debt, hock and slavery (on

---

84 Ibid., pp.114f.
85 On Neh 5:1ff. see also comments on Lev 25:25-28 above. For details on the following, Veerkamp, 1993, pp.75ff.

top of the tribute to the Persian king, which, to make things worse, had to be paid in silver or, in today's terms, hard currency). Nehemiah angrily reprimanded the upper class and officials, urging them, in the name of Yahweh who demands family solidarity (brotherliness), to cancel the debts. And he succeeded. He himself even gave up the taxes earmarked for his gubernatorial administration with its 150 officials.

This example shows that in a transformed society headed by Yahweh it is possible to establish elements of solidarity where a free space, or niche, is granted by the imperial authorities (exacting tribute and therefore basically plundering). Even if granting this space can be seen as part of the ancient Near Eastern tradition of royal acts of mercy (and these are not known to apply to upper classes as a whole), the codified law that emerges in Judaea clearly goes beyond individual acts of that kind and raises questions about the system. Judaea in the Persian period is a transformed society, sustained by the producing peasants (People's Assembly) and their allies in the Council of Elders and College of Priests, under God's kingly rule in a corner of the tributary kingdom of the Persians. It is transformed in the sense that it is not organised as a tributary king-and-temple system but has links with the autonomous and egalitarian society of the pre-state era. But as it is only semi-autonomous because it is subject to the Persian Empire, it has to apply elements of "taming" to the mechanisms of the kingship system – as the example of Nehemiah shows. It is a semi-autonomous counter-culture. Inasmuch as its politico-economic and priestly upper classes turn against solidarity, they contribute to the downfall of the Torah Republic.

I should like to close this review of Judaean attempts to create an alternative, non-tributary society by referring to something that may seem very uneconomic. During the egalitarian first phase after 587 BC, as we saw, those who had remained at home redirected their "tithe", or tribute, not only away from the king to those who had no means of production of their own but also towards the costs of a community festival with a great feast in which all could share: "There you shall spend it as you will on cattle or sheep, wine or strong drink, or whatever you desire; you shall consume it there with rejoicing, both you and your family, in the presence of the Lord your God" (Deut 14:26). Similarly, Ezra says after the people's pledge to keep the Law, Yahweh's Torah:

> "You may go now; refresh yourselves with rich food and sweet drinks, and send a
> share to all who cannot provide for themselves; for this day is holy to our Lord.
> Let there be no sadness, for joy in the LORD is your strength" (Neh 8:10).

Solidarity is not something stiff and sad. A life-sustaining economy (for all) is a joyful matter. We shall meet it again in the early Christian community.

4 Resistance to the totalitarian Hellenistic and Roman Empires and small-scale alternatives in apocalyptic writings

The counterpart to this is *Job*. Ton Veerkamp has shown in a fascinating chapter about the Book of Job that he is the type of the free peasant who is ruined by the toughening of the tributary imperial system in Hellenism.[86] Job represents the Israel of the Torah Republic in the Persian period, which can no longer maintain its semi-autonomous separate identity in the face of the Hellenistic empires after Alexander (330 BC) and their tendency towards totalitarianism. Yet in contrast to his friends he stubbornly refuses to accept as God the arbitrary God that is behind this system. The Yahweh of liberation and solidarity and the arbitrary God of the Hellenistic rulers are absolute opposites. This breaks him – no, before he breaks completely, God turns away from the perversion of himself. He puts aside the form of the arbitrary Greek gods who operate under the *moira*, fate, and installs Job, the just man according to the Torah, in a life of blessedness once more. Job finishes the book with a revolution, in that he introduces for his daughters the right to inherit property. Israel does not give up hope even in the gloomiest night of God's darkness. But there is space here only for so much about the situation of desperation and theodicy which Ton Veerkamp has brought out in masterly fashion.

So we shall turn immediately to the situation in which excess pressure in the boiler led to an explosion in the years 169-167 BC. In 169 BC the Seleucid ruler Antiochus IV Ephiphanes plundered the Temple, which had been rebuilt after the Exile, and entered the Holy of Holies. In 168 he had Jerusalem destroyed, and in 167 he established the cult of Zeus Olympios in the holy place of the Temple. Faced with this total threat to the Jewish faith and alternative community, various forms of theological and practical resistance emerged (against the priestly aristocracy, which had meanwhile conformed to the empires, and the collaborating part of the upper class, both of whom had clearly contributed from within to the collapse of the Torah Republic).

---

86 Ibid., pp.115ff.

Socially, the oppressed Judaeans formed a resistance coalition.[87] Insurrections (200 BC) under the Egyptians, i.e. under the Ptolemaic Hellenistic Empire, had been failures. Now *a broad alliance* was formed, consisting of:

- *country priestly families*, among them the Maccabees, who at once took over the leadership of the opposition;
- *free, landowning peasants*, who saw their existence endangered by the Hellenistic money economy and the consequent accumulation of land in the hand of urban elites;
- *those who had already been uprooted*;
- the party of "pious ones" (*Hasidaeans*), a radical Torah party whose members fought Hellenism as guerillas.

This alliance, which was anti-Hellenistic apart from its socio-economic and political goals, won back Jerusalem in 164 BC by force of arms. The Temple was cleansed and rededicated. But when Jonathan Maccabee aspired not only to become king but also high priest, the coalition broke up. While royal priesthood was the norm in ancient Near Eastern Hellenism, the whole Torah was against it. The *Hasideans* also split up, after the disappointment of seeing the Maccabee rule become Hellenised. When one group withdrew to the wilderness in order to live out an alternative to Hellenism (later to become the *Essenes*, in Qumran and elsewhere), others separated from them in order "to remain ready for political action" as the Torah party (Veerkamp). This breakaway group (*perizim*) later became the *Pharisees*, who in their turn formed a "military wing", the Zealots. In addition there were *messianic fringe groups*, remaining in the tradition of the prophets.

Daniel is the canonical example of apocalyptic resistance theology. There were other late-prophetic and apocalyptic theologies of resistance in the Hellenistic period before the Book of Daniel[88], of which Zech 9-11, Is 24-27 and I Enoch are examples. The groups behind them, mostly from the dregs of society, had had to put up with a marginal existence involving tension with the Judaean majority, even those faithful to the Torah; this situation changed dramatically when the most important groups formed an alliance for common resistance. In the apocalyptic theology of resistance Israel's most important traditions fuse with prophecy.[89]

---

87 On what follows cf. in detail ibid., pp.231ff., and Albertz, 1992, pp.664f.
88 Cf. Albertz, op. cit., pp.633ff.
89 On apocalyptic as a theology of resistance cf. P. Lampe, 1978.

The Book of Daniel[90] contains the most important testimony to this situation. It consists of a part written in Aramaic (2:4b-7:28). This was probably written in the Syrian and Mesopotamian diaspora with recourse to older stories, and was obviously intended to encourage the Maccabean coalition in their struggle. To this a Hebrew part (8:1-12:13) is attached, obviously by Hasideans who were disappointed by the Maccabees, since it includes critical comments about them (11:34). A redactor has also inserted the first chapter in order to show that Daniel and his friends already had to resist pressure to conform (from Hellenism) when they were young.

For our line of questioning we will choose two particularly important chapters from the Aramaic Daniel (3 and 7), in order to clarify the way groups faithful to Yahweh behave in the face of a totalitarian system.

Daniel 3 describes the totalitarian political-economic-ideological system of the Hellenistic kind of empire as a whole: the king (political power) has an image built out of gold (economic power), before which people have to prostrate themselves (ideological power). Veerkamp expresses this crisply:

"The image was of gold. And it was gigantic: 60 ells must be about 30 metres. A golden monster. The gold makes transactions between present and future owners of goods possible; stored it is buying-power and quantified it may be used as a means of measuring value. A means of exchange, a means of preserving value and a measure of value: gold is the centre of gravity for the Hellenistic economy. The king of kings makes an image out of it; he reifies the economy and makes it a cultic object, he fetishises gold. The embodiment of politics (the king) exalts the embodiment of economics (gold) as God of the whole world – that is the process recounted here. So the story describes the unity of politics, economics and ideology in the Hellenistic period. It describes a world economic order."[91]

The background: Antiochus IV had, according to 1 Macc 1:41f., drafted a decree, according to which all the peoples of his Empire had to give up their cultural and legal autonomy and become one imperial people. That means that ideological unity was now to follow the economic (through money) and political (through military power of conquest) unity that had been achieved.

90 On this Veerkamp, op. cit., pp.235ff.
91 Ibid., p.243(tr.).

Everyone falls on their knees, all but three Jewish men: Daniel and his friends. Although they will be thrown into the fiery furnace, they refuse:

> "...be it known to your majesty that we will neither serve your god nor worship the golden image that you have set up." (3:18)

Ton Veerkamp: "This confession, for that is what it is, is their refusal to prostrate themselves before the god of the King and the Empire, *before gold*. The confession is the proclamation of an act, an act of refusal. Therefore they are not reciting a cheap creed but saying what they will do, or rather what they will not do, and they are fully aware of the risk involved in this failure to act."[92]

In this story the men are saved from the furnace by their God, but before that they say: God can save us, but even if he doesn't we declare that we will not fall down. So they are prepared for martyrdom. That is the price to be paid for breaking the arrogant, total power of the world-system. For power cannot exist unless it is worshipped, i.e. unless it is recognised as absolute power. Power cannot exist if its legitimation and loyalty to it are withdrawn. Today that sort of power means that there is no alternative to the capitalist market. We shall come back to this.

Daniel 7 is the great vision of the kingdoms of the world and their overturn by the Kingdom of God. The murderous power of the previous empires is depicted first; in the dream they appear as animals. The neo-Babylonian empire is represented by the winged lion, the Medes as a bear and the Persians as a leopard. The winged lion is a hybrid, symbolising the legacy of the power of Assur (lion) and of Egypt (vulture) under the single rule of Babylon. The piquant thing about this is that these very animals appear in these empires' iconography as heraldic beasts, seen as expressions of strength. Now they take on the fearful aspect of deadly beasts of prey – which they also are. Daniel cannot even find a beast of prey to symbolise the Greek empire. It can only be described as a terrifying monster. It is an absolutist power, leaving no room at all for autonomy. It is the absolute opposite to the God of Israel.

The second part of this vision shows how this terrible being is overcome. One who is "Ancient of Days" ascends the throne, a court is held, the sentence is pronounced, the murderous monster is destroyed and power is handed over to a being "like a son of man". The symbolism is clear: God is the real King, his throne is light and truth. He limits the scope of those who have seized

---

92 Ibid., pp.247f.(tr.).

power for themselves. Daniel sets the being with a human face in contrast to the beasts of prey and the monsters. The human element, human community, is created by God for ever. Who is this epitome of all that is "human"? Daniel makes this clear as he goes through the dream a second time. Judgement is "given in favour of the saints of the Most High"; it brings justice for the oppressed people of God.

> "Holiness in Israel can only be what preserves freedom. The Holy One of Israel is he who sets free; the holiness of Israel is the preservation of freedom, its discipline, the Torah. The one who sets free is the one who makes holy."[93]

That means that the Kingdom of God, which overcomes the murderous kingdoms of the world, is a kingdom governed and shaped by human beings for human beings in freedom and solidarity. That is why it is called eternal: eternal life. How then does Israel react to an economically, politically and ideologically totalitarian kingdom? Different groups react differently. We shall leave aside the conformist priestly aristocracy (later the Sadducees) and the landed and moneyed elite; they simply joined forces with Hellenism. Of those who remain faithful, the Maccabees respond with revolution but afterwards – like Jehu after the first revolution in Israel – they conform to the norm of the power system and themselves become absolutist priest-kings. Two groups stay with the opposition of those faithful to the Torah: the Pharisees, partial objectors who want to remain in the daily business of politics, and the Hasideans who go into the wilderness, total objectors who endeavour to practise human community as a small-scale alternative in anticipation of the Kingdom of God. Finally there are the messianic fringe groups who, in the intense piety of their poverty, wait for the breaking-in of the Kingdom of God.[94] Rejection and small-scale alternatives in expectation of the Kingdom of God: these are the responses of the faithful that Jesus of Nazareth encounters.

---

93 Ibid., p.275(tr.).
94 Cf. Albertz, op. cit., p.676.

5   The Jesus movement and the early Christian messianic communities as the salt, light and leaven of the Kingdom of God in Israel and among the peoples

In view of the Israelites' struggle for over a thousand years against oppressive and life-destroying kingdoms and for an alternative way of life inspired by the liberating God of solidarity, it is not at all surprising that Jesus' life and preaching centres on the Kingdom of God. Kingdom of God (*malkuthYHWH*) means literally "God becomes king". The surprising thing is that in their interpretation and preaching over the years most churches today have stripped the full and fundamental sense of the Kingdom of God in Jesus' message of practically all its economic and political content. Similar false interpretations are usual in relation to Paul, the apostle to the Gentiles, and other writings of the Second Testament.[95]

This is probably also why, as far as I know, there is still no comprehensive sociological-theological presentation of the Jesus Movement and early Christianity which consistently bases its inquiry on Israel's history of struggle with the socio-economic, political and ideological system of the great empires. Such a presentation would have also to make clear how the emergence of the early Christian variants of Judaism relate to Judaism's own history at the time. Happily, however, there are works which offer examples of how one should proceed methodologically.

The brothers Norbert and Gerhard Lohfink provide some magisterial sketches in their books *Das Jüdische am Christentum* (The jewish element in Christianity) and *Wem gilt die Bergpredigt?* (To whom does the Sermon on the Mount apply?)[96] Similar to Lohfink and others, *Wilhelm Haller* has offered a book related to my concern, concentrating on Jesus' basic direction: *Die heilsame Alternative – Jesuanische Ethik in Wirtschaft und Politik* (The salutary alternative –

---

95 I use this expression for the book otherwise known as the New Testament. In view of Christianity's terrible history of guilt towards Jews, every form of expression for the Hebrew Bible that may be misunderstood as denigration, thus even the word "Old" Testament, must be avoided. It is possible here to say "First" and "Second" Testament.
96 N. Lohfink, 1987, specially the chapters "Kingship and Political Power" (pp.71ff.,tr.), "God's Kingdom and the Economy" (pp.103ff.,tr.) and "God on the Side of the Poor" (pp.122ff.,tr.). G. Lohfink, (1988) 1993, particularly Part IV: "Why does the Sermon on the Mount require a Contrast Society?" (pp.99ff.,tr.). Where this term occurs later I owe it to the Lohfinks.

Jesus ethics in economics and politics).[97] From sociological research concentrated on the Second Testament I name here only *Klaus Wengst*: Pax Romana and the Peace of Christ, and *Luise Schottroff: Lydias ungeduldige Schwestern – Feministische Sozialgeschichte des frühen Christentums* (Lydia's impatient sisters – feminist sociology of early Christianity).[98] They complement one another superbly. Wengst gives comprehensive presentation of the Roman Empire in its political, military, economic, cultural and religious dimensions – the macrostructures. Schottroff concentrates on the problem of patriarchy, which has its original setting in the "house", the *oikos*, and thus in the economic, cultural and religious basis of political community.

I choose these as examples because they are oriented towards liberation theology and feminism. In an opening section where she tackles authors like *Theissen* and *Meeks*, L. Schottroff gives reasons why a sociological approach that claims to be neutral is not appropriate for texts which in an asymetrical power situation – like the mainstream of the Hebrew Bible, I would say – take sides unequivocally with the poor and weak. The main line of her criticism is that the usual model in bourgeois social historical exegesis for distinguishing wandering radicals from the (conforming) love-patriarchalism of local congregations obscures the fact that, on the whole, Christian scriptures maintain the tension between the Kingdom of God and its realisation in messianic groups and communities on the one hand, and social reality in the Roman Empire on the other. Helmut Gollwitzer is specially close in systematic theology terms to these tendencies of biblical theology. The title of his last series of lectures, "Liberation for Solidarity", demonstrates this. And what Karl Barth is getting at, in arguing that "the Christian community and the civic community" should be seen as two concentric circles, is the radiating power of the people of God among the peoples.[99]

Hope in the Kingdom of God with a human face, which will remove all the kingdoms which are so like beasts of prey and the totalitarian Hellenistic and now Roman system, stems from the Jewish resistance coalition. The *Essenes* took this hope with them into the desert, and the *prophetic-messianic groups* took it with them to the poor who had gone underground. Before Jesus, *John the Baptist* appears, obviously coming from these circles, and calls the people to repentance and to conversion – for "the Kingdom of God is near".

---

97 W. Haller, 1989.
98 K. Wengst, 1987; L. Schottroff, 1994.
99 H. Gollwitzer, 1984(2), particularly pp.141ff.; K. Barth, 1946.

Jesus accepts this call, but goes a crucial step further. At the same time as he calls people to repentance and announces the coming Kingdom of God he fulfills its coming.[100] "The Kingdom of God is among you", he says (Lk 17:21). That means God becomes king in the midst of the misery that the Roman Empire causes you. A change of power is announced, a fundamental alteration of relationships in the midst of an apparently hopeless situation that reduces people to powerlessness. How?

Let us anticipate the result. Jesus links up with the *Jewish idea* that Israel should be(come) an *alternative society* which is so attractive that all the peoples should come in astonishment to Zion and change in its image, taking on a human face. When we understand this, it also becomes clear that his concentration on changing people in small groups is all about the conversion of Israel, which in turn is about the transformation of the peoples. Through the "pilgrimage of the peoples" which the prophets saw "the Kingdom of God will assume universal dimensions here in this world".[101] In the prophets it says:

> "In days to come the mountain of the LORD's house shall be set over all other mountains, lifted high above the hills. All the nations shall come streaming to it, and many peoples shall come and say, 'Come, let us climb up on to the mountain of the LORD, to the house of the God of Jacob, that he may teach us his way and we may walk in his paths.' For instruction issues from Zion, and out of Jerusalem comes the word of the LORD; he will be judge between nations, arbiter among many peoples. They shall beat their swords into mattocks and their spears into pruning-knives; nation shall not lift up sword against nation nor ever again be trained for war. O people of Jacob, come, let us walk in the light of the LORD" (Is 2:2-5).

> And the post-exilic Trito-Isaiah says of the expected anointed one (Messiah), whom the old prophets hoped for as a new king who would make Israel "autonomous" and "egalitarian" in keeping with the laws for the year of remission (Deut 15) and the year of jubilee (Lev 25)[102]: "The spirit of the Lord GOD is upon me because the LORD has anointed me; He has sent me to bring good news to the humble, to bind up the broken-hearted, to proclaim liberty to (debt-)captives and release to those in prison; to proclaim a year of the LORD's favour..." (Is 61:1f.) "For Zion's sake I will not keep silence, for Jerusalem's sake I will speak

---

100 C. Burchardt in J. Becker et. al., 1987, p.29, talks of "executing" God's rule.

101 N. Lohfink, 1987, p.114(tr.), and in detail G. Lohfink, 1993, pp.142ff.

102 Cf. Albertz, 1992, pp.485ff.; W. Schottroff, 1986, in L. and W. Schottroff (ed.), 1986, pp.122-135.

out, until her right shines forth like the sunrise, her deliverance like a blazing
torch, until the nations see the triumph of your right and all kings see your
glory." (Is 62:1f.)

Jesus obviously did not see himself as a Jewish king in the way this text (and
many of his contemporaries) hoped for, in the sense of a national restoration.
But in his own way he used this text in combination with others from Isaiah
to sum up his mission, and added: today this has come true (Lk 4:17ff.).

"He opened the scroll and found the passage which says, 'The spirit of the Lord
is upon me because he has anointed me; he has sent me to announce good news
to the poor; to proclaim release for prisoners and recovery of sight for the blind;
to let the broken victims go free, to proclaim the year of the Lord's favour.'
...Then he began to speak: 'Today,' he said, 'in your very hearing this text has
come true.'"

And he addresses to his disciples his Sermon on the Mount, the updating of
Israel's Torah for the alternative lifestyle of the "contrast society", on the understanding that:

"You are the salt of the earth... You are the light of the world. A city built on a
hill-top cannot be hidden... Do not imagine that I have come to abolish the Law
(the Torah) or the Prophets. I have come not to abolish them but to complete
them" (Mt 5:13ff.).

N. Lohfink strikingly summarises the mission of Jesus against the background
of the First Testament as follows:

"God wants to change all societies in the world, and he sets before their eyes an
alternative society – the people of God. This universalising happens via a pilgrimage of the peoples. It requires one changed society to trigger it off, and its object
is further social change... What is new in the New Testament, as opposed to the
whole history of the salvation God had wrought previously in Israel, is the claim
that: now the End seems to be at hand. Final Hopes seem about to be met."[103]

The coming of the Kingdom, which Jesus announces and spreads, comes
about in the way he indicates in his parables in Mt 13: a little yeast leavens all

---

103 N. Lohfink, op. cit., p.116(tr.).

the flour (33); seeds are strewn and grow (1ff.); the darnel among the wheat should not be pulled out yet (24ff.); the tiny mustard-seed grows into a big tree (31f.).[104] The *medium for spreading*, the yeast, the salt, the light, the city on the hill-top, are the emerging groups of disciples. G. Theissen has shown in an essay on group Messianism that Jesus' Messianity consists in the fact that he allows his disciples to take part in it. They bear witness to God's rule as a group:

> "Jesus did not only preach it, he did not only enact it, he also awarded his disciples an exalted position in the Kingdom. They were its witnesses. They participated in his Messianity... In the Jesus tradition it is no longer awarded to Israel as opposed to the Gentiles, but to fringe groups in Israel: the poor, children and followers of Jesus. Tax-gatherers and prostitutes are closer to it than the devout."[105]

That says too – just as in the ancient tradition of Israel – that God's new act of liberation and the *building of the alternative society begins among the excluded, the impoverished and the oppressed.* As in Egypt, they must first be set free from fear of the great power:

> "If it is by the finger of God that I drive out the devils, then be sure the kingdom of God has already come upon you" (Lk 11:20).

Like Theissen, Wengst makes the point that demon-possession as a mass phenomenon obviously has to do with situations of oppression.[106] From there it is surely no accident that according to Mk 5:9 a devil that has been driven out introduces itself by the name of Roman soldiers: "My name is Legion, for there are many of us." Thus Jesus sets oppressed people free. "Therefore the Kingdom of God as a counter-reality means struggle for the reality of this world by changing it, so that equivalences of the expected Kingdom may come in the here and now."[107] Although this means Jesus belongs without ambiguity to the category of Judaean liberation movements, he chooses a different strategy from the Zealots, who opt for armed struggle. "He raises up the powerless and lives with them an alternative to the existing order."[108]

---

104 M. Welker, 1992, describes this process, which Jesus discovers and points out in everyday events, as "emergence". In Christological terms one might also speak of the "incarnation" of the Kingdom of God.
105 G. Theissen, 1992, p.122.
106 Wengst, op. cit.
107 Ibid., p.87(tr.).
108 Ibid., p.88(tr).

Coming as he does from a poor manual worker's background in the peripheral area of Galilee, he deliberately lives among the poor and excluded. Theirs is the Kingdom of God.

"How happy are you who are poor; yours is the kingdom of God" (Lk 6:20).

What is ostensibly well known has here to be repeated. The word Gospel, Good News, which we use today in a non-concrete and generalised sense, has its origin unambiguously in the fact that Jesus says he has to bring "good news to the poor". They are the primary receivers and instruments of the lordship of God, which brings them freedom and solidarity and so inspires the spreading of freedom and solidarity. They are the absolutely poor, inwardly and outwardly[109], in Galilee in the first century of our era – economically, socially, politically, religiously, culturally and psychologically. Luise Schottroff and Wolfgang Stegemann have given this topic comprehensive treatment.[110]

In her latest book Luise Schottroff has also convinced me that the Gospel for the poor can only really be understood and practised if *women*, as the poorest of the poor, are the starting-point.[111] So it is today too, in the empire of the world market. In the South, East and North women are always the first to suffer the destructive consequences of the capitalist market and of the neo-liberal economic and social policies. For that reason the issues of patriarchy and imperialism must be treated as having a common origin. The two pervade each other totally. She has also shown convincingly from Mt 24:37-39 and Lk 17:26-27 and 30[112] that Jesus sees unwillingness to repent, which does not accept the newness of the Kingdom of God, to be anchored in the structures of the patriarchal family. Drinking, eating and marrying – that was what people were doing before the Flood. They are doing the same today, before catastrophe overwhelms them in judgement, says Jesus. But those who herald God's great reshaping of the world at the birth of Jesus the Messiah are women – Mary and Elizabeth:

---

109 Cf. L Schottroff, 1994, p.207, against the spiritualising interpretation of the Matthaean version, which pronounces blessed the "poor in spirit".

110 L. Schottroff and W. Stegemann, 1981(2), Jesus von Nazareth - Hoffnung der Armen (Jesus of Nazareth - Hope of the poor; cf. also N. Lohfink, 1987, pp.138ff.

111 Cf. particularly L. Schottroff, 1994, pp.206ff., the section on "The Gospel for the poor and the option for women" (tr.).

112 L. Schottroff, 1994, pp.228ff.

"He has pulled down princes from their thrones and exalted the lowly. The hungry he has filled with good things, the rich sent empty away" (Lk 1:52). L. Schottroff on this[113]: "Mary and Elizabeth proclaim prophetically God's world revolution, his option for the poor which begins as an option for Mary and for women: She is '*of all women...*the most blessed' (Lk 1:42)."

And God's rule belongs to *children* (Mk 10:14f.). With the same tendency to one-sidedness, Jesus calls upon *manual workers* – women and men – and those who do not know how they and their families will get through the next day: "Come to me, all whose work is hard, whose load is heavy" (Mt 11:28).[114]

And the *rich*? In the curses that are appended to the Beatitudes in Luke (6:24), no threat is directed at the rich and no call to repentance is uttered. Their future is simply predicted.[115] "It is easier for a camel to pass through the eye of a needle than for a rich man to enter the kingdom of God" (Mk 10:25). That too is a statement of reality. So much is certain: "The last will be first, and the first last" (Mt 20:16).[116] In the Kingdom of God the relationships that shape society will be reversed. But that does not mean Jesus reacts meanly or vindictively when members of the upper class come to him. Luke in particular reports that there are also rich people who convert (e.g. Ch. 19, the story of Zacchaeus). When they do this they are welcome – as the last comers. But the new society builds up from below, near to God, in clear contrast to the surrounding reality of the Roman Empire, heir to the tributary systems of the ancient Near East.

Jesus says clearly, in a text crucial for our thesis, that in Israel an alternative society for the Gentiles is forming from below out of the groups of disciples. It brings us to the question: What is *the socio-economic alternative* Jesus has in mind? We have already seen that (in Lk 4) Jesus takes up various points from the Torah: the cancellation of debts, the liberation of slaves, non-discrimination and healing of the sick. In the following text Jesus summarises that into one idea: *mutual service.*[117]

---

113 Ibid., pp.281ff.(tr.).
114 G. Theissen, 1989, pp.353ff., has shown very nicely that this word about the "weary and heavy-laden" in this sense expressly means those who work with their hands.
115 Cf. Schottroff and Stegemann, 1981(2), pp.35F.
116 Ibid., p.36.
117 Cf. Wengst, op. cit., and L. Schottroff, 1994, pp.297ff.

"You know that in the world the recognised rulers lord it over their subjects, and their great men make them feel the weight of authority. That is not the way with you; among you, whoever wants to be great must be your servant, and whoever wants to be first must be the willing slave of all" (Mk 10:42ff. and Mt 20:25ff.).

On the one hand, this saying of Jesus summarises a whole polit-economic *analysis*: Rome and its accomplices in the upper class in Palestine's centre and periphery represent nothing but oppression and violent exploitation. Saying this clearly is in itself liberating. It creates distance. It *deprives the system of any legitimation*. It de-ideologises it. The whole Pax Romana is just oppression and exploitation. There is nothing there to tame, nothing worth transforming.

On the other hand, the *alternative* is beginning among you: mutual service. L. Schottroff has shown that *diakonein*, to the extent that it has to do with table service, means the kinds of caring which, under the patriarchal distribution of roles, are done just by slaves and women, never by free men. But here serving – far from meaning organised charitable work in a social system otherwise defined by exploitation and authority – is understood as typifying a counter-culture in which exploitation and oppressive authority are put aside. In the house all are like brothers and sisters. That links up with the family solidarity of the pre-state and post-exilic egalitarian society of peasant families, but it goes beyond that. Even the patriarchal structure of the house itself is to be transformed, although this is only consistent with Israel's egalitarian tendency.

Here equality in principle is assumed, and its vitality is in mutual service. The disciples of Jesus build a counter-model to the world's authority structure.[118]

L. Schottroff points out that Jesus' central idea, loving one's neighbour, meant this kind of family solidarity as early as in Deuteronomy and the Holiness Code. That implies that with Jesus love in the socio-economic sense means precisely acting like brothers and sisters, through which there occurs in the house and between houses a completely equal form of cooperation in mutual service. The term "slave *of all*" signifies that brother-and-sisterliness, mutuality and solidarity do not stop at the borders of the patriarchal house.

118 Wengst, op. cit.

The text in Mark 10 ends by anchoring this new community structure in God's and Jesus' own actions, and here L. Schottroff translates "Son of Man" from Daniel 7 very nicely as "the human one":[119]

> "For even the human one did not come to be served but to serve, and to give up his life as a ransom for many" (Mk 10:45).

The gospels are full of stories with this motif. Particularly telling is Jesus' washing of the disciples' feet before their last meal together. *Meals together* are the heart of brother-and-sisterliness, cutting across the norms of the patriarchal household. *All* are invited. This links up with the joyful feasts held each year in Deuteronomy 14. The Kingdom of God as a feast at which all are satisfied is now no longer purely a universal future. It is beginning, in Jesus' liberating presence, among those who stand on the sidelines and are hungry – through sharing and mutual service. The Lord's Supper in the Christian community, when it involves real sharing, is really the core of the Kingdom of God which Jesus brings.

In the Kingdom of God what counts is the *satisfaction of basic needs*: eating, drinking, having clothes, having somewhere to live, being healed, having freedom. Whether people have helped "the least" to get their share – that is what "the human one" will ask and judge us on when the Kingdom of God is here in its fullness (Mt 25:31ff.). That assumes that where production is concerned Jesus' starting point is simply the ancient Jewish tradition of the peasant/craftsman subsistence economy. That accounts for his radical rejection of the "treasure-storing", money-making economy of the Hellenistic-Roman system. He calls it *Mammon*:

> "No servant can be the slave of two masters; for either he will hate the first and love the second, or he will be devoted to the first and think nothing of the second. You cannot serve God and Mammon" (Mt 6:24).[120]

Just as Elijah called upon people to decide between Baal, the god of the accumulation of land and royal power, and Yahweh, so Jesus calls upon them to

---

119 L. Schottroff, 1994, pp.311f.
120 Cf. appositely D. Pauly, 1988, p.22(tr.): "Under this judgement falls the name of a god called, in the New Testament and elsewhere, 'Mammon'. This means more than 'money', rather the whole interwoven complex of economic, legal, political, social and religious factors. The biblical word 'idols' designates nothing other than bankrupt systems which produce injustice and dissension."

decide between Mammon, a system for accumulating money and power, and God. The poor need not be anxious. For when they take part in the Kingdom of God and the justice of its brother-and-sisterly sharing, they will lack nothing; things to eat, things to drink, things to wear and all the rest will come to them (Mt 6:33).

Ironically, the text always misused as a formula for Jesus' conformity to the politico-economic system of the Empire actually says, in the question about paying taxes to the Emperor, that the disciples of Jesus should refuse to use coins and currency ("the story of Caesar's penny", Mk 12:13-17).[121] Jesus has someone give him a coin – he does not have one himself. He points to Caesar's image on the coin – it belongs to Caesar and should be returned to him. But you people, whose image do you bear? God's – so give yourselves to God. There is no co-existence between the imperial system and the Kingdom of God here.

Jesus also rejects the whole system of Temple taxes and Temple economy, for it only exploits the poor and turns the Temple into a robbers' cave. In a symbolic action he upsets the entire Temple business in the so-called Cleansing of the Temple (Mk 11:15ff.). By this he continues the exilic and post-exilic attempts to set Israel free from the unholy alliance of royal court and state priesthood by lifting the double tribute – though these attempts were increasingly thwarted by the priestly aristocracy in Jerusalem. It is therefore not surprising that the story of the Cleansing of the Temple concludes with the comment: "The chief priests and the doctors of the law heard of this and sought some means of making away with him; for they were afraid of him, because the whole crowd was spellbound by his teaching."

It is no wonder that the upper class of his own people and the Roman empire – the coalition of economic, ideological and political power – wanted to get rid of the inspiration behind this alternative society. *Jesus' Passion* and his *death on* the cross – the Roman punishment for political agitators – are an almost logical consequence of his message, his life and his acts. More a matter for wonder is the fact that the Kingdom of God, which had begun to unfold its power in a new way through Jesus, could not on his death be relegated again to a future world of distant hopes. The disciples were severely disturbed by Jesus' death (only the women had dared to attend his crucifixion at a distance); Jesus' appearances strengthened their belief that in him God had

121 Cf. Wengst, op. cit.; L. Schottroff, 1984, in J. Moltmann (ed.), 1984, pp.15ff.

already brought about the resurrection of the dead for which they all waited in apocalyptic hope. Thus it became evident to them that God had affirmed Jesus and that he was mediating to them the Messianic Spirit again and anew by the power of the resurrection. Theissen says correctly that the messianic groups around Jesus were the origin of the Church.[122]

This is expressed in Luke's *Pentecost story* in Acts 2. The outpouring of the Spirit is presented explicitly there as the opposite to the story of the Tower of Babel (cf. Acts 2 with Gen 11). Babel stands for the empire, whose economic, political, military and ideological-cultural power is symbolised in the "tower" and in the imposition of a single imperial language.[123] In the Pentecost story God has everyone keep their own language but still understand each other (as equals). And the Messianic Spirit falls upon "everyone", including young people, slaves and women, as the prophet Joel (2:28-32) promised.

A new brother-and-sisterly community emerges, sharing everything[124]: the discernment of God through the teaching of the apostles, living fellowship with God through prayer, daily meals together which serve both to remind members about Jesus and to fill stomachs (thus avoiding a division into liturgical and material), and common life. This includes "their giving up private property *voluntarily and according to need* for the sake of communal tasks in the community"[125]. This too, like the joy spoken of in these texts (Acts 2:41ff. and 4:32ff.), reminds us of the feasts and the sharing with the poor of the surplus yield, as described in Deut 14f. There it says only: "Let there be no poor among you" (15:4); but here it says that there were in fact no longer poor among them: "None of their members was ever in want" (Acts 4:34). A life-sustaining economy! That is why between the sentence about the common use of their goods and the one about there being no want, there is another sentence: "The apostles continued to testify to the resurrection of the Lord Jesus with great power, and they were all given great respect" (4:33). Witnessing to Jesus' resurrection, to life's victory over death, occurs when an alternative society succeeds, in the midst of a system of death, of the Horsemen of the Apocalypse (Rev 6), in making provision for the life of all and sharing like sisters and brothers. This is mission among the peoples.

---

122 G. Theissen, 1992, p.122.
123 Cf. H.C. Uehlinger, 1990.
124 L. Schottroff, 1994, pp.316ff.
125 Ibid., p.316(tr.); the term "community of goods" is thus not sharp enough.

Mission to the peoples in the sense of an attractive society in contrast to the Roman Empire with its tributary oppression and exploitation – now, after Jesus' death, that society spills out of its original Palestinian setting and spreads into all parts of the Roman *oikoumene* and beyond. Matthew, the same evangelist who had reported of Jesus that he called his disciples salt of the earth, light of the world, a city on a hill-top, ends his gospel with Jesus' commission to take to all the peoples baptism and the teaching – and for him that means the practice – of the new community shaped by the Sermon on the Mount (Mt 28:16-20):

> "According to Mt 28:19f. the peoples no longer go to Zion in order to be taught, the disciples go to the peoples in order to teach them Jesus' messianic interpretation of the Torah. Outwardly, therefore, the direction of the movement has reversed. Nevertheless, this reversal has not abolished the mental model of the pilgrimage of the peoples. The disciples, sent by the Resurrected One into all the world, are to make the peoples communities of disciples, and these communities, as the New Testament understands it, are what God builds at the end of time out of living stones. So the city on the hill-top is built everywhere in the world where Jesus communities are formed. And since these communities are to fascinate and attract the heathen society round about them, there is again a centripetal direction of the pilgrimage of the peoples. The Church fathers, at any rate, interpreted Is 2:1-5 in precisely this sense."[126]

The apostle to the peoples is *Paul.* Some are of the opinion that he betrayed the direction shown by Jesus and that he conformed to the Roman Empire and patriarchy, spiritualising the Gospel instead of proclaiming its concrete social, economic and political alternative. That is quite wrong. Despite all possible criticism on points of detail, we have to say that Paul did remain true to Jesus' basic direction. Just as Jesus inspired wandering preachers, groups and house-meetings in Palestine, so Paul gives rise to messianic groups and communities through the spreading Jewish diaspora, in the whole Roman Empire and specially in urban settings. Without repeating their argument here, I agree with L. Schottroff and others that the contrast between the Jesus movement and "love-patriarchalism" in Paul is a modern invention.[127] Relevant here are works by José Miranda and Elsa Tamez, who have situated the

---

126 G. Lohfink, 1993, p.145(tr.).
127 Schottroff, op. cit., pp.20ff. and pp.27ff.

Pauline message of God's righteousness clearly in the historical context of the Roman Empire.[128]

First of all, it is clear that Pauline communities consisted overwhelmingly of poor people, social outcasts and manual workers – which, as with the groups around Jesus, did not exclude the possibility of some well-to-do people joining them.[129]

There are those who obscure this clear fact – for which Paul supplies explicit theological reasons – by defending the sociological proposition that Pauline communities simply consisted of a normal cross-section of the population.[130] Yet Paul writes unambiguously to the Corinthian community:

"My brothers, think what sort of people you are, whom God has called. Few of you are men of wisdom, by any human standard; few are powerful or highly born. Yet, to shame the wise, god has chosen what the world counts folly, and to shame what is strong, God has chosen what the world counts weakness. He has chosen things low and contemptible, mere nothings, to overthrow the existing order." (1 Cor 1:26-28)

Thus it is no coincidence that in the hymn of Philippians 2:6ff. Paul does not write simply, "Jesus became a human being", but, "Jesus assumed the condition of a *slave*".[131]

Paul presents his *overall conception* in the *Letter to the Congregation in Rome*, in order to introduce himself before his visit. His object is to show that not only Jews but also Greeks (and all other peoples of the Roman Empire) are, through faith in God's righteousness as revealed in Christ, saved for life and changed, and are thus able to overcome this world, which stands under the power of sin, the law and death. He summarises the reality of the Roman Empire, from which he starts, in this sentence:

"The anger of God is being revealed from heaven against all the impiety (*asebeia*) and depravity (*adikia*) of men who keep truth imprisoned in their wickedness". (1:18)

---

128 J. Miranda, 1974, and E. Tamez, 1993. Cf. also J. Moltmann's attempt to distinguish concretely "Justice for Victims and Culprits" (1994, pp.74ff.tr.).
129 For arguments against softening this basic insight in Meeks, 1983, (despite all need to differentiate) see L. Schottroff, 1994.
130 Cf. L. Schottroff, 1994, pp.224ff., against Theissen and Meeks; on this as well E. Tamez, 1993, pp.61ff.
131 Cf. L. Schottroff, 1994, pp.71ff.

It is important here for us to free ourselves from the inbred inclination to put theology onto the level of universal ideas. "Mankind", "human beings" – anyone who starts, with European patterns of thought in their head, to theologise about, or on the basis of, this idea will understand nothing of the rest of Romans. With bourgeois individualist ideology we will always falsify what Paul means. The situational analysis that follows these verses of Paul is oriented wholly to the ancient Israelite and Jewish approach of linking criticism of idolatry and social criticism. This approach is traditional in that again and again the Israelites and then the Jews applied these strict criteria. But they always did so in a new way, depending on the actual situation. So what does Paul say about the situation in the Roman Empire at the time (Rom 1:19ff.)?

They worship "making" (the creature) instead of their Maker, so God has abandoned them to their degrading passions (*epithymiai*) – the same word by which Plato and Aristotle in their political analyses characterised forms of conduct which are destructive of community, Aristotle particularly highlighting the money-making economy. Not without reason does greed[132] stand high in the list of vices which explains Paul's understanding of injustice. The summary at the end says: "They are...without solidarity ('love' in the sense of Deuteronomy and the Holiness Code) and pity." I cannot do a full exegesis of this passage here.[133] But it is clear, first, that for Paul the whole social reality in the Roman-Hellenistic culture and social order is characterised by injustice and, second, that in this all-perverting reality of structural sin even the good, God-given Torah has been taken captive and the Jews do not obey it. It follows that all are unrighteous before God.

There are specific historical reasons, dating back to the apocalyptic writings, why Paul can and must generalise like that and then draw in the historical Christ event and its concrete effects. The centralised rule (see Aristotle) of the Hellenistic Empire and its almost universal adoption of a monetary system gave rise to an all-pervading, totalitarian order culminating in the Roman Empire. Here there was no escaping the power of sin, which had left its mark on all structures. With that in mind, Israel's series of experiences with empires looked like the single, continuous experience of the whole of humanity since Adam, revealing its inescapable subjection to the power of sin as manifested in

---

132 Cf. L. Schottroff, 1986, in: L. and W. Schottroff (ed.), 1986, p.137.
133 It may be seen as a misfortune in terms of historical effect that Paul here, instead of continuing to detail other social sins, picks on homosexual love as a special example of where "degrading passions" can lead to.

death-bringing structures and behaviour (Rom 5:12ff.). The experience of totalitarian structures in the Hellenistic-Roman system no longer left any niche for Israel's alternative society and even changed the Torah, revealed by God to give them life, into an instrument of death. That is what lies behind this universal statement about humanity from Adam. By going from the specific to the general, Paul has deliberately chosen not to discuss a general idea first and then "apply" it to reality.[134]

By the same token, God's intervention to create justice must occur in equally concrete historical terms. And that is the Christ event, which again does not occur in an abstract heaven of ideas, but is linked inseparably with the gathering of a new humanity among the peoples, a new humanity in Christ (Rom 5:15ff.): which means a messianic humanity. For *Christos* is only the Greek for Messiah, the anointed one of God. What this is about is quite clearly said in Rom 7:14ff.; it is not about a new, general concept of justice. Everyone has that somehow through common sense, indeed, we all want what is just. But how can justice be *done*? This is not possible in the sinful structures of the world as we know it (cf. Rom 12:2) but *is* possible for those who build communities around Jesus the Messiah, and are empowered to act by his Spirit (Rom 8). These structures are driven by the sin of self-love, leading to death; since people cannot set themselves free and obtain justice, God's act of liberation in his Messiah, through his Spirit, is the only way out. Paul calls the acceptance of this act of liberation by the God of Israel faith. This faith is nothing other than opening oneself to God's just-*making* righteousness. God offers this possibility, quite tangibly, in community with the Messiah, without any preconditions that people under the power of sin could not fulfill anyway. So his Spirit floods their hearts (Rom 5:5). This Spirit changes peoples' bodies from being instruments for injustice and death into instruments for justice and life (Rom 6). In the messianic community of the Spirit no-one is excluded any longer, unlike in the Roman system (Rom 8).[135] With these signs of hope, the whole world is being brought by the Spirit out of a slave-

---

134 This is comparable to what Augustine makes of the fall of the Roman Empire in *De Civitate Dei* (On the community of God). Beginning from the concrete historical event of the destruction of Rome (410 AD), he sees the entire history, anthropology and even cosmology together as one story about God's fight against the structures of self-love - a fight which has as its goal a distinctive community by its love for God and one's neighbour. Cf. in addition U. Duchrow, 1983(2), pp.181ff.; J. Millbank, 1990, pp.380ff.
135 This is the core statement of the book I cited by Elsa Tamez.

owner society into the freedom of the children of God; indeed, the whole creation, which now groans beneath human violence and its ruinous consequences[136], is being drawn into the hope of a Spirit-led humanity in Christ. The whole belief in fate engendered by the apparently inescapable system of death and its "powers" is smashed by this certainty: that nothing can separate us from the love, the solidarity of God, which makes us just within the community of the Messiah Jesus, and gives us hope.

The one who does this is the God of Israel (Rom 9-11).[137] Since the way via Israel's attractive alternative society was cut off by the fact that in Jesus' time the whole people could not be converted by God's act of liberation, God in his goodness uses this (partial) refusal in order now to build this "different" society of love and justice directly among the peoples. In this way Israel will in fact be so fascinated by this fulfilment of the Torah among the nations that the entire population will join in after all, in the Last Days. For "the whole law is summed up in love" (Rom 13:10). So here we have the model of the witness people, who attract others to Yahweh and to join them. The signposting of justice in a solidarity-based society – thereby fulfilling the Torah – typifies the relations Paul wants between Christian and Jewish congregations. (After the tragic behaviour of a large part of Christendom towards the Jews over the centuries, right up to the Holocaust, that now sounds more like a word of judgement than of promise.)

> At this point we should perhaps take a closer look at Luther and Neo-Lutheranism. In his anti-monastic struggle Luther stressed Paul's belief that righteousness or justice comes not by works but by faith. In his own day the "antinomians" were already drawing the wrong conclusion that it was all right not to bother about the material realisation of justice since the law had been annulled. Luther tried to counter this fatal misunderstanding in his polemic writings, but the accent on "cheap grace" (Bonhoeffer) has remained characteristic of considerable parts of the Lutheran Church until today.[138]

---

136 Cf. Duchrow and Liedke, 1989, p.52 and p.61.
137 Cf. K. Stendahl, 1976, pp.28ff.
138 Cf. U. Duchrow, 1987, pp.41ff.; with quotations from Luther's writings on the "antinomians", e.g. from *On Councils and Churches*: "For just as these people reject and misconstrue the Ten Commandments, so too they talk loudly of the grace of Christ. But they strengthen and comfort those who persist in their sins by telling them...these sins have all been washed away by Christ. They see people commit notorious and public sins but then let them go on doing so with no change or improvement in their lives. It is

At this point we must reformulate the question about Paul's *overall under-standing of "church"*, and therefore of congregations and messianic groups. W.A. Meeks has given the most detailed description of this in his book *The First Urban Christians*.[139] He brings together carefully all the individual elements, but in my opinion misses the point of the whole. It is not in dispute that for Paul *ekklesia* is the key concept.[140] But what does it mean? In secular Greek it denotes the assembly of the free men of a city republic, e.g. Athens. In the Jewish usage of the Greek Bible (Septuagint) it denotes the institution of the People's Assembly of free peasants in early Israel (*qehal YHWH*, which became popular again after the Exile as the place where the whole people made important decisions, besides the other organs of self-government, the Council of Elders and the College of Priests. Since the synagogue communities of the Jewish diaspora at the time of Paul do not use this term, and since on the other hand Paul does not use the word "synagogue" for Christian communities, it is clear that this choice of term must be deliberate. In other words, in order to characterise the "church" Paul goes back consciously to the initiatives by which Israel tried to build an egalitarian society in contrast to the tributary kingship system – precisely in order to be the witness people of the liberating God.[141]

How exactly is this *ekklesia* structured in Paul? The one *ekklesia* comes into being at all levels, both locally and universally in the whole Roman Empire (the whole *oikoumene*), but also in its individual provinces[142] – and without any hierarchy, in the mutual solidarity of love. The smallest cell of the complete "people's assembly of God" is the house-church (*he kat'oikon ekklesia*), e.g. Rom 16:5,19; Phlm 2). It is ekklesia not only when it meets, however, but

---

quite clear from this that they do not really understand the Christian faith and Christ, abolishing them even as they preach them" (ibid., p.42). Luther sees like Paul that the Holy Spirit brings about the fulfilment of the Commandments, although with him this insight is not worked out ecclesiologically, so that he is not without blame for later misguided developments.

139 W.A. Meeks, 1983, Chap. 3 about the *ekklesia*.
140 Cf. also L. Schottroff, 1994, p.314, and G. Janowski, 1990, pp.20f.
141 In view of this it is not at all confusing, and also legitimate because of secular Greek usage, to think of the Greek cities' attempts at republican democracy when using this word. And indeed the Jewish concept of the qehal *YHWH*, the People's Assembly of free, equal men under the leadership of the liberating God, criticises the ancient Near Eastern tributary social structure much more fundamentally than the Greek democratic structure.
142 Cf. Meeks, op. cit., p.108.

also when, in all areas of life, including economic activities, it reveals that it belongs to the Messiah of the new Israel, to the new creation. All the house-churches and groups in one village or town are one *ekklesia* (e.g. in Corinth, 1 Cor 11:18). It is also possible to address the ekklesiai (plural) of a province together (1 Cor 16:1, etc.).

> It is important to point out that Paul also uses the Jewish word "holy ones" (or "saints") when addressing these alternative cells and their networks locally, in the provinces and in the whole Roman Empire (1 Cor 1:2; Rom 15:25f.; etc.). That means that Paul here picks up the language of the post-exilic priestly document and Deuteronomy, where the expression implies two things: this people chosen from among the peoples is "holy", and thus different from them because it belongs to God, who is holy, i.e. liberating and practising solidarity (1 Cor 16:1, etc.).

Paul explains very graphically how the new humanity in Christ in the shape of messianic, charismatic *ekklesiai* live the justice of God in love and hope of the victory of life over death – focussed on mutuality, brother-and-sisterliness and the support of the weak (Rom 12ff.). I cannot go into this here, but I should like to indicate the detail with which Paul, in the Letter to the Galatians, works out the key differences between this and the dominating, oppressive structures of the Roman system: in the *ekklesia* there is no inequality between different ethnic groups, between masters and slaves and between women and men.

> "For through faith you are all sons of god in union with Christ Jesus. Baptised into union with him (i.e. made part in fellowship with him of one body, inspired by one Spirit), you have all put on (the form of) Christ as a garment. There is no such thing as Jew and Greek, slave and freeman, male and female; for you are all one person in Christ Jesus" (Gal 3:26-28).

By this Paul takes Israel's idea of being Yahweh's egalitarian "different" society another three steps further than Israel itself.[143] 1. Through God's grace in Jesus the Messiah, people from all nations are now made worthy to enter into the inheritance of Israel's alternative way of life and structures of society. From all races people are now called to become a light to the nations, salt of

---

143 Cf. G. Jankowski, 1990, pp.70ff.

the earth, leaven, the witness people of God. There should also be no more ranking among the different peoples. Any false idea that election might serve imperial interests is out. Now no-one is excluded. And no-one must take over other peoples' cultural and cultic monuments. 2. Not just at the macrostructural level but at the microstructural as well, in the household, the domination and exploitation of slavery should not just be softened and then periodically cancelled as in the Torah, but abolished on principle. 3. Even the most subtle of domination relationships, that between men and women, is done away with. In this way within the old humanity, characterised by sin and death, there grows a new humanity, set free by Christ's Spirit, which is one of justice and life at all levels and in all relationships.

That also has far-reaching consequences for our understanding of Paul's *mission* (and, of course, all other aspects of his theology). Building up these alternative cells, extending their number and strengthening their network in the whole *oikoumene*, so that they become a "holy" people witnessing to God, free of domination and exploitation, bound together in love, starting with the weakest – that is mission. This mission-by-fascination no longer happens through one people alone but in many ethnically mixed groups of the Messiah Jesus with no class or gender discrimination, scattered throughout all the nations yet united in one Body.

Now, one must of course ask whether Paul consistently maintained this basic idea of the Church as an alternative society consisting of small *ekklesiai* bound together in the freedom of Christ. With regard to "Jews and Greeks" Paul certainly made his vision work. Building the *universal* "contrast society" among the peoples was his life's task. With regard to slaves and free men, his witness remains fragmentary. In 1 Cor 11 he fulminates against the fact that the common meal to commemorate Jesus excludes from the stomach-filling part slaves who come later because of work. With the solution he proposes, however, that the rich should eat at home, he dangerously separates congregational practice from life in society.[144] And the way he deals with the question of slaves in the Letter to Philemon is certainly a start on the way to an egalitarian society. Clearly the master-slave relationship should indeed be overcome at the personal level. Thus he takes Jesus' way of indirect strategy. Central for him is his request for equality between the messianic communities in the

---

144 Cf. L. Schottroff, 1994, p.316.

matter of collections.[145] He collects money for the "holy ones" in Jerusalem so that there may be equality (*isotes*) in one Body of Christ (2 Cor 8:13).

His position concerning the Roman state is not always consistent with his own theology. To be sure, Rom 13:1-7 does not say what was read into it for centuries. The object of the passage is to give a declaration of loyalty, which was required of all peoples and religious communities in the Roman Empire. He does this very cleverly, in that he limits loyalty to the Roman authorities to what can be checked outwardly, namely criminal jurisdiction and taxes. He expressly omits all reference to the (equally required) main point of public law, worship of the Emperor, which was imposed on all subject peoples in order to test their *absolute* loyalty.[146] This means he judges the situation according to the criterion "bring them all to the test and then keep what is good" (cf. 1 Thess 5:21 and Rom 12:2). Nevertheless, one might wonder if the rather strained theological justification of two parts of the Roman code of public law does not overshoot the target of protecting the congregations from further encroachments by the Roman Empire when he calls tribute collectors "God's servants".[147]

Similarly, various statements about the subordination of women in the church are a step back from Jesus. They are themselves in tension with Gal 3:29. But there too Paul has a rather divided position, for in regarding the unmarried state as superior he adopts a critical attitude towards patriarchal marriage, and goes unequivocally for "brother-and-sisterliness", not power relationships.[148]

I know, of course, that the normal explanation runs like this: Paul did not want to revolutionise the existing order directly but to soften and change it from inside, rather like Jesus' leaven. But that goes for structures other than the congregation! "Among you it is not so," says Jesus. In the messianic communities a clearer transformation of relationships would have been thinkable, in keeping with the "contrast society" which Paul clearly envisaged.

Despite all these slight limitations in its practical application, Paul's whole approach splendidly continued and even surpassed the attempts made again and again since the early days of Israel to create a people of God among the

---

145 Cf. D. Georgi, 1992.
146 Cf. L. Schottroff, 1984, in: J. Moltmann, 1984, pp.15ff.
147 In this I relativise some of my assumptions in U. Duchrow, 1983(2), pp.137ff., but I cannot go into details here.
148 L. Schottroff, 1994, pp.182ff. etc.

peoples. This new people was, through the freedom God effected and willed and through mutual solidarity, to reject the existing structures of oppression and exploitation and to attempt to shape an alternative society free fom the enslaving and deadly idols of power.

Certainly, there are some canonical writings which reflect a more thorough adaptation to Roman society. These include above all the Pastoral Epistles.[149] Particularly crass, however, is the adaptation of the Church to the Empire in the post-canonical First Letter of Clement (about 96 AD), written direct from Rome after the end of Domitian's persecution of Christians.[150] But from the other later writings of the Second Testament and Christian witnesses up to the middle of the second century we can establish clearly that Christian communities were at odds with the Roman Empire and saw themselves as offering an alternative to it.

The sharpest contrast is expressed in the last book of the Bible, the *Revelation of John*, written about 95 AD at the end of Domitian's persecution.[151] Here Daniel's great theme of the kingdoms and the Kingdom of God is taken up openly once more in order to strengthen in endurance and hope the congregations of Asia Minor in their situation of persecution and martyrdom. Ch. 6 gives a pertinent analysis of the Roman system, to the effect that it only has a little time longer in which to rage, before the Judgement comes. The analysis results in the vision of the so-called "horsemen of the Apocalypse", as they are experienced by oppressed people:

"There before my eyes was *a white horse*, and its rider held a bow. He was given a crown, and he rode forth, conquering and to conquer" (6:2). This is none other than the "divine" head of the system, the Emperor.

"Out came another *horse, all red*. To its rider was given power to take peace from the earth adn make men slaughter one another; and he was given a great sword" (6:4). This too is clear: the Roman military is meant.

"There, as I looked, was *a black horse*, and its rider held in his hand a pair of scales. And I heard what sounded like a voice from the midst of the living creatures, which said, 'A whole day's wage for a quart of flour, a whole day's wage for three quarts of barley-meal! But spare the olive and the vine'" (6:5f.). This needs explanation, though here too the meaning is clear: economy, the merchant. But what about the details?[152] The day's wage is what a day-labourer earns. A quart of

---

149 Cf. for example ibid., pp.104ff.
150 Cf. Wengst, op. cit.
151 Cf. ibid.

flour is the amount per head of the daily cereal ration for soldiers. That means that a day labourer has no way of buying for his day's wage the basic nutrition for a whole family. That means wages and prices together are making things extremely expensive for the poor, so that they must suffer hunger. On the other hand luxury goods for the rich, oil and wine, are, cynically, untouched.[153] "There, as I looked, was another horse, sickly pale; and its rider's name was *Death*, and Hades came close behind. To him was given power over a quarter of the earth, with the right to kill *by sword and by famine*, by pestilence and by wild beasts" (6:8). This is death by the violence of the entire system, by war, hunger and epidemic, and it is brought about by "wild beasts". These are kings, i.e. not just the Emperor but also the Emperor's satellites.

John himself unlocks this allegorical language when he says, a few verses on, that the whole society of slavery and violence will face Judgement:

"*Then the kings of the earth, magnates* and marshals, the rich and the powerful, and all men, slave or free, *hid themselves in caves and mountain crags*"(6:15).

As the drama of the Judgement continues, we hear in Ch. 13 of the beasts from the abyss, the Roman Empire and its political and ideological head, the Emperor, and the fact that outside this system no-one can buy and sell. That is why all those who have become rich with the whore of Babylon – the symbol of Rome – fall with her (Ch. 18).

"Your traders were once the merchant princes of the world, and with your sorcery you deceived all the nations. For the blood of the prophets and of God's people was found in her, the blood of all who had been done to death on earth" (18:23f.).[154]

The new heaven and the new earth, which the seer John contemplates and which begins with the persecuted messianic groups, will take the shape of a new Jerusalem. In this city God will live among his people, and there will be no more suffering and death. The city will have no closed gates, and no Temple. In it the water of life will flow (21f.).

---

152 Cf. L. Schottroff, 1994, pp.244f.

153 Cf. K.H. Kroon, 1988, p.71.

154 Cf. P.A. Nogeira de Souza, 1991.

Life is the theme of the last chapter of the Bible, just as it was of the first. What began in the communities of the Messiah amongst suffering and martyrdom – the alternative society with God at its centre – becomes worldwide, creation-wide reality.

Thus the texts I have chosen from the Jesus movement and the early Christian communities show a clear continuity with Israel. They are all about God's alternative society amongst the peoples, which will draw them in, give them freedom and involve them in the justice of mutual solidarity. Even in the context of totalitarianism the approach is, beside dissent, to set up small-scale alternatives and to network between them. After Jesus has been rejected by some of his people and killed by the Romans this widens into a "missionary movement" in the sense that attractive, messianic communities arise among all the peoples. What the Jews began is carried further – now the new communities include all peoples, slaves and women, living together in mutual solidarity as complete equals.

How can we make the riches of the biblical traditions of the First and Second Testaments fruitful for our situation?

Resistance to the kingdoms of the world and alternatives for life – what does it mean today?

The struggle of the freed Hebrew slaves and a new independent, solidarity-based society in early Israel, the prophets' struggle to tame the kingship system, the new beginnings after its failure, and, finally, the resistance struggle and signposting of a wholly new society in the face of empires that have turned totalitarian – biblical traditions show that these events always follow from people recollecting earlier history, relating that to their situation, and attempting to introduce practices and structures consistent with the liberation and solidarity that the recollection revealed.[1] Does this really help us to know what to do today? In technical terms we are now back to the hermeneutical question.[2]

1   Five biblical rules for recollecting the past

1   The key starting point is the *place* from which we ask our questions when, for the sake of our own present and future, we recollect biblical texts. Yahweh does not reveal himself in some neutral place (for example, in the mind of an intellectual, then called a "wise man"), nor in the court or temple of Pharaoh, but in the desert to Moses, the representative of an exploited, oppressed group of slaves (Ex 3). The prophets are persecuted by the royal court and, like Elijah, stay in the home of a poor widow or, like Amos, work with the movements of peasants who are under threat and facing poverty. The post-exilic Holiness Code, for example Lev 25 with its rules about the Jubilee year, seeks to protect the socio-economic interests of specific population groups: slaves, debtors, those forced to sell their houses and so on. The revelation of the

---

1   F. Crüsemann, 1992, p.329(tr.), speaks, in relation to the emergence of the Pentateuch as Israel's foundation document in the Persian Empire, of the linking of "recollecting history and indicating the present", of story and law.

2   Cf. the opening comments to Part II, above.

Kingdom of God with a human face in Jewish apocalyptic writings gives rise
to hope among those oppressed by a universal, ultimately totalitarian system
who live either underground in active or passive resistance, or in exile. Jesus
defines very precisely the place where he, the "human one" of the Kingdom of
God, must be met: with those whose basic needs are unsatisfied, the hungry,
the thirsty, the naked, the homeless, the sick, and those who (above all because of debt) are in prison (Mt 25:31ff.). Here the Bible is quite *clear*. This is
the pattern running through it,[3] and seen from here all its statements about
economics become unambiguous[4] (situations will differ but not the point of
departure). This represents a fundamental problem for theology and the
church in a western middle-class society and thus for me personally, in that I
work – in the official part of my professional role at least – for such a church
and – even if *privatissime et gratis* – with the Theology Faculty of a German
university. The situation must be crystal clear to Latin American liberation
theologians, who do their theological work side by side with popular movements and base communities. It is also not at all surprising that in recent
decades spontaneous reading and understanding of the Bible has occurred,
like a Reformation, among these people at the grassroots. Clearly, the biblical
writings, which were by and large written by those under threat, on the periphery or under pressure from imperial powers, have been taken up and
understood more directly by people in a similar situation than by representatives of countries and classes at the centre. For those the question is: is
there a possibility of coming to the place of clarity, that is to the side of the
poor, the excluded and the oppressed? This we must consider in the Third
Part. But the place is defined clearly and unambiguously.

2 Among the people of Yahweh there are also traditions of personal piety.[5]
But the clear emphasis of faith in God is on celebrating God together and on
corporate efforts to witness, through the development of structures for society
and appropriate practices, to God's liberating and solidarity-creating action.
*Therefore the subject that recollects biblical traditions must always be a com-
munity striving to transpose the Bible's moves towards liberation and solidarity
into the present.*[6] Only in this context can a personal reading of the Bible today
avoid the trap of bourgeois individualism, which ideologises and closes off the

---

3 Cf. W. Dietrich, 1989.
4 Cf. the reflections cited above of T. Veerkamp, 1993, pp.114f.
5 R. Albertz, op. cit., stresses this for all phases of Israel's history.
6 Cf. the clear presentation of this matter in C. Mesters, 1983; also U. Duchrow, 1986.

message of the Bible. In its turn, such individualism is instrumentalised by the predominant capitalist groups, thus becoming an opiate for the people.

3   There is no recollection of the liberating and solidarity-creating God of the Bible without conflict with the economic, political and ideological systems and structures which enslave people and destroy solidarity. This has been clear since the liberation from Egypt, since the criticism and sufferings of the prophets, since the persecution and cross of Jesus and his early messianic groups and communities. For through their suffering and death, the Bible tells us, God creates life for his people and thus proves the truth of their message.

4   Each of these conflicts not only raises questions about structural issues, but also calls the system *as a whole* into question. This is the God-question, whether it is explicit or not.[7] Thus while questioning a system's economic and political structures, we must always ask *what in fact "functions" as God,* even in todays ostensibly "secularized" system.

5   Finally, there is the fundamental hermeneutical question: how can the Christian community relate to the traditions of Israel and how can people, groups, communities and peoples that are neither Jewish not Christian relate to both, Israel and the Church, and vice versa? Assuming rules 1-4, we shall go first to the question of Christian and Jewish Bible readings. We saw that the Hebrew Bible, the First Testament, itself gives pointers on how others, who are not part of the witness people chosen by God, can relate to God's revelations. With this question in mind, Crüsemann and Veerkamp both point at the end of their books to Deut 4, where Moses binds the people to the Torah. There Moses says (vv. 5-8):[8]

> "See, as Yahweh my God has commanded me, I teach you the laws and customs that you are to observe in the land you are to enter and make your own. Keep them, observe them, and they will demonstrate to the peoples your wisdom and understanding. When they come to know of all these laws they will exclaim, 'No other people is as wise and prudent as this great nation'. And indeed, what great nation is there that has its gods so near as Yahweh our God is whenever we call to him? And what great nation is there that has laws and customs to match this whole Law that I put before you today?"

---

7   Cf. Veerkamp, 1993, pp.281ff., etc.
8   Cf. ibid., pp.356ff. and F. Crüsemann, 1992, p.425.

It is their amazement at the Torah (and its implementation) that grants to the other peoples access to it. By this means the identity and special character of Israel's election is respected. But as with the "pilgrimage of the peoples to Zion", learning from the Torah can and should be universal. It is crucial, therefore, to listen, with ever-renewed intensity, to the stories of God's acts of liberation and the laws designed to help preserve freedom (freedom's discipline). Secondly, "understanding" here is not some general common sense, on top of which Israel's specific rules are accepted as a special kind of common sense. "General common sense" is always bound into massive positions of interest, like metaphysics in Aristotle, for example, when he justifies the rule of a single Hellenistic ruler.[9] Israel's common sense is the Torah for the very reason that, in the name of freedom and mutual solidarity, the Torah takes a defensive position against the common sense of the rulers and traders.

Jesus and early Christianity go along with this in that they adopt this same position – in the sense of fulfilling the Torah through the messianic Spirit, which finds people to live out the Kingdom of God. Only by *doing* what justice means and concretely *shaping* an alternative community in the spirit of the Torah do Christian congregations and groups participate in the promise of being a witness people, leaven, salt, light among the peoples – seeking fellowship with Israel without depriving it of its inheritance (Rom 9-11). It is true that acting justly and shaping an alternative community comes by *hearing* the testimony of God's story of liberation. It is also true that all this is a gift of God and cannot be manipulated by human beings. But at the same time the object of hearing is that those who hear may act and be enabled to act (cf. Mt 7:24ff.; Rom 7 and 8). So Israel and the messianic communities and Jesus groups vie to become the salt of the earth and light of the world. The "doctrine of the cross" takes up exactly the Israelite motif of the real *way* of God, on the side of those who are deprived of justice (cf. 1 Cor 1), and makes its object real *living* in the power of the Resurrection.

The Christian community's relation to the peoples is therefore the same as Israel's. It is not some shared common sense or wisdom that brings them together.[10] The wisdom of this world focuses on what is great, mighty and high. God's wisdom, however, chooses the lowly, the weak and the powerless and with them builds a different society of freedom and solidarity. Therefore

---

9 Cf. Veerkamp, ibid., pp.319ff.
10 The idea of "natural knowledge of God" which Paul takes up in Rom 1:19ff. is intended simply to show that all people are inexcusable before God.

the Christian community declares the "doctrine of the cross" to be God's wisdom (1 Cor 1). That is the Good News for oppressed peoples. It can be verified only by testing. Only this can decide the issue of whether life comes from starting with the lowly or with the mighty. The truth about a polito-economic system, and also about other religions, is not decided before the judgement seat of general common sense (who could sit on it?) but by the effect the system has on the actual survival of threatened people and human-kind as a whole.

The obverse of this is that the *name* "Christian" therefore does not matter. In Mt 25:31ff. people come to "the human one" on the judgement seat and say: "Did we not...in your name?" He answers them: "I do not know you." Like-wise, those come forward who have not explicitly called upon Jesus and formed a relationship with him but have responded to the basic needs of needy people. To them Jesus says: "Anything you did for one of my brothers here, however humble, you did for me." That means that Christian groups, communities and churches are the first to be subjected to the ideology critique, or judgement, to put it theologically, in order to prevent word, in-sight and action parting company with each other again.

That takes us back to rule 1: The God of the Jews, the Christians and all the peoples will reveal himself where the oppressed and excluded are. From this place will come forth fundamental criticism of "sinful structures" and the building of alternative structures for society – and the preservation of hope for life.

With the help of these *five rules for recollecting the past* we shall now try to order and evaluate the biblical traditions we have investigated, in order to achieve both perspectives for judging our present situation and possible ways out of it.

2 False paths: "state theology" and "church theology"

These five biblical rules for recollecting the past help first of all to throw into sharp relief two false paths which are already criticized in the biblical writings themselves. The South African Kairos Document calls them the paths of state theology and church theology.[11] L. and W. Schottroff have investigated the biblical traditions from which these theologies claim support.[12] In fact there are *remnants of state theology texts* which try to legitimise kingship according to ancient Near Eastern ideologies of king and empire, e.g. Ps 2 and 72 or Judg 17-21. They come mainly from the time when the monarchy in Israel and Judah had to justify its establishment in the face of resistance from the peasants, i.e. from the time of Saul, David and Solomon. But in many cases they have been reworked later, after the failure of the monarchy. And texts which are critical of the king far outweigh them. In the whole Pentateuch, the five books of Moses, the office of king appears only in Deut 17, in a very "tamed" form. In the Second Testament there is not a single state theology text, although Rom 13:1-7 and the story of Caesar's tax were, as I have shown, incorrectly interpreted in this way. In short: state theology betrays the innermost core of biblical faith in God, it idolises power. We shall have to ask later what it means that since then the centre of power has shifted from the state to capital.

The Kairos Document describes *church theology* as a theology that preaches "peace" and "reconciliation" in a situation marked by injustice and strife. It does not eliminate the fundamental causes of hostility and injustice, because of the institutional interests of the Temple, or later the Church, and indirectly the strong who perpetrate injustice are made stronger. One example is the priestly upper classes in Judaea at the time of Jesus, who collaborated with the Romans. The First Letter of Clement belongs here as well, as it praises the Pax Romana right after the great persecution under Emperor Domitian. Church Theology is about passive conformism to the ruling powers; it suppresses necessary conflict with them, or at least avoids it.

3 Three legitimate approaches to being the Church and to taking steps towards a life-sustaining economy

Each constellation of the history of Israel, Jesus and early Christianity has its particular *kairos*, i.e. its particular opportunities, limitations and challenges to decision-making at its own point in history. In each situation, therefore, people have to analyse the ruling structures, rediscovering – and fighting for – alternative possibilities of life for all. That means there is really no way of systematising things. Those involved have to watch, in keeping with the rules

---

11 Kairos South Africa, 1987.
12 L. and W. Schottroff, 1988.

of recollection, for the burgeoning of freedom and mutual solidarity, and let this bear fruit for the struggle of their time.

Nevertheless, it might help to highlight some of the traits typical of possible constellations of the people of God in their socio-political contexts. I shall select three, without wishing to imply that these are the only ones.

1 Taming political and economic power structures through prophecy and law ("established church" approach);

2 Transforming one society (thus forming a "contrast society") in a corner of the Empire;

3 Refusing to cooperate with totalitarian systems and creating networked small-scale alternatives (the "counter-culture" approach in messianic groups and communities throughout all peoples).

On *1: Taming political-economic power structures through prophecy and law ("established church" approach).* We will start with the most ambiguous constellation. As I have shown, there was a time in Israel and Judah when the fundamental structures of kingship were adopted, along with a class society and the imperial behaviour of a conqueror in external relations. The people wanted "to be like other peoples" (1 Sam 8). Peasants' movements, prophetic movements and individuals who tried to restrain these unjust structures by law (the Book of the Covenant and Josiah's Deuteronomy), endeavoured to give practical expression to their sense of freedom and solidarity inspired by faith in Yahweh, at least in the form of "taming" the power structures. There was one attempt at revolution (Jehu) and one at reform (Hezekiah and Josiah). Both failed. The monarchy collapsed (in 722 in the North, 587/6 in the South). The prophets had predicted these disasters, confining hope for life in the future to just a left-over "remnant", a "stump".

Despite this failure, the part of the Christian Church that lived in the Roman Empire took over this royal-Israel approach almost completely after the Roman emperor Constantine (312) accepted the Christian faith. Shaping itself into an imperial church, later a state church and today also a "national church", this approach may be described as that of a mainstream church or majority church, its object being to get to a situation where people and church-people are as far as possible coterminous. The question before us will be whether it has successfully tamed the structures of kingship and subsequent power systems in the name of Christianity or not, and what that means today.

On *2: Transforming one society in a corner of the Empire (thus forming a "contrast society").* On our journey of recollection through biblical history we came across two constellations in which Israel was able wholly, or partly, to uncouple from the Empires and build a counter-culture involving the whole population group. One was in the early anarchic period, when the marginal groups set free from the yoke of slavery and tribute developed an autonomous and egalitarian subsistence economy in the Palestinian highlands, managing their lives with no state and no Temple. The other was after the fall of the monarchy, first just among the peasants spared from exile and landless people who had come back home, then in semi-autonomy, within the Persian Empire but under the regulations of the Torah, which levelled out economic injustice and organised political self-government.

This approach has also been tried in the name of Christianity, for example in the settlements for the original inhabitants of America, more or less in cooperation with Las Casas in Hispaniola (today's Haiti) and the Jesuits in Paraguay.

On *3: Refusing to cooperate with totalitarian systems and creating networked small-scale alternatives (the "counter-culture" approach in messianic groups and communities throughout all peoples).* This type too found expression in Israel, when there was no longer any niche for the *whole* people. Acting in the apocalyptic hope of the collapse of the totalitarian Hellenistic and then Roman system, a group of the Hasideans, later the Essenes, rejected Hellenism and its permeation of everything, withdrew into the desert and tried, in the spirit of the Kingdom of God which would overcome the world kingdom, to demonstrate an alternative in monastic community.

Similarly and yet quite differently, Jesus, the Jesus movement and the early Christian messianic groups and communities lived out this rejection of the system for small-scale alternatives, linked in networks. They gathered people from out there in the world – beginning with the poor and excluded – and ended up going out into all the world in order to form "attractive" communities in the spirit of God's love and in the practice of sharing, as a signpost to the Kingdom of God. In this way, through small groups and communities in many countries, the Kingdom of God, or "justice, peace, and joy, inspired by the Holy Spirit" (Rom 14:17), was to emerge, putting an end to the unjust relationships between peoples, and between masters and slaves, and men and women, which characterised the Roman Empire as the heir to all Empires (Gal 3:28).

My claim now is that for our global political-economic situation today and the different social constellations in the South, East and West, and also for the role and responsibility of the churches, we can gain vital orientation and inspiration from at least two of these approaches.

THIRD PART

Life-giving economic alternatives – today

Chapter VII

From the empires to the global economy

"Civilising capitalism will only be possible globally, if at all."
Elmar Altvater [1]

In the First Part we tried to outline the origin, structure and development of the modern capitalist market economy over the last few centuries. The Second Part was about developing critical judgement, alternative social approaches and perspectives for action in the face of this economic, political and ideological power system. After all, it is a threat to the life not just of the majority of humankind but of the whole planet. We recalled the biblical traditions since, to my knowledge, there is no tradition in the history of peoples, cultures and religions that is so profoundly critical of unjust and life-threatening social structures as the biblical one. That does not mean that a church adopting these traditions need not engage in frank encounter with representatives of other living faiths. However, it would not do this naively from an allegedly neutral range of reasonable concepts, but according to the "rules for recollecting" gained critically and self-critically from its own tradition, i.e. 1. with a clear location on the side of the victims of the existing power system, 2. as part of communities struggling for justice and life, 3. in conflict with oppressive and life-destroying powers, 4. seeking to find who, or what, is "god", i.e. the power ultimately determining the whole, and 5. in the context of attempts to create alternatives, at least in part or in outline.

Two fundamental problems arise here which need to be tackled before we go on.

- First: we have tried to sharpen our judgement and discover alternatives by analysing the biblical handling of ancient Near Eastern, Greek and Roman empires. Is this relevant at all when we look at the changed context of the modern age, and if so, in what way?
- Second: if they encounter representatives of other religions Christian churches and communities must expect to be asked embarrassing ques-

---

1   E. Altvater, 1992, p.215. Gandhi was once asked, "What do you think about Western Civilisation?" After a moment he replied, "That would be a good idea".

tions about their own past and present[2]. After all they should be the first to be judged according to the criterion of *lived* social alternatives.

1 How can one compare the social configurations of ancient empires and the global capitalist system?

Immanuel Wallerstein begins his classical work on *The Modern World-System* with the words:

> "In the late fifteenth and early sixteenth century, there came into existence what we may call a European world-system. It was not an empire yet it was as spacious as a grand empire and shared some features of it. But it was different, and new ... It is an economic but not a political entity, unlike empires, city-states, and nation-states. In fact, it precisely encompasses within its bounds ... empires, city-states, and the emerging 'nation-states'."[3]

That means that the actual structure of power was no longer a political empire, but a global economic system, comprising and using different political forms. For 5000 years empires have been characterised by political centralisation for the purpose of the forced collection of tribute and taxes. Even where a global economy arose as in China, Persia and Rome, it was turned into an empire. When the Habsburgs attempted this in the emerging European world-economy they failed:

> "What capitalism does is offer an alternative and more lucrative source of surplus appropriation ... In a capitalist world-economy, political energy is used to secure monopoly rights (or as near to it as can be achieved). The state becomes less the central economic enterprise than the means of assuring certain terms of trade in other economic transactions."[4]

---

2   I am not raising the issue of the post-biblical history and present of Israel, since this needs to be raised and dealt with by the Jews. The best basis and reference point for Judeo-Christian dialogue is certainly listening together to biblical traditions. We should remember though that the Jewish state was destroyed by the Romans in the first and second centuries BC. because the Jews were not prepared to adapt to totalitarian political, economic and ideological rule.

3   Wallerstein, 1994, p.15.

4   Ibid., p.16.

In the modern capitalist global economy the economic actors do not need to
cover the political costs of their profits themselves, yet they can take advantage
of state facilities to improve their market opportunities. *There is one feature common to the political economy of empires and the capitalist global economy: they both
are forms of surplus acquisition by those in control of the means of production, at the
expense of the majority.*

Let us recall the quote from Max Weber that capitalism is "masterless slavery".[5] The masters are made invisible behind the mechanisms of the market.
And the latter are regarded as similar to natural law and beyond criticism.
That is precisely why he calls them ethically inaccessible and not subject to
regulation. If we want to critically analyse the mechanisms of capitalist global
economy and seek viable alternatives this can only be done in two respects:
– one can question capitalist mechanisms as such and seek totally different
  forms of common economic activity;
– one can bring to light the hidden elements of political regulation of the
  different forms of capitalist accumulation, that interplay with market
  mechanisms, and then look for ways to intervene.
  In our search for life-bringing economic alternatives we will have to keep
these two approaches in mind.

2 Have the churches the right to speak up at all, in view of their 2000-year history?

Against the background of the biblical perspectives developed above, the basic
problem of European church history doubtless remains the fact that under
Emperor Constantine in the 4th century there was a change from the messianic groups and congregations to the established church model, even constituting an imperial church.

> This is not the place to examine what actual forms of church life were developed
> along the lines of the alternative societies of Jesus and Paul, until this change-
> over, nor to speculate on what caused it.[6] It is clear that up to then the church

---

5 See above, p. 122

kept its distance from the Roman empire, indeed was forced to do so by periodic persecution.

Theologically speaking the problem does not lie in the change-over as such. Even though the great majority of biblical traditions, and certainly the Second Testament, were extremely critical of the monarchy as such, and even more of the empires and their political and economic structures, they had ideas on how it might have been possible to justify theologically an approach of constructive criticism to an empire. Ideally the Pauline vision might have become reality. The cells of the new Messiah-humanity would have been such an attractive alternative to the peoples that they all would have accepted them, and a new, alternative society would have arisen – without centre-periphery structures between peoples and races, without class division of masters and slaves, and without the dominance of men over women. Or there could at least have been the approach of taming the kingship structure through prophecy and law, as exemplified by the Josian reform. Here the emperor would have had to accept a constitutional restriction, and social laws and rights to political participation could have been introduced. However, the danger from the start was that the Christian communities – albeit largely surprised at the change – were so pleased about this "favorable" development that they simply accepted the imperial structure and their new role in it. This entailed the temptation of slipping into a state or church theology to justify, or condone, its political and economic power system. And what actually happened was that the traditions of David and Solomon flourished here again. I will try to briefly explain the institutional and legal instruments that were developed in order to at least try to tame power.

The *first* element was the dual pole of monarchy and (in theory, prophetic) priesthood in the Christian Middle Ages (regnum and sacerdotium).[7] Typical of the Hellenistic-Roman totalitarian order was the unity of the monarchy and priesthood at the pinnacle of the empire, indeed the divinity of the emperor. In the western Middle Ages, by contrast, a duality formed between two "regimens" (potestates) and thus the fundamental independence of a priestly authority vis-à-vis royalty. The possibility of the latter abusing power in turn was something Luther tried to overcome by denying any profane means of

---

6 Cf. the enlightening analyses of L. Schottroff (1994, pp.220f.) on Origen's attempt to refute Celsus's accusation that the church was only a religion for the underclasses.

7 On this and ff. see U. Duchrow, 1983, Chap. III, with further literature.

power to the spiritual regimen (potestas spiritualis) and seeing it as founded in the characteristics of the true church alone, i.e. in word, sacrament, willingness to suffer, prayer and the different forms of expression of exemplary life following God's commands in the power of the Holy Spirit.[8] Proclaiming the gospel to the economically and politically powerful is formulated by Luther as a prophetic task in these classic terms:

"For the princes and 'big shots' find it quite intolerable that the whole world should be criticised if only they themselves are exempted from this criticism. But they must certainly be criticised too and anyone entrusted with the office of preaching owes it to them to point out where they act unjustly and do wrong, even if they protest that such criticism of rulers will lead to rebellion."[9]

Secondly, Luther sharpens the bipolarity of the western Middle Ages in that he denies political institutions the right to call themselves or their own actions "Christian". This may be necessary to de-ideologise and relativise the ruling system, but it had serious consequences with respect to a second element of prophetic action: the constitutive cooperation of prophetic with social movements. According to Jeremiah 22:16, knowing God was identical with helping the poor and weak to enjoy their rights. Luther's dropping the peasants (for whatever reason[10]) was the not the first instance of the problem. The priests and the preachers of the mainline churches in the Middle Ages and the Reformation were not constitutively on the side of the socio-economically and politically weak and oppressed, unlike the prophets and Jesus. Constitutively means that as institutions they should have taken sides for economic and political justice – quite apart from charitable care for the poor.

In another way a *third* element in Constantinian Christianity showed mutual, "horizontal" solidarity with the poor: the monks and the religious orders. In some cases there was literal identification with the poor, e.g. in the case of Francis of Assisi – a protest against the adaptation of the church to wealth and power. In other cases the monasteries and convents did a great deal to develop new forms of agriculture leading to a marked improvement in the economic and social conditions of the poor population.[11] One of the weaknesses of the

8　See U. Duchrow, 1987, pp.41ff.

9　Luther, WA (Weimar edition), pp.28, 360f. (translation David Lewis); cf. U. Duchrow, ibid., p.7.

10　Cf. U. Duchrow, ibid., pp.532ff. and 560.

11　See economist K.G. Zinn, 1989, pp.45ff.

approach of the medieval orders, however, was the fact that it only applied to the "perfect". This weakened the general challenge to ecclesiastical, political and economic institutions on the basis of biblical traditions.

The _fourth_ element of "taming" is comparable with the development of the law in the Israel of the kings. Criteria for organisation and behaviour in these institutions were developed in a long and intensive history of theological work. Biblical tradition was intermingled with Greek philosophy, as were Roman and Germanic law.

> As can be seen on the example e.g. of Thomas Aquinus, this mixture contained critical and conformist elements regarding the system of political and economic power. On one hand, he tries to stop the money-accumulation economy invading the supply-oriented domestic economy, with his analyses of the ban on interest and monopoly or his concept of a just price. On the other, he legitimises the feudal system.[12] In the Lutheran Reformation it was not only the preachers who assessed and decided the political and economic issues as questions of conscience. The heads of families also shared in this, which is why Luther drew up the Large Catechism for them, which contains radical economic points of view (see below). Every Christian was called upon, in their work, to check out the extent to which this participation in political and economic institutions and activities allowed the exercise of love, and to discern when it was necessary to refuse to cooperate. Any involvement in "worldly" institutions was limited by the fact that, if forced to commit sin, you had to "obey God rather than men" (Acts 5:29).[13]

I cannot examine in detail here to what extent, in the Middle Ages and Reformation, these and other elements of the biblical-prophetic attempt to tame the political and economic system of kingdom and empire were carried out under feudal conditions, or to what extent state and church theology prevailed. However, there may be room for a _brief excursion on Luther and Calvin_ since they had interesting things to say about the emergence of early capitalism and their thinking has been used to justify capitalism to this day.

Martin Luther wrote three detailed texts on economic issues, particularly on the problem of interest (usury) and the emerging international, monopolist trading and banking companies (Fugger, Welser etc.) during the Ge-

---

12 See T. Veerkamp, 1993, pp.325ff.
13 Cf. Augsburg Confession, 1530, Art. 16, in: Th.G. Tappert (ed.), The Book of Concord, Philadelphia: Fortress Press, 1959, p.38.

noese-Spanish cycle of capital accumulation. They in turn were deeply entangled in the politics of church and state of their time (against the Reformation).[14] The actual, often unseen theological point in these writings is the alternative of "God or idol", i.e. it is not just a question of ethics. That is best seen in Luther's exposition of the Ten Commandments in the Large Catechism, as brought out by F.M.Marquardt.[15] On the First Commandment, and particularly on the admonition "You shall have no other gods", Luther writes:

> "What is it to have a god? What is God? Answer: A god is that to which we look for all good and in which we find refuge in every time of need. To have a god is nothing else than to trust and believe him with our whole heart ... For these two belong together, faith and God. That to which your heart clings and entrusts itself is, I say, really your God."

These phrases are normally understood in individual terms in our bourgeois tradition, i.e. as relating to individuals – and that is certainly *one* possible meaning. But Luther continues by adding examples of idols people fall victim to. Top of the list is *Mammon:*

> "Many a person thinks he has God and everything he needs when he has money and property; in them he trusts and of them he boasts so stubbornly and securely that he cares for no one. Surely such a man also has a god – mammon by name, that is, money and possessions – on which he fixes his whole heart. It is the most common idol on earth. He who has money and property feels secure, happy, fearless, as if he were sitting in the midst of paradise. On the other hand, he who has nothing doubts and despairs as if he never heard of God. Very few there are who are cheerful, who do not fret and complain, if they do not have mammon. This desire for wealth clings and cleaves to our nature all the way to the grave."

Luther was not thinking of individual persons with particularly terrible vices, but of the early capitalist system. That is clear from the following exposition of the Seventh Commandment, "You shall not steal", where he describes the social-ethical consequences of idolatry:

---

14   Luther, 1519: "The Short Sermon on Usury", WA 6, 1ff. (not in English); 1524: "Trade and Usury", WA 15, pp.218ff. (English: Luther's Works, Philadelphia: Muhlenberg Press, 1962, Vol. 45, pp.244-273) incorporating "The Long Sermon on Usury" of 1520, WA 6, 33ff. (English: ibid., pp.273-308); 1540: "Admonition to the Clergy that They Preach Against Usury", WA 51, pp.325ff. (not in English). Cf. H.-J. Prien, 1992.
15   The Book of Concord, pp.365f. and 395f. (see note 13). See also F.W. Marquardt, 1983.

> "...a person steals not only when he robs a man's strongbox or his pocket, but also when he takes advantage of his neighbour at the market, in a grocery shop, butcher stall, wine and beer cellar, workshop, and, in short, wherever business is transacted and money is exchanged for goods or labour. (p.395) ... In short, thievery is the most common craft and the largest guild on earth. If we look at mankind in all its conditions, it is nothing but a vast, wide stable full of great thieves. These men are called gentleman swindlers or big operators ... they sit in office chairs (= usurers, U.D.) and are called great lords and honourable, good citizens, and yet with a great show of legality they rob and steal ... the great, powerful archthieves who consort with lords and princes and daily plunder not only a city or two, but all Germany" (p.369)

After Luther's usury texts there can be now doubt whom he means here: the big banking and trading companies. But these institutions are only the tip of the iceberg of a system increasingly pervading the whole of society – the system of "devouring" capital.

> "Along with its princes and lords, the whole country and people of Germany will get in the grip of usurers! In the last twenty, even ten years usury has spread so much here that it is enough to make your heart stand still. And it continues to rise, devour and fetter us; the longer it goes on, the more ghastly it is ... So anyone who has a hundred florins in Leipzig now earns an annual forty (in interest, U.D.), which means devouring a peasant or city-dweller. If he has a thousand florins, he earns four hundred in one year, which means devouring a knight or rich nobleman. If he has ten thousand, he earns an annual four thousand, which means devouring a great, rich count in one year. If he has a hundred thousand, which must be the case with big businessmen, he earns an annual forty thousand, which means devouring a great, rich prince in one year. If he has a million, he earns an annual four hundred thousand, which means devouring a great king in one year. And he runs no risk thereby, neither physical nor material; he does no work, but sits by his hearth and bakes apples. In that way a robber can sit comfortably at home and in ten years swallow up the whole world."[16]

This system is not only idolatrous, through its trust in Mammon, but also since

---

16 Admonition to the Clergy, WA 51, pp.364f. and 394-398(tr.).

"... people have wanted to lord it over others since the apple in paradise, where Adam and Eve wanted to be gods in the devil's name. All of us have the same apple in our bellies ... a usurer and miser desires nothing else with all his might than that the whole world should die of hunger and thirst, tears and distress, so that he can have everything for himself alone and everyone else can receive things from him as from a god and become his bondservants for ever. ... So sweet is the poison of the paradise apple that they want to make Mammon their god and raise themselves through his power to become gods over poor, lost and miserable people ..." (ibid., pp.394-8).

Here, as in the First Testament, we see the connection between idolatry and death, hunger and distress. Luther says the same not only about those who charge interest but also about trading companies when they manipulate prices through monopolies – "... just as if they were lords over God's creatures and immune from all the laws of faith and love".[17] In his last work on the topic Luther was clear that he was opposing an enormous power which, to the detriment of all, manipulated people's minds and veiled the truth, so that capital formation through charging interest "no longer wants to be vice, sin or shame, but boasts that it is sheer virtue and honour"[18]. The church also fell for this semblance of virtue, as did the theologians. He calls the Roman theologian Eck a "plutologian", not a theologian[19], and says of the Roman church:

"Basically the whole spiritual governance is nothing but money, money, money. Everything is geared to money-making ...".[20]

That is why, for Luther, there can be no compromise by the true church with those who charge interest, due to the effect on society and the church as a whole:

"Secondly, if you know for a fact that someone is a usurer, remember not to give him either the sacrament or absolution until he repents! Otherwise you will be conniving in his usury and his sins. Then you too will go to the devil with him because of his sins ... Thirdly, be careful that you let the usurer die like a heathen and do not bury him among other Christians! Also that you do not follow him to his grave if he has not repented before! If you do that, you will be conniving in

17 Trade and Usury, Luther's Works, Vol.45, p.270 (see note 14).
18 Admonition to the Clergy, WA 51, p.331(tr.); cf. F.W. Marquardt, 1983, pp.190f.
19 WA 1, pp.304f.; cf. F.W. Marquardt, 1983, p.193.
20 WA 1011, p.125; cf. F.W. Marquardt, ibid.(tr.).

his sins, as I said above. Since he is a usurer and idolater, since he serves Mammon, he lacks credibility, and cannot have or receive the forgiveness of sins, neither the grace of Christ nor the community of the saints. He has damned, isolated and banned himself, until he confesses his sin and does penance."[21]

This text shows that Luther sees the community of the church as an alternative to the capitalist order. That is also reflected in the fact that he challenges it in word and deed (in its own institutional finances) to distance itself from the capital companies and their practices, in order to set a good example to the worldly estates. The church is not worthy of the name if it charges interest like everyone else.[22] At the same time it becomes clear that he does not simply want to solve the problem by confronting the individual usurer, but calls on the whole church to speak out against the social evil. He also calls on the powers-that-be to move to stop the spread of usury. He is realistic, however, in seeing that they are already coopted ("they have a finger in it themselves").[23] The best example here is the dependence of Charles v on the Fuggers. That is why Luther tries to get the congregations and what we would call grassroots groups to combat poverty and its causes, which had an influence on the Protestant church ordinances.[24]

The question of God or Mammon in relation to the economy is with Luther – as with the Bible – inseparably bound up with the effect of economic structures and behaviour on human community or, theologically speaking, on one's neighbour. As we have seen, the first Table of the Law relates to the Second and vice versa (First Commandment – Seventh Commandment). Luther names three legitimate economic courses of action for Christians (in accordance with the Sermon on the Mount): they should allow people to help themselves, and should give and lend freely (without a fee).

"Here there can be no other measure than the urgent need of our neighbour and Christian love."[25]

Here it is clear why Luther perceives a concordance between love (Bible) and reason (Aristotle): the economy is understood and assessed in terms of sat-

21 Admonition to the Clergy, WA 51, pp.367f.(tr.).
22 Trade and Usury, Luther's Works, Vol.45, pp.306ff. (see note 14).
23 Ibid., p.271.
24 See G. Scharffenorth, 1982, pp.331f.
25 Admonition to the Clergy, WA 51, p.393(tr.).

isfying the daily needs of people. One really ought to study the whole contemporary discussion of economic theory against the background of the social and economic situation of Luther's time, and then assess his actual positions. I will confine myself here to a few important statements by Luther and Calvin on interest. The point of departure remains the general premise, supported by the then philosophical and legal traditions:

> "Whoever lends something and takes more money in return is a usurer and damned like a thief, robber and murderer."[26]

In Luther's time, one argument for charging interest was that lending money might lead to the lender making a loss or missing out on a possible profit. Yet Luther opposed the automatic charging of interest:

> "Here one seeks and intensifies one's own loss at the expense of the needy neighbour, wanting to fatten and enrich oneself in lazy and idle debauchery, in other words, to parade other people's work, care, risk and loss."[27]

Only where there has been *real* loss through lending should there be a *subsequent* payment of damages (cautiously, avoiding greed), which is not usury – although it would really be better to write off the whole debt.[28] If old people, widows and orphans can only survive on an income drawn from interest that is only "usury because of need" and should be allowed.[29] It is actually the job of lawyers and the secular authorities to publicise or implement rules of behaviour. However, because they do not do their job properly the poor preachers have to give the matter publicity – in biblical language, exercising their prophetic ministry.[30]

Both Luther and Calvin reject interest in principle, yet show some understanding for *exceptional* credit of the kind that we would today call *productive credit* as against consumer credit. At this point we can find the arguments which, drawn from the theological approaches of the Bible, antiquity and church tradition, also apply today to the modern growth economy or at least to give a clue to transformed criteria. Luther is thinking here of a loan assisting one to work a fertile property. Since the creditor takes part of the profit he

---

26 Ibid., p.367.
27 Ibid., p.351.
28 Ibid., pp.344ff.
29 Ibid., pp.371ff.
30 Ibid., pp.352f.

calls this "buying of income".[31] *Calvin* had the situation of refugees in mind, who came to Geneva without money but with excellent skills, needing financial assistance before they could make a profit in business themselves. Calvin's scattered thoughts on the problem are best summed up in his Commentary on Ezekiel 18:6-8.[32] The conditions and considerations of Luther and Calvin on "productive credit" as an exception can be rendered as follows:

Luther	Calvin
1. Consider the *effect:*	– do not take interest from the poor
– even agricultural loans rarely do your neighbour any good	– have regard for your neighbour (Mt 7:12) and be fair
– borrowing is mostly bad for the land and its inhabitants	– let the result be generally beneficial, not just for personal profit
2. Beware of the *risk:*	
– do not calculate interest "blindly" (no abstract arithmetic!)	– all lenders shall have obligations
– only pay interest on landed property (i.e. considering concrete conditions and results)	– main rules: "not everywhere, not any time, not everything, not from everyone"
– this means *sharing* risk.	
3. Only if both partners are needy *will they both gain*.	– let both make equal gains
4. Even in this exceptional case people mostly charge *too much interest*.	– do not exceed the amount laid down by law (strict *state control*)
5. Even here interest mostly includes gains derived from the work of others.	–
6. –	– observe *the criteria* of the Word of God.

31 The Long Sermon on Usury, Luther's Works, Vol.45, pp.295ff. (see note 14). There is no word in English for *Zinskauf* – a practice that no longer exists. Cf. Luther's Works, Vol.45, Introduction.

32 Calvin, Commentaries on the First Twenty Chapters of the Book of the Prophet Ezekiel, now first translated from the original Latin and collated with the French version by Thomas Myers, Grand Rapids, Michigan: Wm.B. Eerdmans Publishing Company, 1948(tr.).

It is striking that Luther takes a restrictive, even negative tone, while Calvin gives more positive advice, in the form of rules. However, Calvin too is very restrictive in summing up:

> "It is hardly possible that anyone charging interest should not thereby burden his brother, and so it would be good to bury the names of usury and interest and wipe them out of human memory completely. However, since business dealings are not possible without it, one must always be careful to know what is permitted and to what extent it is permitted".

From this you can see how strongly the Reformers looked to the Bible and only accepted restricted elements of a capitalist form of economy with many cautionary rules. The money accumulation market is not simply accepted but linked to tight conditions. Judgement is oriented to the living conditions of the weak. The state is invoked to counter the autonomy of the money-accumulation mechanism. The church is called to exercise corporate rejection, offer resistance and set an example of alternative behaviour. This means that the prophetic approach is maintained so radically that it spills over into a messianic way of being the church.

A similar combination of elements for a church-based counter-strategy can be observed on the Roman Catholic side in *Bartholomé de Las Casas* and like-minded members of religious orders.[33]

- Las Casas formulates the decisive theological alternative: God or gold, the God of life and liberation, or the deadly idol, money?
- He does not limit himself to charitable assistance to the victimised (that would be a sacrifice that God does not accept). Instead he attacks the structural sin of the wars against the native Americans, and the slave system whereby they were "entrusted" (in encomiendas) to the colonists to work in mines and plantations.
- He untiringly pesters the political leaders, in this case the king and emperor, to abolish the encomienda system, give compensation and pass laws to protect the Indios.

This prophetic criticism was swept away by events. The Spanish-Portuguese *conquista* with the plundering of America and genocide of the original inhabitants did not only cruelly continue the *reconquista* of the crusades, but was

---

33 CF. U. Duchrow, 1992, pp.14f. with additional literature.

grounded ideologically in theology. Luther's "plutologian" Eck was for Las Casas the Spanish theologian Sepúlveda.[34] He expressly defended capitalist industry and slavery with pseudo-theological arguments. Since the time of these two theologians, *state theology* – conformist theology in the imperial system – has been joined by *capitalist theology* – conformism to the modern capitalist global economy. But Calvinist theologians also legitimised Dutch and British colonial rule. The missionaries in the competing European colonial empires often worked hand in hand with the governments, the military and the traders. Only in rare cases did they take sides with slaves and the downtrodden. And when, during the industrial, capitalist revolution, colonial methods were transferred onto the working classes of their own European populations, the major churches did not take up their cause. Neo-Lutheranism, in particular in its liberal form, finally even accepted Max Weber's theory on the "autonomy of activities like economics, politics and academic work".[35] Only very few charitable initiatives and even fewer prophetic voices were recorded in the established churches in the 19th century, until the ecumenical movement in the 20th century took up the ideas of religious socialists and their social gospel. Bonhoeffer, the Confessing Church and finally the liberation theologies of Asia, Africa and Latin America also offered capitalism critique, seeking life-bringing alternatives.

By contrast, there are now many theologians and institutes paid by industry and banks (particularly in the United States) to do capitalism theology. One is M. Novak, author of *The Spirit of Democratic Capitalism*. There are also (US-based) capitalist-minded sects flooding Latin America, and now Central and Eastern Europe, with their huge funding and electronic equipment.[36] The history of the Constantinian mainline churches is still to be written from the angle of biblically motivated self-criticism with respect to their position on economic justice. This will be essential if there is to be a new beginning.

Before we turn to the present though, it must be added that there were *minorities* in the Constantinian age believing that it was wrong to have anything to do with the political and economic system of kings, emperors and, later, capitalism. They opted either to be *messianic communities and groups* or a *church living out social transformation.*[37]

---

34 Ibid., p.9.
35 Cf. U. Duchrow, 1987, pp.9ff.
36 M. Novak 1982. Cf. U. Duchrow, 1987, pp.117ff.

These include the Waldensians, the Wiclifites and the (nonviolent) Anabaptists or, in the post-medieval age, the communities of indigenous peoples associated with the efforts of Las Casas in Hispaniola (now Haiti) and the Jesuits in Paraguay: another example is the liberation of slaves under Toussaint Louverture in Haiti at the time of the French Revolution.[38] Transformational biblical impulses have emigrated in view of the shortcomings of the mainline churches and found a home in secular social movements.

In view of these findings there should be a reevaluation of the different form taken by the church in the history of the West. Troeltsch's categories of "institutional churches" and "sects" are largely inadequate since they assume the former are the norm, thereby overlooking all the biblical traditions in their specific social histories.

Let us now take a brief look at *recent history*. In the liberation theologies of the South there has been new work since the late 50s on the intimate connection between biblical faith and economic justice. This connection became clear in the Second Part, but will assist us in the strategic considerations to follow. In the theology of the North the topic has – after long abstinence – been rediscovered under the heading of economic ethics, first by Arthur Rich.[39] Personally I hold the ethical approach to be inadequate, for the reasons given above,[40] which does not mean that some ethical attempts have not been of valuable assistance in providing individual analytical and strategic elements. We can take them up below.

As far as the churches go, the World Council of Churches (and its precursors) have taken up the topic of capitalist economy.[41] The latest publication is the study document "Christian Faith and the World Economy Today".[42] The Vati-

---

37 See U. Duchrow 1992, Part 1.

38 Ibid., pp.17ff.

39 A. Rich, vol. 1, pp.17ff., 1984; vol. 2, 1990. For further literature see U. Duchrow, 1993 (e.g. Y. Spiegel, 1992; F. Hengsbach, 1993; L. Elsner, 1993).

40 That is why I raised the global economy as an issue for a confessing church, i.e. fundamentally bringing in the God question and possible radical rejections. The only book I know of which fully integrates the ethical, theological and economic dimensions of the question is *Capital and the Kingdom* by T.J. Gorringe, 1994.

41 R. van Drimmelen gives a fine survey, 1987; C. Mulholland has collated the work of the Advisory Group on Economic Matters (AGEM) up to 1988.

42 WCC, 1992; the Ecumenical Assemblies of Basel (1989) and Seoul (1990) produced

can issued the encyclical Centesimus Annus to mark the hundredth anniversary of Rerum Novarum.[43] Individual churches in the 80s rose up and opposed the consequences of neo-liberalism: the Anglican Church in face of Thatcherism, and the US Roman Catholic Bishops' Conference and United Church of Christ in face of Reaganomics.[44]

It would be interesting to describe all these – and other – church position papers, and to compare and contrast them in the light of the Bible. All of them express more or less clear concern about the way the market economy is going. These efforts worldwide are an important sign of a turning-away from the churches' previous obliviousness to economic matters. The change began in the churches of Asia, Africa and Latin America, was taken up by the WCC and committed groups and NGOs and finally made headway in the Northern churches in the 80s. The drastic switch to neo-liberal economic policy under Reagan and Thatcher with its obvious social consequences, plus a growth in ecological awareness, prompted a rethink. Amazingly, however, not one of the church statements offers a consistent analysis and criticism of the development of the capitalist market economy. Likewise, the theological justifications tend to be selective and additive, rather than offering a consistent interpretation from biblical sources. So the suggestions made to assist in forming judgements, and the conclusions drawn with regard to the form, action and public position of the churches still lack clarity and commitment. That is seen most clearly in the economic memorandum of the EKD, which falls far short of all other statements within the ecumenical movement.[45]

The very title *The Common Good and Self-Interest* indicates that it basically wants to stay in the tradition of Adam Smith. The memorandum is structured as follows: I. Challenges for the Future. Unsolved global problems are named. II. The Successful Project "Social Market Economy" in the Federal Republic of Germany. III. This tries to fit the Bible and theology into the measure of Adam Smith. "Loving one's neighbour means tying self-interest into an order based on

important statements on this theme.

43 John Paul II, 1991.

44 Faith in the City, 1985; US Roman Catholic Bishops' Conference, 1987; United Church of Christ, 1987 and 1989. For more church statements on economic issues see WCC, 1992, and W. Ellington, 1993.

45 Evangelical Church in Germany, 1991.

mutuality" (§ 139). Part IV postulates that the nationally successful model of the German "social market economy" can be transferred to the world level in order to solve remaining problems.

There is absolutely no awareness here that any analysis and strategy is bound to fail nowadays if it starts from a model of national economy and not from the existing capitalist global economy, in order to test the scope for national and international economic policy from that vantage point. The memorandum bristles with euphemisms about the present situation, e.g. "After numerous hunger revolts... the International Monetary Fund (IMF) and the World Bank are seeking a more development-related strategy of adjustment" (§ 20). This is the only sentence about the IMF in this Northern church memorandum, while the Brazilian Catholic bishops speak of a totalitarian system in view of the victims of the merciless transfer of resources from South to North by the creditors and enforced by the IMF.[46] The Brazilian Lutheran W. Altmann calls the high interest demands on the poor a present-day Auschwitz. This sentence about the IMF in the memorandum is enough to show that we do not worship the same God in our Northern churches as the poor in the South. In addition, the memorandum formulates comments on "social market economy" affirmatively, while all critical questions are worded in the passive, without a subject. No names are given. The memorandum is more of a smoke-screen than a spotlight.

By contrast, what would a life-bringing economy be like, starting from a realistic analysis of the present situation and the recollection of Israelite and early Christian endeavours to found an alternative society? Seeing we are dealing with a complex interplay of a global system and different sub-systems (local, regional, national, global) it seems clear that there can be no simple answer to this question.

In the light of the biblical attempts to find an alternative system, it must first be said that the *option of a wholesale transformation of society* is out of the question. I cannot see that the present state of Israel is such an alternative, or wants to be (naturally there are important smallscale alternatives there, e.g. kibuzzim). But it is not a matter of wanting or not wanting. At present there is no slot available for a nation to set up a genuine alternative, untouched by the global market or even partially autonomous. Cautious experiments such as that of Sandinistan Nicaragua have been mercilessly crushed by US im-

---

46 Publik-Forum, 18.12.92, p.37.

perialism with the aid of low intensity conflict (LIC). And Cuba is now, having lost its allies, finally being throttled by US sanctions. The only halfway functioning attempt to use the market as an instrument, subject to the priority of satisfying basic needs, is China – with the well-known high political costs. It is only in a position to do this because the sheer size of its economic area gives it a certain independence. However, China has to keep to the restrictions, constraints and tributary conditions of the capitalist global economy in its external relations.

Having said that, the two options remain:

- rejection and smallscale alternatives, related to a totalitarian context (biblically speaking, messianic communities in the apocalyptic perspective of hope),
- relative taming of the political and economic system by the vestiges of democratic institutions of criticism and law (biblically speaking, a prophetic approach).

My hypothesis is that we can combine these two approaches into a double strategy, giving central importance to the people of God. Let us first turn to rejection.

Chapter VIII

Rejecting the totalitarian structure of the world economy

If one affirms life and life-bringing economic systems, then one must reject economic systems and structures which bring about death. One objection often raised in this respect says that total dissent would mean losing all political credibility, and that the political possibilities of relative improvement can no longer be seized when one rejects certain basic elements of the capitalist economy. This argument presupposes that the changes in the world's economic system that are necessary for survival can be achieved with the existing political institutions. *Only when* the fundamental, death-inducing mechanisms have been recognised and eliminated can a political strategy be formulated which may be able to help avoid the predictable catastrophes. It is not the desire to constantly criticise but the necessity to avoid illusions when dealing with life-sustaining alternatives for life which compels us to specify what must be rejected, so that the best can be achieved from this firm basis.

Exactly *what* is it that has to be rejected on principle in the present global system, and to which we have to find alternatives for life's sake? It is the mechanisms which, uncontrolled and unimpeded, gear economic activity to the accumulation of money by those who already have it, with the aid of the absolute principle of competition in the global market. Nature and people are, accordingly, subordinated to this end, as far as possible.

In concrete terms, the mechanisms referred to are: the transnational money markets, in so far as they can and do escape national and international controls; national and international institutions, provided they tolerate or favour the pure capitalist market; and also the ideological instruments connected with science, the media, schools, universities and churches, which orientate people towards achieving this goal or whose potential for resistance to the deadly wealth accumulation market is not used. But because the money mechanism only functions with the inclusion of the commodity-money relationship, all people, provided they have money and are consumers with purchasing power, are actively caught up in the machinery of wealth accumulation (incidentally, so are those without much purchasing power, in so far as they – understandably – strive for a share in consumption rather than seeking alternatives to the commodity-money system). That means, however, that although the totalitarian character of the money-orientated system originates from the power of the world market, the market can only exercise this power because so many players, right down to individual human beings, facilitate its operation. Rejection in this case is, therefore, not an attitude adopted with external reference only to identifiable players in the world market. It involves a fundamental change at all levels, including that of the individual.

Before we examine this dimension of rejection more closely, we should consider once more the need for it. From a social point of view, the totalitarian character of the deregulated and competitive world market, centred around wealth accumulation, is leading to dramatic levels of pauperisation and exclusion of more and more people, not only in the South but increasingly in the East and also in the West. Today we have reached a point where at least two thirds of the world's population are either dying of hunger or living on or below the poverty line. These people are subsequently excluded from the formal economy. From an environmental point of view, our planet and the basic conditions for life *will* be destroyed if the transformation of nature into commodities-money for the purpose of wealth accumulation continues to accelerate and intensify. It is, therefore, imperative that the focus of the economy be shifted from money accumulation to the people's needs. A mere 'taming' of the system is not sufficient, although this must be considered when reflecting upon the question of relative political options. The only satisfactory solution can be one that takes into account the lives of not just a few privileged Northerners or even of all people alive today but also of future generations, and ensures that they have the renewable natural resources necessary for survival and procreation. Such a solution would result in the elimination of the money-accumulation economy and its associated structures. This must be recognised before embarking upon any attempt to find concrete alternatives and new regulatory instruments. Any other starting point would be potentially dangerous because it would only create illusions. E. Altvater was right when he said that anybody who maintains that within the framework of a capitalist economy, the environmental catastrophe can be held at bay in the long run is either opportunistic or naive. The same conclusion was also reached by R. Kurz and L. Mayer, who have been quoted already, and, indirectly, H.-Chr. Binswanger.

As Binswanger writes in such a prudent and unideological way, I would like to summarise his views on the present dilemma and the necessity for change which he presents in his book *Geld und Natur* (Money and nature). If one starts from the proposed solution, to gain control of the environmental question within the capitalist economy using the pricing mechanism, then the only result can be that "the demands for better environmental protection increase during periods of economic growth faster than the means available due to this growth" (p.107). If one slows down the growth, then the economy will shrink, which would endanger the current financial structure of the economy. The interest rate can only be cut back to 2.5 per cent. Another form of qualitative growth would be required and indeed possible if the development of technology were to be controlled in a different way. In cases where even this is not sufficient, "the money and financial system must, however, be fundamentally reviewed because of its inherent dynamic" (pp.108f). This is the basic theme of Binswanger's book following the basic Aristotelian comparison between an economy centred on utility value and one centred on money accumulation, under which nature is ignored. There is a reason for this: "the increasing trend to organise economic activity solely for the purpose of obtaining returns on investments, i.e. more money without predefined limits on its expansion and at whose expansion people simply gaze spellbound, blind to the consequent use and abuse of nature around them" (p.194).

It is also possible to describe the murderous basic dynamism which is threatening us in an even more dramatic way, according to R. Bahro in his book *Die Logik der Rettung – Wer kann die Apokalypse aufhalten?*[1] (The logic of rescue – who can stop the apocalypse?). Within the capitalist industrialist "megamachine", he sees a culture bent on self-destruction and a type of "exterminism" at work, and is prompted to ask: "Instead of some form of longing for death, are we not instead driven towards death by trying to run away from it?" (p.110).

Reminding ourselves of the need for a rejection brings us at the same time to the *central points which are to be rejected*. The obsession with living and surviving with the help of the limitless money accumulation system takes the economic form of *competition*.[2] Competitiveness in the competition-based market is the deciding factor between life and death for the players in the

---

1   R. Bahro, 1987.
2   Cf. W. Hoogendijk, 1991; P. Potter, 1992; R. Petrella, 1993a and 1993b; M. Porter 1980 and 1990; The Group of Lisbon, 1993.

economy. The conditions and aims of competition determine the transnational financial markets. Due to the fact that capital only flows to areas where the highest possible returns can be got in the quickest time, working people, whole regions and countries, even continents (Africa, for example), are simply excluded, left to the mercy of relief aid or to hunger and death. Only firms, countries, and continents which stand out through competitive productivity can survive. The competitive cult is characterised by the logic of warfare. Firms "conquer" and "defend" markets. Correspondingly, all that is not competitive is "sacrificed" – the majority of people and of the whole planet. It is very obvious that the competitive chaos stimulated by the transnational money markets is at the heart of the death spiral affecting the economy at present. This then pervades all of society, secondary and tertiary education, research, the media, and collective and individual behaviour.

– As a result, all uncompetitive means of production – even if they are producing useful consumer goods – are eliminated, producing unemployment and other forms of exclusion.

– As a result, society is split into those who have wealth (in hard currency) at their disposal and so become richer, and those who, as dependent workers or having been excluded (individuals, communities, countries, continents), become poorer. For the first time in history, according to Père Léon[3], we have reached a point where the poor are no longer necessary. They are not even exploited any more, they are just superfluous and subsequently ostracised.

– As a result, the dynamic is being stepped up to accelerate and increase the transformation of energy and natural resources into products and waste ('throughput'), with devastating effects on the environment. In terms of economic policy, progress is measured by the growth of the gross national product (GNP) (which conceals where growth is occurring and for whom).

– As a result, democratic participation by the people is being constantly undermined because the politicians are losing their influence over the money markets and financial institutions and have less and less room for manoeuvre. Consequently, it is becoming ever more difficult to structure the conditions governing the interaction between people and their eco-space in a defined community.

---

3   Founder and leader of the "La Poudrière" community in Brussels.

– As a result of what started with the "cut-throat competition" between the northern Italian city-states, the whole of humanity is degenerating into a mass of competing individuals, who no longer accept their mutual limitations and dependence, instead striving endlessly for profit and success – without considering the rising tide of violence and the effects on the weak.

Competitiveness for unlimited money accumulation is the objective and subjective basic structure, the "god" of our market society, which determines the whole. Accordingly, the core of what we must reject is the absolute value attributed to competition and the total absence of limits set on the cancerous growth of capital.

The liberation must, therefore, be comprehensive, just as the 'spirit' of capitalism is comprehensive. In other words, the spiritual side is not one of many dimensions but decisive for the whole. Gerhard Breidenstein makes a similar point in his book *Hoffen inmitten der Krisen*[4] (Hope in the midst of crises). This leads us back to Aristotle, who saw the money-accumulation economy as being driven by the yearning for a life without limits. The same holds true for Jesus, who said that anyone who wanted to win eternal life (through material wealth) would lose it. Mammon (called Baal under agrarian conditions) is, as we saw, not simply 'money' (or 'land') but the whole political, economic and ideological system based on amassing money (or land as a means of production and accumulation), a system which functions as the definitive god for our whole society.

The denial of the mechanisms of the money-accumulation economy, which brings death while seemingly trying to avoid it, is a deeply theological question: should we ultimately trust the illusory god, who presents himself as the only powerful being (free from all laws of faith and love, as Luther once said), or should we trust God, who is so humble as to identify with slaves and with poor widows, and allows Jesus to be crucified – and in so doing helps put human life back on the road to recovery? H. Assmann and F. Hinkelammert have published a detailed analysis of the theo-economic problem of "idolising the market".[5] The unrelenting logic of money accumulation (fetishism) removes the market from its rootedness in the basic needs of society and in-

---

4   G. Breidenstein, 1990.
5   H. Assmann and F. Hinkelammert, 1989; cf. F. Hinkelammert, 1985. See also S. George and F. Sabelli, 1994, on the "visible hands" of the idol.

stead develops an ideology of making sacrifices – just as to the idols in the Old Testament.[6]

Theologians and churches wanting to respond to the liberating and life-creating God have, for theological reasons, to denounce the transnational market that is solely subject to the laws of money accumulation and aspires to total dominance.

> The EKD (German Protestant Church) gives itself away in that its economic memorandum, through its very title *The Common Good and Self-interest*, refuses to make a choice between Yahweh and Baal, and between God and Mammon. This demonstrates that it has not only failed to understand analytically how the present system functions on a global scale, but also what functions as 'God' within this system. This is a great pity, as a clear description and assessment of the present global reality, along with a firm denial of the moloch of a world market based on money accumulation, would have an enormously liberating effect on its victims.

As has already been stated, gods can only survive as long as they are worshipped. Without acceptance and legitimation, power cannot exist. A denial of the untamed commodity-money mechanisms of the world market is, therefore, the most important precondition for a change of direction towards a life-sustaining economy.

There can, however, be no denial of idols without consequences. Whoever does not fall down and worship the golden image will be persecuted (Daniel 3). For Shadrach, Meshach and Abednego at the time of the totalitarian Hellenistic Empire, this meant being thrown into a blazing furnace. It is also what the market has planned for church leaders from Africa, Asia and Latin America, as has been shown by the cases of Bishop Oscar Romero, who paid with his life, and Jean Bertrand Aristide in Haiti, who had to be rescued from several blazing furnaces before being elected president of his country, and who is still being persecuted today. In the North, the market ensures that people who are likely to commit "sacrilege" by condemning transnational deregulated capitalism never even become bishops. But it is not simply a matter of individuals within the church; our aim must be corporate action by the

---

6   Cf. H. Assmann et al., 1984; cf. B. Kern, 1991, pp.174ff., elaborating the link between Latin American liberation theology and the Marxist analysis of fetishism.

church. For this we must first establish the necessary preconditions by enabling it to carry out intensive theological and economic study – and not simply by looking at the alleged consensus of so-called experts. A church which, with regard to a system like the world market with such an asymmetric distribution of power, claims only to be interested in "balance", has already betrayed both the God of the Bible and its own existence as a church.

It is not a matter of lip service, but of the form taken by the church as an economic entity. Like the messianic groups and communities at the time of Jesus and Paul, so the church today – scattered among the peoples – must clearly distance itself from certain capitalist practices and structures. The Barmen Theological Declaration makes the same point in Article III:

> The Christian church is the community of brothers in which Jesus Christ acts presently as Lord in word and sacrament by the Holy Spirit. As the church of pardoned sinners, in the midst of a sinful world, it has to witness by its faith and obedience, its message and order, that it is his alone, that it lives and desires to live only by his consolation and by his orders, in expectation of his coming. We reject the false doctrine that the church is permitted to form its own message or its order according to its own desire or according to prevailing philosophical or political convictions.

The form and structures of our mainline churches are, however, in clear contravention of this biblical and confessional basis:

– The majority of our churches have a passage in their constitution stating that their money must be invested *carefully and profitably*. We must continue to search for an alternative way to deal with this money. Simply continuing to regard the question of investing money to make a profit as being unimportant should no longer be acceptable to Christians, if they want their church to be the Church of Christ. Ton Veerkamp is right when he says that the simple ban on interest payments, a concept found in the Bible, and repeated by Luther, cannot easily be endorsed in a growth economy. The question of interest-rate levels (measured in terms of real growth) remains, however, as does the question of whether church money should be deposited with commercial banks operating transnationally, or more preferable alternatives should be found – even if this means lower "profits".

– Another example is the question of the regulations governing work done within the church, whereby clergymen and other church leaders are paid according to pay scales for civil servants while other employees are taken on and paid as white-collar and blue-collar staff – following the established structure of capitalist society, with its growing gap between the privileged few and the ess well-off.

– A further area for consideration is the growing imbalance, created by the capitalist world market, between the economic weight of churches in the North and the South. Are donations sufficient? Or are they and other economic adaptations to the capitalist society a betrayal of the biblical option to reject allegedly "normal" structures and attitudes in a totalitarian situation – if only symbolically?

These questions involved in the rejection in no way affect only churches, congregations and communities, or Christians solely as individuals, but *all money-owning consumers*, if they feel a sense of responsibility for the life of all present-day people, for vital natural resources and for life of future generations. The obvious first step is not to bypass the tax authorities and deposit one's money in Luxembourg or the Bahamas. But there is still the question of whether strategies can be developed for a general rejection of the financial system, which we can only investigate more closely if we ourselves adopt alternatives.

The same is true for reducing consumption. In a previous book, G. Liedke and I made this point using the examples of meat and energy consumption.[7] The question of living standards is itself in danger of becoming a hobby for those who can afford it. This, however, does not lead to a way of calling into question the basic conditions regarding our handling of money and consumption. The commodity-money mechanism, driven by the yearning for infinite wealth, and made even stronger by the media, is the heart of the problem.

There are special and very effective means of resistance in connection with the question of rejections and new practices where money and commodities are concerned. The example of *boycotts and sanctions* against South Africa has shown that many people and institutions with money and consumer power at their disposal can support freedom movements and the struggle against injustice.

"Shopping basket politics"[8] is only possible if the many small players involved organise themselves. All over the world, many people, encouraged by the liberation

---

7 Cf. U. Duchrow and G. Liedke, 1989, pp.67ff.
8 Cf. E. Stelck, 1980.

movements and linked by the World Council of Churches and solidarity networks, were mobilised and took part in a programme of boycotting South African products and exerting pressure on banks which continued to trade in South Africa. Specific boycotts or threats of such action against transnational companies (TNCs) which continue to cause larger than normal amounts of social or environmental damage have also proved to be very effective. These Goliaths fear that their corporate image could be damaged. Known examples of this are the campaigns against Nestlé (which was exporting artificial baby milk to Third World countries, a practice that had fatal consequences due to the lack of basic hygiene requirements) and against Del Monte (because of socially unjust conditions on its pineapple plantations in the Philippines).[9] In many countries, solidarity groups, religious orders, churches and church-based relief organisations have created cooperative research and advisory facilities, to advise investors and consumers of boycotts and other actions. The best known of these facilities is the "Interfaith Center for Corporate Responsibility" (ICCR) in New York. In Germany, alongside the long-established "Bundeskongress entwicklungspolitischer Aktionsgruppen" (BUKO) (Federal Congress of Development Policy Action Groups), many newer, small "economy workshops" and similar research and advisory groups have been set up. They have to struggle to survive financially, though. Why?

At this point it is necessary to examine the attitude of the churches. Let us take the example of the German Protestant Church (EKD). It represents the classical approach which the South African Kairos document calls "church theology": in cases of clear structural injustice, instead of establishing a clear position leading to clearcut action, it encourages "dialogue".

It is claimed that taking part in boycotts is "not appropriate for churches". As a result, the EKD did not support the action of its women's movement "Don't buy the fruits of apartheid"; it refused to give any of the income from church taxes to the special WCC fund to combat racism, through which humanitarian projects organised by the liberation movements are supported; it did not take part in the action of closing accounts held with banks which traded in South Africa; it pursued a "programme of dialogue" with TNCs[10], instead of demanding clear answers

---

9 Cf. W. Kessler, 1990, pp.141ff.
10 Cf. U. Duchrow, 1993, pp.329ff.

on individual problems as the Dutch churches did with Shell Petroleum; it gives small subsidies to the "economy workshops" and to BUKO through the "Ausschuß für entwicklungsbezogene Bildung und Publizistik" (committee for development education and journalism), but apart from the all-too-small contributions to these groups, it neither has an adequate research and advisory capacity in this area, nor is it prepared to take part in campaigns as mentioned above. Its support is urgently needed today with regard to boycotts against banks that do not write off, or at least substantially reduce, the debts which developing countries have long since repaid, in real terms.

From a theological point of view, it is a clear contravention of biblical tradition on the part of the EKD to dismiss such action as "not appropriate for churches". Exactly the opposite is true: those who do not act when faced with obvious (structural) sins are themselves behaving in a way "not appropriate for churches". This is even part of the Augsburg Confession (Art 16). In the area of economics and politics, campaigns of action are urgently *required* when one is no longer able to conduct oneself in a spirit of solidarity, but instead forced to sin. Here it is a matter of obeying God rather than men (Acts 5:29). The EKD and its member churches have never retracted their view that boycotts are "not appropriate for churches" (despite the fact that it is the only member church of the WCC which still maintains this view). In so doing, they are in direct contravention of the Bible and their own confessional writings. Moreover, from a political point of view it is naive to assume that the capitalist system and governments operating within this system would allow "dialogues" of which the seriousness is not put to the test by action. We will come back to this topic in Chapter X. For now, we should concern ourselves with the question of small-scale concrete alternatives which can accompany a strategy of dissent.

It is important to remember: mechanisms and structures which only serve to accumulate money, and harm the majority of people, nature and future generations, are to be rejected on principle. In practical terms, this means that they are to be delegitimised and influenced through using the power of consumers and savers in the form of boycotts. Here the churches have not only an untapped power for life, but an opportunity to be the church in the biblically legitimate form of "alternative society".

Chapter IX

Small-scale networked alternatives on the basis of a new vision

In biblical times, the resistance groups speaking out in the Jewish apocalyptic writings and the communities of Jesus the Messiah did not only reject the mechanisms of the totalitarian Hellenistic and Roman Empires, i.e. the god of gold and Mammon. They also had a vision of alternatives and put these into practice in the way they led their daily lives. They were sure that these totalitarian systems would soon disappear, having feet of clay and a self-destructive streak capable of destroying themselves from within. This still holds true today: just as the classically liberal world economy collapsed during the great global economic crisis of 1929, so the neo-liberal phase will end in a catastrophe affecting every society, not just those which have already degenerated into a state of chaos, unless a drastic "U-turn"[1] takes place. In both scenarios, alternatives which have been investigated and/or put into practice are of crucial importance. In the event of a complete collapse, they will be a means of survival and the seeds of a new system. In the event of the still awaited U-turn occurring on a macro-level, they will be not only the experimental workshops but also the fundamental support for every political strategy and intervention, as will be shown in Chapter X. It would be very short-sighted to expect political intervention alone to solve all the problems, thereby downplaying the possibilities offered by rejection and alternatives.

The normal question asked when one publicly criticises the present world economy is: "What is the alternative?" Has it not been proved that socialist planned economies cannot succeed? This question is understandable. The propaganda of the interest groups and the economic high priests of the capitalist market economy appears only to propose this false alternative. We have also seen that both private and state capitalist models function according to the same modern mechanisms of the industrial commodity-money relationship, despite all their differences at first glance with respect to the property ownership and distribution of wealth. Are there ways and alternatives beyond the private capitalist market economy and state capitalism?

---

1 Cf. W. Hoogendijk, 1991, pp.81ff.

Although there is no one *single* alternative, we are in the happy position of already having many books on the subject and also the results of practical attempts to implement alternatives – in contrast to the indoctrinated view that there *is* no alternative. Here is just a selection[2]:

Some authors take as their starting point environmental alternatives (land or technology) and go on to deal with social and environmental questions. Among these authors, after the classic by E.F. Schumacher, *Small is Beautiful*, there are: Hazel Henderson, *Creating Alternative Futures* and *The Politics of the Solar Age*; H. Daly and J. Cobb jr., *For the Common Good – Redirecting the Economy Toward Community, the Environment and a Sustainable Future*; E. Altvater, *Der Preis des Wohlstands oder Umweltplünderung und neue Welt(un)ordnung* (The price of prosperity or environmental plundering and the new world (dis)order). A special variant on the environmental approach is eco-feminism, a theme concentrated on by Maria Mies, *Patriarchat und Kapital – Frauen in der internationalen Arbeitsteilung* (Patriarchy and capital – women and the international division of labour). Others begin with alternatives in the working world, e.g. W. Kessler, *Aufbruch zu neuen Ufern – Ein Manifest für eine sozial-ökologische Wirtschaftsdemokratie* (Setting off for new shores – a manifesto for a socio-environmental economic democracy). Some authors concentrate on the money mechanisms, for example Margrit Kennedy, *Interest and Inflation – Free Money*; H. Creutz, *Das Geldsyndrom – Wege zu einer krisenfreien Marktwirtschaft* (The money syndrome – ways to a market economy free from crisis). Kennedy and Creutz are writing in the tradition of Silvio Gesell, who proposed that every kind of savings should be taxed instead of having interest paid on them; W. Haller, *Die heilsame Alternative – Jesuanische Ethik in Wirtschaft und Politik* (The salutary alternative – Jesus ethics in economics and politics); and most importantly, the authors who, alongside Daly/Cobb, have put forward a comprehensive concept of an alternative economy: W. Hoogendijk, *The Economic Revolution – Towards a Sustainable Future by Freeing the Economy from Money-Making*; J. Robertson,

2   E.F. Schumacher, 1973; H. Henderson, 1978 and 1981; H.E. Daly and J.B. Cobb jr., 1989; E. Altvater, 1992; M. Mies, 1988; W. Kessler, 1990; M. Kennedy, 1988; H. Creutz, 1993; W. Haller, 1989; W. Hoogendijk, 1991; J. Robertson, 1990; P. Ekins (ed.), 1989[2]; G. Breidenstein, 1990; New Economics Foundation (NEF), Vine Court, 112-116 Whitechapel Rd., London E1 17E, publishes the main magazine, "New Economics", connected with this topic and provides a library service for English-language books in this field; NEF also organises, together with other NGOs, an annual counter-summit called "The Other Economic Summit" (TOES) to coincide with the annual economic summit of the G7 nations.

Future Wealth - - New Economics for the 21st Century, P. Ekins (ed.), *The Living Economy*, and *Real-life Economics* with M. Max-Neef (ed.). (The last four authors have links with the London-based New Economics Foundation, an important centre for work on alternative economic concepts and models.) Finally, one can look at the idea of a complete alternative from the basis of the spiritual question of a release from "egocentricity", as G. Breidenstein does in *Hoffen inmitten der Krisen – Von Krankheit und Heilung unserer Gesellschaft* (Hope in the middle of the crisis – a remedy for the malaise affecting our society). It must be added that in 1992, at a conference organised by Non-Governmental Organisations (NGOs) parallel to the UNCED Summit in Rio, a number of "treaties" for an alternative economy were concluded. These documents are fundamental for any further consideration of the topic because they reflect the widest consensus of the social movements.[3] Moreover, especially encouraging is the fact that there is one branch of the UN which – to a certain degree at least – is working on the same basis as all these alternative approaches: the United Nations Development Program (UNDP) with its annual *Human Development Report*.

There remains the question of how is it possible to politically implement such alternative approaches in the face of the gigantic, existing power complexes. We will look at this in the next chapter, but we should also keep the question in mind while presently investigating the alternative visions and practical endeavours. In connection with this, it is important to realise that economies are a result of the constant interplay between any number of local, regional, national and global factors. We should always remember which level we are dealing with. Something which works at community level, or lower, need not yet be workable at a much higher level in the whole system.

1 The vision of an economy for life

The above studies and facilities and many others, all work from one basic assumption: in contrast to the present dominant system, the new economy must be life-sustaining in three respects:

---

3   In: Sutherland (ed.), 1992; cf. T.W. Fatheuer, 1992, pp.27ff., referring to the unbalanced and partly contradictory statements in the various treaties and to the common trend, summarised in nine points.

- the life of all present-day people, i.e. it must satisfy their basic needs;
- the life of all our fellow creatures on Earth;
- the life of future generations.

In other words, priority must be given these three dimensions, which are currently only variables as opposed to the invariable of wealth accumulation. The economy must serve them, not the other way round. This means that an "economy from below" must replace an "economy from above". This is why all the approaches I have mentioned are based on people and the earth. The social and environmental perspectives, therefore, are always fundamentally related to a democratic perspective. In the new system, people are players, not economic objects.[4]

This immediately leads us to another change. Instead of defining competing individuals as its starting point, the new economy will be based around the "person in community".[5] The crucial factor in Aristotle's work is thereby rediscovered: the "household", i.e. the formerly smallest unit of production and consumption is the reference point for the economy.[6] All larger units in the economy must be geared to meeting basic needs, although today there are other units apart from the nuclear family (that did not exist in Aristotle's time anyway) and which must be taken as the local starting points. We will return to this subject shortly.

Let us take the *NGO Forum treaty on Alternative Economic Models*[7] from Rio as a comprehensive basis for further detailed study. After a preamble containing basically the same criticisms of the present world economy as I have already made, there are a number of *principles:*

"Our vision of the alternatives to the current economic models is grounded on the following principles:

1 The fundamental purpose of economic organization is to provide for the basic needs of a community, in terms of food, shelter, education, health, the enjoyment of culture, as opposed to a concentration on the generation of profit and on the growth of production for its own sake. Economic life must

---

4 This is also the central theme of the 1993 UNDP Human Development Report. It should be remembered, however, that these annual UNDP reports remain ambiguous and undecided – presumably so they do not lose the financial support of the West. They often raise critical questions but construct answers around neo-liberal reality. cf. the fundamental criticism by T. Kunanayakam, 1993.
5 Cf. Daly and Cobb, 1989, pp.159ff.
6 Ibid., pp.138ff.
7 In: Sutherland (ed.), 1992.

also be organised in such a way that it enhances rather than destroys the environment and safeguards natural resources for the use of future generations.

2   An alternative to the current system must be based on indigenous, community-based, people-empowering models that are rooted in peoples' experiences, history, and eco-cultural reality. This implies, incorporating diversity of alternative production systems, decision-making processes, and technologies, especially those drawn from indigenous peoples and peasant communities.

3   An alternative economic model must recognize and institutionalize a central and equal role for women in shaping economic life.

4   An alternative economic model should be based on the relative self-sufficiency of communities, regions, and nations, rather than on free trade, the world market, and large domestic and transnational corporations as the central institutions that determine production and distribution.

5   Economic life must be informed by bottom-up development strategies, in which people and communities have the power to make economic decisions that affect their lives, in contrast with the dominant model which marginalises grassroot communities and fosters international economic relations in which the center subjugates the periphery.

6   One of the central ethical foundations of an alternative economic model is the interdependence of all peoples and the interdependence of peoples and communities and the non-human material world. This interdependence demands a system of sharing resources based on autonomy, equality, participatory democracy, and solidarity. As members of a community, individuals must also take responsibility for living within the limits of the earth's resources, in contrast with the Northern model of excessive consumption.

7   Human and economic development indicators should no longer exclusively or principally reflect material growth and technological advance but must take into account individual, social, and environmental well-being. Such indicators would include health, gender equalities, unpaid family work, equalization in the distribution of income, better care of children, and the maximization of human happiness with minimal use of resources and minimal generation of waste.

8   In an alternative economic system, the state will be transformed from being chiefly a facilitating agent of the present economic system that is dominated by domestic and transnational corporations, into a mechanism that genuinely represents and serves the people's will and promotes a strategy of relatively self-reliant, community-centered development."

Of course, the feasibility of these principles has yet to be properly investigated. Much attention, however, should be given to point 7 because it is one of the fundamental questions connected with this vision: the so-called *indicators of development* or, put another way, the *yardsticks for measuring the success of the economy*. We have already seen that the current measuring instrument, the GNP, concentrates solely on the quantitative growth of the economy and therefore exactly who the winners and losers are is unclear.

Victor Anderson offers the most formulated version of alternative indicators in his book *Alternative Economic Indicators*.[8] It is not possible here to refer to and discuss in detail the on-going debate about possible alternatives to the use of the GNP as a yardstick. Daly and Cobb give an overview, as does the 1993 Human Development Report.[9] Because this report, as a UN publication, is the most representative on the subject, although not the most radical, I would like to briefly summarise its arguments.

The UNDP differentiates between two separate indices: the Human Development Index (HDI) and the Human Freedom Index (HFI). The HDI is defined as follows: "Human development is a process of enlarging people's choices. In principle, these choices can be infinite and change over time. But at all levels of development, the three essential ones are for people to lead a long and healthy life, to acquire knowledge and to have access to resources needed for a decent standard of living. If these choices are not available, many other opportunities remain inaccessible". The report stresses the fact that this is only a minimum. Besides the three-sided concept of human development, there are, of course, a number of possibilities regarding the measurement of the three indicators. Among these are: life expectancy, healthcare, nutrition for a long and healthy life; education, from literacy to research; incomes, with respect to poverty, labour, the status of women and children, social security and the environment. As a result of these factors, economic success can be measured in diverse ways, which shows that the environment does not have the same prominent status as it has in other alternative approaches that have been mentioned. Despite this, it is clear that this approach represents a great improvement over the present system, where the measuring instrument, the GNP, is centred around the value of money.

8　V. Anderson, 1991.
9　Daly and Cobb, 1989, pp.62ff; Human Development Report 1993, pp.10ff. and pp.104ff. (detailed discussion of the economic debate).

Satisfying the basic needs of people in the community, and maintaining the natural conditions for life, especially for future generations – how can these goals be achieved?

2 An economy for life in community

In the description of an alternative economy, it is possible to follow the traditional division of labour, land and capital and subsequently ask: "How would an alternative economy look with regard to these production factors?", "How would distribution be organised?", and "How would one design a form of consumption that enhances life?". In posing these questions, however, the damaging approach of the traditional economy would right from the outset be introduced into the description of the alternative and conceal the more important aspects, despite the fact that the alternative must provide answers to all this as well. It is far more appropriate, in my opinion, to start with constituting community and society at different levels, from the local to the global.

The small units of the messianic communities under the totalitarian Roman Empire, as we have seen, shared everything such that, through their common life and household management, nobody lacked anything and, most importantly, there was a sense of equality and happiness. The same principle lives on today in the form of *base communities*. Instead of describing the elements of such a community in an abstract way, I would like to use an example: the "La Poudrière" community, which is situated in and around Brussels.

"La Poudrière" consists of five communities which have developed out of the original community over the last 35 years. They were inspired by Abbé Pierre and the Emmaus movement. Homeless and unemployed people got together to work on all kinds of waste from our affluent society, selling repaired goods to other poor people. They have taken the initiative and can support themselves with this ecological recycling activity. They needed a van to collect bulky waste, which they also use to do removals, another source of income. They now have over 100 members in all and also run a removals firm. They have renovated an old brewery and factory for their recycling activities, vehicle repairs and all kinds of manual jobs. Parts of the works premises have been renovated for accommodation, as have derelict houses. Most of their food comes from their own farm.

The group of five communities, present in the city and the country, is an autonomous cell of poor people for the poor in a totalitarian global economic system – and so richer and fitter than those deriving their wealth from the "whore of Babylon" (Rev 18), who will meet their doom when disaster strikes her. The main thing is that people are living a life in community which is impressive in its wholeness, and marked by joy and healing, as can be seen from the many people at risk who have made a new beginning there. In front of the large kitchen there is a big terrace on the garage roof, so that children can play there in sight of their parents. Meals take place around one or two large tables, made from timber from the farm. In the house of the first community there are five artistic stained glass windows over the tables in the dining room. They depict the five *goals* of the community: presence, friendship, justice, utopia and hope, and self-discipline. Here is a short explanation taken from the community's newsletter (May 1993):[10]

> At first we had a very clear goal: to be present...incarnate...in the neighbourhood, among the masses...with ordinary people living just like them...to be a leaven, a festive ferment.
>
> At the same time we discovered the meaning of friendship...and tried to offer it without expecting anything in return. As we grew we had to renovate a cellar and then an old house over the way – and we said that if friendship is to remain possible there has to be more justice.
>
> Two tendencies emerged: some wanted to become involved in politics and parties, while others just wanted to be present, without trying to become an activist every time. Instead of just fighting for the "great evening", already they wanted to be a "small morning"... "...Those who then left the community called the others 'utopian', dreamers...and so our Utopia (believing in the whole person) became a programme!...We also discovered that we had to change ourselves in order to change society and others. So we realised the importance of self-discipline..."

The argument about whether the community should be a lived example of an alternative, or means to the end of political struggle, is central to the concern of this book and to the strategy discussion within the social movements. Do we want all or nothing, politically, or to live our lives differently where we are? Are rejections and small-scale, lived alternatives in a totalitarian context more

---

10 La Poudrière, Bulletin de Liaison, mai 1993, p.10(tr.).

important than the prophetic use of possibilities offered by limited political influence? This question will remain with us to the end of the book.

Firstly, let us go back to the example of "La Poudrière". Besides its stated goals, the community tried to define the *means* by which these goals could be achieved: work; a shared life and communal use of goods; a simple lifestyle; trust in others and in the goals...simple resources, available to everyone...no-one is excluded, be it for reasons of their past, class background, religion, situation or job training.

In such cases, there is no ethnic exclusiveness, no masters and no slaves, and no dominance of men over women. Everyone is involved in the decision-making process, everyone receives the same financial allowance, and everyone is free to go on the main annual holiday excursion and to participate in cultural events. A small group celebrate Mass every morning, a larger group every Sunday and everybody joins in the periodic celebrations. The houses are always open to guests – the modern-day equivalent of the Pauline messianic communities, as are monasteries.

All over the world, a broad diversity of such base communities, and other types, demonstrate how to live differently. Many are constituted as orders. Among these are the Sisters of Grandchamp, in Switzerland, and the Brothers of Taizé, in France. Others live as Christian communities, in Germany, for example, in Wulfshagenerhütten, Wethen, Imshausen, the Mennonite community in Bammental and the traditional Hutterer brotherhood in the Eifel. On a European level, the Christian base communities have formed themselves into a network called the European Collective of Christian Base Communities. Their small head office is in Holland.[11] There are also communities with no religious links, however, often connected with self-administrated concerns like "Werk Selbstverwalteter Projekte und Einrichtungen" (agency for self-managed projects and facilities) in Neustadt an der Weinstraße. Many of them are taking part in "Project A", creating a network of contacts and publishing a pamphlet, using project funds, so that those interested can contact groups in their local area.[12]

Such autonomous communities based on solidarity form the bedrock of the new society. This will remain, even if the attempts to bring about a complete change in society fail or the destruction which the present system has

---

11   European Collective of Christian Base Communities, Mariahoek 16-17, Postbus 19 170, NL-3501 DD Utrecht.

12   C/o Pro A-Gruppe, Frankfurter Str. 2a, 35037 Marburg.

brought to the South, and is currently bringing to the East and parts of the West, leads to complete disaster.

Going beyond the "leaven community", the *level of the local community* and the small region are central to a life-sustaining economy. All the endeavours and proposals so far referred to agree that the economy of the future must, as far as possible, use the local community as its base. The basic supply structure, especially, must be organised as much as possible at the local level. Of course, this means a new urban-rural partnership must be formed in strongly urbanised areas. Producer-consumer cooperatives are a model for this. Daly and Cobb urge that regional planning in future should ensure towns and cities become smaller. The key element of this perspective is, as far as possible, to make local communities self-sufficient and immune to the damaging effects of the world market. With regard to trade, only that which can be produced due to special resources in a certain area and is surplus to domestic requirement should be put on the market. At present, local authorities are increasingly being forced to take on the burden of caring for those who have been excluded from the formal world market economy – while at the same time receiving fewer funds with which to do so. The reason given is that Germany, Britain, Europe etc. must remain competitive!

This leads to a basic issue of which few are aware: the division of economic power between

– non-financial (household) economy
– the state economic sector
– the global market economy.

Hilkka Pietilä has produced a study for the South Commission that not only shows the surprisingly strong links between these economic sectors, but also allows for strategic reflection.[13] Household economy she calls "free economy" because labour is not rewarded by financial payment but is also voluntary because it directly serves the welfare of the family. The state economy for local markets and its own domestic market, as well as the public service and public spending, is called the "protected economy" because the state takes as many political measures as possible to protect these areas from the intervention of the world market. She calls the world market economy a "fettered economy" because the transnational market calls the shots – this is, therefore, an appropriate description of the actual

---

13 H. Pietilä, 1991.

situation in contrast to the ideological distortion which talks of "free" economy and "free" trade precisely in connection with the global economy.

In 1980 the Finnish national economy showed the following division between these economic sectors:

	Time	Money
A. Free (household) economy	54%	35%
B. Protected (state) economy	36%	46%
C. Fettered economy	10%	19%

This means, therefore, that even in an industrialised country like Finland, free (household) economic activities can be responsible for more than half of all economic performance – naturally not accounted for by the GNP.

At this point, however, a number of differences should be pointed out. It must be made clear how this free (household) economy interacts with the *informal economy* and the *subsistence economy*.[14] The concept of the informal economy is the opposite of the formal economy, where labour is regulated by pay and contracts, workers are organised in trade unions and the Welfare State guarantees benefits to those who need them. In the neo-liberal phase of Fordism, more and more workers are being excluded from these regulated conditions. In the main, the informal sector reflects the deformalisation of the economy. In the Two-Thirds World, there has never been a time when all workers were included in the formal economy. Not only there but also in the North, the deformalised sector is rapidly expanding. Under this system – in contrast to subsistence economies – production is based around market needs, and not only at the local level. The informal economy is often brutally abused by the formal economy because it is the lowest link in a cheap supply chain for production for the world market. In addition to this, exploitative Mafia networks often spring up. Under the influence of the world market, the informal economy is characterised by a constant struggle for survival. It is not a self-contained free sector.

Despite similarities, there is a difference between the informal sector and a subsistence economy, which has an approach based on self-sufficiency. But as Marx saw, such an economy is also capable of being abused within the frame-

---

14 Cf. E. Altvater, 1987, pp.44ff., and the excellent article by Gudrun Kochendörfer-Lucius, 1991.

work of the capitalist system, due to the unpaid and therefore exploited work done in reproducing the workers for the formal and informal sectors.

So we cannot just assume that informal and subsistence economies are free. It is all the more important to protect them and enable them to become truly creative, community-inclusive economic areas. Hilkka Pietilä is of the opinion that "we should improve the conditions for revival of free economy".[15] The International Wages for Housework Campaign is working towards such an improvement.[16] J. Robertson has collated further proposals with regard to taxation, land use and education etc.[17]

In this field, one must consider the question of economic discrimination against *women* and how the special contribution of women towards an alternative economy can be fully utilised. The role division between housework and paid work must be broken down, and so the upgrading of housework to a form of paid employment would be one component in the renewal of the economy, and an important step towards eliminating discrimination against women.[18]

To summarise, the challenge is to improve protection for the informal economy of the poor, while using this system as a testing ground for an alternative, life-sustaining economy. This is a field where people can become less dependent on the world market and in so doing gain strength for their political struggle. That brings us now to the question of alternative micro-economics and micro-financial systems.

3 Alternative micro-economics

If we look at the informal economy not only as a desperate form of survival economy, but as a testing ground for a future life-sustaining economy, it must be in the light of learning from mistakes or wrong developments so far.

Economic dimensions are normally divided into consumption, production and distribution.

In the case of *consumption*, there is one main alternative:

---

15 H. Pietilä, op. cit., p.8; cf. J. Robertson, op. cit., pp.35f.
16 International Wages for Housework Campaign, c/o King's Cross Women's Centre, P.O.Box 287, London NW6 5QU.
17 J. Robertson, op. cit., pp.36f., in connection with Scott Burns, 1975.
18 Cf. also H. Ludwig, 1987, pp.28ff.

- Consumption should not be orientated around the satisfaction of boundless desires and "preferences" (which only serve money accumulation), but around basic needs and, moreover, around that which is not harmful to people and the planet. This means that when it comes to "demand", a micro-economy must concentrate on utility goods, essential services, and culture.

Production, which orientates itself around the demand for utility goods, has several dimensions:

- With regard to *labour*, industrial capitalism has alienated the workforce in three ways: firstly, by separating them from the means of production; secondly, by subjecting them to increasingly stressful working conditions; and thirdly, by the fact that they have no say in the final product. As a result, we should be on the lookout for companies in which the workers are co-owners, and in which the workers are not faced with over-demanding working conditions and participate fully in the process of deciding what they produce.
- With regard to *technology*, the current trend is to become bigger, more complex, more expensive, and more harmful (to people and planet). An economy for life must, therefore, aim to develop suitable technology which is on a smaller scale and has a simpler form, as well as being less capital intensive and less harmful.[19]
- With regard to *land* and the biosphere, it is a matter of producing environmentally sustainable industrial goods and following organic methods of agriculture. The question of *scale* is of central importance here, too.
- With regard to *money*, it is vital to largely eliminate money as a means of preserving value and to redefine it as a medium of exchange for utility goods and as a form of production loan, with fair or no interest rates, as a function of the productive power of the producer.

Finally, from the very outset, the micro-economy should aim to create a different form of distribution. The development of a gap between rich and poor, as in the case of the present macro-economy, will then not be possible because of the participation in production by the workers.

There are examples of all of this. W. Kessler calls them "germ cells" of an alternative economic policy – a good description for the vision of a future economy.[20]

---

19 Cf. E.F. Schumacher, 1979, pp.54ff.

3.1 Alternative companies and company networks

J. Robertson rightly draws our attention to the fact that alternative companies which are linked by having the same economic, social and environmental aims, are doing away with a myth of the classical economy. This myth says that companies must create wealth to be distributed and consumed – by wages, and also by the redistribution methods of the state, such as taxation and employment schemes. This myth also forms the basis of Keynesianism. The latter long disguised the fact that, because of this model, an increasingly disproportionate share of the created wealth finds its way straight into the pockets of the owners of capital. In today's neo-liberal reality, and indeed since the 1980s, this has been obvious for all to see; likewise the redistribution is reaching more and more people only in the form of minimal monetary transfer payments. These people are, therefore, no longer participants in the economic process. Indeed, they are excluded from it with all the individual and (a)social psychological consequences this entails. In the face of current widespread structural unemployment, the time has come to end the separation between wealth creation and redistribution as a basic model for capitalism.

There is one more matter to be dealt with in this respect. This model, in its Fordist-Keynesian form, presumed that the disproportionate accumulation of capital and simultaneous mass welfare could only be guaranteed by continuing to boost growth. This idea was not only disproved in the 1970s by the problem of overproduction but is also unjustifiable on principle for environmental reasons. Further growth of the Fordist kind, with its associated squandering of resources and overproduction of waste, would not produce sufficient financial profit to pay for the elimination of environmental damage. From both a social and an environmental perspective, therefore, the division between wealth creation and socio-environmental remedies is, in reality, a thing of the past – even if economists and politicians are still working mainly with these old, inappropriate concepts.[21] These preliminary remarks illustrate the importance of experimenting with alternative company structures all over the world, whether or not these experiments are successful.

----

20 Cf. W. Kessler, 1990, pp.108ff.; see also J. Robertson, op. cit., pp.47ff.; P. Ekins, 1986, pp.264ff.
21 Yet certain proposals by Keynes regarding political regulatory instruments at the national and international levels contain important elements, which will concern us in the next chapter.

One of the oldest and most successful European examples in this century has been Mondragon in Spain's Basque Country.[22]

> In 1941 the priest Don José Maria Arizmendiarrieta, with the help of a popula-
> tion still recovering from the effects of the civil war, began building a technical
> college. The first self-managed cooperatives soon followed in the Leniz valley. A
> credit cooperative was set up to fund the venture. By 1986, the system of coopera-
> tives in the region consisted of: 103 industrial cooperatives (with high quality re-
> search centres), 8 agricultural cooperatives, 4 service cooperatives (including
> medical care), 1 consumer cooperative, 17 housing cooperatives, and 46 educa-
> tion cooperatives with, in total, around 20,000 working members. All these
> workers and their families see themselves not only as owners but also as co-re-
> sponsible creators of this continuously expanding enterprise, in which economic
> (wealth creating) and social components are integrated.

By 1990, there were between 12,000 and 15,000 self-managed companies in Germany with around 100,000 workers.[23] Of these, W. Kessler examines the Blätterwald Cooperative in Oberursel and the Panda shoe factory in Naila. There are also examples of original ways of shortening working hours, as at Hewlett Packard and the Canstatter Volksbank. The integration of social aspects in the economic organisation and production is important in all these companies, as is participation, inclusion of the disabled, and pay on the basis of need and availability, not the maximisation of profits.

From the United States, M. Phillips has written about an amazing model for networking – the Briarpatch Network, consisting of 315 small firms in the Bay Area of San Francisco.[24] They are all united in their goal of a simple lifestyle, open and honest book-keeping and management styles, as well as mutual cooperation. The network needs only two co-ordinators and provides its members with business and legal advice, and medical and education services. By means of this cooperation, the companies are able to free themselves

---

22 The Caja Laboral Popular in Mondragon (tel. 79 10 44) offers special courses for
visitors. The information below is drawn from their documents; cf. also U. Reifner and
J. Ford (ed.), 1992, pp.201ff. This model is now affected by unemployment problems
caused by the conditions imposed by the world market.
23 Cf. W. Kessler, loc. cit.; cf. also the details about "Project A", already referred to.
24 In: P. Ekins, 1986, pp.272ff.

to a large extent from dictatorial market forces and are, moreover, a great source of innovative production.

3.2 *Alternative technologies*

Alternative companies have not only social, but also environmental aims. We have been reminded of this fact by the example of the "La Poudrière" community.

> W. Kessler has written about Ernst Winter & Son, a Hamburg company which is the largest producer of diamond and borazon tools in the Western world.[25] This company has not only made its own factory environmentally friendly, but has set up a German association for environmentally benign materials management. Another example is the Follman & Co. chemical factory in Minden, which not only organises its production around environmental criteria, but has also, along with 60 other firms in the local area, established the Pro Future lobby which obliges its members to have an ecological management style.

I have deliberately begun with examples from the industrialised nations because capitalist ideology frequently maintains that an "alternative economy" means a return to the Stone Age. However, it is vitally important that the vast majority of the world's population stay on the lookout for alternatives to Western technology, which due to capital intensity is prohibitively expensive for them. Moreover, by using alternative technologies, people can often put their own resources and abilities to better use and take into account their own cultural needs.

The Development Commission of the World Council of Churches carried out an important experimental study in this area in the 1970s and early 1980s. Pascal de Pury summarises the situation in *People's Technologies and People's Participation*:

> "Technologies which help the poor to survive with their own resources, but also and above all to organise themselves and become (or become again) a people able to make their own choice of society and guide them towards liberation and development, are also defined as 'People's technologies'."[26]

---

25 W. Kessler, 1990, pp.115ff.

One example is the project of Ebenezer, an Indian engineer. He had been engaged in working on President Reagan's SDI Programme but quickly became frustrated and returned to India where, with Indian farmers, he developed the "pedal power" system.[27] He constructed bicycles that could also be used for powering other small, purpose-built machines, for example, for threshing or grinding. As a result of this, villages were able to increase their production and at the same time use the bicycles to deliver their products to local markets. In the next section we will look at more examples from agriculture.

At this point we should once more point out the great importance of alternative technologies. This raises the topic of *alternative energy*, especially solar energy, which most authors see as being fundamental for the future (see H. Henderson or E. Altvater). This question, of course, goes beyond the realm of micro-economics. It is *the* high-tech problem of the future. However, if it were resolved it would lead to a vast improvement in local economic possibilities precisely in the hot countries of the Two-Thirds World. For this reason it is both irresponsible and short-sighted on the part of a country like Germany to continue to invest far more in research in the area of nuclear power than in the development of solar energy and other alternative sources of energy.

3.3 Alternative land use

If there is one area where the absurdity of the present system must be obvious, it is European and North American agriculture, which is organised purely around the profit motive and has been industrialised to the point today where it is machine-intensive, chemical-intensive, and capital-intensive. The motto seems to be "expand or perish". The repercussions have had damaging effects in a number of areas: on smallholders; on taxpayers, who have to bear the costs of subsidies and storage costs as a result of overproduction; on farmers in the Two-Thirds World, who cannot compete with the subsidised dumping prices of the EU; and on the soil and drinking water, which have been contaminated by over-fertilising. Only the biggest players have survived: the banks; the transnational companies, and the most prosperous farmers. We are

26 P. de Pury, 1983, p.10.
27 J. Ebenezer, Pedal Power, in: Impact, Albuquerque Journal Magazine, 23/4/85, pp.4ff.

not yet talking here about the aims and strategies of political struggle against this madness, but about a different basic approach and the small-scale alternatives seeking to escape from this destructive system.

The alternative basic model is called *sustainable agriculture*. It is based on the principles of the NGO treaty of the same name which was agreed in Rio (here is a selection):

11. Sustainable agriculture is a model of social and economic organization based on an equitable and participatory vision of development which recognizes the environment and natural resources as the foundation of economic activity. Agriculture is sustainable when it is ecologically sound, economically viable, socially just, culturally appropriate and based on a holistic scientific approach;

12. Sustainable agriculture preserves biodiversity, maintains soil fertility and water purity, conserves and improves the chemical, physical and biological qualities of the soil, recycles natural resources, and conserves energy. Sustainable agriculture produces diverse forms of high quality foods, fibers, and medicines;

13. Sustainable agriculture uses locally available renewable resources, appropriate and affordable technologies, and minimizes the use of external and purchased inputs, thereby increasing local independence and self sufficiency and insuring a source of stable income for peasants, family and small farmers and rural communities. This allows more people to stay on the land, strengthens rural communities, and integrates humans with their environment;

15. Women play a key role in providing the largest proportion of the world's food resources, by growing, buying and selling.

It is clear, of course, that every situation is different due to local circumstances (climate, availability of land, etc.) and therefore no single definitive form or ideal system can be established. Sustainable agriculture can and must adapt to these local circumstances. A classic example: a nomadic lifestyle is appropriate if limitless amounts of land are available. If this is not the case, then over-grazing can be the result. Common land use can also lead to this problem. But even if one model cannot be universally applied, it can at least serve as an example of alternative approaches.

In this context, W. Kessler refers to the producer-consumer cooperatives in Germany, which number over 100.[28] In most of these cases, environmentally aware small firms have formed links with consumer groups in their local

---

28 W. Kessler, op. cit.

area. As a result, they become less dependent on the Common Agricultural Policy, run less risk of not finding outlets and are not so reliant on middlemen. The small farms keep their workers, the consumers are able to buy healthier foodstuffs, the soil is less contaminated by pesticides, overproduction is checked, and farmers in the developing world are not forced to contend with foreign imports at dumping prices.

The coalitions, however, go further and include environmental and one-world groups, as is shown by the Aachen Declaration from 1987 and the Altenkirchen Theses called "Small Scale Agriculture does have a Future" from 1989.[29] These documents are especially important for political strategies, which we will look at later. With regard to small-scale alternatives, the decisive step forwards would be a community-region integrated agricultural policy that concentrates on using local resources to cover the needs of the population of a region.[30] Models for this are the Community Land Trust (CLT), and the Cooperative Land Banks[31] which lease land to poor people to build houses, or to small-holders to put to agricultural use, as well as looking after the local infrastructure. These models are of fundamental interest because they remind us of the biblical message that land is not a commodity to be bought and sold, but an asset to be used. They have also shown that, in practice, land need not be used to reap profits for a few or to serve the inefficiency and nepotism of a centrally planned bureaucracy, because a third way is possible, linking solidarity and initiative.

Many traditional communities in Asia, Africa and Latin America have been able to defend what is left of their culture from the predatory market regulations. It is now a matter of strengthening and expanding these cultures, taking into account each situation and new environmental insights.

In India, initiatives of this kind are often in many ways linked to Gandhi's ideas for the development of village communities and cottage industries.[32] In the con-

---

29 A copy of the Aachen Declaration can be found in: U. Duchrow, 1992, pp.52ff.; further statements in this direction include the proceedings of the People's Parliament held by Kairos Europa in 1992, pp.1ff.

30 Cf. Daly and Cobb, 1989, pp.268ff., in favour of agriculture in the USA being based as much as possible on independent smallholdings at local and national levels.

31 Cf. P. Ekins, 1993, p.16, regarding the Community Land Trust which is run by the Institute for Community Economics in Massachusetts; cf. also P. Ekins (ed.), 1986, pp.181ff.

32 Cf. M. Gandhi, 1990, pp.13ff.

text of the increase in the number of coalitions among the indigenous people of Latin and South America in 1992, the question of land and an independent economy has become crucial.[33] It is to be hoped that the newly won power of resistance will lead to a lasting and successful movement campaigning for the release of more land. As we have seen, even in biblical times, the approaches to an alternative society were founded on the struggle of the smallholders against large-scale ownership and tributary power. One especially interesting model of how traditional, community-based agriculture can lead to modern, environmental understanding and can then be linked to it, has been developed in the last decade in Tanzania and Rwanda. In these countries it was even possible to claim back agricultural land from the desert by traditional, environmental recultivation.[34]

Let us remember: such small-scale approaches are not yet capable of changing entire agricultural systems, but they do point to alternatives that can then serve as a stimulus and basis for new political perspectives.

3.4 Alternative micro-financial systems

Many people are today united in their criticism of the capitalist economy and its mechanisms and institutions at every level. But how can we find alternatives in the field of finance? On this topic, the critics are far from united. In the next chapter we will look at the possibilities for politically taming and controlling the existing capitalist system. We must first examine the fundamental possibility of other ways of approaching the issue, especially at the level of micro-economics.

Silvio Gesell put forward a new approach 100 years ago in his book *Natürliche Wirtschaftsordnung* (Natural economic order).[35] *Two recent books by M. Kennedy and H. Creutz*[36] *explain the position of Gesell's modern-day supporters.*

---

33 T.W. Fatheuer, p.46, offers a good example of sustainable agriculture in the Amazon region.
34 Cf. K. Egger, 1990. This is only one example of the importance of socio-cultural factors in a new community-oriented development model; cf. M. Büscher, 1989; and P. Rottach (ed.), 1988.
35 Cf. S. Gesell, 1986.
36 M. Kennedy, 1991; H. Creutz, 1993.

In true Aristotelian tradition, this free economic theory sees the main problem as the use of money in the capitalist market economy not only as a means of exchange, but as a means of preserving value and accumulating wealth. It proposes, therefore, that instead of rewarding wealth accumulation by paying interest (which is behind the compound interest mechanisms, redistributing from the poor to the rich, and destructive economic growth), exactly the opposite should take place and accumulated money should be taxed (decreasing money). So that the rich do not simply switch to land ownership to continue to earn speculative profits, a land reform programme should make available "free land" to ensure land is used and not just accumulated.

If we put to one side for a moment the problem that the implementation of such a system would be politically impossible under present conditions (Gesell thought simply in terms of implementation through parliaments), it could be of great significance at a local level, as shown by the experiment in Wörgl in Austria[37], where such a system created so much employment and had such a beneficial effect on local prosperity during the economic depression after the First World War that it was eventually outlawed by the Dollfuss government (financial monopoly of the state).

W. Kessler offers a basic economic criticism of the approach of the Gesell school of thought.[38] He acknowledges the criticism of the effects of unjust distribution of interest but questions the deduction that the problem has only one cause. The cause of the problems of the capitalist economy lies in the linking of private property to the means of production, the principles of competition and profit. The subsequent inequality is only made worse, not produced, by the system of interest payments. Conversely, other negative economic effects caused by "decreasing money" would not be avoidable: *1.* the flow of wealth into material assets, *2.* the favouring of capital intensive production, *3.* the outbreak of a frenzied period of consumption (throw-away economy) – all effects which would not lead to an environmentally-based economy. As a result, a number of measures must be taken at a micro- and macro-economic level to bring capitalism under control or even transform it completely. I am of the opinion that Kessler should not simply leave out measures aimed at politically controlling interest rates and money supply. The only elements Kessler refers to in connection with money are the alternative banks in the area of micro-economics.

---

37 Cf. A. Richter, 1993.
38 W. Kessler, 1992, pp.14ff.

The most impressive of the world's alternative banks is the Grameen Bank (GB) in *Bangladesh*.[39] It began in 1975 as a piece of applied research by the economist Dr Muhammad Yunus into the question of whether poor people with no land, who would not normally be eligible for credit (due to a lack of collateral) according to the normal criteria of the banks, could restart or increase their contribution to the economy by saving and by receiving small loans. This experiment was not only successful, the results of its widespread implementation bordered on the miraculous. By the end of 1992, the GB co-operative had over 1.4 million members, of whom 93 per cent were (landless) women, from amongst the poorest of the poor. They are organised in about 50,000 "centres", each of which includes between 6 and 10 local savings/credit groups. US$475 million has so far been lent out, of which 98 per cent was repaid within two years. Nearly 157,000 families have been able to replace their huts in the slums with simple houses, send their children to school for the first time, improve the standard of their food and clothing, etc. Above all, women have been able to free themselves from their traditional position of dependency and have become a growing social and political force. How has this marvel been possible?

The key to success lies in the fact that the poor have been shown a better way of meeting their basic needs: by saving in small amounts (one handful of rice per meal); by organising themselves (group discipline replaces collateral); by a common decision-making process and education; by disciplined repayment of credit; and by cooperative conduct similar to that of small businesses. In addition to this is the process of integrated developmental education, laid down in the bank's 16 resolutions. M. Masud Isa relates the example of Momota Begum, a woman who, after four years with the GB, was able to buy 600 m^2 of land (0.15 acres) and two dairy cattle, build a small house with a corrugated iron roof, see her two daughters marry without dowries, pay for medical treatment for her sick husband, and still save 7000 Taka (about US$134). The infrastructure costs are relatively high because the educational and organisational elements make the process person-intensive (and it therefore creates jobs). The costs are subsidised by favourable rates of credit from the government and by aid agencies. However, it is planned that this dependency will cease to exist from 1995.

---

39 Cf. M. Malkamäki, 1991; M. Masud Isa, 1993.

In the light of the biblical studies in the second part of this book, the work of the Grameen Bank among the poor reminds us of Deuteronomy 14, where we are told how the remaining poor reorganised their tithes after the collapse of the kingship system in Judah. The tithes, which had been demanded by kings as a tribute, were now used to the benefit of the poor themselves. They used their productive resources to redistribute among themselves and saw themselves as an alternative model to the exploitative system of the times – in a tiny corner of the empire. However, the Grameen Bank, which gives surplus value produced by careful management back to the poor, is not (yet?) capable of revolutionising a whole country. It is "only" an attractive, small-scale, practical and organisational model (including a number of culturally-specific conditions which cannot easily be imitated) which can act as a leaven among the peoples and be of liberating inspiration to the poor elsewhere.[40]

In Europe it is practically impossible to find such an example among the poor. The phenomena of mass pauperisation, mass unemployment and mass indebtedness are too recent. Moreover, they affect only one third of the population, who are still protected by a social net (in which the holes are getting bigger). There is, however, a programme of cooperation among 35 alternative banks – the International Association of Investors in the Social Economy (INAISE).[41]

A comprehensive work analysing the present position of these efforts has been published by U. Reifner and J. Ford, *Banking for People. Social Banking and New Poverty, Consumer Debts and Unemployment in Europe – National Reports*.[42] The resource material *Geld, Zins und Gewissen. Neue Formen im Umgang mit Geld* (Money, interest and conscience – new ways of using money) produced by W. Kessler presents an excellent summary of chances, problems and examples related to the situation in Germany.[43]

---

40 It would be interesting to investigate whether the biblical traditions were better preserved here by the Islamic rather than the Christian religion. In any case, the concept of a ban on interest payments still exists in the Islamic banking system, even if it has not survived the global capitalist economy.

41 INAISE, 63 Rue Montoyer, B-1040 Brussels.

42 U. Reifner and J. Ford (ed.), 1992; I would especially like to mention a successful Swedish credit cooperative called "JAK" (Fjällgatan 23A, S-11628 Stockholm).

43 W. Kessler (ed.), 1993 (tr.). Kairos Europa is preparing a manual on alternative micro-finance for 1996.

It is important that the limitations imposed on the humanisation of the money transaction system under present conditions be made clear right from the outset. They include legal requirements, high costs and the protection of savings. The main result of this is that alternative banks cannot devote all the capital at their disposal to alternative purposes. Just like any other bank, they must deposit (interest-free) a certain percentage of the money they lend with the central bank, which then feeds this money into normal circulation. Moreover, most alternative banks usually deposit any unused capital with other commercial banks – albeit according to ethical investment criteria.

On the other hand, alternative banks do have considerable *scope* for introducing new initiatives:[44]

– Their business policy can be made more transparent, so that a mutual relationship can be built up between owners, employees, savers and borrowers. As a result, it would be possible, for example, for those with savings accounts to support plans they consider to be life-enhancing in social and environmental terms by investing in them.

– Conversely, savers are able to prevent their money being lent to the arms industry, firms whose actions destroy the environment, governments which support systems of apartheid and/or which contravene basic human rights.

– Finally, savers can opt to receive only partial or no interest so that poor, democratically self-administered undertakings or environmental research units can benefit by receiving cheaper loans.

The oldest "alternative" bank among the more recent experiments in Germany is the GLS cooperative bank which has its head office in Bochum. The idea goes back to 1961 and the bank itself was set up in 1974. It has an anthroposophical background and promotes, above all, projects concerned with alternative technologies and environmental and community issues. W.Kessler explains that the aim of the cooperative bank is to encourage people to actively commit themselves and their money to the pursuit of common goals. In this way, money can be transformed from being a tool of thoughtless egotism to being an instrument of mutual help and support. According to the bank's management, customers are then better placed to protect their investments, "by no longer thinking of money purely in terms of security and instead committing themselves and their

---

44 Ibid., pp.33ff.

available funds in cooperative contexts. As a result, they also cast off the illusion
that banks and their protective systems can protect abstract currency values.
They put their trust in individuals and the social context created. In this way, the
money invested has a definite, long-term contextuality and does not simply
become a *roving object of trade or speculation.*"[45]

This way of phrasing things hits the nail on the head. The small-scale alternatives
are not in a position to be able to transform the entire financial system into a
life-enhancing system, but they are starting a process of removing money from a
cycle based on wealth accumulation and the destruction of life, and using it for
life-sustaining projects.

Other examples are the Ecobank, which has its headquarters in Frankfurt, and
the Ecumenical Development Cooperative Society (EDCS), which has its
main office in Amersfoort and branches in many countries.[46] There are also
interesting examples to be found in Switzerland[47] and other European countries, further information about which can be found in INAISE documents
and the book by Reifner and Ford. We cannot here assess each individual
alternative bank and point out which aspects each one concentrates on and
whether it offers more possibilities with regard to social, environmental,
democratic and financial policy factors than the others.[48] Our concern is to
emphasise the fundamental possibility of clearly signposting positive action,
despite restrictions when it comes to the money itself, all of which is summarised by Kessler:

"After this survey of the possibilities of a 'more humane money transaction system', squeezed into the corset of current pressures, surely nobody can maintain
that the entire money transaction system can be channelled into a more humane
form using a few 'alternative' elements. This would be just as illusionary as the
belief that 'alternative' banks can remain absolutely true to the spirit of their ethical objectives while conducting their business. Yet it would be utterly wrong to
give up the search for alternative ways of investing capital. Quite the opposite.

---

45 Ibid., p.41(tr.).
46 Ibid., pp.37ff. and 44ff.
47 Cf. Aktion Finanzplatz Schweiz-Dritte Welt (Action for alternative financial
cooperation between Switzerland and the Third World), 1993.
48 There is an increasing amount of literature on this subject to be evaluated by the
forthcoming manual of Kairos Europe.

Even under the present conditions, small institutions are capable of giving clear signs pointing to a more humane economy."[49]

To be clear signs – that is the role of small-scale alternatives, in conjunction with a rejection of the deadly totalitarian system of money accumulation for its own sake. And just as churches must back this rejection – if they want to be or become churches – they must also seize upon these symbolic alternatives.[50] Ulrich Luz sums it all up when he discusses Jesus' speech in Matthew 10, in which he sends out his disciples as messengers but tells them not to take any money, and explains what this means for us today:

"Jesus' missionary instructions apply first and foremost to the disciples, the 'wandering radicals' and 'followers' in the literal sense of the word. Are we therefore talking here about a special case of discipleship? Matthew was writing for a sedentary society. But he does not differentiate between the original '12 Apostles' and the disciples, who become representative of the community. We suspect that in his eyes, missionary preaching is a task for the whole community, and, accordingly, the life of a 'wandering radical' is a way of life for every member of that community. Because by living as a pacifist and being poor, one is putting into practice the teachings from the Sermon on the Mount (see 5:38-42, 6:25-34), it is important that each individual, in his/her free time, should do as much as possible to help the cause of justice. In any case, the community identifies itself to a large extent with the 'wandering radicals' and their task.

How can all this be brought forward into the present? First of all we should consider the rest of the New Testament. For instance, Paul's renunciation of the apostolic right to have his keep paid, the renunciation of the traditional style of 'wandering radicalism' in the large cities of Greece and Asia Minor, and the later transition to 'on the spot' missionary preaching to communities attest to a large degree of freedom in dealing with Jesus' teachings. For our own situation in Western Europe, where mainline churches have, by complex means, become a factor and ferment in the whole of society, this is even more relevant. On the other hand, history has shown, quite drastically, that with regard to this 'glorious freedom' of Jesus, everything is explained away. The fact that 'gospel' means the binding words of Jesus is part of the fundamental thrust of Matthew's Gospel. Proclamation means these words take shape in the life and works (5:16) of the

49 Ibid., p.35(tr.).
50 From among the diverse basic literature on this subject cf. Ökumenische Initiative Eine Welt (One World ecumenical initiative), 1990; D. Schirmer and P. Neumann, 1991.

preacher. Perhaps Matthew would deny the claim of West European churches to be preaching the 'gospel of the kingdom', not because of their manner of preaching, and not because they have not taken on his form of church, but because they are hardly moving in his intended direction any more. They hardly show any signs of poverty, homelessness and powerlessness, signs which would reveal 'better righteousness' and thus the Gospel."[51]

In the same context, as has already been mentioned, Luther said that a church that simply participates in the (early) capitalist interest system should cast off the name "church", because the church should "set a good example to the worldly estates". Setting a good example means giving a sign, showing that there is another way. It is important that the church not only do this with respect to individuals or small activist groups, but as a *corporate whole*, as a congregation, as a church district, as a regional church and diocese, or at the national level. I am aware of the enormous upheaval that this would involve. It would also certainly not take place overnight. But the *direction* must be clear. Then, step by step, the huge amounts of capital at the church's disposal can be diverted into alternative, life-enhancing investment projects. The missionary effect in our society and worldwide would be greater than a hundred thousand inconsequential sermons. Certainly income would fall as many of the well-off would not go along with it. The wages priests and pastors receive would have to be cut, which would make it even more necessary e.g. to revise the hierarchical structure of German church pay scales. The church would again be the "city on the hill", the "salt of the earth" and the "light to the peoples" and be just as attractive as the Pauline communities of Jesus the Messiah under the totalitarian Roman Empire. And last but not least, the political endeavours towards gaining control of the current destructive financial system, which we will look at in the next chapter, would receive considerable backing.

---

51 U. Luz, 1990, p.103(tr.); cf. same, Die Kirche und ihr Geld im Neuen Testament (The church and its money in the New Testament), in: W. Lienemann (ed.), 1989, pp.525ff.

3.5 *Alternative trade*

In Germany, alternative north-south trade has been carried out for more than
twenty years under the guidance of the political movement "*Aktion Dritte
Welt Handel*" (for fair trading with the Third World) – as in many other
countries.[52] The movement's aims are:
–   to portray the injustice present in global trade using the examples of indi-
    vidual products,
–   to urge consumers to be more aware of what they are buying,
–   to support self-help and producer groups in their economic, social and
    cultural struggle against dependency and exploitation,
–   to gain more direct influence over commercial companies by increasing its
    own influence over the market.

The movement is supported by 600-700 fair-trade shops and several thousand
action groups. During the 1991 financial year, all the alternative import organisations had a combined turnover of around US$42 million. Churches also belong
to these and the biggest organisation, GEPA, saw its turnover increase from US$12
million in the financial year 1989-90 to nearly US$17 million two years later and
has now set its sights on achieving a turnover of US$ 42 within the next five years.
The contentious issue connected with this expansion into the retail trade lies in
the question of whether the main focus on critical information is thereby being
neglected. The point about necessary exertion of influence has, however, been accepted. Alternative trade in coffee has increased due to the part played by TRANS-
FAIR (an association for the promotion of fair trade with the South) and following the example set by the Max Havelaar campaign in Holland.

Compared with figures for world trade, these figures are more pitiful than tiny
David confronting the giant Goliath. Nevertheless, this sign is of enormous
importance in indicating the *direction* in which the changes must go, if the
destruction of an ever larger proportion of the world's population by "free"
trade is not to lead to an even more catastrophic state of affairs. For example,
the price of coffee on the world market is so low that it does not even cover
production costs in many countries. Moreover, the repercussions of the destruc-

52 G. Young, 1990, pp.24f., gives examples and addresses in New Zealand, Australia,
Canada, United Kingdom, USA, The Netherlands. See also B. Coote, 1992.

tion of the economic potential of many Southern countries will cause an increase in drug trafficking and migration, which will, in turn, boomerang and have an effect on the Northern countries responsible for causing the problems in the first place (Susan George). The practicality of this approach makes it especially well suited for root groups. So this is one of the few approaches that, in traditional church communities, at least serves to promote the beginnings of awareness of the problem, and changes in behaviour patterns.

A completely new area of alternative trade is emerging unnoticed because of increasing numbers of migrants. Because of their strong traditions of family solidarity, they are developing among themselves an informal trade sector between groups here and their country of origin. The result is not only development work, but the formation of trading networks based on solidarity, in which solidarity groups are increasingly being included. The European initiative Kairos Europa is currently developing a project at a European level which hopes to build on this starting point.[53]

Less well known are the LETS and barter systems for local and regional communities.[54] LETS means Local Employment and Trading System. It combines the creation of a local/regional currency and credit system with the exchange of local/regional goods and services. Barter may also avoid money altogether and nowadays use (computer-controlled) information systems to coordinate exchanges between those offering goods and services (supply) and those looking for them (demand).

However, all this still does not solve the problem of unjust world trade. This must be tackled politically. But awareness of the problem on the part of people and institutions can be increased by small-scale projects. They can also create a local base for an alternative vision and for political strategies, quite apart from their very real importance in themselves.

4 Alternative consumption

The two areas in which every individual has real but barely-recognised power are *money* and *consumption*. For every individual, in some way, takes part each

---

53 Contact address: David Forbes, c/o Praxis, Pott Street, London E2 OEF.
54 Cf. e.g. R.V.G. Dobsan, 1992, esp. pp.77ff.

day in the key sectors of the capitalist economy via these two areas: products and money. But this power is fettered.

In considering rejection, we have already seen that the heart of the problem was recognised by Aristotle: the desire for ever more (artificial products and money) has replaced the primary importance of the basic needs of life in the community. And the neo-liberal form of the capitalist market economy aims automatically at the – unquenchable – satisfaction of customer preferences. I recently heard an advertising slogan that ran: "For all those who want everything – fast", then came the offer of credit.

Apart from the unfulfilled basic needs of the poor, another result of consumption in developed countries is a situation which is environmentally unsustainable. This is a truism. What remains unclear, however, is how to initiate the necessary self-restraint on the part of the population. This may well be impossible, considering that we are not just dealing with normal desires, but with a serious problem of addiction, made worse by the huge amounts spent on advertising each day. G. Breidenstein compares this situation with that of patients who have a headache. They are advised by the doctor to eat less but ignore the advice and simply accept the headache.[55] In the aftermath of the Chernobyl nuclear disaster, it seemed that people were ready to turn away from nuclear power. As soon as the acute headache had gone away, nuclear power was once more acceptable, although every scientist knows that due to the large number of nuclear power stations worldwide, a disaster on the scale of Chernobyl, statistically speaking, will happen every twenty years. It is clear that the social and environmental catastrophes must become even more catastrophic, until more and more people are so shocked that they seek therapy for their addiction to consumption. The small, "lived" alternatives serve as points of reference, as G. Breidenstein explains:

> "If the comparison with individual addiction therapy is to some extent correct, then one must say that, in the current advanced stage of our dependency on expansionism and on patriarchal, technocratic and imperialistic dominance, a form of therapy based on rational insight can no longer be expected to work. The pleasure people derive from consumption far outweighs the present disadvantages, or at least those visible at first glance. It is probably only a considerably greater degree of suffering that will cure us of our deep-seated egocentricity, the real cause of our current affliction.

---

55 G. Breidenstein, 1990, p.114(tr.).

But why should we wait for the nadir of our physical, emotional and social decline? Perhaps we would need a lesser degree of suffering to make us change if
our decision were to be supported by an insight into the deeper correlations. And
how many of us have already suffered for a long time under present conditions
and how many have already set themselves on the road to liberation? On the
fringe of society, in the many, diverse alternative movements, the self-healing of
society has long since begun."[56]

It is clear to see that we are dealing here with a problem which Paul the Apostle
describes in Romans 7:14ff: we already have insight and willingness, but under
the completely dominant power of unrighteousness and desire ("sin" theologically speaking), we cannot put into practice in society what we understand
and want to do. Paul's answer is that in the messianic community there is a
spirit abroad through which it is possible to turn intentions into action and
hope remains alive, despite all the pressure of world powers. The individual is
powerless if no U-turn can be brought about in society. The therapy, therefore, is one of experiencing alternative society. Those who have already experienced such communities know that the feeling of joy found therein is so
strong that the required self-discipline is not a burden at all. Addiction to
consumption is the pathological answer to the collective withdrawal of love
caused by the capitalist system and its isolating function, precisely because it
concentrates on competition for the sake of money accumulation. Communities based on solidarity are the clearest answer. We have seen another
example in the form of producer-consumer cooperatives helping in the production and local marketing of healthier foodstuffs.

When such communities, and other types, organise themselves, they can
become movements. Maria Mies calls them "Konsumbefreiungsbewegun-
gen" (freedom from consumption movements).[57] They can contribute not
only to their own liberation but also to the liberation of others. In addition,
there are various kinds of boycott and organised consumer power. We have
already referred to the "Don't buy the fruits of apartheid" action by the German Protestant women's movement and the "Nestlé kills babies" campaign,
and there are many other examples. Alongside these special campaigns, criti-

---

56 Ibid., p.115(tr.).
57 M. Mies, 1988, p.213.

cal consumers are required in general; in this connection, the Third World Shops movement distributes a guide to supermarkets.[58]

As far as the church is concerned, there are countless Christian individuals and groups who are working seriously towards alternatives and careful practice in the area of consumption. With regard to the corporate practice of congregations and institutions, however, there is still a lack of unambiguity and clarity. Only a readiness to object in clear cases of injustice and environmental destruction can lead the small, alternative projects out of inconsequential anonymity to become symbols of a fundamental U-turn away from consumerism based on money-accumulation.

5 Fairer distribution of income

The distribution question only seems to have been rediscovered in Germany since the federal government used the opportunity offered by reunification to do what the Reagan/Bush administrations in the United States and the Thatcher government in Britain had already achieved in the 1980s, namely giving political backing to the enormous redistribution of wealth from salaried workers and the increasing number of people mainly excluded from the formal economy to the rich.[59] Under the Fordist-Keynesian accumulation model it has long seemed that, in periods of constant economic growth, capital could fulfill its accumulation function and there would still be enough cake left over – at least in the industrialised nations – to satisfy the needs of employees (presuming full employment exists). This certainly includes the elimination of over-exploitation of nature and the Two-Thirds World, but this area is left to environmental and solidarity groups and regarded as being playground for altruists and idealists. Now, however, the world system is in our own backyard. As a result, the struggle has begun over positional goods (i.e. those which not everybody can get) and over the distribution of income.

We do not yet want to examine political strategies in this situation; we are still looking at the question of further small-scale alternatives. We have already seen that some self-managed companies have expressly set themselves

---

58 Council for Economic Priorities, Shopping for a Better World, annual.
59 Cf. Hickel et al., 1993; Huster, 1993; E. Altvater, 1993.

the aim of a fairer distribution of income – and have achieved this with a degree of success. There are also base communities and other Christian communities by whom this same distribution is a matter of course. And in this respect there is no escaping the biblical approach to an alternative society or, theologically speaking, an organisation or institution which bears the name of Jesus, the Messiah of the poor.

From this perspective, as we saw when referring to dissent, it is clearly against biblical intentions when the large churches in Western Europe use the pay scale system of the capitalist society, divided into civil servants, white-collar staff and blue-collar workers. And indeed the saddest fact is that churches in former East Germany, which had relatively consistent and, in relation to their society, low wage levels, have now been incorporated into the West German system after pressure from western financial experts. This means that a number of church initiatives pressing for a U-turn take on special significance. The most important of these are the Berlin-Brandenburg initiative "PfarrerInnengehalt – Ökumenisches Teilen" (pastors' wages – ecumenical sharing) and the Baden initiative "Solidarischer Lohn – Ökumenisches Teilen" (solidarity pay – ecumenical sharing).[60] These initiatives have two purposes: on the one hand, they are attempting to get the church, via synod proposals, to adopt a uniform, equalising pay structure, and on the other, they are leading the way with voluntary self-taxation.

Due to the fact that an egalitarian pay structure in the sense of "wages according to needs" is hardly likely to succeed faced with the growing chasm between the mainline churches and the Gospel, by taking one step forward of the kind proposed by U. Luz in relation to Matthew's Gospel, we would be trying to change the present pay scale at least at its highest and lowest extremes and finance groups within the church which are working carefully towards an alternative economy. In so doing, jobs within the church will at the same time be created in the areas of rejection, small-scale alternatives and prophetic political influence for an alternative economy. Secondly, part of the money to be redistributed would be made available for ecumenical sharing in the field of international justice (see below). Initiative groups are looking for as many volunteers as possible from the clergy who are prepared to support these steps. In Berlin, already nearly 100 out of 900 ministers are taking part. In Baden, the figures are smaller because

---

60 Cf. C.-D. Schulze, 1989.

the initiative only started properly in 1993. Every time these pastors receive a pay rise, they subtract the increase, up to 10 per cent, and pay it into a fund used to finance the activities referred to above, already operating on a voluntary basis.

We should take another look at *sharing within the church on a global level.* Churches and members of the church in the rich western nations donate large amounts of money. It is clear, however, that in most cases, these donations come from superfluous money, not money that is used by individuals or institutions for their own needs. On the other hand, it is not simply a matter of pumping more money into churches in the South and the East. The worst cases are when this money is actively tied to political aims, as is the situation with regard to a few neo-Pentecostal and evangelical groups in the USA, who even work in cooperation with the CIA in Central and Latin America, and now also in the East, supplying people with opium religion while at the same time actively combating the struggle of social, liberating grassroots projects. But well-meaning donations can also lead to quarrelling within these churches, and between them and their poor surroundings, if the donations are linked with the flow of money from the West, which itself is permanently being sucked from the societies in which they live. Remember UN figure of around US$ 500 billion per year lost by the South to the North! The necessary money transfer to the South must, therefore, be subject to a number of conditions if it is not to have a destructive effect. Here are some of these *conditions*:

– Church aid funds must come not only from voluntary donations, but also money from their own personnel costs. Hence the above-mentioned linking of ecumenical sharing to solidarity pay. The *sign* of justice shown there is at least as important as the money itself. Without this link, the donated money would even entail the temptation to disguise the actual question of justice because it eases the giver's conscience.

– A further symbol of the linkage of money transfer to the question of justice is the active rejection of unjust structures, as described in Chapter VIII. A church that does not publicly reject the injustice of the world economic order by taking firm action is hiding the question of the fundamental causes of the poverty of the churches in the South and East behind its donations.

– An important practical element of the conditions is the embedding of donations in partnership structures, by which the recipient churches have the opportunity to participate in the financial decisions of the donor churches. We now have a global world economy in which the dominant western transnational banks and companies and the international economic and financial institutions which are dominated by these banks and companies with the help of western governments have the final say on the economic and cultural fate of people in those countries receiving money. As a countermove, within the framework of the ecumenical movement, western churches should develop decision-making structures according to which churches in those societies bled dry by 500 years of western domination are able to actively influence the economic decisions of churches in the North, which have become rich by participating in the exploitation.

– Conversely, there should be no money transfers that bring about or consolidate cases of injustice in the churches receiving the money or between the churches and their local communities. Ideally we should support processes that work from below in which churches participate, like lending for self-reliance as promoted by the Grameen Bank. Another crucial factor is the participation by churches in the struggle of those people who have been sidelined by or even excluded from society. Within the framework of this common struggle in the respective context of the North, the South or the East, ecumenical sharing is better placed to avoid the dangers connected with money in this regard.

Small-scale redistribution cannot, of course, solve the problem of distribution on a global scale. It can, however, serve as a symbol and basis for the necessary political changes.

6 The networking of small-scale alternatives

Interestingly, W. Kessler gives headings to his summaries of grassroots initiatives working towards a new life-sustaining economy which remind us of the biblical traditions we have already looked at: "Germ cells of a new economic policy" and "Alternatives to traditional economic policy".[61] Despite the totalitarian structure of the world economy, it is still possible to reject certain structures and develop small-scale alternatives.

Yet individual or isolated groups have practically no chance of survival in view of the enormous pressure applied by the system. This is why totalitarian systems attempt – with some success, unfortunately – to play the victims off

---

61 W. Kessler, 1990, pp.147ff.(tr.)

against each other and to isolate them. The Romans called this principle *divide et impera* (divide and rule). The Boers in South Africa called it *apartheid* (division). Even today, the unemployed are played off against immigrants while well-trained workers are played off against those with little or no training. In this way, the typical climate of the capitalist system is strengthened: everybody against everybody, look after number one, and every man for himself! In this situation, it is crucial to find methods of mutual encouragement and support.

The simplest form, and hardest for totalitarian systems to get a grip on, is reciprocal visits. This was the method chosen by the early Christian communities under the Roman Empire. It is also still practised today. Base groups working towards an alternative economy and democratic self-organisation visit one other, exchange information, support each other, strengthen each other through positive stimuli, and form loosely – or more tightly – organised networks: ecumenical networks, solidarity networks of all types, and research networks. This is happening at all levels: first locally and then at a national and European level, with countries always split into clearly-defined regions. During the UNCED in Rio in 1992, a large meeting of NGOs also took place. In June 1993, the World Council of Churches hosted an international meeting of those networks which had carried out programmes of action marking "500 years of oppression and resistance". The theme of the meeting was that of the Asian networks (People's Plan 21): Alliances of Hope. There are innumerable examples, in many diverse forms, of such alliances. What unites them is the concept of a just, peaceful and environmentally friendly co-existence.

We should in no way idealise these alliances. They are relatively weak and fragile. Organisation beyond the local level costs money and sufficient finances are scarce. Rivalries sometimes develop, and personality clashes. Often too much is left in the hands of too few people because resources do not stretch to better organisational facilities. One of the main problems is that it is easier for single-issue groups to network with each other than with groups dealing with different issues, although their problems are all interrelated and can only be solved by working together. Nevertheless, the "political economy of the Holy Spirit" is at work here.[62] Against the background of the biblical traditions we have already looked at, it is therefore of crucial importance to define the relationship between the *Church of Jesus Christ and these movements*.

---

62 Cf. J. de Santa Ana et al., 1990.

The *first* point in keeping with our "biblical recollection rules" is clear: the place of the church is with these movements. If the institutionally organised churches are not present, then they are not where Jesus the Messiah is and are taking his name in vain. Building community – locally and globally – with those presently sidelined or excluded, is the process by which the Bible speaks to churches as the Word of God. Their biblical mission is to work with such people in rejecting systemically unjust structures and shaping symbolic life-giving alternatives. That is the *second* point. The conflict with the dominant economic and political powers must also be continued at their side. That is the *third* point.

What is the special role of churches, congregations, and Christian action groups and base communities in this area, in this struggle and conflict? They are able to comprehend what exactly functions as the oppressive and destructive god of our society and to discover the liberating counterforces present in their own God of the Bible. For where a clear view is clouded by disinformation, cover-ups or taboos, they can – if they are part of the church and therefore present in the community with all Jews who believe in the Torah and the prophets – use the Torah, the prophets, and Jesus and his first Messianic communities as their compass, as their light. They cannot "have" the God referred to. He is "only a voice".[63] He does not manifest himself in images – of a church, an institution, a dogmatic or ethical formula, and certainly not in the name of a political party with "Christian" in its name. God raises up "servants" from any nation, people who serve him like the King of the Medes, Cyrus, who liberated the Jews from the Babylonian dominance. Every Christian should be ashamed that the fiercest resistance against the destructive Western cultural and financial dominance has come from the indigenous peoples of the Americas and from fundamental Islamic groups. But we can "hear the voice" and carry it further, after it has reached us. And we come together round one table in memory of Jesus and in hope for the future of God's kingdom. We call this Communion or the Lord's Supper because Jesus had his last meal with his disciples on the eve of his crucifixion by the Romans. We also call it the Eucharist, i.e. thanksgiving, because we receive food from God to feed us and to share. Christians celebrate this to this day. Where they celebrate in the name of Jesus, there is no difference between the sharing of bread and wine at the altar and the sharing of food (the means of life) in everyday economic and social life.

---

63 Cf. T. Veerkamp, 1993, pp.356ff.(tr.).

Conversely, if they fight alongside the victims of social marginalisation, rejecting injustice and building small-scale alternatives, then they are also celebrating Communion, the Eucharist. For me, the image that illustrates this most graphically is the daily routine of the "La Poudrière" community in Brussels. All its members, whether they are Christians, Muslims, Buddhists or atheists, are independent and equal and participate in the fully democratic process of shaping their economy for life. Every morning, before work begins, a small group – which is open to all members but nobody is forced to attend – meets in a renovated underground vault to hear the Word of God and share out bread and wine, before going to communal breakfast (on Sundays they go to communal lunch after celebrating Mass). In addition, there are always a couple of extra places at the long wooden table, made of wood from the farm, in case a visitor from another messianic community or a homeless person arrives (Matthew 25).

After his description of grassroots initiatives as germ cells for a new economy, W. Kessler states: "The decisive step towards changing the whole economy still remains to be taken."[64] But what are the reasons "why economic development cannot be fundamentally altered by an 'economic policy from below' alone"? "Grassroots initiatives are seeds of a new economic policy at the micro-level but they (can) change general economic conditions only if they spark off change at the macro-level." The bridge between rejecting unjust global mechanisms and setting up small-scale alternatives, on the one hand, and the necessary political strategies, on the other, is the networking of initiatives among themselves, and between themselves and institutions which in principle could be independent of capital forces – e.g. trade unions and churches. If we could practise rejection and new departures on a small scale together, the foundation would be laid for political action at a higher level – in what is ultimately a totalitarian system.

---

64 W. Kessler, 1990, p.148(tr.).

Chapter x

Alternative economic policy for life

1 Chances for political action under a totalitarian system or the relationship between prophetic and apocalyptic voices

We began this Third Part by inquiring whether there can be any comparison at all between ancient Near Eastern structures and capitalist structures of surplus acquisition and oppression; this led us to examine the asymmetric accumulation structures and their political, military and ideological safeguards. After a short outline of the problem in the light of church history, we then suggested that in the present situation, a *double strategy* is necessary and possible: rejection and small-scale alternatives, on the one hand, and the exertion of political influence wherever possible, on the other. This raises a number of fundamental questions which we must answer before turning our attention to actual political aims and methods.

Within early coalitions known from early Jewish and Christian texts, we found different approaches and even disputes about the correct strategy for resistance. To begin with, it was agreed by all that the totalitarian foreign yoke of the Hellenistic ruler Antiochus IV must be shaken off. The Maccabean revolution succeeded but kings, temple officials and the majority of the upper classes adapted increasingly to the conditions of Hellenistic economy and its form of rule. So some people (Essenes) went into the desert, some (Pharisees and Zealots) tried to exert as much political influence as possible in the name of the Torah, and others formed small, clandestine, radical-prophetic groups waiting for the dawning of the messianic kingdom; they wanted a king in the tradition of David, but a king of the poor and thus of a "tamed" kingdom in the spirit of Deuteronomy. For his part, Jesus set his hope in messianic groups to leaven the lump, and he vehemently attacked the temple aristocracy and the Judaean upper classes; he never went to the lengths of directly confronting the puppet king Herod or representatives of the Roman Empire. In other words, he did not expect a reform of the totalitarian empire and its substructures to be possible, waiting instead for a (self-inflicted) collapse of the type mentioned in Daniel 2 and 7, as well as simply preparing for a new age with the forces of God's imminent kingdom emerging from below.

Reflecting upon the net results of western church history we could also conclude that it does not make sense to simply try to tame the power systems. Churches with structures of political and economic power, first as imperial churches, then as national or regional churches, and also as large church dioceses, have failed in most attempts to tame the structures of power and money by raising their prophetic voice. The power systems have emerged victorious and, in the worst cases, churches have adapted to capitalist or state theology, or have followed the path of "church theology" and therefore, in a situation of asymmetric power, compromised themselves and the Gospel in order not to endanger the institutions themselves. This failure can be seen as analogous to the failure of the kingdoms in Israel and Judah, although the Western system seems to have triumphed and the coffers of the temple are still well filled. The decline in church membership is spreading but up to now there have been no recognisable signs to suggest that, corporately, there is a need for a change drawn from the teachings of the Bible. Rather, the all-pervading spirit of preserving the status quo can be seen in this action. The appeals of the ecumenical movement for churches to become confessing and prophetic have gone unheeded. The conciliar process for justice, peace, and the integrity of creation has hardly, if at all, led to decisions and practical consequences with regard to their own structures and corporate action, although there are undoubtedly many people *within* the church who are waiting for a breakaway from the fleshpots of Egypt and are themselves working towards this.

I can well understand that from the analyses of the world situation and from the plight of the church in a biblical light, many people conclude that a combination of rejection and small-scale alternatives is the only way forward at present. Nevertheless, I would like to explain why I am in favour of a *double strategy*, including political intervention, and in what sense.

According to our first and second rules for biblical recollection, the starting point for any judgement is cooperation with the poor. At least in the South which has been mostly destroyed by the North – people are crying out not only for rescue, but also for a struggle based on solidarity. The impoverished are fighting themselves for their relative political aims, and doing so from the periphery. Should not those living in the power centres fight the system too? A third of western society has also been sidelined, or excluded from productive activity; the fact that it is not (yet) crying out, but is hiding and finding expression in speechless violence, says nothing about the pain, which can be even greater when it remains silent. I do not see how we can escape this cry to join in their political struggle. Our sharpest weapons are, of course, dissent, with which we can cut through the web of lies, spun every day by the system, and the signs which show that small-scale alternatives have a future and that the prospect of the consummation of God's kingdom maintains hope against all hope. But can we give up before we have tried and exhausted every possibility of political action?

The second reason why I favour a double strategy is as follows: the capitalist market economy has totalitarian tendencies but it has shown in the past that it reacts to countervailing power. The history of the workers' movement is proof of this. Without this movement's long struggle, no social improvements would have been wrung out of capitalism. Now we have reached a point where a proportion of the working class has thereby become relatively rich and a – sometimes even stabilising – part of the system, and where capital is in a position to be able to avoid the increasingly weak pressure exerted by the organised workforce. So we cannot expect the workforce alone to exert enough pressure to bring about social, environmental and democratic reforms in this neo-liberal phase of the capitalist market economy. The heart of the problem is that we are not so much confronted by exploitation now as by exclusion. Whole population groups, countries and, in the case of Africa, continents simply do not count any more. They are out of the picture and no longer have an effective part to play with regard to the main principle of capitalism – accumulation of capital. As Karl Marx said: they are not just the underclass but lumpenproletariat, with whom it is not possible to stage revolutions or apply pressure for reform. Is this really true?

This defeatism is contradicted by one of Polanyi's observations, mentioned above. He rightly points out that since the 19th century not only the working class but all of society has reacted to the destructive effects of the capitalist market when they become perceptible. These effects are becoming visible in ever more fractures and inconsistencies and are affecting all walks of life.

Realistically, and taking history into account, one must admit that this situation may produce fascist reactions. At the moment it seems as if the result could be similar to that of the great global economic crisis of 1929. Not only in Russia but also in Western Europe there are increasing indications that the losers can be seduced into a new form of fascist state capitalism by the winners. It must be recognised that our economy in the West is so geared to exports that neo-fascism would only be economically feasible given a parallel imperialisation of foreign policy. In fact, there are enough signs of a move in this direction – most importantly, the intervention troops projected in the European Union.

Nevertheless we have to fight for alternatives. This can only happen through coalition-building between all groups negatively affected by the global capitalist economy (and perhaps enlightened minorities in the more privileged classes). The goal would be the formation of countervailing power at all levels in order to place the transnational economic and financial systems under democratic control. In this context there are also secondary goals.

This has an eccentric and pointless ring to it. It may be that it is pointless. But first of all we must realise that all over the world, many people have *actually* got together in *new social, environmental and democratic movements*: women's movements, homeless movements, farmers' movements, indigenous movements, environmental movements, peace movements and so on. Some have already formed international networks. They often work in close cooperation with the old social movements – workers' movements and trade union movements. In many cases, churches have joined these alliances at least through Christian grassroots movements.

There are also people with the same aims in political parties, above all among the Greens and democratic socialists; such parties as these have not opted out of the capitalist market economy because they are seeking to have an effect from within the system. This shows, however, that within the global totalitarian capitalist system there are some partially democratic institutions whose scope with regard to changing the market could be extended, given sufficient pressure.

It is interesting to note that not only those who are working to bring about structural change in the global economic and financial systems see the concept of social movements as being fundamental. This is also true now of the players in the system itself. An article was published in *The Economist* of 30.5.92 under the heading "Pressure Politics". This article about networks like Greenpeace and Friends of the Earth claims that when the big pressure groups are taken together, their role in bringing ideas onto the political agenda is clearly significant (p.36).

A.G. Frank and M. Fuentes-Frank have devoted a book to the phenomenon of social movements in the context of the capitalist world economy: *Wider-*

stand im Weltsystem – Kapitalistische Akkumulation, staatliche Politik, soziale Bewegung (Resistance in the world system – capitalist accumulation, state policies, social movement).[1] With regard to practical help, the most useful book is that by the American *Bill Moyer: The Movement Action Plan. A Strategic Framework Describing the Eight Stages of Successful Social Movements.*[2] Instead of describing his approach verbally, I shall reproduce his own summaries, which speak for themselves (see pages 284, 285, 286 and 287).

We should take a short look at *some individual questions* linked with the political part of the double strategy. One practical problem connected with forming coalitions is that, faced with the complexity of the entire global system, those concerned and their root groups are often too busy with everyday chores to carry out analyses or to put their efforts into forming national or international coalitions. On the other hand, specialised NGOs are becoming so professionalised that they may lose contact with the grassroots. In this area much patient liaison work remains to be done regarding planning and organisation. But we should not immediately rule out the possibility that politically effective, coordinated intervention might lead to progress on the road towards our main goal, as indicated in Moyer's Movement Action Plan.

Another question concerns the possible role of churches and communities. In the light of biblical recollection, prophetic methods could provide a stimulus. The first group to be addressed must be God's people themselves. Working in cooperation with social movements – as was the case with the prophets and the (peasant) farmers' movements – churches and communities must convince their members of the need for this political struggle on the basis of their faith. If they expressed dissent, symbolic difference and a clear identification with the social movements, churches and congregations would gain credibility, and so enjoy untold opportunities to prophetically challenge the power structures.

Up until now, the official strategy of most of the mainline churches has been to pursue "dialogues" with those holding economic and political power – and behind closed doors at that. This overlooks the fact that we are dealing here, in the words of Max Weber, with a form of "slavery without slaveowners" and are there-

---

1 A.G. Frank and M. Fuentes-Frank, 1990; cf. also R. Kurz, 1991, pp.259ff.
2 B. Moyer, 1987.

fore dealing with structures which cannot be influenced by individuals alone. Only when the churches participate in a double strategy, and go about it seriously, by saying "no" where necessary and offering alternatives, thus participating in the creation of social counterforces, can their "dialogues" take on a limited meaning within the strategy as a whole. And this is not – I repeat – a secondary question of "social ethics", but *the* theological question with regard to their existence as churches after the clear failure of the Constantine model of the established church.

Let us summarise: it could be that we are in for a major global disaster. Then rejection and small-scale alternatives will be the seed of something new. However, should prophetic intervention bring about (partial) success, then the interplay of both alternatives in resistance and political involvement (the double strategy) will have been worth it for people and creation. Hope lies in the former, otherwise political strategy would be pointless; no-one can say whether, in view of the power situation and collective delusions and obsessions, it will succeed. What can such a political strategy aim at? What are the absolute and relative goals of political and economic alternatives? The general goal is aptly put by Kessler: to move from capitalism to socio-ecological economic democracy.[3]

Outlines for such a socio-ecological economic democracy are available from various national and international contexts.

They include works that have already been mentioned: in a German context, W. Kessler[4]; in Holland, W. Hoogendijk[5]; in Britain, P. Ekins and J. Robertson[6]; and in the USA, H.E. Daly and J.B. Cobb jr.[7], who have very firm proposals on this subject. All these works also include stimuli for the local community and the global level. There are also a number of important alternative outlines specialising in the topic of a global restructuring of the political economy available: the UNDP *Human Development Report*; the "treaties" resulting from the conference of NGOs at the time of the UNCED Rio Summit in 1992; the study commissioned by the EC Commissions's FAST Programme, *Towards a New Bretton Woods* (ed.

3   W. Kessler, 1990, pp.151ff.
4   Ibid.
5   W. Hoogendijk, 1991.
6   P. Ekins, 1986 and 1992; J. Robertson, 1990.
7   H.E. Daly and J.B. Cobb jr., 1989.

Eight stages of the process of social movement success

2 Prove failure of official institutions
- Many new local opposition groups.
- Use official channels: Courts, government offices, commissions, hearings ... Prove they don't work.
- Become experts; do research.

3 Ripening conditions
- Recognition of problem and victims grow.
- Public sees victim's faces.
- More active local groups.
- Need pre-existing institutions and networks available to new movement.
- 20-30% of public oppose powerholder policies.

I Critical social problem exists
- Violates widely-held values.
- Powerholders support problem:
- "Official Policies" tout values
- Real "Operating Policies" violate values.
- Public is unaware of the problem. Support powerholders.
- Problem/policies is not a public issue.

Characteristics of movement process:
- Social Movements are composed of many sub-goals and sub-movements, each in their own MAP stage.
- Strategy & Tactics are different for each sub-movement, according to the MAP stage each is in.
- Keep advancing sub-movements through the eight stages.
- Each sub-movement is focused on a specific goal (eg, for civil rights movements: restaurants, voting, public accomodations).
- All of the sub-movements promote the same paradigm shift (eg, shift from hard to soft energy policy).

Public must be convinced three times:
1. That there is a Problem. (Stage 4)
2. To oppose current conditions and policies. (Stages 4, 6, 7)
3. To want, no longer fear, alternatives. (Stages 6, 7)

- Focus more on other sub
- New social movements as

by Bill Moyer 24 November 1991

4 Take-off

Trigger event

– Dramatic nonviolent actions/campaigns.
– Actions show public that conditions and policies violate widely-held values.
– Nonviolent actions repeated around country.
– Problem put on the *social* agenda.
– New Social Movement rapidly "takes off".
– 40% of public oppose current policies/conditions.

5 Perception of failure
– See goals unachieved.
– See powerholders unchanged.
– See numbers down at demonstrations.
– Despair, hopelessness, burnout, dropout, seems movement ended.
– Emergence of Negative Rebel.

6 Majority public opinion
– Majority oppose present conditions and powerholder policies.
– Show how the problem and policies affect all sectors of society.
– Involve mainstream citizens and institutions in addressing the problem.
– Problem put on the *political* agenda.
– Promote alternatives.
– Counter each new powerholder strategy.
– Demonology: Powerholders promote public's fear of alternative.
– Promote a Paradigm Shift, not only reforms.
– Re-trigger events happen, re-enacting stage 4 for a period.

WERHOLDERS

Continuation
Extend successes (ex: even stronger civil rights laws).
Oppose attempts at backlash
Promote paradigm shift.
Focus on other Sub-issues.
Recognize/celebrate successes so far.

7 Success
– Large majority oppose current policies and no longer fear alternative.
– Many powerholders split off and change positions.
– End game process:
  Powerholders change policies (its more costly to continue old policies than to change) are voted out of office, or slow invisible attrition.
– New laws or policies.
– Powerholders try to make minimal reforms, while movement demands social change.

Chart I

Four roles of activism

Ineffective

- *Naive Citizen:*
  Believes the "Official Policies". Does not yet realize that powerholders & institutions serve special elite interests at the expense of the less powerful minorities and the general welfare.

or

- *Super-patriot:*
- *Blind Obedience to powerholders and the country.*

Effective

- Promote positive American values, principles, symbols, e.g. democracy, freedom, justice, nonviolence.
- Normal citizen.
- Grounded in center of society
- Protect against anti-American charges.

CITIZEN

REBEL

Ineffective

- *Anti-American, anti-authority, anti-organization rules & structure.*
- *Self-identity as radical militant, a lonely voice on society's fringe.*
- *Any Means necessary: especially disruptive tactics and violence to property or people when "necessary".*
- *Tactics without realistic strategy.*
- *Isolated from mass-base grassroots.*
- *Victim atttitude and behaviour: angry, aggressive, judgmatic, dogmatic, powerlessness ...*
- *"Politically correct", absolute truth, moral superiority.*
- *Strident: acts out strong personal upset emotions, needs & freedom, regardless of movement's needs.*
- **Negative rebel** *is indistinguishable from* **agent provocateur.**

Effective

- Protest: say, "NO!" to violation of positive American values.
- Nonviolent direct action & attitude, including civil disobedience.
- Target: official powerholders & institutions
- Puts problems & policies in public spotlight and agenda.
- Strategy & tactics.
- Exciting, courageous, risky.

By Bill Moyer 1990

Effective

- Parliamentary: Use official mainstream system & institutions, e.g. courts, Congress, city hall, corporations to get movement goals,
  values, alternatives adopted into official laws, policies, & conventional wisdom.
- Use variety of means: lobbying, lawsuits, referenda, official rallies, candidates, etc.
- Professional Opposition Organizations (POOs) are the key movement agency.
- Watchdog successes to ensure enforcement, expand success, and protect against backlash.

Ineffective

- *"Realistic Politics": Promotes minor reforms that might be more acceptable to the powerholders.*
- *POO limitations: patriarchal, hierarchical organization leadership & structure; organizational maintenance needs replace movement needs/goals; dominant power undermines democracy with the movement and disempowers the grassroots.*
- *Cooptation: POO staff identify more with official powerholders than they do with the movement's grassroots.*
- *Does not advocate paradigm shifts.*

REFORMER

CHANGE AGENT

Effective

- People Power: educate, convince, involve majority of ordinary citizens & whole society in change process.
- Mass-based grassroots organizations, networks, activists.
- Put issue on political agenda.
- Promote strategies & tactics for waging long-term social movement.
- Nurturer role: empower grassroots.
- Create permanent organizations and support & nurture activists.
- Promote alternatives and paradigm shift.
- Promote paradigm shift.

Ineffective

- *Utopian: Promote visions of perfection or live alternatives in isolation from the practical political & social struggle.*
- *Promote only minor reform.*
- *Movement leadership & organizational patriarchy & oppressive hierarchy.*
- *Tunnel vision: advocate single approach, while opposing those doing all others.*
- *Patriarchal & oppressive movement organizations & leadership.*
- *Ignore personal issues & needs of activists.*

S. Holland)[8]; the study by the Transnational Institute/Amsterdam, *Beyond Bretton Woods. Alternatives to the Global Economic Order* (ed. J. Cavanagh)[9]; and the most recent books by E. Altvater who deals especially with the European level in his book *Gewerkschaften vor der europäischen Herausforderung* (Trade unions and the European challenge).[10]

If it is true that the decisive power in the present system rests with the transnational capital markets, then the starting point of any counter-strategy must be to discover alternatives to the way they are regulated on a global scale. Implementing these alternatives will require national, regional and community-based strategies. This will define the structure of the following sections of this book – always assuming that a coalition of victims from the South, East and North/West offers the best chance of changing and perhaps taming the global system from below, if it is possible at all.

2 Alternatives to the current world economic and financial (dis)order

2.1 *The UN and the Bretton Woods institutions (IMF, World Bank, GATT)*

The issue at the global level now is the *assignment of tasks and division of labour between the United Nations and the Bretton Woods (BW) institutions.*[11] The strategy of the North is clear and extremely dangerous: in development issues the UN is only to be responsible for peace and social policy. Finance and economic policy are to be decided globally by the BW institutions. The reason is clear. They are plutocratically controlled by the rich industrialised countries alone, while in the UN context the latter would be accountable and have to bow – ideally – to common decisions. The practical tactics of the North are

---

8   EC-Commission, 1993.
9   J. Cavanagh (ed.), 1994.
10 E. Altvater, 1992[2], 1992, 1993; for more details concerning the European level cf. U. Duchrow, 1992; for information about the global dimension of the problems facing the environment cf. E.U. von Weizsäcker, 1994.
11 Cf. South Centre, 1992. Other recent publications on the reform of the global institutions include J. Cavanagh, M. Arruda and D. Wysham (ed.), 1994; J. Bruin (ed.), 1994; U. Duchrow and M. Gueck, 1994 and 1995.

aimed at strengthening the powers of the BW institutions and weakening, or undermining and instrumentalising, the UN institutions, particularly the United Nations Conference on Trade and Development (UNCTAD) and the United Nations Development Programme (UNDP).

By contrast, the strategy of the South, admittedly flagging in the face of the brutal approach of the North, aims at integrating the BW institutions into the UN system, to be made even more democratic, and at campaigning meanwhile for democracy, pluralism and universality in the BW institutions. All social movements, non-governmental organisations (NGOs) including the churches, and all responsible people in the North are called upon to join in this campaign. What are the *actual goals and demands?*

In its 1992 Human Development Report, the UNDP put forward a comprehensive plan for a *new international economic and financial order.*[12]

> It is based on the observation that the present international economic order is undemocratic, against the interests of the majority of the world population, and thus extremely dangerous. (p.78)

This observation is of vital importance. Any *political* strategy in the present situation must first start from the rejection and delegitimation of the existing undemocratic disorder and plutocracy. The social movements and NGOs have done this, even the World Council of Churches Assemblies in Vancouver (1983) and Canberra (1991) and the European Ecumenical Assembly in Basel (1989) and the global convocation in Seoul (1990). But most individual churches have not been as forthright. The UN now supports this strategy but are the churches prepared to do likewise? This would be an important step. The withdrawal of legitimation can only be achieved by the movements and UN development agencies, which do not have much power anyway, when recognised social institutions like churches and unions widen their political base in the population.

> The report sets out two basic principles on which a new system should be based: "First, a set of rules and procedures that all nation-states accept as governing their actions and interactions. Second, a fair and effective system for enforcing such rules on nation-states." (p.78)

---

12 UNDP, 1992; cf. also UNDP, 1994.

The reason for these principles is clear. In the present disorder the strong countries have the power to govern the economies of the indebted and weak countries directly, by means of the BW institutions. They do not have to undertake structural adjustments themselves and can escape the decisions of UN organisations by different tricks.

> The United States has simply refused to accept a number of adverse decisions by the International Court of Justice, e.g. that it should pay US$3 billion in compensation to Nicaragua because of the undeclared war it waged on that country. When UNESCO wanted to adopt a New International Information Order the US stopped paying its dues until a new director-general was installed and the plan was dropped. So it is plain why the UNDP report lays down these principles.

Its plan distinguishes between a long-term goal and an overarching transitional strategy.

> – The long-term goal provides for a global central bank. It would have the task of creating a common currency, maintaining price and exchange rate stability, providing for a global adjustment of surpluses and deficits and for equal access to international loans – and giving poor nations liquidity and borrowing assistance. (pp.78f.)

This proposal is basically a revival of Keynes' ideas as expressed at Bretton Woods in 1944, which were rejected under pressure from the United States and replaced by the present system of the IMF and World Bank, with the dollar as world currency.

> – The second long-term element is a system of progressive income tax – "to be collected automatically from the rich nations, and to be distributed to the poor nations according to their income and development needs. The administration of this tax would have to represent equally the interests of both donors and recipients. And funds would be allocated on the basis of a shared policy dialogue, rather than a system of formal conditionality." (p.79)

This revolutionary proposal of a global progressive tax goes further than Keynes, but is in line with his theory: the international community would have to take on functions of the nation state, i.e. introducing taxation to redistribute the profits accumulated unequally through the mechanisms of the market economy.

- Third, an international trade organisation is needed – "to ensure free and equal access to all forms of global trade, to manage commodity stabilisation schemes and to do research and make recommendations for commodity policies. This new organisation would merge the current functions of GATT and UNCTAD, but it would also be strengthened by effective regulatory powers and by a small and manageable executive board." (p.79)

This proposal also corresponds to the ideas of Keynes, likewise dropped when the industrialised countries had achieved what they wanted with the setting up of GATT, which they originally intended to be provisional. The UNDP proposal would now be an important instrument, if implemented to counter-act the constant deterioration of the terms of trade.

- Fourth, the UNDP proposed a strengthened UN system, with "a new Development Security Council, which would establish the broad policy framework for all global development issues. These issues range from food security to ecological security, from humanitarian assistance to development assistance, from debt relief to social development, from drug control to international migration." (p.79)[13]

This proposal is also new, compared with the original Bretton Woods proposals. It takes account of the fact that since the end of the East-West conflict the actual security problem has lain in the destruction of social and ecological resources by the present global economic system.[14]

The *transitional strategy* aims to reform the existing institutions until long-term proposals can be put into practice. Let us look at the *IMF*.

- First, the *adjusting of external accounts* is exclusively at the expense of the deficit countries in the present system. The deficit countries have to destroy their societies with painful adjustment burdens, while the surplus countries "feel no corresponding obligation to increase their imports". The IMF should thus reactivate Keynes' original proposal that it become an International Clearing Union with the possibility of imposing "a penalty on surplus countries – 1 per cent of

---

13 Cf. also UNDP, 1992, pp.82f. and UNDP, 1994, calling for an "Economic Security Council" (p.84).
14 See also the demands of the 1993 and the 1994 UNDP reports with regard to expanding the concept of human security from the security of nations to the security of people.

the surplus per month to encourage them to make adjustments too. (...) The current system is both inefficient and unjust". (p.79)

This proposal of Keynes would be a powerful corrective to the growing gap between poor and rich countries and should be strongly supported by solidarity groups in the industrialised countries. Another key issue is the development of alternative models for structural adjustment.[15]

- *Second*, the IMF gives assistance with *liquidity*. In 1967 it created Special Drawing Rights (SDR) by analogy with Keynes' proposal of an international currency ("bancor"). However, instead of mainly making them available to the central banks of the weaker countries, it gives them to industrialised countries – which only increases the gap between rich and poor. (The astronomic debt of the United States weighs particularly heavily here.)
- The *third* role of the IMF, to exercise functions of a world central bank, has been effectively sabotaged to date. And yet that role is "desperately needed", in view of the growth of cross-border lending. (p.80)

The lack of regulation of transnational capital markets is the cancer of the present system. This is something that even European parliamentarians, like the President of the European Commission, Jacques Delors, seem to feel, when they repeatedly consider imposing controls on capital movement in Europe in order to counteract the mobility of speculative finance. There is a deep contradiction here between ideology and the reality of the transnational "free market". Genuinely free movement would only be possible with the aid of international regulation. The deregulated market is so destructive that even strong industrial regions like Western Europe need to consider introducing restrictions. Admittedly, it is also clear that solutions cannot be found at the national or regional levels alone.

The *World Bank* is the second Bretton Woods organisation. According to the UNDP proposal, "The World Bank must rediscover its original mandate as well – to mediate between the capital markets and the developing countries" (p.80).

The UNDP proposes two measures which will not be described in detail here.[16]
First, the World Bank should become an International Investment Trust. "This

---

15 A main emphasis of the Bretton Woods Reform Organisation (BWRO), Grenada, Green Street, St. Georges.
16 See UNDP, 1992, pp.80ff.

would enable it to sell bonds (safe ones, though with a lower rate of return, U.D.) to surplus nations and lend the proceeds to developing countries" on terms they could afford (p.80). Second, the World Bank should set up an Intermediate Assistance Facility which would not be bound to the quota policy which the US forces on the BW organisations (so as not to change the voting structure to its own disadvantage). Surplus countries like Japan could offer more resources for lending without the US having to reduce its voting power in the World Bank as a whole. The resources available on special conditions could also be extended, which now only represent 30 per cent of World Bank lending to the poorest countries (administered by the International Development Association).

This proposal falls short of that of Keynes who put forward the idea not of a development bank but of a fund. However, the expansion of favourable credit facilities offered to poorer countries should be welcomed. In addition, NGOs are calling for a reform of the undemocratic character of the World Bank and its lack of accountability and transparency. The NGOs have different possible models in mind when calling for an independent *appeals authority*, with access to all bank information and with the right to express criticism and be heard by the bank.[17]

The call for democratisation, transparency and participation by those involved is central to both the IMF and World Bank. Moreover, the UNDP report rightly calls for them to be fundamentally reorientated away from purely financial and economic growth to a policy of human development and the preservation of natural resources.

The *world trade system*, currently controlled and manipulated by the industrialised countries through GATT (now: World Trade Organisation/WTO), is in urgent need of reform, according to the UNDP report (p.82).

First, there is the question of the stabilisation of commodity prices. That means, in practical terms, that the GATT rules should be extended to cover all products, including agricultural and tropical products. That would include textiles, also a strength of developing countries. Further, the question of intellectual property

---

17 This proposal builds on the critical Wapenhans Report on the World Bank. For more alternative features of the WB see Cavanagh/Arruda, 1994, pp. 111ff.

rights must be settled so that developing countries are not disadvantaged. Also, GATT/WTO must receive powers to enforce rules even against the strong countries, which at present can use all rules to their own advantage without submitting to them themselves. Moreover, after the conclusion of the Uruguay negotiations, the NGOs are now demanding an immediate new round of GATT talks to discuss how to adapt to the social and environmental requirements ("sustainable development").

In the *ecological field*, the UNDP report proposes the strengthening of existing environmental facilities, and the development of new ones. The Global Environmental Facility administered by the UNDP, UNEP and World Bank must be supplemented by *international environmental taxation* (eco-tax).

At the same time, the report urges the creation of a *global security system*, a radical disarmament policy and the channelling of proceeds to development and environmental policy as a peace dividend.

Finally, the report appraises the *importance of the people involved and NGOs* in developing this international order, which includes an appropriate reform of the UN. The question of participation in the structures and decision-making is the emphasis of the 1993 UNDP report. It must be seen that the UNDP reports are divided in themselves and ambiguous, since their proposals stem from a traditional growth policy and a liberal free trade context.[18] Yet the UNDP research team has shown courage in telling these unpleasant truths directly to the plutocratic major powers of the global economic system. Its efforts will have been in vain if the social institutions and the general public in the industrialised countries do not wake up and urge their own governments to accept these proposals.

2.2   Ending modern-day debt slavery

If there exists a direct analogy to biblical situations, demands and strategies, then it is here in the indebtedness of the Southern countries, which were once colonies and are now controlled in a neo-colonialist way. The mechanisms themselves have, of course, changed. But the heart of the problem lies in the fact that weaker countries and peoples were oppressed, had to pay "tribute" to

---

18 Cf. T. Kunanayakam, 1993.

their masters and thereby fell into debt. Now they are deep in debt (partly due to their own corrupt rulers, who were usually installed and supported by the colonial powers), they are having everything mercilessly taken away from them – seemingly without end – including the lives of many people.[19] What can be done?

There have been many radical demands by the NGOs, churches and Southern nations, all of which cannot be discussed here in detail.[20] Professional NGO lobbies and the Southern states are naturally forced to tone down their demands, so that the present power cartels of the banks, international financial institutions, and creditor states are still prepared to listen. By contrast, grassroots movements, churches and other agencies, can in principle act independently of this cartel; they should raise demands and alternatives that are as far-reaching as possible, tackling the problem at its roots and creating as much new political latitude as possible for those who have to manoeuvre within the system. I will confine myself to the demands made by the NGO conference in Rio in 1992, and the demands of the People's Parliament (1992) and the Hearing on "The Political Responsibility of the European Union for the International Financial Order with Respect to Sustainable Development on Social Justice" (1994) held by Kairos Europa, and choose ten of these:[21]

1 As a first immediate measure, regulations regarding insolvency must be drawn up for countries which are hopelessly in debt, based on regulations which already exist in cases of individual debt. Kunibert Raffer has put forward proposals for such a move drawn from the model of US insolvency law.[22] These regulations would mean that in the case of unrepayable debt, a community or a state could file for bankruptcy, exactly as a bankrupt firm can today, and cannot, therefore,

---

19 The NGO treaty on the debt question begins with the phrase: "Considering that the foreign debt is the most recent mechanism of the exploitation of Southern peoples and the environment by the North, thus adding an extra burden to the historical, resource and cultural debt of the North to the South…".

20 An excellent survey of the question of debt relief can be found in: H.-B. Peter et al., 1990, pp.35ff. I am assuming, as described in the first part of this book, that all the proposals regarding international crisis management simply amount to rescuing creditors from the crisis of the capital accumulation system and withdrawing control over important resources and economic facilities from debtor countries by methods like "debt-for-equity swaps".

21 Cf. Kairos Europa, 1992, pp.96ff.; U. Duchrow and M. Gueck, 1994 and 1995.

22 K. Raffer, 1990.

be made to pay back exorbitant sums it requires for basic survival. In our context, this demand must be addressed to western governments and the EU.

2   Every fundamental strategy for combating the debt of Southern nations must start from the assumption that in most cases the debt was not only illegitimate, but in some cases even illegal. Most of the debts have been accumulated by illegitimate governments. This weighs even heavier since these regimes were sometimes installed with the illegal help of the US government and subsequently supported and kept in power by the US and other Western governments (as in the case of Brazil, Chile, and Argentina). Moreover, these debts have been repaid many times over in the meantime but due to the compound interest mechanism, their nominal value continues to increase. Support should, therefore, be lent to the assertions of Latin American lawyers who are currently claiming before the International Court of Justice that 90 per cent of Brazil's debts are illegitimate.[23]

3   Pressure should be exerted on governments and banks to give due consideration to finding a democratic way of solving the debt question. This includes transparency and the release of information pertaining to each individual debt situation and agreement, as well as the participation of organisations representing the debtors and of NGOs. They should also demand the right to cooperate with the UN in setting up a conference to deal with a solution to the debt question and at which all the players in the debate (debtors, creditors, social movements, and NGOs) would be present.

4   The subject of the recognition of the debts of the North with respect to the South must be examined, as must colonial and neo-colonial exploitation and environmental debt.

5   It must be demanded that all debts are written off, even if a large reduction is all that is feasibly possible. The starting point must be those debts which are clearly illegal. Moreover, governments should force banks to take over the decisions of the "Paris Club" and to release the debtor countries from at least 50 per cent of their debt obligations as the Dutch ABN-AMRO Bank has done voluntarily. In any case, an immediate end should be put to the criminal process of the poor countries transferring US$ 50 billion (net) to the industrialised nations every year through the debt mechanisms.

6   Conversely, strong pressure must be applied to the rich nations urging them to give 0.7 per cent of their GNP to Southern nations as development aid towards socio-environmental and participatory development.

---

23 Cf. J.L. Duboc Pinaud, 1992.

In order that the poor nations should not fall back into debt immediately after their debts have been written off, the terms of trade between industrial goods and raw materials must be improved to the benefit of the latter and the protectionism practised by the industrialised nations with regard to goods from developing countries must be abolished.

8 The structural adjustments that have been imposed on the South by the IMF must be implemented on a fundamentally different development model, i.e. an approach based on people and the environment, not on financial and economic growth alone. At the same time, structural adjustments must also be imposed on Northern nations – of course alternative ones, i.e. socially just ones (compare this with the demands of the UNDP above).

9 With regard to banks, governments must be urged only to give tax deductions on unrepayable loans to those banks which pass on this tax relief to their debtors.[24] In addition, governments should also be pressed to make banks obliged to reveal information about flight capital, as they are already obliged to do in the case of drug-related money.

10 Social movements and NGOs are calling on people and especially churches in the industrialised nations to boycott banks that do not write off their Third World debt – similar to the programme of withdrawing accounts and investments held with banks that continued to trade in South Africa under the apartheid regime.

In order to achieve all these aims, social movements, professional organisations, churches, trade unions, etc. should form coalitions to mount a coordinated campaign to increase the participation among people in the West in the process to liberate the South from its debt slavery. In this context, it would be useful to adopt the arguments used by Susan George in her book *The Debt Boomerang* to remind the people in the North that this matter also concerns them.[25] Moreover, Kairos Europa is trying to highlight the link between the pauperisation mechanisms inside and outside Europe in a campaign that will be looked at later in this book.

---

24 This proposal has got wide support in the European Parliament.
25 S. George, 1992.

2.3   *Combating capital and tax flight and all economic crime*

Capital and tax flight are the strategic points that directly link the debt of developing countries, with all its devastating consequences for people and the environment, with the public debt and pauperisation of one third of people in the rich nations. In the First Part we saw how Germany, for example, is falling deeper into debt and the government cut about 20 billion DM from its budget for social welfare and job creation schemes in 1994, while in the same year at least 60 billion DM left the country in unpaid taxes on financial assets alone. Much could be done to rectify this situation by a socially aware government less responsive to the interests of the rich than the present coalition government. It should simply be prepared to finance more investigations into tax evasion, a practice that would soon bring returns far greater than the initial expense. Ultimately, however, we must strive for new international regulatory and control systems, with the governments of the richest industrialised nations taking the lead.

The *Treaty on Capital Flight and Corruption* from the NGO conference in Rio is one important step towards making people aware of the problem and developing firm strategies.

> Capital flight and corruption are some of the main causes of the poverty in the South. Without capital flight and corruption the debt crisis would not exist in its current form.
>
> More than half of the Southern countries' debts are in the form of private capital deposited in the tax havens controlled by the banks of the North. The five leading countries that host this type of capital are Panama, Cayman Islands, Switzerland, Luxembourg and the USA.
>
> There exist at least a dozen different forms of corruption, such as bribing, fraudulent enrichment of public authorities, tax evasions, etc...
>
> The financial centres and the tax havens play a crucial role in international financial relations. In order to effectively combat these procedures, the explorers must find a national, regional and international legal base. Many countries, among them the tax havens, do not provide international juridical assistance. The Marcos and Duvalier affairs and other financial scandals indicate that the existing juridical procedures are inoperative.
>
> It is not possible to continue tolerating the role played by the Northern and Southern elites. A new legal base aimed at addressing the diversion of public funds is needed.

There is of course the question of how to go about effectively combating the theft of public money by rich individuals and the ensuing pauperisation of large numbers of people in the South, East and West. Firstly, what are the precise aims? The NGO treaty defines a number of *pledges:*

1 There is a need to introduce legislation to act against passive and active capital flight and tax evasion.

2 There is a need for the creation of a mechanism which will force the banks to become transparent. Transparent statistics on the transfer of capital by banks must be sent to the country of origin.

3 In order to combat corruption we need an International Legal Assistance System. Legal procedures for any act of corruption should not exceed six months.

Which *strategies* can help to achieve these aims?

1 We will put pressure on governments to adopt new regulations and laws in order to combat corrupt practices. This can only be achieved with NGO collaboration.

2 We need to create a specialized "economic Interpol" in order to investigate capital flight and corrupt practices.

Proposals 3 and 4 concern the support of public campaigns by NGOs – like the Berne Declaration – which seek to make political issues of capital and tax flight and economic crime and corruption. Proposals 5 and 6 are aimed directly at national and international political institutions.

5 We believe it is necessary to undertake legal action against the public authorities which have committed criminal capital flight. In this sense, it would be useful to set up a coalition of NGOs interested in undertaking such legal action.

6 In order to avoid the transfer of capital from one financial center to another, we will demand that the United Nations, through its Vienna-based institution specialized in criminal prevention, undertakes to harmonize all the existing laws regarding the subject.

Correspondingly, NGOs must form coalitions to influence governments and banks in this respect. I see this question as being central to the debate, yet it is hardly raised in public discussion.[26] Elections must be used to put this question onto the political agenda because the governments are currently misleading people by concentrating on other topics like immigrants, abuse of social

---

26 Only recently has a left-wing SPD group, the "Frankfurter Kreis" (Frankfurt circle), taken up this question as a topic for the 1994 election campaigns in Germany.

benefits, overly high wage levels or crime prevention instead of the real causes of the present economic and financial problems (or the "arch-thieves" as Luther called them).

2.4 Riding the tiger, or, can TNCs be tamed?

Along with the control of the transnational money markets, the control of transnational corporations (TNCs) is the most serious unsolved problem facing us today and under the present conditions it is likely to remain unsolved. Neither individual national governments nor the existing international institutions have the power to monitor all the activities of TNCs. In fact, the final outcome of the GATT talks and the tendency of TNCs to infiltrate UNCTAD have led away from this goal instead of towards it. The NGO treaty from Rio entitled "Democratic Regulation of the Behaviour of TNCs" contains principles and a preliminary approach for developing a strategy to gain influence in this area. Here are some of the *principles*:

> TNCs have the duty to respect national sovereignty, respect the health and environmental rights of the public, and refrain from financial, pricing or technological activities that cause socio-economic difficulties to host countries.

> International mechanisms should hold TNCs liable for the harmful effects caused by their operations in all countries of operations. Contractual clauses binding TNCs to agreements with host governments and communities should be enforceable in home and host countries.

This demonstrates that no single international institution can presently be said to have powers of control and supervision over TNCs. We should therefore refer back to the reasons behind the earlier proposals for a reform of the UN. New institutions based on these ideas would have such powers. The NGO treaty contains further principles:

> TNCs should be held to the highest environmental, health, safety and labor standards in all countries of operations.

> Workers and unions have the right to representation and participation in environmental and health audits. Workers have the right to training, control and to negotiate social economic health and environmental conditions in North and South.

> Freedom of information for all citizens, environmental groups, labor unions and governmental agencies, including the names and quantities of chemicals on site,

data on emissions, access to waste streams for independent sampling and analysis, access to environmental assessments and audits, should be guaranteed and
take precedence over proprietary information and trade secrets.

Clear production methods and technologies should be used for all new TNC projects, environmental assessments will determine if a proposed project will use
clean production. For existing operations, environmental audits will be the basis
for planning a conversion to clean production.

TNCs shall not trade in wastes, banned or unregistered products, and shall not
transfer obsolete or hazardous technologies. Workers displaced by conversion to
ecologically sound practices should be retrained and compensated by TNCs.

The precautionary approach, which places the burden of proof of no harm on
the potential polluter rather than on the environment or potential victims,
should govern TNC practices.

The NGO treaty also puts forward several proposals in connection with how
the internationally coordinated supervision of the activities of TNCs can be
organised and consolidated by NGO networks. Coalitions between NGOs,
consumer associations, trade organisations, citizens' initiatives and other
grassroots initiatives can be formed when action proves necessary. The development of material for resolving the problem and mobilising large numbers
of people should be extended.

This shows once again how little international legal control can be exerted
over TNCs. They operate transnationally and as such are outside the bounds of
the existing public institutions. "Civil society" must organise itself either to
directly influence TNCs (since they rely on a positive public image which
serves as a sort of legitimation) or to exert pressure on individual governments
or the EU to take steps against practices like eco-dumping. But under the
present structure of the capitalist world market, the possibilities for an effective means of control are very limited. We have not yet found the path leading
to a worldwide economic democracy.[27] There is still a lot of spadework to be
done.

---

27 The Heidelberg Economy Workshop has put forward further proposals for
intervention strategies against multinational companies in its publication "Multis,
Markt und Krise" (multinationals, the market and crisis), 1992.

3　Strategies for life at local, national and European levels

3.1　The local level

Even today, most people seem to be of the opinion that it is possible to leave global and international questions to a few enthusiasts, who are idealistic in caring for the "Third World" and the rainforests. This opinion must and can be radically altered. Originally in the United States, then in Britain and now increasingly in the remainder of Europe, neo-liberal policies have meant that the environment and the weakest in society have to bear the pressure of global market forces. Large-scale processes of pauperisation, exclusion and destruction have followed, most noticeably at the local level. It is here that the unemployed gather, along with economic migrants who have seen their livelihoods stripped away; it is here that farmers are falling deeper into debt; it is here that the potential for violence among neglected youngsters is present; it is here that those receiving social security benefits are seeing their handouts reduced; it is here that despair and subsequent cases of alcoholism are rife; it is here that the rent hikes which bring about further homelessness and debt are to be paid; it is here that the potential for racism and fascism is most prevalent; it is here that education and culture are declining; it is here that rubbish levels are increasing; and it is here that the air, water and soil are being polluted. And at the same time, subsidies for local authorities are being cut. Jobs are being lost and there is no recourse.[28] And all this is happening while the rich engage in tax evasion on interest from money assets – not to speak of their vast profits from speculation on the transnational money markets. The discrepancy here is something the ordinary person can easily understand.

But can people convert these insights into political action? Yes, but only when coalitions are formed between those directly affected and the other forces of civil society. This is precisely the point at which the old class analysis and class struggle models are outdated and yet can be constructively overhauled. Workers are no longer the only ones to be exposed to the perils of capitalism. It is imperative that, in all attempts to form coalitions, they try to convince the unions of the futility of an isolationist, unpolitical outlook con-

---

28　In Mannheim, the job cuts have meant that even the person responsible for debt advice has been laid off. The reason given is that this problem has grown so much that ten counsellors would be needed.

centrated solely on pay levels and that they should join forces with the poor, the excluded, and environmental groups in campaigning for a global regulation of capital. The forming of coalitions between the groups of victims and supportive elements in civil society is the only opportunity we have to persuade political institutions at all levels to take action against the deregulated forces of capital. Of course, in this respect, it must be remembered, as we saw in Chapter IX, that all concerned must try out alternatives to their own handling of consumption and money, both to explore new avenues and to remain credible. Here is *an example from Mannheim.*

Since 1991 the Mannheim church district has been trying to involve congregations in the project on "Poverty, Wealth, Justice". A facilitator tries to bring about coalitions between the parishes and marginalised groups in their suburbs. They include unemployed people, refugees, social welfare recipients, single parents, and victims of rent speculation. The project is assisted by a qualified committee. It includes the Diakonisches Werk (Protestant social services), the church youth department, the urban industrial mission, the regional office for mission and ecumenics, providing international reference points, and a representative of the city of Mannheim responsible for its "social atlas". Only seven parishes have agreed to participate but they are working hard. At "plenaries" the different groups hear about one another, there are workshops to shed light on the economic and financial grounds for impoverishment and enrichment processes, and the church district is kept regularly informed.

The next step was a "City poverty conference", also known as a "communal social policy offensive". There is already a National Poverty Conference to which the different agencies belong. Now a larger alliance is forming at the local level. It includes the self-help groups, the association of relief agencies and social welfare organisations in Mannheim, the trade unions and the churches. In 1994 there was a "Social Initiative Day" to protest against social cutbacks. This led to a new structure of Round Tables for applying pressure on governmental and capitalist institutions. A similar day was held in Liège in Belgium. Now Kairos Europa is organising a process of networking between community alliances like these at a European level.[29]

---

29 Coordination: Industrie- und Sozialpfarramt, Nietzschestrasse 8, D-68165 Mannheim

Is it not conceivable that, throughout Germany and other EU member states, civil society will become a key player at the local level when it comes to putting a life-sustaining economy on the political agenda? What are the chances of the introverted, conformist mainline churches reverting to their biblical calling of building attractive cells of an alternative society in the spirit of God's kingdom? And where else, if not at the local level, should the urgent radical reforms begin? Where else than at the level at which Jesus promised to show himself: the domain of the marginalised groups and those whose basic needs have been trampled underfoot?

In keeping with the necessary double strategy, this is also the place to link small-scale alternatives and political strategies. This will require training for people on the ground and organising things at the local level so as to free up resources for networking.

3.2   *The national level*

The next step concerns *economic policy and the formation of coalitions at the national level.* In his book *Aufbruch zu neuen Ufern* (Setting off for new shores), W.Kessler gives an excellent survey of goals and measures on the way towards a socio-ecological economic democracy in a national context.[30] First he indicates two clear *restrictions*:

– A policy like the present one of merely trying to reduce the damage done by the capitalist market economy (usually unsuccessfully) is definitely not enough.

– In a democracy which fundamentally accepts the free market economy, no government can ultimately force industrialists, employees, consumers and share-holders to act in a socially and ecologically responsible way.

Nevertheless, it is *possible* for a government in such a system to have a policy aiming at bringing about socio-ecological economic democracy, if this policy ensures:

– that private ownership of means of production is broadly based and subordinate to the participatory claims of employees and

---

30 W. Kessler, 1990, pp.151ff.(tr.) In respect of other national contexts, refer to the books already mentioned, especially Daly and Cobb, 1989.

- that the market processes in one's own country and internationally are subject to social and ecological regulation "so that the economy develops in harmony with the people involved, and with nature" (p.152).

He names the following individual goals and measures:

- eco-taxes leading to an ecological production and the creation of new jobs (pp.152ff);[31]
- a guaranteed basic income ("basic wage for all"), in order to overcome poverty, unemployment and economic dependence (pp.158ff);
- revolutionising ownership "peacefully" through more participation and the promotion of worker-managed businesses (pp.168ff);
- an employment policy targeted at disadvantaged groups (pp.179ff);
- a new financial policy with the goal of redistribution for a socio-ecological economic democracy (pp.192ff).

Here, Kessler puts his finger on the crucial point when he contradicts the prima facie objection that none of this would work due to shortage of finance.

> "A second look will reveal the real reason why there is a lack of funds in certain social and economic areas: the unequal distribution of economic wealth. (...) The diverse processes here are not evidence of a general lack of capital, but of a most unequal distribution of economic wealth. (...) That is why new financial policy criteria are essential for a fundamental change-over to a socio-ecological economic democracy with the goal of reconciling economics and ecology and creating more social justice and eventually more democratic ownership in business. The approach must be three-pronged: *surplus capital from productivity gains and interest, along with spending on luxury goods, must be redistributed for the greater good of society.*"

So there should not be just a lower limit to ensure people's livelihood, but also an upper limit for wealth.[32] Kessler envisages a profit levy on companies, an effective tax on interest with a clear and practicable obligation on the banks to give appropriate information to the inland revenue authorities, and a doubling of VAT on luxury goods. Only if the giant profits are redistributed for social and ecological purposes will it be possible to solve future problems.

---

31 Cf. also E.U. von Weizsäcker, 1994, pp.159ff.
32 Cf. also B. Goudzwaard and H. de Lange, 1995; E.-U. Huster, 1993.

Kessler points out that politicians do not have the courage to take the necessary steps because of pressure from the lobbies representing the winners under the present system. They have huge resources at their disposal, while those people suffering under the same system are badly organised, if at all, and – most importantly – are constantly fed misleading information. From our analysis, however, it is clear that the necessary political changes at the national level alone cannot lead to success. The lobbies do not only use powerful rhetoric and, in a few cases, bribery, but they also simply transfer capital to where it will make the largest profit and be subject to the least social and economic restrictions. In euphemistic management jargon, this is called the "location question". Any country is said to lose its attractiveness as a financial centre and as an industrial location if it pays better wages and maintains jobs. Companies are being forced to bow to the pressures of competition within the world market, so the argument runs.

Who is it that allows this same competition to crack the whip on the world's population and the whole planet? In the front line are those economic players who are responsible only to the owners of capital, not to the majority of people. This is the reason why Brazilian bishops speak of a worldwide totalitarian system. But it is not only our banks and TNCs which are participating in this undemocratic, dictatorial system on behalf of the owners of capital, but also our governments, which we elect democratically. They – primarily the German, Japanese and United States governments – have ensured that the present plutocratic institutions of the world economy (the IMF, the World Bank, GATT/WTO and G7) still exist and have not been replaced by democratic institutions which can exert efficient controls over the markets and their players.

To put it plainly: at present the national governments we elect in the industrialised countries are acting dictatorially at the international level. They should be voted out by the majority of their populations if they do not develop democratic controls on capital at the international level. Only then will it be possible at the national level to organise social, ecological and democratic structures, and guide economic processes. That means, however, that the national level is of crucial importance not just for its own sake but in terms of global conditions for the future of life on this planet. Here the nature of financial systems becomes a central issue.[33]

3.3 The European level

With regard to the European level, I have already analysed the situation in detail after the introduction of the Single Market in 1992 and put forward strategies.[34] My concerns were the consequences of this neo-liberal project ("Europe must be competitive in the world market"): the concentration of economic power in face of rising unemployment; division into rich and poor regions; victims among the smallholders; increasing divisions within society; environmental dumping; the growing imperialisation of European defence policies and the development of "Fortress Europe"; and the dismantling of democracy. All these arguments will not be repeated here.

In view of the present analysis, there can be no doubt that with the European Union we need more political unity, not less. Only if the political institutions are strengthened can regulatory mechanisms be developed which are able – given the political will – to confine the market to a framework of conditions concerning local and regional needs, and to redress the balance of unequal distribution (caused by the market in the first place) to the benefit of weaker individuals, groups and regions.

The most serious shortcomings of the Maastricht Treaty are that the European Parliament has still not received any full legislative powers and the Social Union has fallen foul of British opposition. In other words, Maastricht does not yet allow for a truly democratic constitution or for a binding social policy for the European institutions. It came, therefore, as a timely reminder when the Danes firstly rejected the treaty in a referendum and at the second attempt the majority in favour was by no means overwhelming – admittedly for a variety of reasons, some of which have been referred to here. Perhaps this shock will contribute to the treaty being developed further with the aim of creating more democracy and greater potential for socio-political and environmental intervention. This is the aim which all social and environmental movements should work towards.

---

33 In this context one must also re-examine the question of whether the central bank should have such a powerful, politically-independent position. It now seems to be responsible only to those with money at their disposal, because of the question of stability of value, and in addition it has no democratic legitimation. On the other hand, the central bank has a number of very important tasks to perform in so far as it has a statutory regulatory function over banks.

34 Cf. U. Duchrow, 1992.

It will have become clear that the question of financial systems is of crucial importance – but in a different form to that in which it is being discussed in Germany, where the primary concern is that the standing of that fetish, the German Mark, will be weakened by a European currency union. After all, a strong currency bears witness to an important position in the unjust global economic system. That it capitalises thereby on the weakness of others is secondary. The Maastricht Treaty now aims to replace other European currencies with the ECU, which would result in all member states having to make many difficult structural adjustments in order to be incorporated into the new hard currency system. What would be the consequences of this?

I support the argument put forward by W.Hankel[35] that this solution would only leave us with two negative options. Either the economically weaker countries or regions within the EU would be forced to make enormous social sacrifices on the altar of hard currency (as shown by the difficulties faced by the formerly two Germanies in trying to unify their currencies after reunification), or very few countries would take part in the system, the others paying for social cohesion with inflation; the EU would be monetarily divided. Hankel's own proposed solution, like the proposals of Keynes in connection with the IMF, is to introduce the ECU as an artificial currency parallel to all other European currencies. The ECU would then remain stable as a world currency, alongside the dollar, while the individual currencies would fluctuate according to their economic strength and could give more weight to stability or socio-environmental interests according to the circumstances. I am not an expert and so cannot judge whether this solution is the right one, but what is clear is that the negative social consequences of a common currency that have been pointed out by Hankel must be publicly discussed, and avoided.

At this point I would go one step further. What sort of policy will the EU pursue in the international monetary system after the introduction of the common European currency? Will it simply be one of competition, which also seems to figure prominently in Hankel's ideas? Or will the EU in its future currency policy favour the equalising and socially responsible intentions which Keynes wanted to bring to express in his original proposals for the Bretton Woods institutions? In other words, will Europe now simply pursue the former policy of the United States, intensified further by the introduction of the ECU to compete with the dollar and the yen as world currency? Or will

---

35 Cf. W. Hankel, 1992.

we see the setting up of an international financial system and corresponding global institutions with regulatory and democratic functions, which will turn money into an instrument for socially and ecologically sound business activity instead of being an end in itself and an instrument of control? The answer to this question will have a direct influence over whether countries in Eastern Europe continue to decline like those in the South or have a chance of becoming self-reliant.

1994 was the year in which precisely these questions were put on the agenda, since 1994 saw the fiftieth anniversary of the setting up of the Bretton Woods institutions. Social movements and NGOs used this opportunity to bring about a public debate over these questions. One example is Kairos Europa, the network I have already mentioned of self-help organisations and solidarity groups. It has launched a campaign, calling for the creation of a link between the struggles for a just economy inside and outside Europe. This plan will now be described in brief terms. The campaign has the goal of *finding alternatives to the economic and financial system which creates pauperisation mechanisms in the South, East and West.*

After gathering appropriate data[36] in the first phase (1993 – June 1994) victims of poverty and debt within Europe and outside have been working in local groups and in four international teams, looking at their own experiences of pauperisation and its causes within the economic and financial system. Among those having taken part are: farmers who have fallen into debt, jobless people, trade union members, and migrants, as well as experts who are working with them. The "Poverty, Wealth, Justice" and "poverty conference" projects in Mannheim can serve as examples in this respect. In the first half of 1994, international teams organised mobile seminars in Brazil, the Caribbean, Germany and Poland, and Switzerland and Italy.

Their experiences were collated at an evaluation conference in Brussels in June 1994 followed by the "Brussels Action Days" under the motto "Save Planet and People – Control Money". A rally took place in front of the stock exchange in Brussels, followed by a public hearing with representatives of the European Commission and the European Parliament. The main topics included the European political responsibility for reforming the Bretton Woods institutions, controlling

---

36 See the consultation document *Transnational Financial Markets and the European Currency System – Their Effects on Poor Countries and Population Groups*, Kairos Europa (Hegenichstr. 22, D-69124 Heidelberg), 1993.

the transnational financial markets and bringing the debt crisis to an end, as well as raising demands for a socio-environmental reform of European internal financial policy.[37]

In the second phase, a double strategy will be pursued with the intention, first, of influencing national governments in this respect and the general public in the EU member states, and, second, of developing a network of economic and financial micro-alternatives on European and international levels. As a first step Kairos Europa sent a letter to all finance ministers and presidents of central banks in the EU with the questions and proposals from the Brussels hearing. At the same time, churches and communities in Europe should be involved in the handling of these questions and – as far as possible – in the campaign, in preparation for the planned second European ecumenical assembly in 1997.

By linking local, national and European levels in a worldwide context, this whole process is intended to contribute to the establishment of broadly based "alliances of hope". They will give an opportunity to try out life-sustaining economic activities and will at the same time help create the necessary political conditions for an alternative economy at the macro-level.

Let us, finally, put this double-strategy approach in the perspective of Giovanni Arrighi's long cycles of capital accumulation. The financial expansion and increasing competition we have experienced since the 1970s is, from that point of view, at the same time a sign of the decline of the hegemonic power of the USA and for the emergence of a new epicentre of the next cycle of accumulation. Arrighi locates it in East Asia. Japan has become the leading economic and financial force, having been built up by the United States itself during the Cold War. In manufacturing industry it has been developing new forms of business organisation centred on cost reduction, combined with the advantage of plentiful industrious cheap labour in East and South East Asia. Financially it has been gathering vast amounts of surplus capital, particularly because of leaving the protection cost of military defense to the US.

However, this makes it impossible for the new global finance centre to take over the hegemonic role. Arrighi compares Japan with Genoa. It needs a territorial political power partner, which for him could be the USA. (Astonish-

---

37 The events in Brussels were organised in cooperation with the Bretton Woods Reform Organisation, the World Council of Churches and other European, Latin American and Caribbean church councils and agencies. The documentation is available from the Kairos office (see previous footnote).

ingly he does not reflect about the possible role of China which could add a dragon to the four tigers around Japan). In this situation he sees three options (pp.355ff.):

- "...the old guard... may well be in a position to appropriate through force, cunning, or persuasion the surplus capital that accumulates in the new centers and thereby terminate capitalist history through the formation of a truly global world empire."

- "East Asia capital may come to occupy a commanding position in systemic processes of capital accumulation." But without state- and war-making capacities "the underlying layer of the market economy would revert to some kind of anarchic order".

- "Finally...before humanity chokes (or basks) in the dungeon (or paradise) of a post-capitalist world empire or of a post-capitalist world market society, it may well burn up in the horrors (or glories) of the escalating violence that has accompanied the liquidation of the Cold War world order. In this case, capitalist history would come to an end but by reverting permanently to the systemic chaos from which it began six hundred years ago and which has been reproduced on an ever-increasing scale with each transition. Whether this would mean the end just of capitalist history or of all human history, it is impossible to tell".

To be sure, there are signs in all three directions: the "New World Order" with the global intervention forces of the West; the chaotic, criminal and corrupt character of the transnational markets; the chaotic proliferation of increasingly lethal weapons through (and throughout) these markets, creating more and more victims every day.

In the perspective of the double strategy put forward in this book all three options certainly call for resistance and small-scale alternatives. The political scenario is daunting. But it can also give direction. The movements in civil society and also the churches in the South, in North America and in Europe will have to concentrate more on linking up with civil society in Japan and East and South-East Asia. There is also a particular point in linking up networks in the USA, Japan and Europe: In the present power structure these three regions will be responsible for creating either socially and ecologically viable global institutions or the horror visions of Arrighi's three options.

What we need, therefore, is a networked *global economic civil rights movement*.

4 Summary

I A		**REJECTION / DELEGITIMISATION / COUNTER-INFORMATION**
Against whom/ what? **For whom/ what?**	1	**Economic** Deregulation mechanisms of limitless money accumulation via totalitarian – global money markets } oriented to competitiveness for – global industrial markets } profit instead of real life
	2	**Political** Institutions to support the mechanisms of limitless money accumulation – global: IMF/World Bank – European: single market without political-social-ecological monitoring and control – national: neo-liberal policy of deregulation and social cuts
	3	**Military** – LIC and MIC
	4	**Ideological** – Neo-liberal ideology in media, education, churches
How?	1	**Boycotts** – Money: – against banks (which e.g. do not cancel 3rd world debt, finance arms industry) – against market interest – Consumption: – against TNCs (e.g. injustice in 3rd world) – against luxury products and unfair trade – Distribution: – against unjust pay systems
	2	**Delegitimation of system and counter-information**
I B		**SMALL-SCALE ALTERNATIVE NETWORKS**
Vision		**Oriented to real life** – everyone basic needs, ecology, community, – nature } participation, from below (local) – future generation to above (global), alternative indicators
Alternatives	1	**In production and trade** – alternative companies – alternative technology ⟹ – low-interest loan – alternative banks – alternative agriculture ⟶ – producer-consumer coopera – alternative trade – fair trade
	2	**In consumption** – simple and ecological – products from fair trade
	3	**Income distribution** – breaking the income-divide (e.g. in churches) – ecumenical sharing
	4	**Security** – social defence – networking of alternatives for mutual strengthening
Goal		**FOR A LIFE-SUSTAININ**⬤

the life-threatening global capitalist economy

III STRUGGLE FOR A SOCIAL-ECOLOGICAL ECONOMIC DEMOCRACY

1 **Economic**
   - Internationalisation of countervailing power of trade unions
   - Internationalisation of countervailing power of civil society
   - Internationalisation of control and taxation of transnational markets and actors

2 **Political**
   - global: – reformed UN – instead of Bretton Woods institutions (democratisation)
              – cancellation of debts, change of terms of trade and taxation of interest
   - European: political-social-ecological conditions of single market
   - national: framework for markets against monopolies, tax flight, social cuts
   - local: priority of social issues and a sustainable local economy

3 **Military**
   - Struggle against imperial intervention troops and arms export, for arms conversion
     and using the peace dividend for global social polity

4 **Ideological**
   - Counter-offensive in media, education, churches

- -

1 **Active involvement in elections**
   - via media
   - via all social sectors

2 **Professional lobbying of non-governmental organisations**

3 **Forming a civil rights movement on the global economy**
   - local/communal
   - national   ⎫   alliances of victims and solidarity groups
   - regional (European) ⎬ to create pressure from below
   - global   ⎭

4.2   Responses of the people of god to politico-economic power systems

Social forms of the church	Basic theo-logical orien-tation	A Biblically legitimate theologies in the perspective and power of the kingdom of god
		– when open space: 1. **Taming of the power systems** 2. **Transformed "Contrast Society" as example**

		LITURGY	PROCLAMATION
aa.	**Local Congregations**	– **Eucharist**: – God's sharing – our sharing – **Vision** of God's Kingdom – **Praise of God of love, not of mammon and competitiveness** – **Confession and forgiveness** of guilt and sin – **Intercession** for victims, actors and profiteers – Relational **spirituality** and spirituality of combat	– **Delegitimisation** of idols (mammon) – **Counter-information** – **Empowerment** through faith in God's justice – **Challenge** of God's law of love for power sharing – **Inspiration** of God's law of love for power sharing – Sustaining **hope** in God's Kingdom of Justice (in unfolding the **Bible** as the "Memory Book of the Poor")
ab	**Local Christian groups/ communities**	The same	The same
ba	National/ regional **Churches**	The same at the national/regional level	The same at the national/regional level
bb	**National/ regional networks** of Christian groups/ communities	The same at the national/regional level	The same at the national/regional level
ca	**Universal Church**	**The same at global level ...** of local/national/regional churches... **to face global power structures ...**	
cb	**Global networks** of Christian groups	The same by **challenging the universal church structures ...** and to **link up with the marginalised and ...** in order to resist/tame/transform ...	

mpires/capitalist global economy)

		B. "State theologies"/ capitalist theologies	C. Church theology
In cooperation with:	– civil society actors for self-help and solidarity – reasonable actors in institutions		
In struggle against			
when systems get closed/totalitarian: resistance against systems and attractive alternatives		**Active assimilation** (supports injustices up to persecution of the true church)	**Passive Assimilation** (neutral or rhetoric towards injustices)
ACONIA	KOINONIA (community)		
Economic literacy **Mutual service** versus domination and exploitation (cf. Mk 10, 42ff.) Letting the **marginalised** of society be the **central subjects** of the congregation Support for **self-help and solidarity groups** **Lobbying** the municipal institutions – – – – – – – – – – – – **Linking** marginalised with congregations Radical **Praxis** for justice, peace, creation (JPIC)	– Moving towards **alternative forms of community/** relationships esp. re: dealing with money, land, work and power	"Church struggle"	
e same at the national/regional vel and **participation in ruggles of civil society** – – – – – – – – – – – – **Linking** marginalised and social/ecological movements with institutional churches by challenging these towards decision and action beyond rhetoric	– **Alternative** dealing with – money (salaries and capital) – land, buildings – work (e.g. no unemployment) – Developing community of communities and **networks**		Invitation Inspiration Communication Challenge
by furthering the capacity and Christian movements and further alternatives	– Furthering of **conciliar community** among traditions and forms of local/national/ regional churches and Christian movements		
to move towards decision and action social/ecological **movements** global plutocratic structures	– Living out ecumenical unity		

Conclusion

In the First Part of this book we examined the global mechanisms which are bringing about pauperisation and environmental destruction in the South, East and West. We identified these mechanisms above all in the deregulated transnational capital markets, which are centred purely around money accumulation, and in the plutocratic institutions which do nothing to halt their advance.

In the Second Part we then recollected traditions from the Bible because they can point the way to new attempts to construct an alternative society based on solidarity to counter the unjust politico-economic systems, especially the ancient Near Eastern, Hellenistic and Roman empires. The heirs of these attempts should be the churches, which should urgently use the "conciliar process for justice, peace and the integrity of creation" (that they themselves started) to fulfill their biblical calling and to support the people's struggle against pauperisation and environmental degradation. This would also renew church life. However, most of the resolutions passed at the ecumenical assemblies in Basel (1989) and Seoul (1990) have not yet been put into practice. The Second European Ecumenical Assembly, planned for 1997, should therefore start by looking at alternative forms of action and practicable examples for restructuring the economy. In this context, the Bible offers two approaches. When we are faced with totalitarian systems, resistance based on dissent and small-scale alternatives are both necessary and possible. When political influence can be brought to bear, prophetic intervention is called for.

A look at present circumstances showed that both situations are interlinked and so both biblical approaches can, and should, be usefully combined in a double strategy. We are currently faced with a totalitarian, plutocratic and therefore undemocratic system in the shape of the transnational capital markets and international financial institutions like the IMF and the World Bank. The transnational capital markets are only accountable to the small proportion of the world's population with large amounts of money at their disposal and so merely seek the short-term accumulation of profit. They no longer have any sense of responsibility towards the majority of people or the environment. They embody the mechanism of the capitalist market. The international financial and economic institutions (i.e. the IMF, the World Bank and WTO) are dominated by the governments of the industrialised countries and therefore support the interests of the players in the transnational capital markets. Some of the functions of the governments which we in the West elect are therefore dictatorial. Rejection and networked small-scale alternatives are the appropriate – and, in the case of churches, theologically necessary – answer to this totalitarian part of the global system.

Everybody in the western industrialised nations has their political rights to exercise in the space left to them by capital. This space is not clearly defined but depends on the degree to which the victims of the system make their voices heard. The crucial question is whether social and environmental movements can win sufficient support from among the victims and their sympathisers, and from other groups and institutions in society, to use and expand this space. The main aim must be to create global democratic political institutions which are capable of monitoring the transnational capital markets and forcing them to operate according to socio-environmental standards. In order to achieve this aim, we have tried to set out approaches for a double strategy at local, national, European, and global levels. The choice is before us. Either we allow the dominance of money accumulation caused by the world market and based on cut-throat competition, accompanied by the consumption of luxury goods by a privileged few, the consequence being death and chaos for the majority of people, societies and the planet itself; or money is placed under strict control and used to satisfy the basic needs of people and to bring about social equality and environmental awareness – in short, to create an economy with a human face, an economy that sustains life.

Bibliography

AKTION FINANZPLATZ SCHWEIZ-DRITTE WELT, 1993, Andere
Bankenkonzepte, Schriftenreihe 1, Bern, Gerberngasse 21 a

ALBERTZ, R., 1992, Religionsgeschichte Israels in der alttestamentlichen Zeit,
Vandenhoeck & Ruprecht, Göttingen

ALTVATER, E., 1987, Sachzwang Weltmarkt: Verschuldungskrise, blockierte
Industrialisierung, ökologische Gefährdung – der Fall Brasilien, VSA-Verlag,
Hamburg

ALTVATER, E., 1992, Der Preis des Wohlstands oder Umweltplünderung und
neue Welt(un)ordnung, Westfälisches Dampfboot, Münster

ALTVATER, E., 1992², Die Zukunft des Marktes: Ein Essay über die Regulation
von Geld und Natur nach dem Scheitern des "real existierenden Sozialismus",
Westfälisches Dampfboot, Münster

ALTVATER, E., MAHNKOPF, B., 1993, Gewerkschaften vor der europäischen
Herausforderung: Tarifpolitik nach Mauer und Maastricht, Westfälisches
Dampfboot, Münster

ANDERSON, V., 1991, Alternative Economic Indicators, Routledge, London/
New York

ARMSTRONG, K., (1988) 1991, Holy War: The Crusades and their Impact on
Todays' World, Anchor Books, New York

ARRIGHI, G., 1994, The Long Twentieth Century: Money, Power, and the
Origins of Our Times, Verso, London/New York

ASCHINGER, F.E., 1978, Das neue Währungssystem: Von Bretton Woods bis zur
Dollarkrise 1977, Frankfurt

ASSMANN, H., u.a., 1984, Die Götzen der Unterdrückung und der befreiende
Gott, edition liberación, Münster

ASSMANN, H., HINKELAMMERT, F.J., 1989, A Idolatria do Mercado: Ensaio
sobre Economia e Teologia, Vozes, Sao Paulo

ASSMANN, J., 1990, Ma'at: Gerechtigkeit und Unsterblichkeit im Alten Ägypten,
C.H. Beck, München

ASSMANN, J., 1992, Politische Theologie zwischen Ägypten und Israel, Siemens
Stiftung, Themen LII, Bonn

BARINCOU, E., (1958) 1988, Niccolò Machiavelli, rororo, Hamburg

BARNET, R.J., CAVANAGH, J., 1994, Global Dreams: Imperial Corporations and the New World Order, Simon & Schuster, New York/London/Toronto/Sydney/Tokyo/Singapore

BARNET, R.J., MÜLLER, R.E., 1974, Global Reach: The Power of the Multinational Corporations, Simon & Schuster, New York

BARTH, K., 1946, Christengemeinde und Bürgergemeinde, ThSt (B), 20, Zürich

BEAUD, M., 1981, A History of Capitalism 1500-1980, MACMILLAN, London

BECKER, J., u.a., 1987, Die Anfänge des Christentums: Alte Welt und neue Hoffnung, Kohlhammer, Stuttgart/Berlin/Köln/Mainz

BELLO, W., 1993, Dark Victory: The United States, Structural Adjustment and Global Poverty, TNI and Pluto Press, London/Boulder, Colorado

BINSWANGER, H.C., 1982, Geld und Wirtschaft im Verständnis des Merkantilismus. Zu den Theorien von John Locke (1632-1704) und John Law (1671-1729), in: Studien zur Entwicklung der ökonomischen Theorie II, Duncker & Humboldt, Berlin

BINSWANGER, H.C., 1991, Geld & Natur. Das wirtschaftliche Wachstum im Spannungsfeld zwischen Ökonomie und Ökologie, Edition Weitbrecht, Stuttgart/Wien

BINSWANGER, H.C., 1994, Money and Magic: Critique of the Modern Economy in the Light of Goethe's Faust, University of Chicago Press, Chicago

BINSWANGER, H.C., FABER, M., MANSTETTEN, R., 1990, The Dilemma of Modern Man and Nature: An Exploration of the Faustian Imperative, in: Ecological Economics, vol. 2, International Society for Ecological Economies, Amsterdam

BOERMA, C., 1979, Rich Man, Poor Man – and the Bible, London

BREIDENSTEIN, G., 1990, Hoffen inmitten der Krisen: Von Krankheit und Heilung unserer Gesellschaft, Fischer, Frankfurt

BREUER, S., 1987, Imperien der Alten Welt, Kohlhammer, Stuttgart/Berlin/Köln/Mainz

BRUIN, J., 1994, The South and the Bretton Woods Institutions, c/o YWCA, Geneva

BUDHOO, D.L., 1990, Enough is Enough: Open Letter of Resignation to the Managing Director of the International Monetary Fund, New Horizons Press, New York

BUKO AGRAR INFO, 1992, Aktion Dritte Welt Handel – weder müde noch entbehrlich, Nr. 16, September, Bundeskongress entwicklungspolitischer Gruppen, Hamburg

BURCHARD, C., 1987, Jesus von Nazarath, in: Becker, J., u.a., Die Anfänge des Christentums: Alte Welt und neue Hoffnung, Kohlhammer, Stuttgart/Berlin/Köln/Mainz, pp. 12ff.

BURNS, S., 1986, The Household Economy, Beacon Press, Boston

BÜSCHER, M., 1989, Socio-cultural Factors in Economic Development, in: Intereconomics, March/April, pp. 79ff.

CAVANAGH, J. , ARRUDA, M., WYSHAM, D. (ed.), 1994, Beyond Bretton Woods: Alternatives to the Global Economic Order, Transnational Institute, Pluto Press, London

CHOMSKY, N., 1985, Turning the Tide, Boston

CHOMSKY, N., HERMAN, E.S., 1979a, After the Cataclysm: Postwar Indochina and the Reconstruction of Imperial Ideology. The Political Economy of Human Rights, vol. ii, South End Press, Boston

CHOMSKY, N., HERMAN, E.S., 1979b, The Washington Connection and Third World Fascism: The Political Economy of Human Rights, vol. i, South End Press, Boston

CLAIREMONTE, F.F., 1989, Mechanics of Finance Capital: Merger Mania and Insider Trading, (wcc/ccpd Occasional Study Pamphlet) Geneva

COCKETT, R., 1994, Thinking the Unthinkable: Think-Tanks and the Economic Counter-Revolution 1931-1983, Harper Colling Publ., London

COOTE, B., The Trade Trap: Poverty and the Global Commodity Markets, Oxfam Publications, Oxford

COUNCIL FOR ECONOMIC PRIORITIES, annual publication, Shopping For a Better World

COUVRAT, J.-F., PLESS, N., 1988, La face cachée de l'économie mondiale, Hatier, Paris (enlarged version in German: 1993, Das verborgene Gesicht der Weltwirtschaft: das internationale Geschäft mit Drogen, Waffen und Geld, Westfälisches Dampfboot, Münster)

CREUTZ, H., 1993, Das Geld Syndrom: Wege zu einer krisenfreien Marktwirtschaft, Wirtschaftsverlag Langen Müller/Herbig, München

CRÜSEMANN, F., 1978, Widerstand gegen das Königtum: Die antiköniglichen Texte des Alten Testaments und der Kampf um den frühen israelitischen Staat, Neukirchener Verlag, Neukirchen-Vluyn

CRÜSEMANN, F., 1983, Bewahrung der Freiheit: Das Thema des Dekalogs in sozialgeschichtlicher Perspektive, Kaiser, München

CRÜSEMANN, F., 1992, Die Tora: Theologie und Sozialgeschichte des alttestamentlichen Gesetzes, Kaiser, München

DALY, H.E., COBB, J.B., 1989, For The Common Good: Redirecting the
Economy Toward Community, the Environment, and a Sustainable Future,
Beacon Press, Boston

DIE GRÜNEN IM BUNDESTAG, 1990, Auf dem Weg zu einer
ökologisch-solidarischen Weltwirtschaft: Konzept für eine grüne
Aussenwirtschaftspolitik, Bonn

DIETRICH, W., 1989, Der rote Faden im Alten Testament, in: Ev. Theologie 49,
München, pp. 232ff.

DOBSON, R.V.G., 1992, Bringing the Economy Home from the Market, Black
Rose Books, Montreal/New York/London

DONNER, H., 1984, Geschichte des Volkes Israel und seiner Nachbarn in
Grundzügen, 1, Vandenhoeck & Ruprecht, Göttingen

DÖRING, D., HANESCH, W., HUSTER, E.-U., 1990, Armut im Wohlstand,
Suhrkamp, Frankfurt

DREHER, C.A., 1993, Die "Auslandsschulden" in der Geschichte Israels, in: Texte
& Kontexte, Nr. 57, April, alektor, Berlin, pp. 17ff.

DRIMMELEN, R. van, 1987, Christian Reflection on Economics, in:
Transformation, vol. 4 nos 3 and 4, Philadelphia

DUBOC PINAUD, J.L., 1992, Divida contra o direito, CEDI, Sao Paulo

DUCHROW, U., 1981, Conflict over the Ecumenical Movement: Confessing
Christ Today in the Universal Church, WCC, Geneva

DUCHROW, U., 1983^2, Christenheit und Weltverantwortung, Klett-Cotta,
Stuttgart

DUCHROW, U., 1986, Was können wir von den Basisgemeinden in Brasilien
lernen?, in: Pastoraltheologie, Göttingen, pp. 229ff.

DUCHROW, U., 1987, Global Economy: A Confessional Issue for the Churches?,
WCC, Geneva

DUCHROW, U., 1992, Europe in the World System 1492-1992: Is justice possible?,
WCC, Geneva

DUCHROW, U., 1993, Theologie, Ethik und Wirtschaft: Ausgewählte
Neuerscheinungen, in: Pastoraltheologie, Göttingen, pp. 319ff.

DUCHROW, U., 1994, Biblical Perspectives on Empire: A View from Western
Europe, in: the ecumenical review, vol. 46, January, WCC, Geneva

DUCHROW, U., EISENBÜRGER, G., HIPPLER, J., 1990, Total War Against
the Poor: Confidential Documents of the 17th Conference of American Armies,
New York Circus Publications, New York

DUCHROW, U., FÜLLKRUG-WEITZEL, C., RAISER, K. (Hg.), 1989, Geld für wenige oder Leben für alle? Ökumenisches Hearing zum Internationalen Finanzsystem, Berlin, 21.-24.8.1988, (Publik-Forum-Dokumentation) Oberursel

DUCHROW, U., GUECK, M., 1994, Economic Alternatives: Responding to the Fifty Years of the Dominant Financial Systems Established at Bretton Woods, Kairos Europa, Budapest/Brussels/Heidelberg

DUCHROW, U., LIEDKE, G., 1989, Shalom: Biblical Perspectives on Creation, Justice and Peace, WCC, Geneva

EATWOT, 1992, Life Affirming Spirituality: Source of Justice and Righteousness, Voices from the Third World, vol. XV, no. 1, June, Colombo

EC-COMMISSION, 1992, Progress Report "Über die Beteiligung der EG am Prozess der strukturellen Anpassungen in den AKP-Staaten", Document SEC (91) 2320 final v. 8.1., Brussels

EC-COMMISSION, 1993, Towards a New Bretton Woods: Alternatives for the Global Economy: A Report for the FAST Programme by St. Holland, Document FOP 325, Brussels

EC-PARLIAMENT, 1992, Neue Weltpartnerschaft, Document PE 201.304, Brussels/Strasbourg

EGGER, K., 1990, Ecofarming: a synthesis of old and new, in: ILEIA Newsletter for Low External Input and Sustainable Agriculture, 2, pp. 3ff.

EKD (Evang. Kirche in Deutschland), 1991, Common Good and Self-Interest: Economic Activity and Responsibility for the Future, Hannover

EKINS, P. (ed.), (1986) 1989[2], The Living Economy: A New Economics in the Making, Routledge, London/New York

EKINS, P., 1993, Living Economies: Can you reconcile community and markets?, in: New Economics 26, London, 16

EKINS, P., MAX-NEEF, M. (ed.), 1992, Real-Life Economics: Understanding Wealth Creation, Routledge, London/New York

ELLINGSON, E., 1993, The Cutting Edge: How Churches Speak on Social Issues, WCC and Eerdmans, Geneva/Grand Rapids

FAITH IN THE CITY, 1985, A Call for Action by Church and Nation: The Report of the Archbishop of Canterbury's Commission on Urban Priority Areas, Church House Publishing, London

FANON, F., 1986, Les damnés de la terre, petite collection maspero, Paris

FATHEUER, T.W., 1992, Nach Rio (FASE), Rio de Janeiro

FATHEUER, T.W., 1993, Ein roter Stern am Amazonas, in: Lateinamerika Nachrichten 227, Berlin, pp. 46ff.

FAY, M.A., 1980, The Influence of Adam Smith on Marx' Theory of Alienation: A Reexamination of the 1844 Economic and Philosophic Manuscripts (with Emphasis on Manuscript 1), University Microfilms, Michigan

FINKELSTEIN, I., 1989, The Emergence of the Monarchy in Israel: The Environmental and Socio-Economic Aspects, JSOT 44, pp. 43ff.

FRANK, A.G., 1988, American Roulette in the Globonomic Casino: Retrospect and Prospect on the World Economic Crisis Today, in: Research in Political Economy, vol. 11, 33ff., JAI Press Inc.

FRANK, A.G., FUENTES-FRANK, M., 1990, Widerstand im Weltsystem: Kapitalistische Akkumulation – Staatliche Politik – Soziale Bewegung, Pro Media, Rieden

GALEANO, E., 1971, Las venas abiertas de America Latina, Universidad de la Republica, Montevideo

GANDHI, M., 1990, Die Lehre vom Schwert und andere Aufsätze aus den Jahren 1919-1922, Rolf Kugler Verlag, Oberwil b. Zug

GEORGE, S., 1988, How the Other Half Dies: A Fate Worse than Debt, Penguin Books, London

GEORGE, S., 1992, The Debt Boomerang: How Third World Debt Harms Us All, Pluto Press, London

GEORGE, S., SABELLI, F., 1994, Faith and Credit: The World Banks Secular Empire, Penguin Books, London

GEORGESCU-ROEGEN, N., 1971, The Entropy Law and the Economic Process, Cambridge/Mass. and London

GEORGI, D., 1992, Der Armen zu gedenken: Die Geschichte der Kollekte des Paulus für Jerusalem, Neukirchener Verlag, Neukirchen-Vluyn

GESELL, S., 1986, Die natürliche Wirtschaftsordnung: Kurzausgabe, Rudolf Zitzmann Verlag, Lauf

GOLLWITZER, H., 1984[2], Befreiung zur Solidarität, Kaiser, München

GORRINGE, T.J., 1994, Capital and the Kingdom: Theological Ethics and Economic Order, SPCK and Orbis Books, London/Maryknoll, N.Y.

GOTTWALD, N.K., 1981[2], The Tribes of Jahwe: A Sociology of the Religion of Liberated Israel 1250-1050 B.C.E., New York

GOUDZWAARD, B., DE LANGE, H., 1995, Beyond Poverty and Affluence: Toward an Economy of Care, WCC and Eerdmans, Geneva/Grand Rapids

GRANADOS, G., GURGSDIES, E., 1985[3], Lern- und Arbeitsbuch Ökonomie, Verlag Neue Gesellschaft, Bonn

GREIDER, W., 1987, Secrets of the Temple: How the Federal Reserve Runs the Country, Simon & Schuster, New York/London

GROSS, B., 1980, Friendly Fascism: The New Face of Power in America, South End Press, Boston

GROTH, U., 1991[8], Schuldnerberatung: Praktischer Leitfaden für die Sozialarbeit, Campus, Frankfurt/New York

GROUP OF LISBON, The, 1993, Limits to Competition, Gulbenkian Foundation, Lisbon

GRÜNDER, H., 1992, Welteroberung und Christentum: Ein Handbuch zur Geschichte der Neuzeit, Gütersloher Verlagshaus, Gütersloh

GUTIERREZ, G., 1989, Dios o el oro en las Indias: Siglo XVI, Instituto Bartolome de las Casas, Lima

HALLER, W., 1989, Die heilsame Alternative: Jesuanische Ethik in Wirtschaft und Politik, Peter Hammer, Wuppertal

HAMELINK, C., 1991, Media Magnates Are Turning Their Backs on Freedom of the Press, in: Global Affairs, 10 May, Society for International Development/SID, Amsterdam

HANESCH, W. et al., 1994, Armut in Deutschland, ed. Deutscher Gewerkschaftsbund and Paritätischer Wohlfahrtsverband, rororo, Hamburg

HANKEL, W., 1992, Dollar und ECU: Leitwährungen im Wettstreit, Fischer, Frankfurt

HARDES, H.-D., RAHMEYER, F., SCHMID, A., (1971) 1986[15], Volkswirtschaftslehre: Eine problemorientierte Einführung, J.C.B. Mohr, Tübingen

HEILBRONNER, R.L., 1988, Behind the Veil of Economics: Essays in the Worldly Philosophy, W.W. Norton & Co., New York/London

HEILBRONNER, R.L., THUROW, L., (1982) 1994[3], Economics Explained: Everything You Need to Know About How the Economy Works and Where It's Going, Touchstone, New York

HENDERSON, H., (1978) 1980, Creating Alternative Futures, G.P. Putnam's Sons, New York (reprint)

HENDERSON, H., (1981) 1988, The Politics of the Solar Age, Ind. Knowledge Systems, Indianapolis

HICKEL, R., HUSTER, E.-U., KOHL, H. (Hg.), 1993, Umverteilen – Schritte zur sozialen und wirtschaftlichen Einheit Deutschlands, Bund Verlag, Köln

HINKELAMMERT, F.J., 1985, The Politics of the Total Market: Its Theology and Our Response, North and South Dialogue, EPICA, Washington, Vol. 1, Number 1.

HINKELAMMERT, F.J., 1986, The Ideological Weapons of Death: A Theological Critique of Capitalism, Orbis Books, Maryknoll, N.Y.

HIPPLER, J., 1985, New Deal Planning, 1933-1935: Die unzureichende
    Modernisierung des Staatsapparates im organisierten Kapitalismus,
    maschinenschriftl. Diss., Bonn

HIPPLER, J., 1994, Pax Americana? Hegemony or Decline, Transnational Institute
    Series, Pluto Press, London/Boulder, Colorado

HIPPLER, J. (ed.), 1995, The Democratisation of Disempowerment: The Problem
    of Democracy in the Third World, Pento Press, Londen/Boulder, Colorado

HIPPLER, J., LUEG, A. (ed.), 1995, The Next Threat: Western Perceptions of
    Islam; Transnational Institute Series, Pluto Press, London/Boulder, Colorado

HIRSCH, J., 1990, Kapitalismus ohne Alternative? Materialistische
    Gesellschaftstheorie und Möglichkeiten einer sozialistischen Politik heute, VSA
    Verlag, Hamburg

HIRSCH, J., ROTH, R., 1986, Das neue Gesicht des Kapitalismus: Vom
    Fordismus zum Postfordismus, VSA Verlag, Hamburg

HOBBES, T., (1651) 1986, Leviathan, (Penguin Books) Harmondsworth

HOOGENDIJK, W., 1991, The Economic Revolution: Towards a sustainable
    future by freeing the economy from money-making, Green Print/Jan van Arkel,
    London/Utrecht

HOPKINS, D.N., CUMMINGS, G. (ed.), 1991, Cut Loose Your Stammering
    Tongue: Black Theology in the Slave Narratives, Orbis Books, Maryknoll, New
    York

HUSTER, E.-U., 1993, Reichtum in Deutschland: Der diskrete Charme der
    sozialen Distanz, Campus, Frankfurt/New York

ICDA (International Coalition for Development Action), 1995, An Alternative
    Report on Trade. An NGO Perspective on International Trade, Brussels

INGRIM, P., WILLIAMSON, R., 1994, Towards the Peace Economy: The Oxford
    Manifesto, Complementary Texts and Call to Action, Oxford Research Group,
    Oxford

JANKOWSKI, G., 1990, Friede über Gottes Israel: Paulus an die Galater, in: Texte
    & Kontexte 13, Nr. 47/48, pp. 20f., alektor, Berlin

JOHN PAUL II., 1991, Centesimus Annus, Catholic Truth Society, London

KAIROS EUROPA, 1992, Documentation from the "People's Parliament",
    Strasbourg, 5th-10th June, The Aisling Scriptorium Press, Aran Islands, Ireland

KAIROS EUROPA, 1993, Transnationale Finanzmärkte und Europäisches
    Währungssystem – Ihre Auswirkungen auf arme Länder und
    Bevölkerungsgruppen, Dokumentation einer Fachkonsultation vom 2.-4. Juli in
    Frankfurt, (Hegenichstrasse 22) Heidelberg

KAIROS EUROPA, 1995, The Political Responsibility of the European Union for the International Financial System with Respect to Sustainable Development and Social Justice, Documentation of the Kairos Europa-Hearing in the European Parliament, June 27, 1994, (Hegenichstr. 22) Heidelberg

KAISER, O. (Hg.), 1982ff., Texte aus der Umwelt des Alten Testaments, Bd. 1, Gütersloher Verlagshaus, Gütersloh

KEGLER, J., 1992, Das Zinsverbot in der hebräischen Bibel, in: Crüsemann, M., Schottroff, W., Schuld und Schulden: Biblische Traditionen in gegenwärtigen Konflikten, Kaiser, München, pp. 17ff.

KENNEDY, M., 1988, Interest and Inflation Free Money, Permaculture Institute Publications, Steyerberg

KERN, B., 1991, Theologie im Horizont des Marxismus: Zur Geschichte der Marxismusrezeption in der lateinamerikanischen Theologie der Befreiung, Matthias Grünewald, Mainz

KESSLER, R., 1992, Staat und Gesellschaft im vorexilischen Juda, Leiden

KESSLER, W., 1990, Aufbruch zu neuen Ufern: Ein Manifest für eine sozial-ökologische Wirtschaftsdemokratie, (Publik-Forum-Dokumentation) Oberursel

KESSLER, W., 1992, Freies Geld für freie Bürger?, in: Publik-Forum Nr. 22, 20.11., Oberursel, pp. 14ff.

KESSLER, W. (Hg.), 1993, Geld, Zins und Gewissen: Neue Formen im Umgang mit Geld, (Publik-Forum-Materialmappe) Oberursel

KEYNES, J.M., (1935) 1991, The General Theory of Employment, Interest and Money, A Harvest/HBJ Book, San Diego/New York/London

KIPPENBERG, H.G., 1977, Die Typik der antiken Entwicklung, in: ders. (Hg.), Seminar: Die Entstehung der antiken Klassengesellschaft, Suhrkamp, Frankfurt

KIPPENBERG, H.G., 1978, Religion und Klassenbildung im antiken Judäa, Vandenhoeck & Ruprecht, Göttingen

KIPPENBERG, H.G., 1991, Die vorderasiatischen Erlösungsreligionen in ihrem Zusammenhang mit der antiken Stadtherrschaft, Frankfurt

KLARE, M.T., 1991, Krieg den Aufsteigern: Die neue US-Doktrin der Konflikte "mittlerer Intensität" (MIC), in: Blätter für deutsche und internationale Politik, 3, Bonn

KOCH, K., 1976, Gemeinschaftstreu/heilvoll sein, in: Theol. Handwörterbuch zum Alten Testament, Bd. II, München/Zürich, col. 507ff.

KOCHENDÖRFER-LUCIUS, G., 1991, Der "Informelle Sektor": Schattenwirtschaft oder Wirtschaft der Zukunft, in: Jahrbuch Dritte Welt, hg. v. Dt. Übersee-Institut, Hamburg, pp. 61ff.

KRÖLLS, A., 1988, Das Grundgesetz als Verfassung des staatlich organisierten Kapitalismus, Deutscher Universitäts Verlag, Wiesbaden

KUHN, T.S., 1967, The Structure of Scientific Revolutions, University of Chicago Press, Chicago

KUNANAYAKAM, T., 1993, Globaler Markt kontra menschliche Entwicklung, in: epd-Entwicklungspolitik 19, Frankfurt, pp. b-h

KURZ, R., 1991, Der Kollaps der Modernisierung: Vom Zusammenbruch des Kasernensozialismus zur Krise der Weltökonomie, Eichborn, Frankfurt

KUTTNER, R., (1991) 1992, The End of Laissez-Faire: National Purpose and the Global Economy After the Cold War, University of Pennsylvania Press, Philadelphia

LA POUDRIERE, 1993, Bulletin de Liaison, Mai, Brussels

LAMPE, P., 1978, Die Apokalyptiker – ihre Situation und ihr Handeln, in: Eschatologie und Frieden, Bd. 11, Texte und Materialien der FEST, Heidelberg

LANTZ, G., 1977, Eigentumsrecht – ein Recht oder ein Unrecht? Eine kritische Beurteilung der ethischen Argumente für das Privateigentum bei Aristoteles, Thomas von Aquino, Grothius, Locke, Hegel, Marx und in den modernen katholischen Sozialenzykliken, Uppsala

LE GOFF, J., 1988, Wucherzins und Höllenqualen: Ökonomie und Religion im Mittelalter, Klett-Cotta, Stuttgart

LOCKE, J., (1690), 1988 (reprinted 2nd ed.), Two Treaties of Government, ed. P. Laslett, Cambridge University Press, Cambridge

LOHFINK, G., (1988) 1993, Wem gilt die Bergpredigt? Zur Glaubwürdigkeit des Christlichen, Herder, Freiburg/Basel/Wien

LOHFINK, N., 1987, Das Jüdische am Christentum: Die verlorene Dimension, Herder, Freiburg/Basel/Wien

LUDWIG, H., 1987, Arbeit durch Einkommen statt Grundeinkommen ohne Arbeit: Die Weidener Erklärung der KAB Süddeutschlands "Arbeit durch Solidarität", in: Wiss. Arbeitsstelle der Diözese Aachen, Hg., Arbeiterfragen Nr. 3, Aachen

LÜTHI, H., 1967, Variationen über ein Thema von Max Weber: Die protestantische Ethik und der Geist des Kapitalismus, in: ders., In Gegenwart der Geschichte, Köln/Berlin

LUZ, U., 1989, Die Kirche und ihr Geld im Neuen Testament, in: Lienemann, W. (Hg.), Die Finanzen der Kirche, München, pp. 525ff.

LUZ, U., 1990, Das Evangelium nach Matthäus, 2. Teilband, Mt 8-17, Evang.-Kath. Kommentar zum Neuen Testament 1/2, Neukirchener Verlag, Neukirchen-Vluyn

MAALOUF, A., 1983, Les croisades vues par les Arabes, Paris

MACAFEE BROWN, R. ed., 1990, Kairos – Three Prophetic Challenges to the Church, Eerdmans, Grand Rapids

MACHFUS, N., 1990, Die Kinder unseres Viertels, Zürich

MACPHERSON, C.B., 1962, The Political Theory of Possessive Individualism: Hobbes to Locke, Oxford University Press, Oxford

MALKAMÄKI, M., 1991, Banking the Poor: Informal and Semi-Formal Financial Systems Serving the Microenterprises, Helsinki

MARQUARDT, F.W., 1983, Gott oder Mammon aber: Theologie und Ökonomie bei Martin Luther, in: Einwürfe 1, Kaiser, München, pp. 126-216

MARX, K., 1844, Ökonomisch-philosophische Manuskripte aus dem Jahre 1844, in: Marx Engels Werke (MEW), Erg.Bd. 1, Berlin 1968

MARX, K., ENGELS, F. (ed.), 1974, Capital: A Critique of Political Economy, Vol. III: The Process of Capitalist Production as a Whole, Lawrence & Wishart, London

MARX, K., 1990, Capital: A Critical Analysis of Capitalist Production, Karl Marx and Friedrich Engels Gesamtausgabe (MEGA), II. Abteilung, Vol. 9, Dietz Verlag, Berlin

MASSARRAT, M., u.a. (Hg.), 1993, Die Dritte Welt und wir – Bilanz und Perspektiven für Wissenschaft und Praxis, Freiburg

MASUD ISA, M., 1993, The Access to Credit Makes the Difference: The Grameen Bank Experience. Prepared for the International Conference of Anthroposophically Oriented Bankers in Kassel, Fed. Rep. of Germany, February 18-21

MAYER, L., 1992, Ein System siegt sich zu Tode: Der Kapitalismus frißt seine Kinder, (Publik-Forum-Dokumentation) Oberursel

MEEKS, M.D., 1989, God the Economist, Fortress Press, Minneapolis

MEEKS, W.A., 1983, The First Urban Christians: The Social World of the Apostle Paul, Yale University, New Haven/London

MESTERS, C., 1983, Vom Leben zur Bibel – Von der Bibel zum Leben, Bd. 1 u. 2, Kaiser und Grünewald, München/Mainz

MIES, M., 1988a, Die Krise ist eine Chance: Subsistenz statt "Entwicklung", in: Altvater, E., u.a., Soll und Haben: Strategien und Alternativen zur Lösung der Schuldenkrise, Konkret Literatur Verlag, Hamburg

MIES, M., 1988b, Patriarchat und Kapital – Frauen in der internationalen Arbeitsteilung, Zürich

MILBANK, J., 1990, Theology and Social Theory: Beyond Secular Reason, Basil Blackwell, Oxford

MINNAAR, A. et al. (ed.), 1994, The Hidden Hand: Covert Operations in South Africa, Human Sciences Research Council, Pretoria

MIRANDA, J., 1974, Marx and the Bible: A Critique of the Philosophy of Oppression, Orbis Books, Maryknoll, N.Y.

MIRANDA, J., 1982, Communism in the Bible, Orbis Books, Maryknoll, N.Y.

MIRES, F., 1989, Im Namen des Kreuzes: Der Genozid an den Indianern während der spanischen Eroberung: theologische und politische Diskussionen, Exodus, Fribourg/Brig

MIROW, K.R., 1978, Die Diktatur der Kartelle: Zum Beispiel Brasilien. Materialien zur Vermachtung des Weltmarktes, rororo, Reinbek b. Hamburg

MONCAYO, H.-L., 1994, From GATT to the multilateral trade organisation: a new world order, in: Free or Fair Trade? Latin American and Caribbean trade alert, vol. 2, 8-9, Bogota

MOYER, B., 1987, The Movement Action Plan: A Strategic Framework Describing the Eight Stages of Successful Social Movements, Revised Edition of the Dandelion, Cambridge, MA

MULHOLLAND, C. (Hg.), 1988, Ecumenical Reflections on Political Economy, WCC, Geneva

MÜLLER-ARMACK, A., 1956, Soziale Marktwirtschaft, in: Handwörterbuch der Sozialwissenschaften, Bd. 9, pp. 390-392

NAIR, K., OPPERSKALSKI, M., 1988, CIA: Club der Mörder: Der US-Geheimdienst in der Dritten Welt, Lamuv, Göttingen

NELSON-PALLMEYER, J., 1992, Brave New World Order: Must We Pledge Allegiance?, Orbis Books, Maryknoll, N.Y.

NEU, R., 1992, Von der Anarchie zum Staat: Entwicklungsgeschichte Israels vom Nomadentum zur Monarchie im Spiegel der Ethnosoziologie, Neukirchener Verlag, Neukirchen-Vluyn

NOGUEIRA, P.A. de SOUZA, 1991, Der Widerstand gegen Rom in der Apokalypse des Johannes: Eine Untersuchung zur Tradition des Falls von Babylon in Apokalypse 18, theol diss. in manuscr. form, Heidelberg

NOVAK, M., 1982, The Spirit of Democratic Capitalism, American Enterprise Institute/Simon & Schuster, New York

O.M.G.U.S. (Office of Military Government for Germany, United States), 1985, Ermittlungen gegen die Deutsche Bank 1946/1947, Nördlingen

O.M.G.U.S., 1986, Ermittlungen gegen die I.G. Farben, Nördlingen

PAULY, D., 1988, Bekehrung des Managements: Bibelarbeit zu Lukas 16,1-13, in: Weissenseer Blätter, H. 6, Berlin-Brandenburg

PETRELLA, R., 1993a, L'évangile de la compétitivité, in: Le Monde Diplomatique (Manière de voir 18), Mai, Paris

PETRELLA, R., 1993b, Le culte de la compétitivité, in: Tendances (Belgien) v. 9.9.

PIETILÄ, H., o.J. (ca. 1991), Doing Justice – The Best Thing we Could Give: A paper prepared for the South Commission, Helsinki University, Dept. of Development Studies

POLANYI, K., 1945, Origins of Our Time: The Great Transformation, Gollancz, London

PORTER, M., 1980, The Competitive Strategy, New York

PORTER, M., 1990, The Competitive Advantage of Nations, London

POTTER, G.A., 1988, Dialogue on Debt: Alternative Analyses and Solutions, Center of Concern, Washington, DC

POTTER, P., 1993, The Global Economic System in Biblical Perspective, in: M. Reuver (et al. ed.), The Ecumenical Movement Tomorrow, KOK Publishing House and WCC, Kampen/Geneva, pp. 13-35

PRIEN, H.-J., 1992, Luthers Wirtschaftsethik, Vandenhoeck & Ruprecht, Göttingen

PURY, P. de, 1983, People's Technologies and People's Participation, WCC/CCPD, Geneva

RAFFER, K., 1990, Applying Chapter 9 Insolvency to International Debts: An Economically Efficient Solution with a Human Face, in: World Development 18/2

RAISER, K., 1994, Ecumenism in Transition: A Paradigm Shift in the Ecumenical Movement, WCC, Geneva

REICH, R.B., 1991, The Work of Nations: Preparing Ourselves for 21st Century Capitalism, Vintage Books, New York

REIFNER, U., FORD, J. (ed.), 1992, Banking for People: Social Banking and New Poverty. Consumer Debts and Unemployment in Europe – National Reports, Walter de Gruyter, Berlin/New York

RICH, A., 1984, Wirtschaftsethik. Grundlagen in theologischer Perspektive, Gütersloher Verlagshaus, Gütersloh

RICH, A., 1990, Wirtschaftsethik II: Marktwirtschaft, Planwirtschaft, Weltwirtschaft aus sozialethischer Sicht, Gütersloher Verlagshaus, Gütersloh

RICH, B., 1994, Mortgaging the Earth: The World Bank, Environmental Impoverishment, and the Crisis of Development, Beacon Press, Boston

RICHTER, A., 1983, Das Wirtschaftswunder von Wörgl, in: Arbeit & Wirtschaft, Wien, März

ROBERTSON, J., 1990, Future Wealth: A New Economics for the 21st Century, The Bootstrap Press, New York

RODNEY, W., 1972, How Europe Underdeveloped Africa, Bogle-L'Ouverture Publications/London and Tanzania Publishing House/Dar es Salaam

ROTTACH, P. (Hg.)., 1988, Ökologischer Landbau in den Tropen, Karlsruhe

SABET, H., 1991, Die Schuld des Nordens: Der 5°-Billionen-Coup, Horizonte Verlag, Bad König

SACHS, W., 1992, Von der Verteilung der Reichtümer zur Verteilung der Risiken: Sicherheit: zum Aufstieg eines neuen Leitbegriffs, in: Universitas, H. 9

SANTA ANA, J. de, RAISER, K., DUCHROW, U., 1990, The Political Economy of the Holy Spirit, WCC, Geneva

SCHÄFER, H., 1992, Protestantismus in Zentralamerika: Christliches Zeugnis im Spannungsfeld von US-amerikanischem Fundamentalismus, Unterdrückung und Wiederbelebung "indianischer" Kultur, Peter Lang, Frankfurt/Berlin/Bern/ New York/Paris/Wien

SCHARFFENORTH, G., 1982, Den Glauben ins Leben ziehen: Studien zu Luthers Theologie, Kaiser, München

SCHILLER, H.I., 1989, Culture, Inc: The Corporate Takeover of Public Expression, New York/Oxford

SCHILLING, P.R., 1993, Mercosur – Integration oder Beherrschung?, ela Verlag, Berlin

SCHNEIDER, R., (1952) 1990, Las Casas vor Karl V., Suhrkamp, Frankfurt

SCHNEIDER, U., 1993, Solidarpakt gegen die Schwachen: Der Rückzug des Staates aus der Sozialpolitik, Knaur, München

SCHOTTROFF, L. u. W., 1988, Biblische Traditionen von "Staatstheologie, Kirchentheologie und Prophetischer Theologie" nach dem Kairos-Dokument, in: dies., Die Macht der Auferstehung: Sozialgeschichtliche Bibelauslegungen, Kaiser, München

SCHOTTROFF, L., 1984, "Gebt dem Kaiser, was dem Kaiser gehört, und Gott, was Gott gehört": Die theologische Antwort der urchristlichen Gemeinden auf ihre gesellschaftliche und politische Situation, in: Moltmann, J. (Hg.), Annahme und Widerstand, Kaiser, München, pp. 15ff.

SCHOTTROFF, L., 1986, Die Befreiung vom Götzendienst der Habgier, in: Schottroff, L. u. W. (Hg.), Wer ist unser Gott? Beiträge zu einer Befreiungstheologie im Kontext der "ersten" Welt, Kaiser, München, pp. 137ff.

SCHOTTROFF, L., 1994, Lydias ungeduldige Schwestern: Feministische Sozialgeschichte des frühen Christentums, Kaiser/Gütersloher Verlagshaus, Gütersloh

SCHOTTROFF, L., STEGEMANN, W., 1981², Jesus von Nazareth – Hoffnung der Armen, Kohlhammer, Stuttgart

SCHOTTROFF, W., 1986, Das Jahr der Gnade Jahwes (Jes 61,1-11), in: Schottroff, L. u. W. (Hg.), Wer ist unser Gott? Beiträge zu einer Befreiungstheologie im Kontext der "ersten" Welt, Kaiser, München

SCHUBERT, A., 1985, Die internationale Verschuldung, Suhrkamp, Frankfurt

SCHULZE, C.-D., 1989, Kursänderung – Die Berliner "Initiative PfarrerInnengehalt/Ökumenisches Teilen", in: Mitteilungen der Ev. Landeskirche in Baden, Juli/August, Karlsruhe

SCHUMACHER, E.F., 1973, Small is Beautiful, Blond & Briggs, London

SCHUMACHER, E.F., 1979, Good Work, Harper & Row, New York

SCHWANTES, M., 1991, Das Land kann seine Worte nicht ertragen: Meditationen zu Amos, Kaiser, München

SEE, H., 1992, Kapital-Verbrechen: Die Verwirtschaftung der Moral, Fischer, Frankfurt

SEGHERS, A., 1981⁴, Die Hochzeit von Haiti: Karibische Geschichten, Sammlung Luchterhand, Darmstadt

SMITH, A., (1776) 1976⁴, An Inquiry into the Nature and Causes of the Wealth of Nations, 1776 ed. R.H. Campbell et al., Indianapolis/O.U.P. 1976

SOUTH CENTRE, 1992, The United Nations at a Critical Crossroads: Time for the South to Act, Geneva

SPIEGEL, Y., 1992, Wirtschaftsethik und Wirtschaftspraxis – ein wachsender Widerspruch?, Kohlhammer, Stuttgart/Berlin/Köln

STELCK, E., 1980, Politik mit dem Einkaufskorb, Peter Hammer, Wuppertal

STENDAHL, K., 1976, Paul among Jews and Gentiles, Fortress Press, Philadelphia

STRAHM, R.H., 1985, Warum sie so arm sind, Peter Hammer, Wuppertal

SUTHERLAND, W. (ed.), 1992, The Rio Treaties of the Global NGO Movement: documentary source book, Adamantine Press, London

TAMEZ, E., 1991, Contra Toda Condena: La justificacion por la fe desde los excluidos, DEI, San José, Costa Rica

THEISSEN, G., 1992, Gruppenmessianismus: Überlegungen zum Ursprung der Kirche im Jüngerkreis Jesu, in: Jahrbuch für Biblische Theologie, Bd. 7, Neukirchen-Vluyn

THEISSEN, G., 989, Jesusbewegung als charismatische Wertrevolution, in: New Test. Stud., vol. 35, pp. 343ff.

TODOROV, T., 1985, Die Eroberung Amerikas: Das Problem des Anderen, Suhrkamp, Frankfurt

TUNSTALL, J., PALMER, M., 1991, Media Moguls, London/New York

U.S. CATHOLIC BISHOPS CONFERENCE, 1987, Economic Justice for all: A Pastoral Letter on Catholic Social Teaching and the U.S. Economy, in: Building Economic Justice (National Conference of Catholic Bishops), Washington, DC

UEHLINGER, H.C., 1990, Weltreiche und eine Rede, Vandenhoeck & Ruprecht, Göttingen/Fribourg

UNDP (United Nations Development Programme), 1992, 1993, 1994, Human Development Report 1992, 1993, 1994, New York/Oxford

UNITED CHURCH OF CHRIST, 1987, Christian Faith and Economic Life: A Study Paper Contributing to a Pronouncement for the 17th General Synod, ed. A.Ch. Smock, New York

UNITED CHURCH OF CHRIST, 1989, Christian Faith: Economic Life and Justice. A Pronouncement from the 17th General Synod, New York

VALLELY, P., 1990, Bad Samaritans: First World Ethics and Third World Debt, Hodder & Stoughton, London

VEERKAMP, T., 1983, Die Vernichtung des Baal: Auslegung der Königsbücher (1.17-2.11), alektor, Stuttgart

VEERKAMP, T., 1988, Die Schulden fressen den Sozialismus: Eine neue Bedrohung der Sicherheit in Europa?, in: Junge Kirche, Bremen, pp. 423ff.

VEERKAMP, T., 1989, Nachdem die Schulden den Sozialismus gefressen haben, erweisen sie sich als demokratieresistent, in: Junge Kirche, Bremen, pp. 572ff.

VEERKAMP, T., 1993, Autonomie & Egalität: Ökonomie, Politik, Ideologie in der Schrift, alektor, Berlin

WALLERSTEIN, I., 1974, The Modern World-System: Capitalist Agriculture and the Origins of the European World-Economy in the Sixteenth Century, Academic Press, New York/San Francisco/London

WEBER, M., 1953, Gesammelte Aufsätze zur Religionssoziologie, 1, J.C.B. Mohr, Tübingen

WEBER, M., 1972⁵, Wirtschaft und Gesellschaft, J.C.B. Mohr, Tübingen

WEIZSÄCKER, E.U. von, 1994, Earth Politics, Zed Books, London/New Jersey

WELKER, M., 1992, Das Reich Gottes, in: Ev. Theol. 52, München, 497-512

WENGST, K., 1987, Pax Romana and the Peace of Christ, trans. John Bowden, Fortress Press and SCM Press, Philadelphia/London

WERKSTATT ÖKONOMIE, 1992, Multis – Markt & Krise: Unternehmensstrategien im Strukturbruch der Weltwirtschaft, Heidelberg

WILLIAMS, E., 1967², Capitalism and Slavery, André Deutsch, London

WILLIAMS, E., 1971², From Columbus to Castro: The History of the Caribbean 1492-1969, Vintage Books, London

WINK, W., 1984, Naming the Powers, Fortress Press, Philadelphia

WINK, W., 1986, Unmasking the Powers, Fortress Press, Philadelphia

WINK, W., 1992, Engaging the Powers, Fortress Press, Philadelphia

WOLF, E.R., 1982, Europe and the People without History, University of California Press, Berkeley/Los Angeles/London

WORLD COUNCIL OF CHURCHES, 1992, Christian Faith and the World Economy Today: A Study Document from the wcc, Geneva

YOUNG, G., 1990, Fair Trading, in: New Internationalist, Febr., pp. 24f.

ZIEGLER, J., 1992, Die Schweiz wäscht weisser: Die Finanzdrehscheibe des internationalen Verbrechens, Knaur, München

ZIEGLER, J., 1993, Le bonheur d'être Suisse, Paris

ZINN, K.G., 1989, Kanonen und Pest: Über die Ursprünge der Neuzeit im 14. und 15. Jahrhundert, Westdeutscher Verlag, Opladen

Additional bibliography

COCKETT, R., 1994, Thinking the Unthinkable: Think-Tanks and the Economic Counter-Revolution 1931-1983, Harper Collins Publishers, London

DOUTHWAITE, R., 1996, Short Circuit: Strengthening Local Economies for Security in an Unstable World, Liliput Press, Dublin

GREIDER, W., 1997, One World, Ready or Not: The Manic Logic of Global Capitalism, Simon & Schuster, New York

GREY, M., 1997, Beyond the Dark Night: A Way Forward for the Church?, Cassell, London

HAMELINK, C., 1995, World Communication, Zed Books, London

KORTEN, D.C., 1995, When Corporations Rule the World, Kumarian Press/Berrett-Koehler Publishers, West Hartford/San Francisco

MYERS, C., 1995[2], Who Will Roll Away The Stone? Discipleship Queries for First World Christians, Orbis Books, Maryknoll/New York

MYERS, C., 1994[7], Binding The Strong Man: A Political Reading of Mark's Story of Jesus, Orbis Books, Maryknoll/New York

PIXLEY, J., 1989, The Bible, the Church and the Poor, Orbis Books, Maryknoll/New York

ROWBOTHAM, M., 1998, The Grip of Death: A study of modern money, debt slavery and destructive economics, Jon Carpenter Publishing, Charlbury (UK)

RUSSELL., H., 1995, Poverty Close To Home: A Christian Understanding, Mowbray, London

SASSEN, S., 1996, Losing Control? Sovereignty in an Age of Globalization, Columbia University Press, New York/Chichester

KAIROS EUROPA

Towards a Europe for Justice...
is a network of marginalised people
and groups, networks, NGOs and church
organisations in solidarity with them. Its goal is
to unite the struggles for more economic, social,
racial and gender justice within Europe and with networks in other continents. Kairos Europa works at the local, national and European level. Major
events have included the "People's Parliament" in Strasbourg (1992), the hearings on the "Political Responsibility of the European Union for the International Financial Order in View of Sustainable Development and Social Cohesion" and "The European Monetary Union in the Context of Mass Unemployment, Social Degradation, and the Globalisation of Capital Markets
(1996) in Brussels.

Ongoing programme lines are:
– Alternatives to the economic and financial mechanisms of impoverish-
   ment and debt.in South/East/North.(coordination in Heidelberg)
– Migration (coordination in Birmingham)
– Identity (coordination in Ireland)
– Spirituality of resistance and solidarity (coordination in Austria/Hungary)
– Kairos Jeunesse (coordination in Brussels)

There are national and regional coordinations
General coordination: Kairos Europa, International Office
3 Avenue du Parc Royal
B - 1020 Bruxelles
phone: +32 3 - 479 9655, fax - 476 0650

The Newsletter: Gyula Simonyi
Pf. 7
H - 8003 Székesfehérvár
phone: +36 22 - 327 263, fax - 343 823, e-mail: bocs@c3.hu
homepage: http://bocs.hu

Kairos Europa Publications and Working Materials

(some titles are available in German, Swedish, Hungarian, Korean)
Europe in the World System 1492-1992: Is justice possible?, World Council of Churches, Geneva 1992   *Ulrich Duchrow*

Economic Alternatives: Responding to the Fifty Years of the Dominant Financial Systems Established at Bretton Woods, Budapest 1994   *Ulrich Duchrow and Martin Gueck*

Documentation of the Hearings:
"The Political Responsibility of the European Union for the International Financial Order in View of Sustainable Development and Social Cohesion", Brussels 1994;
"The European Monetary Union in the Context of Mass Unemployment, Social Degradation, and the Globalization of Capital Markets", Brussels 1997 *edited by Martin Gueck*

Documentation of the European meetings 1994-1997:
Communal Alliances Against Social Degradation and for the Local Agenda 21 (in German)   *edited by Jutta Wenz*

The European Kairos Document for a socially just, life-sustaining and democratic Europe (in at least eight European languages)

Kairos Center Heidelberg-Mannheim
Hegenichstrasse 22
D - 69124 Heidelberg
phone: +49 6221 - 712 610, fax:781 183
e-mail: KAIROSHD@aol.com
(This book is available now also in German, Indonesian, Korean and Spanish)